# CRITICAL INSIGHTS

## Sherman Alexie

Editor
**Leon Lewis**
*Appalachian State University*

Salem Press
Pasadena, California      Hackensack, New Jersey

PS
3551
.L35774
Z85
2012

**Library of Congress Cataloging-in-Publication Data**
Sherman Alexie / Editor, Leon Lewis.
    p. cm. -- (Critical insights)
    Includes bibliographical references and index.
    ISBN 978-1-58765-821-1 (set : alk. paper) -- ISBN 978-1-58765-822-8 (set-pack A : alk. paper) -- ISBN 978-1-58765-823-5 (vol. 1 : alk. paper)
    1. Alexie, Sherman, 1966---Criticism and interpretation. I. Lewis, Leon.
    PS3551.L35774Z85 2012
    818'.5409--dc23
                                                                2011018805

PRINTED IN CANADA

# Contents

# Resources_____

# About This Volume

Leon Lewis

One indication of an author's impact on the zeitgeist can be registered in terms of the extent of editions published in languages other than the one in which his or her works were written. Noticed initially as a Native American author, Sherman Alexie has achieved a reputation as a significant figure in the American literary landscape that has blossomed through the first decade of the twenty-first century as commentators have drawn Alexie into the conversation concerning writers whose work is not dependent only on a particular ethnic identity. Barry Harbaugh's commentary on Alexie's work in "The *Paris Review* Perspective" in this volume compares Alexie's first short-story collection, *The Lone Ranger and Tonto Fistfight in Heaven,* to Jhumpa Lahiri's *Interpreter of Maladies* "as a seminal book of assimilation fiction," and the extent of interest in Alexie's work beyond national boundaries can be measured by the proliferation of translations that are appearing and by the range of response to the work by scholars throughout the world of letters. Michel Lederer's translation into French of *The Lone Ranger and Tonto Fistfight in Heaven,* for instance, was published as *Phoenix, Arizona et autres nouvelles* (from the title of the story "This Is What It Means to Say Phoenix, Arizona"—followed by "and other stories") in 1999. Lederer's translation of *The Toughest Indian in the World* appeared as *La Vie aux trousses* (roughly "life on the edge") in 2000, and Alexie's collection of poetry *The Summer of Black Widows* was translated into Italian by Giorgio Mariani as *L'estate delle vedove nere* in 2005. Alexie's work has also been translated into Hungarian, Hebrew, Japanese, Icelandic, and Swahili, among an expanding list of languages.

In a correlation with these editions, scholars in other countries have similarly begun to examine Alexie's work. A volume titled *Kulturelle Selbstentwürfe in zeitgenössocher indianischer Literatur: N. Scott Momaday, Sherman Alexie, und Wendy Rose* (cultural self-projection in contemporary American Indian literature) was published in Germany in 2003. While all of the essays appearing in this volume were written in English, the diversity of the contributors reflects the transnational perspective on Alexie that has marked the response to his work, as his prominence among American writers has increased steadily to its current pinnacle of interest and engagement. A typical example is Åse Nygren's interview with Alexie. Nygren is a Swedish scholar whose doctoral dissertation "Tracing Trauma: The Narration of Suffering in Sherman Alexie's Fiction" is an indication of the manner in which current modes of critical inquiry have been applied to Alexie's work. Nygren, whose interview originally appeared in *MELUS: Journal of the Society for the Study of Multi-Ethnic Literature of the United States*, states that she approached Alexie as a "European white female scholar," and her conversation with Alexie illustrates how Alexie's work is illuminated by the range of references that Nygren's asute queries require.

Initial responses to Alexie's writing focused on the areas of concentration that coincided with the particular points of interest that the commentators found captivating. Gloria Bird, a contributing editor at the *Wicazo Sa Review* and a member of the Spokane tribal grouping that includes the Wellpinit reservation, where Alexie was born, calls Alexie "an enigma on the literary scene" in her 1995 essay "The Exaggeration of Despair in Sherman Alexie's *Reservation Blues*," reprinted in this volume; Bird addresses a fundamental issue for Native critics when she states, "This review questions the assumption that because someone is Indian what they produce is automatically an accurate representation." A continuing controversy, highlighted by Alexie's refusal to be restricted to *any* projection of American indian reality other than his own, is given expression by the distinguished scholar Sean Kicummah Teuton when he asks, "What right does Alexie have to share with general readers our most painful realities of poverty and social dysfunction?" Teuton's judicious exploration of this query, in the selection from his landmark *Red Land, Red Power: Grounding Knowledge in the American Indian Novel* included here, is an illustration of one of the most provocative and persistent issues that Alexie's work has emphasized.

Proceeding past identification to a direct engagement with the issue, Tammy Wahpeconiah's new essay in this volume, "Navigating the River of the World: Collective Trauma in *The Absolutely True Diary of a Part-Time Indian*," provides an illuminating account of a Native scholar's work with her students—the vast maority non-Native—and her perceived responsibility to herself, her heritage, and Alexie's writing. Nancy Van Styvendale's "The Trans/Historicity of Trauma in Jeanette Armstrong's *Slash* and Sherman Alexie's *Indian Killer*," reprinted here, widens and deepens the ways to approach this vital aspect of Native scholarship by showing that "cumulative, collective, intergenerational, and intersubjective, the trauma of Native peoples, when understood as trans/historical, exceeds any attempt to fix its location or define its event, even as it demands our attention to historically specific atrocities." Van Styvendale argues that Alexie's depiction of a "present citation" of trauma is "not only-ever a repetition of the past but instead has its own materiality, its own conditions of production, its own traumatic effects," offering an explanation of how Alexie's work can be regarded as a version of an "accurate representation" even as it differs from other persuasive portrayals, even those preferred by some respected critics.

Carrie Etter's essay "Dialectic to Dialogic: Negotiating Bicultural Heritage in Sherman Alexie's Sonnets" takes this issue into Alexie's poetry, the genre acknowledged by Alexie as the "original fire" (to appropriate the title of Louise Erdrich's collection) that ignited his creative flame. In her discussion of the ways in which Alexie "modifies the English sonnet" to negotiate "between his cultural inheritances," Etter stresses the ways Alexie restructures the sonnet to "upset the reader's expectation of resolution and thus promote the idea that the Indian dilemma is never a matter that can be easily or hastily solved." Her discussion offers a good entrance into a less popular but absolutely crucial component of Alexie's artistic vision. Jennifer Gillan's "Reservation Home Movies: Sherman Alexie's Poetry" combines two areas of interest for Alexie, locating themes and stylistic techniques in the short fiction and poetry Alexie published at the moment when he was emerging into national consciousness as an original voice from what was generally regarded as a small subdivision of American culture. Gillan traces the ways that Alexie was perceived by literary critics who were troubled by his disruption of genres and his apparent challenge to conventional versions of "Indian" existence. Citing poet Donald Hall's dictum that "poems embody the coexistence of opposites that together form an identity," she calls Alexie a "twentieth-century fancydancer" who "makes music by fingering all the discordant strings of his life."

Douglas Ford, in "Sherman Alexie's Indigenous Blues," also draws on Alexie's juxtaposition of poetry and prose fiction in an examination of *Reservation Blues*, where "the blues speak not just an African American history and identity, but instead seem to generate from a Native American point of reference." Ford argues that the ethos of the novel is controlled by "a distinct blues-tone" and that "prominent blues images" function to "facilitate the cultural intersection for which the blues serve as trope." Scott Andrews's "A New Road and a Dead End in Sherman Alexie's *Reservation Blues*" supports and explores further many of Ford's central suppositions, illustrating some of the ways in which the processes of scholarly inquiry acknowledge, evaluate, and extend insight and judgment. Andrews's ideas about hybridity, cross-cultural intermixture, and what he calls "Alexie's paradigmatic despair" widen the scope of study of Alexie's first novel, delving into some of the more substantial matters that Alexie's book introduces, aspects that were initially neglected as reviewers responded to the most immediately striking features of narrative and character.

As Alexie's collections of poetry were published, scholars felt obligated to take into account the entire cultural context that his writing encompasses. Laura Arnold Leibman is attentive to this trend, but her "A Bridge of Difference: Sherman Alexie and the Politics of Mourning" is designed as a close reading of *The Summer of Black Widows* both as "witness to the power of stories" and as a consideration of the ways that Alexie has borrowed "from oral tradition, elegiac conventions, and formal poetic structures." Leibman's reading follows a path that is extended as Cindy M. Spurlock carries the conversation about Alexie's poetic modes toward the present in her employment of the instruments of rhetorical analysis for an enlightening examination of Alexie's development as a poet in *Face*, supporting the assessment that Alexie should now be regarded as a singular and significant voice in contemporary American poetics. In her new essay "The Rhetorical, Performative Poetics of Sherman Alexie: Critical Reflections on Affect, Memory, and Subjectivity," Spurlock utilizes astutely chosen selections from *Face* to demonstrate the range of invention and capability with form that Alexie has attained.

The course of critical scrutiny that followed the publication of Alexie's books is ably assessed by Tammy Wahpeconiah in her new essay "Postmodern Magic, Traditional Rage: The Critical Reception of Sherman Alexie's Work," in which she reaches back to Alexie's early life to lead into the beginning of his appearance in print and then continues on as he becomes a part of a visible literary landscape and then a prominent point in its topography. Touching on representative critical responses, Wahpeconiah indicates the ways in which issues have been raised, disputes have developed, and patterns of meaning have become more pronounced. Her essay includes discussion of the work of scholars reprinted in this volume as well as that of others whose commentary has become a vital component of Alexie's evolving literary legacy.

Michael Wilson's overview of the cultural and historical context referred to by every commentator on Alexie's work, "'Doesn't everybody belong to a subculture?': Community and History in Sherman Alexie's Writing," is an appropriate complement to Wahpeconiah's investigation. Some of the most contentious issues raised by Alexie's writing, filmmaking, and public appearances are given a sensible and perceptive airing as Wilson traces Alexie's "full evolution . . . from youth to maturity, from a singular focus on self and individual ethnicity to a multifaceted, compassionate, and often sharply comedic exploration of human nature." As it became apparent that this "evolution" constituted a *career*, full-length studies of Alexie began to seem like plausible projects. Daniel Grassian's *Understanding Sherman Alexie*, in the respected University of South Carolina series, is a reliable overview, represented here by the chapter on *Indian Killer*. Meredith K. James uses Alexie's work as writer and director of two films, the collaboration with Chris Eyre on *Smoke Signals* (1998) and his own *The Business of Fancydancing* (2002) as a basis for her book *Literary and Cinematic Reservation in Selected Works of Native American Author Sherman Alexie*. Her chapter "'The res has missed you': The Fragmented Reservation of the Mind in *The Business of Fancydancing*" considers that film within the record of Hollywood efforts (and revealing failures) to make films from American Indian history.

The scholarship devoted to Alexie's work has established a foundation for the kinds of studies that take account of the ways that Alexie—writing with a sort of sustained energy emblematic of an artist hitting full stride—continues to define the dimensions of a postmodern man of letters in twenty-first-century America. Lisa Tatonetti's "Sex and Salmon: Queer Identities in Sherman Alexie's *The Toughest Indian in the World*" recapitulates the publishing history of works about "Two-Spirit Native peoples" and then provides an illuminating, careful reading of Alexie's candid rendering of sensitive and previously forbidden terrain. In her new essay "Articulations of Difference: Minority Existence in White America in Sherman Alexie's *Indian Killer* and Toni Morrison's *The Bluest Eye*," Constance Bracewell delineates the points of correspondence between these two works, not only showing the ways that both novels "map out the psychological, emotional, and experiential pain of being 'different'" but also revealing strategies of narrative progression, thematic insertion, and authorial control that justify the comparison of Alexie with a Nobel laureate.

Richard Sax's new essay "A Rez Kid Gone Urban: Sherman Alexie's Recent Short Fiction" traces the transition in Alexie's work from the stories in his stunning debut collection, with its now iconic title *The Lone Ranger and Tonto Fistfight in Heaven,* to the PEN/Faulkner Award-winning *War Dances* of 2009, explaining and illustrating how, while still involved with issues on "the rez," Alexie's characters are now living on the entire continent, though not as American Indians once did. In his essay "Half Child/Half Adult: Sherman Alexie's Hybrid Young Adult Fiction," Mark Vogel, writing with an expert's understanding of the field of young adult literature, is able to account for the impressive success of Alexie's *The Absolutely True Diary of a Part-Time Indian* by showing how the work recalls some of the classic tropes of young adult writing while presenting a fresh and vibrant take on archetypal elements. In the final reprinted work in this volume, Margo Rabb, herself a successful author of national repute, engages Alexie in a high-spirited, revealing discussion of his current plans and future possibilities.

Alexie's work, as serious scholars, inquisitive interviewers, and fascinated readers report, emerges in the form of imaginative expressions of his eventful life, and Georgie L. Donovan, in her biographical sketch of Alexie, provides a lucid and incisive guide to many of the most noteworthy incidents and circumstances that inform its essence. The combination of controversy, compelling writing, and a dynamic personal presence has projected Alexie into a unique position in contemporary American culture, and his work has reached a much wider range of readers than would have been anticipated even by the supportive and discerning editors at Hanging Loose Press when they received, unbidden, his first poems.

Amid the abundance of substantial scholarship devoted to Alexie's work, the process of selection of reprints for this volume required thoughtful scrutiny, and April McGinnis provided valuable assistance with this task. The essays in this volume have been chosen to address the interests and needs of a broad range of readers, from students seeking further insights into stories and poems that call to them to teachers who hope to deepen their understanding of books that they want to share with their students, to scholars who wish to join a conversation among their peers that touches some of the most vital, current issues of literary and cultural studies. In his citation of *War Dances* as the winner of the PEN/Faulkner Award, poet Al Young said that the book "taps every vein and nerve, every tissue, every issue that quickens the current blood-pulse," lauding Alexie for "the caring, eye-opening beauty of this rollicking, bittersweet gem of a book." The intention and purpose of this volume is to provide critical insights worthy of that achievement.

# CAREER, LIFE, AND INFLUENCE

# On Sherman Alexie:
## American Man of Letters_____

Leon Lewis

> And there is always one more story
>
> —Simon J. Ortiz, *A Good Journey*, 1977

The fracturing of the consensus concerning a common American culture and the proliferation of factions contending for prominence within the American literary cosmos have not entirely removed the tendency toward the anointment of a single figure as the face of a cultural community. Especially for emerging literary cohorts, it has been a convention of convenience to designate one writer to represent everyone. While the concept of a "main current" of American literature has been reconfigured toward what Ishmael Reed has identified as an "ocean" with many separate streams, the inclination to recognize an African American writer, a Latino (or Latina) American writer, and—since the 1960s—a "Native American writer" of special distinction has continued the categorization that mingles respect with regionalist confinement.

J. J. Phillips, one of Reed's coeditors of *The Before Columbus Foundation Poetry Anthology*, summarizes the foundation's intentions by commenting that contrary to "the negative, exclusionary paradigm advanced by those who cling with desperate tenacity to the myth of a western European-American monoculture . . . multiculturalism is all embracing." The streams and eddying currents that Reed navigated contributed to the charting of a much more elaborate map than that which had been drawn on the assumption of an Anglo/American ascendancy, a map assembled point by point, or person by person, since so many of the sites on the new map were marked by names and works familiar primarily to those members of that particular group or gathering. Among other distinct streams, the foundation recognized works by American Indian writers for the Before Columbus Foundation

American Book Awards from the first awards in 1980, beginning that year with Leslie Marmon Silko's *Ceremony* (1977), followed by Peter Blue Cloud's award for *Back Then Now* in 1981, the year after its publication, then Duane Niatum's *Song for the Harvester of Dreams* (1982), Maurice Kenny's *The Mama Poems* (1984), and William Oandasan's *Round Valley Songs* (1985), volumes hardly noticed by other national organizations, academic journals, or anthologies beyond specific themed collections or token inclusions of items from ostensibly exotic fringe minorities.

The writers recognized were, at that time, relatively unknown and their introduction to wider readership was instrumental in the acknowledgment, if not full acceptance, of Reed's assertion that "American literature is an ocean." An examination of the list of awards from 1980 to 1990, published in *The Before Columbus Poetry Anthology* (1992), indicates just how prescient Reed and his coeditors were. Louise Erdrich's *Love Medicine* (1985), Harvey Pekar's *American Splendor* (1987), and Henry Louis Gates's *The Signifying Monkey: A Theory of Afro-American Literary Criticism* (1989) are illustrations of works now regarded as almost "classic" whose authors were relatively obscure at that time. For American Indian writers, however, an appearance in the wider literary cosmos did not result in much more attention to their work by scholars or readers beyond a few notable exceptions such as Erdrich, Silko, and N. Scott Momaday, whose Pulitzer Prize for *House Made of Dawn* in 1969 was a landmark moment in terms of a national awareness of Native writers.

The foundation's goal was, in Robert Duncan's apt observation, "the opening of the field," and although awards also imply a kind of hierarchy, a deliberate effort was made to avoid any ordering of precedence. This laudable aim, however, is contrary to the "best list" inclinations of so many other elements of contemporary American culture. The work of American Indian authors was almost entirely invisible beyond a small community of initiates prior to the publication of Momaday's *House Made of Dawn* in 1968, and there was an understandable although drastically flawed assumption that the most easily recognizable name must belong to the "best" American Indian writer. Momaday's compelling narrative in conjunction with his affable projection of wisdom in many public appearances initially established him as *the* American Indian—or, as was the convention at the time, *the* Native American—writer, a mantle he neither sought nor exploited but that enhanced his position. The opportunity for Native writers to participate in a publishing practice that had been in existence only in limited form from the early eighteenth century was a welcome phenomenon.

To use Catherine Rainwater's formulation, native writers had joined "the tribe of pressed leaves," her designation for "the steadily increasing tribe of 'books' such as those by Erdrich and other Native American writers that aim to revise not simply the record of the past but the shape of the future." Momaday was thrust into a kind of prominence that he handled so impressively that the kind of rivalry that has afflicted many other "schools" (an inexact but common collective term for any loose affiliation of artists) was mostly subdued, if inevitably arising. The appearance of such a competent and appealing spokesman was primarily positive, but it also meant that unless someone heard Simon J. Ortiz read his poetry, or Erdrich talk about her unique meld of native and German/American experience, or Gerald Vizenor examine trends in American Indian literature with original insight and intellectual rigor equal to academic commentators speaking about much more familiar specialties, there was just one spokesperson for/of, in William Oandasan's phrase, "the voice of an ancient age/ dreaming of breath." As Craig Womack notes, "By 1990, though more than two thousand books had been authored by Native people in twenty years, a huge proportion of critical attention had been focused on the same five Native authors over and over again," and during that era, Momaday was known to many more people than Erdrich, Vizenor, Silko, and James Welch. Womack claims that the following twenty years have not resulted in much of a change, in that "with an occasional bow to Louis Owens, Sherman Alexie, maybe one or two others at best," the literary journals that run special issues on Native literature continue their concentration on the favored authors. Womack might be underestimating the conversation about a writer such as Welch, notably lauded on his homeground, and Silko, whose national reputation has been growing steadily, but his assertion is not inaccurate.

Four decades after Momaday's breakthrough, no really significant change has taken place in the way a public perception of American Indian culture is formed, although the role of notable *Native American* has now been taken by Sherman Alexie, who, as the face of American Indian culture, is more recognizable than any other artist, if perhaps not the equal of pop-culture icons such as Kevin Costner, who appeared to dance with wolves, or "Iron Eyes Cody," whose tears helped to expunge vague feelings of guilt among non-Native citizens. From his numerous appearances to read his work in all kinds of settings to his performances as poetry slam champion, to his energetic and entertaining visits to television programs such as *The Oprah Winfrey Show* and *The Colbert Report*, Alexie has attained a kind of visibility and celebrity that has begun to edge into the area occupied by minor athletes, actors, and musicians. Womack, in 2008, wondered about the dangers of celebrity corrupting Native studies, and, in terms of the compilation of an anthology of "unfamous" Native writers, remarked that he had thought that "all of us were 'unfamous' anyway," since he could not "imagine that even someone like N. Scott Momaday has ever been plagued by paparazzi," before reflecting "but I could be wrong." There has been some predictable resentment in response to Alexie's prominence, but more significant than the negative reactions to Alexie's fame are the ways in which it might detract from his accomplishments as a writer. In the true meaning of the term, Alexie should be understood not only as an exemplar of an important strain of American literature but also as an American "man of letters," a distinction that previously has been reserved for writers who more closely (if perhaps superficially) resemble the august presences of English writers of previous centuries.

Even if the whole concept of a "man of letters" reeks of an antique attitude—Is there a corresponding category for the "woman of letters"?—the appellation has some appealing aspects, especially in an era when honorifics reflect brands as much as achievements. The original usage implied a degree of literacy in a fundamentally nonliterate society, which meant the mind as a living record of a culture's continuity. It had a particular resonance in a preprint era, when memory and orality were crucial for the survival of civilized society, and as widespread literacy became the standard for relatively advanced nations, it was replaced by the less felicitous "public intellectual." Momaday had something of this in mind in his essay "Man Made of Words," which deals with a historic recapitulation of Kiowa culture in which an engagement with the roots of language reveals layers of history. The Enlightenment concept of belles lettres carries some of the same implications, and the sense of something beautiful indicates a respect for a writer's ability to create something linked to positive qualities in both the human and the natural universe, entities that writers have been fascinated to comprehend in a harmony of intersections.

To see Alexie in this fashion is to emphasize the range of his literary inventions and to recognize his roots in a variety of traditional and esoteric linguistic practices, as well as to acknowledge his desire to be an active participant in a serious social agenda. Poetry, short fiction, novels, essays, screenplays, meta-autobiographical excursions, broadsides, dialogues/conversations, scraps from notebooks, sketches, pages defying genre and categorization—all have been a part of his *production*, although that word conveys grind-it-out tenacity rather than an urge to write that cannot be contained. While it is somewhat simplistic to equate an author with any of his characters, it is hard to separate some of Thomas Builds-the-Fire's dynamic determination to give form to the stories that shape his spirit from Alexie's writing paths. In an oft-noted passage in *Reservation Blues*, Thomas's stories "climbed into your clothes like sand, gave you itches that could not be scratched. If you repeated even a sentence from one of those stories, your throat was never the same again. These stories hung in your hair and clothes like smoke"—a powerful expression of the enduring effect that is at the heart of writer's desire, the deeper need deflected by Alexie's sardonic comment in an interview about the rewards for a writer: "Money and attention," and when the interviewer prompted, "Beside that," Alexie answered, "Don't let any writer fool you."

Alexie's apparent confession of abrupt candor is a verbal shield to protect the sincerity of Thomas's urge to satisfy the impossible goal of doing justice to his need to be "the self-proclaimed storyteller of the Spokane tribe." It is an admission that echoes James Joyce's young artist's aspiration to "forge in the smithy of my soul the uncreated conscience of my race." The colossal hubris of Stephen Dedalus's declaration risks the accusation of arrogance, and Alexie has had to face such accusations, but anything less would be like settling for the acceptable, which diminishes the goal from the Promethean to the merely practical. In 1999, Alexie said that "Thomas and Victor are a very high percentage of me," and in 2007, he reaffirmed the linkage to Thomas ("in the very first short story I ever wrote"), saying, "I just know that I'm doing now what I would have been doing 200 years ago," traveling the world telling stories. But there is Victor as well, the would-be warrior who sees counting goals in the basketball arena as a modern version of "counting coups," who could be the guitar-hero of the rez rock band, who is overflowing with the kind of anger that led to *Indian Killer*, and who needs the injection of humor that is a major component of Alexie's stand-up-comic, antic strategy for psychic survival. Introducing an element that he insists is a part of a more private dimension of Indian tradition, Alexie insists, "Maybe my stories have more dick jokes in them but they're still traditional." He has strenuously maintained that his way of being an Indian is as valid and viable as that of any other Native artist.

One of the main issues of contention among Native scholars has been the definition of *Indianness*, a vitally important consideration for a community that has had its identity suppressed, assaulted, determined by outside agencies, and nearly obliterated. The issuance by the federal government of the United States of permits to set up gambling operations has added another layer of economic incentive to the lawsuits over mineral rights on lands subject to reclamation by the tribes who held original possession of them. The resulting legalistic intratribal disputes—a contemporary continuance of historic tribal warfare—are reflected in the active discussions among scholars about what has been called "essentialism," the idea that there is an *authentic or essential* Indian identity. The initial enthusiasm for this position has been altered or eroded by an insistence on the complexity of "Indian diversity across and within tribes." Alexie's approach to this intense conversation is exemplified by "An Incomplete List of People I Wish Were Indian," one of the subsections in the opening "chapter"—"The Unauthorized Biography of Me"—of his hybrid collection *One Stick Song* (2000). This "chapter" is a declaration and exposition of individual identity, and the list is startling in its choices, proposing a reconsideration of value and validity, its serious intent modulated by the juxtapositions of people whose attributes suggest sharp contrasts and then more subtle correspondences. It begins with heroic originators

Kareem Abdul-Jabbar
Adam
Muhammad Ali

whose names denote their self-created identities; then a gender expansion, with a tilt toward the political

Susan B. Anthony
Jimmy Carter
Patsy Cline

followed by artists in various fields

Robert De Niro
Emily Dickinson
Isadora Duncan
Amelia Earhart

and onward, resisting any easy patterns of organization before winding up with

John Steinbeck
Superman
Harriet Tubman
Voltaire
Walt Whitman

Alexie has made the primacy of poetry an important part of a personal credo, and the appearances of a basketball player and a singer near the top of the list are designed to reveal two of his life passions, both of which figure prominently in *Reservation Blues*, a fictional projection of achievement in the absence of any available historical account. Alexie's story of the rise of the reservation garage band Coyote Springs, highlighted by a symbolic basketball game acting as an emblem of combat between cultures, is presented as an imaginative deliberation on the integrative aspects of American Indians with the main lines of American culture from which separation is impossible. Victor, his search for his father close to a conclusion in *Smoke Signals*, summarizes their intricate relationship with the story of a basketball game—he in his youth with his father against Jesuit priests ostensibly offering education and instruction on the rez—and the ball in his hands for the last shot with the game on the line. This parallels the game in *Reservation Blues* where two Indians—the legendary rez superstar of an earlier generation, Samuel Builds-the-Fire, Jr. (Thomas's father), and the very ordinary Lester FallsApart, just another guy on the rez—are matched with a six-man team of tribal cops (who must claim some Indian blood to qualify—*Which side are you on?*). Complementing

Samuel's otherworldly shot making, which keeps his team in the game, Alexie develops a running dialogue of trash talk that picks up on memorable moments in Anglo/Indian history:

> Samuel cut behind Lester, took a handoff, shrugged off Wilson and William, and launched a thirty-foot jumper.
> "For Crazy Horse," Samuel said as he released the ball.
>
> SAMUEL AND LESTER—2
>
> TRIBAL COPS—0

The game is not simply the aggrieved against the ascendant. As the game continues:

> The Chief threw the ball to Art Heavy Burden, who missed a jumper, but the Chief followed the shot and put the rebound back in.
>
> TRIBAL COPS—6
>
> SAMUEL AND LESTER—3
>
> "That shot was for every time one of you drunk ass Indians told me I wasn't real," the Chief said. "That was for every time you little fuckers think pissing in your pants is a ceremonial act."

With the tribal cops one basket away from victory, Samuel "stole the ball, drove down the court, and went in for a two-handed, rattle-the-foundations, ratify-a-treaty, abolish-the-income tax, close-the-uranium-mines monster dunk":

> "That was for every one of you Indians like you Tribal Cops," Samuel said. "That was for all those Indian scouts who helped the U.S. Cavalry. That

was for Wounded Knee I and II. For Sand Creek. Hell, that was for both the Kennedys, Martin Luther King and Malcolm X."

The shifting focus of sympathy that rides with Samuel "flying four feet above the basketball court" is a mix of history, hope, desire and, ultimately, defeat. "You never told us who won that game between your father and the tribal cops," Chess says to Thomas. "Who do you think?" Thomas asks. "Who do you think won that game?" he demands, blending the mythmaking capacity of his stories with the grip of reality that is riveted into tribal memory.

From the start of his entrance into the world of letters, Alexie has devoted his life to the promotion and encouragement of Native cultural events, utilizing the increasing popularity and prominence of his written work as an opportunity to take part in every aspect of American Indian life. There is a rough parallel between Alexie's developing role as a supporter, encourager, adviser, and celebrator and that which Allen Ginsberg grew into as each man became both the visual embodiment and the conservator of a bourgeoning literary culture initially dismissed, even despised, by the arbiters of the literary establishment. In a direct statement of his commitment to an ongoing exploration of his heritage, Alexie says:

> I made a very conscious decision to marry an Indian woman, who made a very conscious decision to marry me.
>
> Our hope: to give birth to and raise Indian children who love themselves. That is the most revolutionary act.

For Alexie, the familial extended toward the tribal, and his willingness to respond with characteristic friendliness to requests from every corner of American Indian life is a testament to the sincerity of his sentiments. Alexie's first entries into print were in small, local journals publishing near Spokane, Washington, as he sought acceptance for his early work, and then in small journals anywhere when he could find editors astute enough to recognize an emerging writer of unusual ability, as well as a cultural perspective not shared by many other contributors or the magazine's readership. Prior to the publication of his break-out book, *The Business of Fancydancing: Stories and Poems* (1992), by Hanging Loose Press in Brooklyn, he placed poems in the press's journal, and following the positive response to the book, he used the increasing opportunities of his modest prominence to assist other writers and to participate in what he regarded as activities designed to introduce and direct attention to what was still an almost invisible or misunderstood but thriving Native artistic enterprise.

Alexie's fourteen-"stanza" poem in the spring 1992 issue of *Blue Mesa Review* was like an extension, or continuance, of the poetic modes he had been pursuing in *Fancydancing*, designed as a commentary on the political themes that his stories and poems explored. The journal was designated "Special Issue: 1492-1992" and on the back cover listed Alexie among Paula Gunn Allen, Adrian C. Louis, and Leslie Marmon Silko at the moment when a signal publication of each author had recently appeared—Allen's short fiction *Spider Woman's Granddaughters* (1989), Louis's poems *Among the Dog Eaters* (1992), and Silko's *Almanac of the Dead* (1991, reviewed by Joy Harjo in the issue). Alexie's poem "Imagining the Reservation" is dedicated to Louis and alternates single statements ("3. Survival = Anger × Imagination;" "4. Imagination is the only weapon on the reservation") with paragraphs of exposition. The assertive nature of Alexie's imaginative social constructs ("1. Imagine Crazy Horse invented the atom bomb in 1876 and detonated it over Washington, D.C. Would the urban Indians still be sprawled around the one-room apartment in the cable television reservation?") were provocative in the manner of a call to an awakening of honest introspection, prevalent queries pushing past the familiar kind of intraethnic "circling the wagons" sadly common among beleagured minorities. When Alexie asked in section 6, "How do we forgive our enemies when the battle is Indian versus Indian?" he was voicing the forbidden, and the negative reactions were not unexpected. This kind of unrestrained honesty, however, was tempered by Alexie's readiness to respond to the requests for collaboration that arrived with increasing frequency as his visibility expanded. His interview with Charlene Teters in the spring 1998 issue of *Indian Artist*, "the Magazine of Contemporary Native American Art, Music, Literature, Film, Photography, Theater & Dance," announced on the cover with a striking photo of Alexie reaching—or possibly dispatching a signal—toward the reader, is an example of the kind of open, friendly conversation Alexie was ready to have with almost everyone interested in his work, regardless of their backgrounds. If the photo on the cover is somewhat confrontational, the full-page photo preceding the interview is endearing—Alexie, arms crossed, looking up and leaning out of the page, his warm smile glowing, his books in front of him (amid biographies of Vladimir Nabokov and Beryl Markham) offered as a gift to the reader.

Alexie understood that different occasions and publications would provide forums for the illumination of different phases of his work. His contribution to the fall 1994 issue of *Zyzzyva* followed the editor's distribution of a "layout board" upon which each artist "was asked to work directly." This gave Alexie a way to discuss some of his individual methods of composition. "Writer's Notebook, The" began with an explanatory essay:

> My "notebook" is actually a U-Haul cardboard box where I toss every scrap of paper that I've ever touched with a pen, pencil, crayon, or typewriter, hotel stationery, paper, envelopes, etc. I fill these pages with poem ideas, rough drafts of rough drafts, story ideas, "great themes" I should be addressing, jokes, cartoons that become jokes in my reading routines (my secret wish is to be a stand-up comic), character sketches, outlines, random thoughts, grocery lists, telephone numbers, and other stuff.

This is the characteristic congenial, open, and high-spirited voice that is Alexie's way of beginning conversations—straightforward, not particularly self-conscious but appealingly self-aware, and clearly pleased to be sharing something of importance with someone who is interested. The page after the "layout board," however, immediately calls attention to Alexie's central subject. The single word "Airplane," handwritten, appears. A few spaces beneath it, Alexie has written:

> Up here, where no Indian was ever meant to be
> I carry small things . . . to insure my safety:

A theme, attitude, location, and cultural foundation are included in the couplet. The next page has a column of figures from a "Stephanie Inn" (Cannon Beach, Oregon) notepad, plus, in response to the query "What does an Ocean smell like?" the thought "Sex + death." Then another four pages of ideas (World Cup Soccer = poem?) lead to a page with a rough sketch of two people (Indians, since each has a long feather on his head) at the CHEZ POWWOW, where the waiter is asking, "Would you like that fry bread with white wine sauce or the vinaigrette?" This is followed by a two-page spread from the calendar for April 1992, each day/box filled with directive or summative notes, a brief diary of a perhaps typical month in a writer's life. The final four pages are "Short Story Idea" on stationery from Lewis & Clark College/Business Office; an evaluation form (YOUR THOUGHTS ARE IMPORTANT!!) asking, for instance, "What did you like best about the conference?" with Alexie responding:

> There were ghosts
> in my hotel room, but they were boring

"What could be improved?"

> and didn't know any stories I hadn't heard
> before

Then, a letter from a friend (April 92) denoted "a found poem!" with Alexie's reply:

> Dear Aaron—
> I know.
> Love—
> Sherman

And finally a page from a local newspaper, the second story on the page headed "Writing Congress is 'No-No' for Tribal Staff" with a note from Alexie running up the left margin, an arrow pointing toward the story, "found poem!?—epigram(ph)—short story!-uggh!"

Energized by the response to *The Lone Ranger and Tonto Fistfight in Heaven*, with the novel *Reservation Blues* on the way toward publication (referred to as *Coyote Spring* in the notes about the author), Alexie is assuming that there is at least a small and discerning readership curious about his writing practices. "The Writer's Notebook" is a typical sample from a transitional time when Alexie began to use his relative national prominence to lead Native cultural events toward a wider audience while continuing to place poems in journals, on broadsheets, and on DVDs whose focus was more specific in intent. The first scene of an Oregon Public Television documentary in 1993 shows Alexie as he speaks lines from his poem "Horses of Their Own Making," which was used for the title of the film and which established its theme of spiritual regeneration. A DVD from Evergreen State College in 2003 called "Under a Silver Sky: Poetry and Place in the Pacific Northwest" includes a poem from Alexie along with work from other "regional artists" such as Raymond Carver, Carolyn Kizer, Denise Levertov, Theodore Roethke, and Gary Snyder, as well as many less well-known poets. A broadsheet from Midnight Paper Sales in an edition of ninety, separately numbered, each copy signed by Alexie, has the poem "HE STOOD THERE IN THE DARK" to mark the occasion of a reading at the Hungry Mind bookstore in 1996. Alexie offered the poem "Father and Farther" (from *The Summer of Black Widows*) to the book *Will Work for Peace: New Political Poems* (1996), a multiethnic collection from a wide spectrum of poets including established writers such as Donald Hall and W. D. Snodgrass and many less familiar writers.

At the same time that his work as a screenwriter was bringing him into contact with one of the centers of American popular culture, Alexie expanded his participation in Native projects, writing an introduction to a chapbook, *Coyote Laughing: Poems from Earl Thompson* (2003) from Real Change Press in Seattle, an organization that "provides income opportunity to poor and homeless people through publication and street sales of a bi-weekly, urban-issues newspaper," and an introduction to a large-format book of photographs, *Real Indians: Portraits of Contemporary Native Americans and America's Tribal Colleges* (2003), from Melcher Media and the W. K. Kellogg Foundation. Alexie's heartfelt response to the skillful portraits is both a celebration of achievement and an invitation to the non-Native viewer to share an aspect of a world he is proud of. His foreword to *How to Rise: Or, I Put My Heart into the Close* (2009), "a collection of personal narrative, short fiction, and poetry by forty-six seniors from Ypsilanti High School in Michigan," stemmed from a visit to a juvenile detention center and is based on his belief that "the reading and writing of books will save us. It has always saved us. Storymaking and storytelling is that powerful." This is another version of a credo that is at the core of Alexie's writing life from the start, central to American Indian experience since it is central to human experience. And in a confluence of interests—rock music/poetry/movies—Alexie wrote an introduction to a new edition of P. F. Kluge's novel *Eddie and the Cruisers* (1980), the basis for the film of 1983, in 2009. As Alexie explains:

> I first saw the film in VHS while I was in high school, along with my basketball teammates, and most of them hated it. It was too romantic and nostalgic for most teenage boys. . . . But a few of us quietly loved the flick. My best friend Steve and I became obsessed with it.

And at the end of a characteristically vibrant, insightful, and very personal essay, he concludes:

> Yes, this is a novel about sex, drugs, rock and roll, murder and the caesura. How could one not love it?

In his introduction "Hope and Grace: The Poetry of Earl Thompson," Alexie recalls that when he was "twenty-one years old and a junior at Washington State University," although he was a "Spokane/ Coeur d'Alene Indian bookworm who grew up on the Spokane Indian Reservation, I'd never before read any poem written by any Native American." In Thompson's poetry, he "recognized the coyote humor, aching sadness and lyrical beauty" and "saw myself in his work." Alexie has not, himself, written about the Coyote figure very often, but the shape-shifting, protean aspects of this archetypal entity endlessly associated with Native people while eluding constricting definition have some correspondence with Alexie's life. In "Tuxedo with Eagle Feathers," a poem he published among a group of five in issue 16 of *Smartish Pace* in April 2009, Alexie gleefully and ruefully acknowledges the turmoil of impulse and inclination that drives his poems, yet another (or actually recurring) "chapter" in the ongoing "Unauthorized Biography of Me" (as he puts it in *One Stick Song*). The unexpected juxtaposition of formal dress with tribal style in the title is a familiar trope for Alexie, two aspects of his essential self, and his employment of a poem to rebuke one of his persistent adversaries stems from his conviction that whatever else he may be/do, he, like W. B. Yeats in a similar attempt at explanation, has "cast my heart into my rhymes."

Alexie's writing life begins with poetry, returns continually and relentlessly to poetry with a sometimes fearful urgency blended with a fierce joy—this is why he is so adamant about the critique from Elizabeth Cook-Lynn, his chosen figure for the "swarm of professional locusts" who, he insists, have been resisting "the individual Indian artist's right to be an eccentric bastard." He sees himself as superbly prepared to use poetic power in an attack/rebuttal that incarnates the warrior spirit never completely absent from his work—and life:

> Let me slap Cook-Lynn upside her head with the right hand of John Keats and the left hand of Emily Dickinson. Let me kick her in the shin with the left toe of Marianne Moore and the right toe of John Donne. I wasn't saved by the separation of cultures; I was reborn inside the collision of cultures.

Alexie, one might speculate, would be pleased to see Cook-Lynn come back with a similarly barbed response using a vernacular mostly avoided by academic critics—if she were so inclined and had the linguistic capacity for that kind of reaction. It could be something akin to Samuel and the Chief, their clash on the basketball court epitomized by their verbal ability to accentuate action with exposition. True sovereignty is a condition of freedom wherein Cook-Lynn can say what she wants—and so can Alexie.

As Momaday has spoken of a "man made of words," Alexie has earned the accolade "American man (made) of letters," reviving and redefining the traditional term for his time, an honored practice sustaining a country's culture through the power of an individual's engagement with the "complexities and contradictions inherent in American society," as Tammy Wahpeconiah ably describes Alexie's work. He is supported in this task by his commitment to his original intention to be a storyteller of the Spokane tribe who dances with words in the world of language.

# Biography of Sherman Alexie _____

Georgie L. Donovan

Soon after Sherman J. Alexie, Jr., was born on October 7, 1966, in Wellpinit, Washington (Spokane Indian reservation), he underwent brain surgery for hydrocephalus, a life-threatening excess of cerebrospinal fluid gathered in the brain. The surgery, which can itself cause death or mental impairment, successfully saved his life; however, his first seven years were marked by epileptic seizures, doses of powerful sedatives, and frequent medical interventions to ensure his healthy intellectual development. In interviews, Alexie credits early intense attention to his brain development by health professionals with affording him the opportunity to learn to read by age three and to begin devouring the literature that would later shape his career as a writer.

## Reservation Life

This concentration on Alexie's early childhood health and education stands in contrast to the experience of others living in Wellpinit, Washington, on the Spokane Indian reservation where he grew up, fifty miles northwest of Spokane. Grappling with enduring symptoms from a long history of persistent oppression and genocide of Native Americans, the members of his community were plagued by poverty, violence, and substance abuse. When he is criticized for portraying stereotypes of alcoholism or violence among Native Americans, Alexie scoffs at any "romantic fool" who has not seen the damage caused by alcohol abuse and this environment of poverty and despair ("Author").

These problems did not miss Alexie's own family. Neither of Alexie's parents, Sherman Joseph Alexie (a Coeur d'Alene Indian) and Lillian Agnes Cox Alexie (of Spokane, Flathead, and Colville heritage), graduated from high school. Within his own family, alcoholism was widespread. In one interview, he described its impact: "My dad wasn't violent, but he would leave us to go drinking, and would sometimes be gone for a few weeks. He was completely undependable and unpredictable. My wife's father was a scary and unpredictable alcoholic, charming and funny one moment, violent and caustic the next" (Thiel 138). His older sister and her husband died in a mobile home fire. This atmosphere of violence, alcoholism, and poverty pervades much of Alexie's writing whether the setting is on or off the reservation.

Though Alexie lays bare the distressing realities of reservation life without idealization, he nevertheless is fiercely proud of and connected to his heritage and his people, and he is ever protective of the authentic presentation of Native Americans in writing and pop culture. "The responsibilities of being an Indian writer are enormous," he has observed (Purdy 50). Life on the reservation and the culture of his people are driving forces in his life and his writings: "I grew up on the Spokane Indian reservation, and my tribe heavily influences my personality and the ways in which I see the world" (Nygren 146). Alexie particularly emphasizes his multitribal identity, especially when reacting to the rise of fundamentalism in the world since the events of September 11, 2001: "I think fundamentalism is the mistaken belief that one belongs to only one tribe; I am the opposite of that" (Davis and Stevenson 190).

## Education

As an example of Alexie's unflinching gaze at both the positive and the negative aspects of his culture, he recognized at a young age that it would be difficult to obtain a rigorous education in the poorly funded school of the reservation and among members of the community who held a certain disdain for success. Alexie has described a situation among members of his tribe where peers ostracized him for being bookish and others in the community viewed him as arrogant and an overachiever: "Loving books, loving school, the concept of school, was seen as being white. The notion of any sort of success was seen as being white" (Cerna). As he grew up, Alexie's interest in books distinguished him from others in his community. He began reading novels at an early age—such as Steinbeck's *The Grapes of Wrath* by age five—and made it through all of the books in the small reservation school library by the time he was in the fifth grade (FallsApart.com). Often, his intellectual curiosity led to isolation from others and provoked bullying from his classmates, fellow Spokane tribal members.

In his seventh-grade math class, he opened up the textbook at the beginning of the year to find his mother's maiden name inside the cover as a previous owner of the book. Alexie refers to this incident as the tipping point in his realization that he would have to leave the reservation for a better education. He transferred in the eighth grade to a white border-town school off the reservation, which he attended for the remainder of high school. These years, when he was a high school basketball player and the only Native American student at his school, prefigure the experiences of Arnold, the protagonist of *The Absolutely True Diary of a Part-Time Indian* (2007), who also struggles with adapting to both white and Native American societies.

After graduating from high school in 1985, Alexie went to the Jesuit-run Gonzaga University, dropped out, and eventually transferred to Washington State University in 1988. In interviews, Alexie has stated that he dropped out of Gonzaga because of an inability to afford the tuition. He also briefly intended to enroll at the University of Washington, but he never actually became a student there. When he began school again, this time at Washington State, his intent was to study medicine and become a doctor or similarly esteemed professional. However, he quickly learned he was incapable of stomaching the requisite human anatomy courses in the premedicine curriculum. While taking an eclectic range of classes that earned him a degree in American studies, Alexie happened upon a creative-writing course that changed his life. He originally signed up for the course because it was the only one available during a specific time slot he had to fill after dropping out of an anatomy course. The creative-writing professor,

Alex Kuo, gave Alexie a poetry anthology of works by Native American writers titled *Songs from This Earth on Turtle's Back: Contemporary American Indian Poetry*, edited by Joseph Bruchac, which would change his life.

Reading writers whose backgrounds and stories were similar to his opened up a new world for Alexie, and he soon realized his passion and drive for writing. Although he began drinking heavily after high school, he stopped drinking entirely at the age of twenty-three. Like the majority of his family members, he struggled with drinking and is a self-professed recovering alcoholic. His decision to quit drinking coincided with the advent of his career as a writer, when his first book of poems, *The Business of Fancydancing*, was accepted for publication by Hanging Loose Press, a small Brooklyn firm that had published some of his individual poems in its magazine. Since that time, Alexie has proved a prolific writer of poetry and fiction, publishing numerous books and contributing widely to journals, magazines, and anthologies, working on films and screenplays, and leading outreach projects focused on Native American issues.

## Life's Work

Once Alexie began publishing, he stopped pursuing other careers and became a full-time writer. The turning point occurred in 1992, when Alexie won a prestigious National Endowment for the Arts fellowship for poetry ($20,000) and *The Business of Fancydancing*, a collection of poems and short stories, became his first published book. That same year, the book was reviewed in the *New York Times Book Review* alongside other Native American writing, and Alexie was heralded as "one of the major lyric voices of our time" (Kincaid). Following the attention he received from the reviews of *The Business of Fancydancing*, he found it easier to publish and work as a writer, with publishers increasingly interested in his work.

While Alexie can be considered first and foremost a poet, having published numerous books of poetry, he is better known among many readers for his stories and novels. His first major book of fiction, *The Lone Ranger and Tonto Fistfight in Heaven*, was published in 1993 by Atlantic Monthly Press. The book tells of the lives of residents of the Spokane Indian reservation, weaving together serious and living history with elements of modernity that any American teenager would recognize. The book features both poetry and fiction, a rare marriage of genres. Alexie describes this blending of format as an unintentional pairing made by a first-time author, although he defends its use, stating, "I think that fusion is just natural, maybe even reflexive" (Thiel 136).

Alexie's first major novels were published soon after; these include *Reservation Blues* (1995) and *Indian Killer* (1996). *Reservation Blues* features some of the same characters as in *The Lone Ranger and Tonto Fistfight in Heaven* and has a similar tone, weaving together humor, reality that is at times heartbreaking, and poetic language and imagery. *Indian Killer*, however, is more bleak. In the shape of a murder mystery, the book focuses on themes of massacre—the systematic genocide of Native Americans and the murders committed by the central character, who is himself Native American. Both these works received wide attention in the press, and *Granta* magazine named Alexie one of the "twenty best American novelists under the age of 40" in its 1996 issue.

Approached by a young Cheyenne/Arapaho filmmaker named Chris Eyre, Alexie began turning some of the characters and one of the stories from *The Lone Ranger and Tonto Fistfight in Heaven* into a screenplay, and then into a movie. *Smoke Signals*, the resulting film, was released in 1998 at the Sundance Film Festival. The film relates the story of Spokane young men Victor and Thomas on a journey to collect the ashes of Victor's father, who has died in Phoenix, Arizona. Victor's father had left his family ten years earlier, and Victor struggles with an inability to forgive him for his alcoholism, abusive nature, and abandonment. The screenplay is based on the story "This Is What It

Means to Say Phoenix, Arizona" and weaves in other characters from *The Lone Ranger and Tonto Fistfight in Heaven. Smoke Signals* received significant critical and public attention, and the film garnered awards for the cast and crew from Sundance, other national and international film festivals, and the Independent Spirit Awards.

Alexie has described working in the medium of film as "so fun, and so intense, so immediate"; he sees film as the ideal medium for reaching large audiences, including Native American people (Purdy 38). His work in films includes screenwriting for the short documentary *49?* (2003) and writing and directing *The Business of Fancydancing* (2002). The importance of this work cannot be underestimated, for, as Dan Georgakas has noted in an article and interview in *Cineaste*, "Hopefully, [*Smoke Signals*] will prove to be the first of a new wave of diverse Native American films. The ethnic group that has been featured more than any other in the history of American films is finally beginning to speak in its own voice" (qtd. in West and West 61).

Since 1992 Alexie has published a book of poetry every few years, and he has also been recognized as a performer of poetry, perhaps most notably by the World Poetry Bout Association, which hosted competitive poetry slams for twenty-two years. Featuring three of Alexie's favorite elements—competition, humor, and art—poetry slams feature two poets facing off. Alexie first won the championship in 1998 and then went on to become the only four-time winner of the competition, taking on poets such as Jimmy Santiago Baca to become the "World Heavyweight Poetry Champ."

Alexie's poetry is a study in interlacing textures. He entwines formal structures (sonnets, rhymed couplets, and other forms) with prose poetry and informal verse. He knits together political or cultural observations with wit, storytelling, anger, love, and pain. Often, the speaker of the poems runs passionately from one emotion to another, offering grave sincerity followed by cutting critique followed by humor. Alexie's works are often on reviewers' year-end lists of best poetry books and have earned popularity far beyond the world of contemporary poetry. Among poetry books from small presses, Alexie's works account for four of the top five best-selling works of 2000-2009: *One Stick Song, The Business of Fancydancing, First Indian on the Moon, Old Shirts and New Skins*. His poetry collection *Face*, released in 2009, is viewed as an especially important piece of Alexie's work, and it was also the Small Press Distribution's best-selling poetry book of 2009 (FallsApart.com).

Perhaps Alexie's best writing is found in his short stories. His story collections *The Toughest Indian in the World*, published in 2000, and *Ten Little Indians*, published in 2003, have both gained praise and major awards from the literary community. *The Toughest Indian in the World* marks a transition in Alexie's writing from a reservation focus to stories of Indians living in urban settings or moving between the two worlds. As Alexie has observed, "Sixty percent of all Indians live in urban areas, but nobody's writing about them" (Chapel 97)—a fault of contemporary publications that the book consciously corrects. Alexie's short stories may also be among his favorites of his own writing. In a 2007 interview, when pressured to name which were the best among his publications, he admitted to satisfaction with the story "What You Pawn I Will Redeem" from *Ten Little Indians* and "about eight stories. I've written about eight stories that measure up to just about anybody's stories. Probably ten or fifteen poems. That's probably it" (Weich 174). Among his most recent honors, Alexie won the 2010 PEN/Faulkner Award for Fiction for his short-story and verse collection *War Dances*. The book, published by Grove Press in October 2009, includes intensely personal stories of "ordinary men on the brink of exceptional change" (FallsApart).

Alexie returned to novels in 2007, publishing two books about Native American teenagers, but with very different experiences. The first, *The Absolutely True Diary of a Part-Time Indian*, is often read in high schools and by young adults. The story resembles Alexie's own story of going off the reservation to attend high school in an all-white community; the central character, Junior, fights to integrate his new world with his home life and to find human connection in both. The work won many awards, including the 2007 National Book Award for young people's literature. That same year, the book *Flight* was published. Zits, the main character, grapples with the foster care system and a future portending great violence. At the moment before murdering a host of strangers, Zits is jolted once and then again into the bodies of those in the past: figures with pivotal roles in a history of murder and death. Their lives suggest the recurrent legacy of Native American history and inspire an identity crisis for Zits that echoes a universal conflict encountered by all those seeking a path through modern life.

## Public Performance

Sherman Alexie's writings and public speaking engagements are colored with a wide range of emotions, often moving swiftly from heartbreak to hilarity. Coming to the heart of emotion is fundamental to much of Alexie's work, which wrestles with combining storytelling (fiction) and revealed reality of human experience (nonfiction). Alexie demonstrates a commitment to telling the story of Native American experience—particularly the Northwest Native American experience—to a wider audience. He points graphically to the past and present genocide and holocaust of Native peoples and speaks of the damage done without victimizing, or sacrificing the humanity of, his characters. While he attempts to narrate this experience for outsiders, Alexie's work also respects and shields that which is sacred or private among Native American peoples. For example, he resists narrating the details of Native American cultural and religious ceremonies for a white audience, stating in at least one interview that "spiritual matters should be private" ("Border Talk"). These seemingly distant threads can be tied together as a theme of the negotiation of Native American identity. Alexie's intense commitment to Native Americans—to their survival, their stories, and their lives—is coupled with a need to communicate and have other people understand these stories.

## Authenticity

Alexie's commitment to authenticity allows him to speak from a position of strong wisdom, as when he exposed a forgery by an Anglo author posing as a Native American. In his anger and grief over the situation, he wrote: "So why should we be concerned about his lies? His lies matter because he has cynically co-opted as a literary style the very real suffering endured by generations of very real Indians because of very real injustices caused by very real American aggression that destroyed very real tribes" (Alexie). In several interviews, he has critiqued Anglo writers who write about Native Americans to great acclaim from the literary community, when it is such a struggle for Native Americans to tell their own stories and have them heard by any audience. His interest in centering on a truthful narrative of Native experience drives his writing and also his criticism.

Sherman Alexie has lived in Seattle since 1994 with his wife Diane (married in 1994) and two sons, Joseph (born in 1997) and David (born in 2001). He travels widely to speak and read publicly at poetry festivals, universities, and libraries, and he maintains an active, informative, and fascinating Web site at FallsApart.com.

## Works Cited

Alexie, Sherman. "When the Story Stolen Is Your Own." *Time* 29 Jan. 2006. 5 Aug. 2010. http://www.time.com/time/magazine/article/0,9171,1154221,00.html.

"Author Sherman Alexie Targets Young Readers" (transcript). *Morning Edition*. Renee Montagne, host. NPR 21 Sept. 2007. http://www.npr.org/templates/transcript/transcript.php?storyId=14586575.

"Border Talk: Sherman Alexie." *POV*. PBS. 13 Sept. 2010. http://www.pbs.org/pov/pov2002/borders/talk/dialogue010_sa.html.

Cerna, Enrique. "Enrique Cerna Interviews Author and Poet Sherman Alexie" (transcript). *KCTS 9 Website* 11 July 2008. 13 Sept. 2010. http://kcts9.org/programs/productions/conversations/transcript/alexie.

Chapel, Jessica. "American Literature: Interview with Sherman Alexie." *Atlantic Unbound* 1 June 2000. Rpt. in *Conversations with Sherman Alexie*. Ed. Nancy J. Peterson. Jackson: UP of Mississippi, 2009. 96-99.

Davis, Tanita, and Sarah Stevenson. "Sherman Alexie." *Finding Wonderland Blog*

7 Nov. 2007. Rpt. in *Conversations with Sherman Alexie*. Ed. Nancy J. Peterson. Jackson: UP of Mississippi, 2009. 187-91.

FallsApart.com. Official Sherman Alexie site. 20 Aug. 2010. http://www.fallsapart.com.

Kincaid, James. "Who Gets to Tell Their Stories?" *New York Times Book Review* 3 May 1992: 1, 24-29.

Nygren, Åse. "A World of Story-Smoke: A Conversation with Sherman Alexie." *MELUS* 30.4 (2005): 149-52. Rpt. in *Conversations with Sherman Alexie*. Ed. Nancy J. Peterson. Jackson: UP of Mississippi, 2009. 141-56.

Purdy, John. "Crossroads: A Conversation with Sherman Alexie." *Studies in American Indian Literature* 9.4 (1997): 1-18. Rpt. in *Conversations with Sherman Alexie*. Ed. Nancy J. Peterson. Jackson: UP of Mississippi, 2009. 36-52.

Thiel, Diane. "A Conversation with Sherman Alexie." *Crossroads: The Journal of the Poetry Society of America* 64 (2004): 4-7. Rpt. in *Conversations with Sherman Alexie*. Ed. Nancy J. Peterson. Jackson: UP of Mississippi, 2009. 135-40.

Weich, Dave. "Revising Sherman Alexie." *Powells.com* online author interviews May 2007. Rpt. in *Conversations with Sherman Alexie*. Ed. Nancy J. Peterson. Jackson: UP of Mississippi, 2009. 169-79.

West, Dennis, and Joan M. West. "Sending Cinematic Smoke Signals: An Interview with Sherman Alexie." *Cineaste* 23.4 (1998): 28-31, 37. Rpt. in *Conversations with Sherman Alexie*. Ed. Nancy J. Peterson. Jackson: UP of Mississippi, 2009. 59-70.

## The *Paris Review* Perspective_____

Barry Harbaugh for *The Paris Review*

Sherman Alexie should not have lived into adulthood. His brain at birth was floating in an excess of cranial fluid that had leaked from his spinal column, a rare and usually fatal condition called hydrocephalus. The disease makes an appearance in two of his books, in his young adult novel *The Absolutely True Diary of a Part-Time Indian* (2007), a fictitious chronicle of Alexie's childhood that won a National Book Award, and in the title story from *War Dances* (2009), a hybrid collection of fiction and poetry that won the PEN/Faulkner Award.

Alexie's life story is the foundation for his prolific output (collections of poetry, collections of short stories, novels, and films). He was born in 1966 on the Spokane Indian reservation in Wellpinit, Washington. His father, a truck driver, was Coeur d'Alene Indian, his mother Spokane—making young Alexie, like one of his characters, "a goofy reservation mixed drink." Alexie claims, on the garrulous biography page of his Web site (FallsApart.com), to have read *The Grapes of Wrath* at age five and the entire collection of the reservation's library by the time he was twelve. A year or so later he fled for an all-white high school in nearby Reardan, where he stood out on the school's basketball team, the Indians.

Even though Alexie has not lived in Wellpinit for more than a few weeks since then, the bleakness of reservation life figures prominently in his work. In "Imagine the Reservation," an Indian boy has his fingers blown off while playing with an M80 on the Fourth of July, but still "has a thumb left to oppose his future." In another story, Alexie describes a moment of silence as "a reservation kind of quiet, where you can hear somebody drinking whiskey on the rocks three miles away." But his stories pair an often despairing vision of the future—what good is hope when it all shakes out the same, anyway?—with an earnest mission of preservation and remembrance, as in the story "Jesus Christ's Half-Brother Is Alive and Well on the Spokane Indian Reservation," where the dread of oblivion retains a bit of mysticism: "There they were and suddenly they were forgotten for just a second and for just a second nobody thought about them and then they were gone."

Those three examples are all from his debut collection, *The Lone Ranger and Tonto Fistfight in Heaven*, which he wrote in a three-month stretch in 1993, when he was twenty-seven. The book brought him fame and critical praise: he was chosen by *Granta* as one of the twenty best fiction writers under forty in 1996. The collection stands beside Bernard Malamud's *The Magic Barrel*—or, for a more contemporary comparison, Jhumpa Lahiri's *Interpreter of Maladies*—as a seminal book of assimilation fiction in the United States, which in the last thirty years has become if not the trunk of American literature then a formidable branch, from Amy Tan to Junot Díaz to Edwidge Danticat to Yiyun Li to David Bezmozgis to Gary Shteyngart, and on and on. The Native American population that Alexie represents both resists and embraces the world of Nike sneakers, Ford pickups, and gangsta rap that they see on television and all around them. The contemporary references and dark humor that Alexie brings to his stories set him apart from the writers of the Native American Renaissance such as Leslie Marmon Silko and Louise Erdrich. In a generational shift that brings to mind the distaste that writers such as Richard Wright and Ralph Ellison had for books like Zora Neale Hurston's *Their Eyes Were Watching God* (a book that Wright called "a minstrel-show"), Alexie told his publisher after *Lone Ranger* had debuted, "I'm not from the eagle-feather and corn-pollen school."

Alexie followed up *Lone Ranger* with a novel, *Reservation Blues*, that took many of the characters from his collection and set them loose in the world—both on and off the reservation. Even when he seems to leave Wellpinit behind, as in *Indian Killer*, a novel about a serial killer set in Seattle, or in many of the stories in *The Toughest Indian in the World*, the insular community they left behind seems to lurk just off-stage, still exerting its influence on everyone who has left. In his most recent book, *War Dances*, though, Alexie's characters rarely refer to the reservation explicitly. Most of the stories feature middle-aged men facing typical middle-class American crises: health scares, home invasions, the sexual precocity of one's children, and so on. In "The Ballad of Paul Nonetheless," our man Paul, a purveyor of expensive vintage denim in Seattle who has been estranged from his wife and daughters for "fucking someone on eBay," has a near breakdown that recalls the haunting lines from "Jesus Christ's Half-Brother"; "I don't want to be forgotten," Paul weeps. "I don't want to be forgotten. Don't forget me. Don't forget me. Don't forget me. Don't forget me." Fear of being lost and neglected, it seems, is not only the preoccupation of the reservation.

## Bibliography

Alexie, Sherman. *The Absolutely True Diary of a Part-Time Indian*. New York: Little, Brown, 2007.

_____. *The Lone Ranger and Tonto Fistfight in Heaven*. New York: Grove Press, 1993.

_____. *Reservation Blues*. New York: Grove Press, 1995.

_____. "Smoke Signals: A Film by Somebody." *Zoetrope: All-Story* 8.4 (Winter 2004).

_____. *The Toughest Indian in the World*. New York: Atlantic Monthly Press, 2000.

_____. *War Dances*. New York: Grove Press, 2009.

Egan, Timothy. "An Indian Without Reservations." *New York Times Magazine* 18 Jan. 1998.

# CRITICAL CONTEXTS

# Navigating the River of the World:
## Collective Trauma in *The Absolutely True Diary of a Part-Time Indian*_____

Tammy Wahpeconiah

Reservations were created by white people for the Native Americans/ Indians to live on and they were plots of land that no body [*sic*] wanted and were just god-awful. White people didn't want the land and had to move them somewhere so they chose the worst land they could find and gave it to the Indians. They did not care about them (and still don't in a way) and pretty much just wanted them dead. The land was not nice, pretty, or easy to live off of [*sic*]. They couldn't do much with the land, so staying alive was very hard. The Indians couldn't just up and leave; they had no where to go, no energy to do so, and the fear of the white people killing them forced them to stay put where they were allowed. Mr. P was the first person who told Junior that "'If you stay on this rez . . . they're going to kill you. I'm going to kill you. We are all going to kill you. . . . You're going to find more and more hope the farther and farther you walk away from this sad, sad, sad reservation'" (43) which means that *the reservation is a place where nothing good happens. There are no dreams, no ambitious people, no motivation and the people who live there are sad, lonely, isolated, and usually end up dying, mostly from alcohol.* This makes the reservation a death camp. Junior finally realizes it when he says "reservations were meant to be prisons. . . . Indians were supposed to move on reservations and die. We were supposed to disappear" (216) and this means that he knows that where he is from is a place where nothing good will happen and no one besides his tribe will know who he is. This is just like a death sentence. *The reservation is just like prison. People who are bad go there, where their humanity is taken away.* (Student response, fall 2009; emphasis added)

The English department at the midsize state university in western North Carolina where I teach offers two lower-level classes with a focus on minority literature: African American Literature and Ethnic American Literature. The Ethnic American Literature course attracts mostly white, mostly non-English majors who take the course to fulfill the literature portion of their humanities requirements. The parameters of the course require those of us who teach it to provide coverage of various American ethnic groups. Recently, my students have read Junot Díaz's *The Brief Wondrous Life of Oscar Wao*, Edwidge Danticat's *The Dew Breaker*, Octavia E. Butler's *Kindred*, Jhumpa Lahiri's *The Namesake*, and the work of Sherman Alexie.

The response quoted above came as my Ethnic American Literature class finished reading Alexie's *The Absolutely True Diary of a Part-Time Indian*. I am always concerned each time I teach a Sherman Alexie novel, and each time I hope that I will not run into the same issues. And each time, I am disappointed.

Before I address the problems I have, let me preface this essay with an expression of my admiration for Alexie's writing, his humor, his raising of important issues, and his ability to tell a compelling story. I believe he is an important voice in Native American contemporary literature, and, more important, my students love him. When you are teaching non-English majors, this is not an insignificant point.

Unfortunately, a majority of students have had no exposure to anything Native American other than film, television, and stereotypes that have existed for centuries. If Indians show up in film or on television, they are mostly seen in a historical light, as figments of a quasi-national past that no longer exists, if it ever did. The most recent "Indian-centered" film I have seen is *Bury My Heart at Wounded Knee*, a 2007 made-for-television film based on Dee Brown's novel. The screenplay takes vast liberties with the original text, showing Indians as mainstream media have always seen them: as vanishing savages whose only choices were complete annihilation or complete assimilation. It seems as though there is no room for the contemporary Indian in mainstream entertainment.

If I asked my class to list Native American writers, whom would they name? How about the titles of books?[1] Granted, reading has become a lost art for many of our college students, but they are aware of classic American and British authors and texts, such as Nathaniel Hawthorne, Charles Dickens, *Huckleberry Finn*, and *Hamlet*. This is not to say that they are any more familiar with African American or Hispanic American writers and texts, but I would argue that they are more familiar with certain aspects of the above-named cultures than they are with contemporary Native American culture.

With the 1992 publication of *The Business of Fancydancing*, several influential critics hailed Sherman Alexie as an important new voice in Native American literature. Later works, especially *The Lone Ranger and Tonto Fistfight in Heaven* (1993), garnered Alexie both critical and mainstream success. Stephen F. Evans points out, "Much of the praise bestowed on Alexie . . . [focuses] on the author's unflinching bold depiction of the dysfunctional nature of contemporary reservation life and the fragmented, often alienated 'bicultural' lives of characters who daily confront the white civilization that encaptives their world—physically, historically, spiritually, and psychically" (46). Very true. Indians on reservations have not literally vanished, but they have vanished from the minds of American society. Furthermore, we often fail to see how history is actively present in the lives of certain peoples. We are, broadly speaking, a forgetful nation, and what we do remember, we remember selectively.

Therefore, Alexie has positioned himself to do what no other contemporary Native writer has done: reach a non-Native audience. I would argue this is especially true with his 2007 young adult novel *The Absolutely True Diary of a Part-Time Indian*, which won the National Book Award for young people's literature. Critics writing for major publications such as the *New York Times*, *Los Angeles Times*, *Chicago Tribune*, *Newsday*, and *Publishers Weekly* all gave positive reviews of the novel. In his review in the *New York Times*, Bruce Barcott stated:

For 15 years now, Sherman Alexie has explored the struggle to survive between the grinding plates of the Indian and white worlds. He's done it through various characters and genres, but "The Absolutely True Diary of a Part-Time Indian" may be his best work yet. Working in the voice of a 14-year-old forces Alexie to strip everything down to action and emotion, so that reading becomes more like listening to your smart, funny best friend recount his day while waiting after school for a ride home. (39)

*Publishers Weekly*, in a starred review, claimed, "Screenwriter, novelist and poet, Alexie bounds into YA with what might be a Native American equivalent of *Angela's Ashes*, a coming-of-age story so well observed that its very rootedness in one specific culture is also what lends it universality, and so emotionally honest that the humor almost always proves painful" (Rev.). Both reviewers praised Alexie's novel for its ability to reach all of us, Indian or not.

Granted, this is what good literature is supposed to do: speak to each of us and remind us what it means to be human in the world. However, I would also argue that artists, especially writers, have a great responsibility, as their creations can become a certain type of truth for their audience. Thus other scholars and critics, with this in mind, have pointed out that Alexie's dependence on stereotypes, both white and Indian, leads to the creation of caricature instead of character. Louis Owens argues that Alexie

too often simply reinforces all of the stereotypes desired by white readers: his bleakly absurd and aimless Indians are imploding in a passion of self-destructiveness and self-loathing; there in no family or community center toward which his characters . . . might turn for coherence; and in the process of self-destruction the Indians provide Euramerican readers with pleasurable moments of dark humor or the titillation of bloodthirsty savagery. Above all, the non-Indian reader of Alexie's work is allowed to come away with a sense . . . that no one is really to blame but the Indians, no matter how loudly the author shouts his anger. (79-80)

Owens believes that Euramerican readers want the same Indian from Native writers as they do from white writers, "Indians who are romantic, unthreatening, and self-destructive. Indians who are enacting, in one guise or another, the process of vanishing. Borrowing from William Faulkner, that epic poet of inexorable, tragic history, I'll call this the 'Chief Doom' school of literature" (82).

In many ways, Arnold Spirit, the protagonist of *The Absolutely True Diary*, Arnold's best friend, Rowdy, and Arnold's father fit Owen's description. Arnold enacts the process of vanishing as he leaves the rez to attend Reardan High School. His experience at a school "whose mascot was an Indian, thereby making [him] the only *other* Indian in town" (56) is difficult, but Alexie never paints it as being as difficult as Arnold's life on the rez. He is the butt of one racist joke and his white peers ostracize him for a short time, but he miraculously befriends both the most popular girl and the most popular boy at the high school. Penelope is "the prettiest girl [he] had ever seen" and he falls in love with her, even after discovering (and maybe because) she is bulimic. Arnold fights with Roger, and even though, as Arnold tells us, Roger's record is "five wins and one hundred and twelve losses" (62), he manages to frighten "the farm boy who carried squealing pigs around like they were already thin slices of bacon" (64). Arnold becomes the star basketball player on the varsity squad, even with his physical limitations, and his wealthy white friends provide both economic and psychological support.

However, the most damning aspect of Alexie's novels, of all his writing, is the prevalence of alcoholism. To be fair, Alexie has said that what he writes is what he knows. His parents were both alcoholics, as were many other friends and family on the Spokane reservation. And we cannot argue that a writer should not write what he or she knows. But, as Uncle Ben tells Peter Parker, "with great power comes great responsibility." Thus, if Alexie is the best-known Native American writer and his writings contain a multitude of alcoholic Indians, what is the uneducated or unfamiliar reader going to glean from these characters?

Now, let's discuss the uncomfortable realities of alcoholism. Alcohol affects Native Americans disproportionately; the 2001-2005 age-adjusted alcoholism mortality rate for Native Americans is approximately three times the rate for the U.S. population as a whole, according to the Centers for Disease Control and Prevention. The CDC study found that 66 percent of the men whose deaths were attributed to alcohol were younger than fifty years old ("1 in 10"). What we need to understand is that physical and social environmental factors have as much influence on human health as do purely biological forces. Therefore, the epidemic of alcoholism is primarily a function of explicit cultural values and practices set in a particular historical and economic context.

In areas north of what are now the states of Arizona and New Mexico there were no significant traditions of fermented or distilled beverages before European contact, and alcohol's effects were largely unknown throughout much of North America. Thus the indigenous peoples of North America in the early days of European contact had no role models for drinking behavior, nor did they have mechanisms for dealing with the negative consequences of drinking. Alcohol was also used as a diplomatic and economic tool between Europeans and Indians.

But this is historical information—although important, it does not fully explain what is happening on reservations in contemporary U.S. society. What we as a society often do is blame the individual. We believe that alcoholism is a choice, that the person is weak, lazy, or just plain ignorant. Blaming someone for being an alcoholic is like blaming someone for having cancer. We need to remember that becoming an alcoholic is not a choice, just as becoming a diabetic is not one either. Yes, the diabetic may be "responsible" for her illness, but we would never tell her to "suck it up," or "tough it out" the way we do alcoholics. Alcoholism is a problem, yes. It is a problem in almost every family, but it is especially a problem among the impoverished, and it is especially a problem for many Native American communities.

So, what do I do? Avoiding assigning Alexie's works to my students is not the answer, as avoidance does not erase or undermine the stereotypes the students may hold, nor does it allow them to learn anything about Native Americans, either contemporary or historical. In addition, as an Indian woman teaching Ethnic American Literature, I feel a sense of responsibility to provide the fullest and most accurate picture of contemporary Native life as I possibly can. And Alexie's picture of his life is accurate. Therefore, the responsibility lies with me and not with Alexie; it is up to me to find a way into his texts that provides students with the tools they need to understand not only his life experience but also all the experiences we read about over the course of the term.

Although the use of the term "epiphany" is somewhat clichéd, it offers the best approximation of what I experienced when I read Kai Erikson's definition of "collective trauma" in his essay "Notes on Trauma and Community":

> By collective trauma . . . I mean a blow to the basic tissues of social life that damages the bond attaching people together and impairs the prevailing sense of communality. The collective trauma works its way slowly and even insidiously into the awareness of those who suffer from it, so it does not have the quality of suddenness normally associated with "trauma." But it is a form of shock all the same, a gradual realization that the community no longer exists as an effective source of support and that an important part of the self has disappeared. . . ."I" continue to exist, though damaged and may even permanently changed. "You" continue to exist, thought distant and hard to relate to. But "we" no longer exist as a connected pair or as linked cells in a larger communal body. (187)

This idea of collective trauma resonates clearly within *The Absolutely True Diary of a Part-Time Indian*. Junior is the damaged "I," and the others living on the Spokane reservation are the "You" to whom he can no longer relate. He is able to leave the reservation to attend an all-white high school because the " 'we' no longer exists as a connected pair."

However, Erikson's discussion of collective trauma focuses on a distinct event that occurs to the community, causing the breakdown. Nancy Van Styvendale takes issue with the idea of "extraordinary occurrence" as the focus of trauma theory, especially as it pertains to Native peoples. Using a trans/historical approach, Van Styvendale argues that the systematic oppression of Native Americans calls for another definition of trauma that includes "cumulative, collective, intergenerational, and intersubjective" (203) as terms to help us understand a trauma that is "centuries old and nations wide" (204). When the focus is on only a discrete event, Euro-American responsibility is erased, and the current situation of Native life is believed to reside "in an indigenous rehearsal of the forgotten past" (207). Thus the ability to represent the Native American experience is made unreadable, because, as Jacques Derrida illustrates, the unreadability

> stems from the violence of foreclosure, exclusion, all of history being a conflictual field of forces in which it is a matter of making unreadable, excluding, of positing by excluding, of imposing a dominant force by excluding, that is to say, not only by marginalizing, by setting aside the victims, but also by doing so in such a way that no trace remains of the victims, so that no one can testify to the fact they are victims. (qtd. in Goodspeed-Chadwick 268)

Because Native trauma is said to exist in the distant past, we marginalize the peoples whose trauma Euro-American colonialism has caused. In this way, as Derrida says, we erase any trace of the victims and thus ignore the *events* (not a discrete event) that caused their victimization.

To understand how trauma affects a people throughout a historical period, we can turn to Claire Stocks's overview of the work of Nicholas Abraham and Maria Torok along with that of Malcolm Bull. One of the main tenets of psychoanalysis as it pertains to trauma victims is based on the Freudian theory of the integrated self. The traumatic event creates a second, yet altered, self, and that traumatized self is considered to be in a pathological state. Psychoanalysis seeks to return the patient to a state of psychic unity through language, the patient's ability to verbalize the loss "into a coherent and linear life narrative" (Stocks 76). What Freudian psychoanalysts fail to consider are those people who believe neither in the Western construction of the individual nor in the linear life narrative. As Stocks points out, Abraham and Torok view the self as "permeable and open to various 'others'" and posit that an individual's "identity is inherently formed around a kernel of an 'other' lodged in the unconscious" (78). More important to the work of Alexie and other Native writers is their theory of the "transgenerational phantom," wherein "unresolved and silenced issues that disrupt one person's psychic life may be unconsciously transmitted through the generations" (79). This phantom reappears again and again, enacting continual reverberations over time. These reverberations affect the child through the "inheritance of the parental unconscious," and the "initial dual union of parental unconscious and that of the child . . . provides the means by which the shameful secret might be transmitted from one generation to the next" (81).

Malcolm Bull focuses on the "specific cultural conditions in which identity is established" and how that identity may lead to a multiplicity of selves, similar to W. E. B. Du Bois's theory of "double consciousness" (Stocks 88). Although Du Bois was speaking in particular of African Americans, his theory works well for other minorities, including Native Americans, who are always aware of themselves as individuals and of themselves as seen through the eyes of mainstream America. As Bull describes it, one creates identity in recognizing that "the identity of others also requires the acknowledgement of subordinated aspects of one's own identity, the other in the self" (qtd. in Stocks 87). Thus a Native American sees herself as both colonist and colonized, as part of and yet outside American culture, as living person and historical memory. To create a linear life narrative required for the integrated self, therefore, may not be possible for one whose history is interrupted and incoherent. Narratives that exist outside the Western construct allow the individual to achieve a catharsis that is rooted not in integration but rather in the multiplicity of the self.

In turning to *The Absolutely True Diary of a Part-Time Indian*, we see Junior constructing a narrative that heals through the creation of a multiple self. Furthermore, we observe Junior and other characters dealing with the continual reverberations of the "transgenerational phantom." The unresolved and silenced issues manifest themselves in heartbreaking ways because of the collective and cumulative trauma visited on Junior's community.

The novel is written in the first person, symbolizing the "talking cure" that is the foundation of psychoanalysis. The reader thus becomes the witness to Junior's recovery, establishing a relationship that is necessary for the "testimony to trauma" to exist (Radstone 20). Reader and narrator create a dialogic meaning-making to remake an Indian identity that moves beyond the trans/historical accumulation of trauma. Junior begins his story by telling the reader of his hydrocephalus and the life-threatening surgery he endured at six months old. Although he surprised the doctors not only by surviving but also by surviving with no brain damage, he suffered throughout his childhood from seizures. To make matters worse, he had forty-two teeth, or, as he tells it, "ten teeth past human" (2). Thus the cumulative and collective trauma manifests itself on Junior's body.[2] We can read his seizures as the "gap within the psyche" revealing the loss unspoken by the community. Junior's additional teeth, which make him inhuman, are the "intrapsychic tomb," or the radical denial of loss that is an "artificial unconscious lodged like a prosthesis, a graft in the heart of an organ, within the divided self" (Derrida qtd. in Stocks 79).

Junior is a cartoonist because words are "too unpredictable" and "too limiting" (5). His cartoons are understandable to everyone, unlike his speech, which is fractured and incoherent as his stutter prevents clear communication between him and members of his community. Junior's art allows us to see how he views himself as well as those around him. The first self-portrait shows us a cross-eyed, dentally challenged, hydrocephalic Junior, evidently in the midst of a seizure, with a speech bubble illustrating his stutter. The second self-portrait is even more telling, with Junior juggling a book, a rabbit, and a chain saw, begging the reader to love him. Other cartoons show a rage-filled Junior, and in several illustrations, anger is physically manifested around Junior's body. What we are seeing is the evidence of transgenerational trauma written on Junior's body as text. His cartoons are his search for truth and are an act of talking, of dialogue with the reader. As Cathy Caruth explains, "The attempt to gain access to a traumatic history . . . is . . . the project of listening beyond the pathology of individual suffering, to the reality of a history that in its crises can only be perceived in unassimilable forms" (156). Thus we see Junior attempting, through both writing and drawing, to show us the history that, heretofore, has been suppressed.

We cannot confine transgenerational trauma to one event, and Junior evidences this fact: "I think the world is a series of broken dams and floods, and my cartoons are tiny little lifeboats" (6). His world, therefore, is made up of continual catastrophes, both human-made and natural. Erikson points out that we see human-made, or technological, disasters as preventable, and we feel especially vulnerable. We also expect "something similar to what lawyers call punitive damages" (192), and when we are denied, we come to see inhumanity as a "natural feature of human life" (194). To see the world as a series of natural and human-made disasters can only create a sense of hopelessness and inevitability.

Junior describes the community's sense of despondency and inexorability in his theory of Indian poverty: "My parents came from poor people who came from poor people who came from poor people, all the way back to the very first poor people. Adam and Eve covered their privates with fig leaves; the first Indians covered their privates *with their tiny hands*" (11). One cannot escape Indian poverty because, according to Junior, God created Indians as poor. And, as with original sin, Indians carry poverty with them throughout the generations. The knowledge, however erroneous, that poverty is passed down in Indian DNA does not free one from a negative self-image. Junior goes on to say:

> It sucks to be poor, and it sucks to feel that you somehow *deserve* to be poor. You start believing that you're poor because you're stupid and ugly. And then you start believing that you're stupid and ugly because you're Indian. And because you're Indian you start believing you're destined to be poor. It's an ugly circle and *there's nothing you can do about it*. (13)

We cannot help but notice Junior's agency in his understanding of poverty, and yet, conversely, his poverty is out of his control. He believes that he deserves to be poor because he is Indian and the destiny for all Indians is to be the negative of what American society desires most—beauty, intelligence, and wealth. In other words, the attributes we most desire are denied to Junior and his community because of their DNA.

Junior takes on the subject of desire and denial in the story of his parents. His mother desired a college education and if she had been "*given the chance*," she would have gotten one (11; emphasis added). Junior's father wanted to be a musician, and if he had been "*given the chance*," he would have done so (13; emphasis added). But, as Junior says, "we reservation Indians don't get to realize our dreams. We don't get those chances. Or choices" (13). The incapacity to make choices, to "have a chance," as it were, comes not from personal inability but from mainstream society's refusal to allow them the chance. However, as Van Styvendale points out, mainstream society insists on adhering to the "accident model of trauma" and "an indigenous rehearsal of the forgotten past" rather than acknowledging the "ongoing situation of domestic colonialism" (207). This allows society to "displace and assuage Euroamerican guilt for the existent colonial situation in North America" (208).

Junior comes face-to-face with colonialism, both historical and current, in the person of his geometry teacher, Mr. P. Teachers, Mr. P tells Junior "were supposed to kill the Indian to save the child. . . . We were supposed to make you give up being Indian. Your songs and stories and language and dancing. Everything. We weren't trying to kill Indian people. We were trying to kill Indian culture" (35). Mr. P is invoking the educational philosophy of Richard Pratt, founder of Carlisle Indian School, who believed assimilation could only happen with the destruction of Indian culture.

Mr. P confesses his pedagogy to Junior after Junior is suspended for throwing a textbook at Mr. P. Junior's rage-filled reaction comes from seeing his mother's name in his textbook, "a textbook that was at least thirty years older than [he] was" (31). Junior is saddened and angered at seeing the "old, old, old, *decrepit* geometry book" (31). It hits him with the force of a nuclear bomb, and he asks, "What do you do when the world has declared nuclear war on you?" (31). At this moment, Junior is able to grasp one aspect of the trans/historical trauma that has been visited on his people. The educational policies are directly connected to—not a remnant of—the Indian boarding schools.

Mr. P offers Junior advice that goes right to the heart of Spokane culture. He tells Junior that he has to leave the reservation forever. Junior must turn his back on his community in order to survive: "'If you stay on this rez,' Mr. P said, 'they're going to kill you. I'm going to kill you. We're all going to kill you. You can't fight us forever'" (43). Mr. P establishes that the threat to Junior resides not only in the white teachers but also in Junior's own people. The horrors historically perpetrated on the Spokane are now perpetrated by the Spokane. This residue of destruction is the transgenerational phantom "re-emerging in what seems to be an inescapable pattern of endless repetition" (Stocks 80). The only way to avoid this "death" is for Junior to "take [his] hope and go somewhere where other people have hope" (43). Junior can only find hope, according to Mr. P, "the farther and farther [he walks] away from this sad, sad, sad reservation" (43). Written on both the body and the land are pain and despair that Junior can escape only by leaving his community.

Unfortunately, the only place to which he can escape is Reardan, the all-white high school in the "rich, white farm town that sits in the wheat fields exactly twenty-two miles away from the rez" (45). As his parents tell him, the people who have the most hope are white people, so Junior must abandon his community to enter the center of his transgenerational trauma. As Erikson explains, "Trauma has both centripetal and centrifugal tendencies. It draws one away from the center of the group space while at the same time drawing one back" (186). Although Junior needs to leave to avoid a psychic death, the community reacts strongly and negatively, enacting the centripetal tendency. His parents warn him of the community response, saying, "The Indians around here are going to be angry with you" (47). Their prediction falls far short of the reality. Junior's best friend, Rowdy, screams, the worst scream Junior has ever heard. "It was pain, pure pain" (52). A few months after Junior begins attending Reardan, a group of children attack him on Halloween night:

They shoved me to the ground and kicked me a few times.

And spit on me.

I could handle the kicks.

But the spit made me feel like an insect.

Like a slug.

Like a slug burning to death from salty spit.

They didn't beat me up too bad. . . . Mostly they just wanted to remind me that I was a traitor. (79)

The rage and pain that Rowdy and the others feel is the residue of transgenerational trauma. Their inability to articulate this pain through language are what Hayden White describes as trauma that "cannot be simply forgotten . . . but neither can [it] be adequately remembered" (qtd. in Radstone 21). Since the traumatic events cannot be adequately remembered, all that is left is "a gap in the unconscious" (Stocks 80), the silence of the previous generations. "The tombs of others" (Stocks 80) haunt Junior, Rowdy, and all the other Spokane.

Punctuating Junior's time at Reardan are events that mimic and represent the ongoing domestic colonization of Native peoples. The school's mascot is an Indian, making Junior "the only other Indian in town" (56). A girl tells him he talks "funny" because of his "reservation accent," which makes everything he says "sound like a bad poem," and silences him for six days (61). The jocks in the school keep their distance because, as an Indian, Junior is "still a potential killer" (63). They call him "Chief," "Tonto," and "Squaw Boy." In the most egregious instance, one of the kids tells him a horrible and insulting joke that Junior calls "the most racist thing I've ever heard in my life" (64). Thus, in his movement from the reservation to Reardan High School, he becomes "the opposite of human . . . something less than less than less than Indian" (83). All the effects of domestic colonialism manifest themselves in Junior's experience at Reardan. He is reduced to a stereotyped symbol, reduced to the representative for a forgotten people who exist no longer in the national consciousness except as a subject to belittle.

However, Junior finds a way to move through the trauma to a place where his multiplicity of selves are integrated "into a contradictory co-existence producing recognisable . . . multiple identities within a single self" (Stocks 87). For Alexie's characters, one way to integrate these multiple selves is through humor. Junior and his family laugh at the seeming contradiction in celebrating Thanksgiving, joking that Indians "should give thanks that they didn't kill all of us" (102). Junior learns that his white friends are dealing with different kinds of issues, but those issues cause pain as well. He finds friendship and acceptance from people who are "a little bit racist" and yet "pretty damn amazing" (129). He comes to realize that the world is not "broken down by tribes. . . . By black and white. By Indian and white. . . . The world is only broken into two tribes: The people who are assholes and the people who are not" (176). And those tribes are not exclusive in their racial makeup.

More important, Junior learns to integrate the historical pain of his people, and, in doing so, he incorporates yet another of his multiple selves. In a significant basketball game, Junior's Reardan team beats Wellpinit, his former team, by forty points. Instead of feeling happy and proud, Junior feels "suddenly ashamed that [he had] wanted so badly to take revenge on them. [He is] suddenly ashamed of [his] anger, [his] rage, and [his] pain" (196). He becomes fully aware of how trans/historical trauma has affected his community.

> I knew that two or three of those Indians might not have eaten breakfast that morning.
>
> No food in the house.
>
> I knew that seven or eight of those Indians lived with drunken mothers and fathers.
>
> I knew that one of those Indians had a father who dealt crack and meth.
>
> I knew two of those Indians had fathers in prison.
>
> I knew that none of them were going to college. Not one of them. (195)

What he sees in his community is the impact of poverty and the lack of opportunity available to the community members. Junior has had to wrest opportunity from a world that would not willingly give it to him. He realizes that his ability to choose a different life is an anomaly, not the norm.

Although he must leave the community to create the life he wants, Junior understands it is the community that provides him the ability to succeed. As Erikson points out, "It is the community that offers a cushion for pain, the community that offers a context for intimacy, the community that serves as the repository for binding traditions" (188). For Junior, community means both the Spokane reservation and Reardan High School. He realizes he belongs to the Spokane Indian tribe, but also "to the tribe of American immigrants. And to the tribe of basketball players. And to the tribe of bookworms. . . . And the tribe of teenage boys. . . . And the tribe of poverty. . . . And the tribe of beloved sons" (217). In accepting seemingly contradictory selves and communities, Junior achieves integration.

By introducing the ideas of transgenerational and trans/historical trauma, I hope to be able to help my students become readers who can fully understand and empathize with the characters and issues Sherman Alexie presents in his fiction and poetry. I do not want to create a guilt-ridden reader, but rather a learned reader who understands the complexities and contradictions inherent in American society. In achieving the ability to help students navigate and understand cultures different from their own, I, too, can learn to integrate my own transgenerational trauma and accept the contradictory selves that make up my identity.

## Notes

1. I did ask my fall 2009 Ethnic Literature class. One student named Alexie and his novel *The Lone Ranger and Tonto Fistfight in Heaven*.

2. I fully understand that *The Absolutely True Diary* is a semiautobiographical novel, and I do not wish to argue that Alexie's very real and serious childhood health problems are a metaphor. However, I would argue that reading Junior's physical problems as the results of transgenerational trauma opens the novel up for readers unfamiliar with Native American peoples, cultures, and writings.

## Works Cited

Alexie, Sherman. *The Absolutely True Diary of a Part-Time Indian*. New York: Little, Brown, 2007.

Barcott, Bruce. "Off the Rez." Rev. of *The Absolutely True Diary of a Part-Time Indian*, by Sherman Alexie. *New York Times* 11 Nov. 2007, late ed.: 7.39.

Caruth, Cathy. "Recapturing the Past: Introduction." *Trauma: Explorations in Memory*. Ed. Cathy Caruth. Baltimore: Johns Hopkins UP, 1995. 151-57.

Erikson, Kai. "Notes on Trauma and Community." *Trauma: Explorations in Memory*. Ed. Cathy Caruth. Baltimore: Johns Hopkins UP, 1995. 183-99.

Evans, Stephen F. "'Open Containers': Sherman Alexie's Drunken Indians." *American Indian Quarterly* 25.1 (2001): 46-72.

Goodspeed-Chadwick, Julie Elaine. "Derrida's Deconstruction of Logocentrism: Implications for Trauma Studies." *Theory After Derrida: Essays in Critical Praxis*. Ed. Kailash Baral and R. Radhakrishnan. New York: Routledge, 2009. 264-79.

"1 in 10 Native American Deaths Alcohol Related." *Associated Press* 28 Aug. 2008. Web. *MSNBC*. 19 June 2010.

Owens, Louis. *Mixedblood Messages: Literature, Film, Family, Place*. Norman: U of Oklahoma P, 1998.

Radstone, Susannah. "Trauma Theory: Contexts, Politics, Ethics." *Paragraph* 30.1 (2007): 9-29.

Rev. of *The Absolutely True Diary of a Part-Time Indian*, by Sherman Alexie. *Publishers Weekly* 20 Aug. 2007.

Stocks, Claire. "Trauma Theory and the Singular Self: Rethinking Extreme Experiences in the Light of Cross Cultural Identity." *Textual Practice*. 21.1 (2007): 71-92.

Van Styvendale, Nancy. "The Trans/historicity of Trauma in Jeanette Armstrong's *Slash* and Sherman Alexie's *Indian Killer*." *Studies in the Novel* 40.1-2 (2008): 203-23.

# "Doesn't everybody belong to a subculture?"
## Community and History in Sherman Alexie's Writing

Michael Wilson

An American writer of American Indian descent, Sherman Alexie arrived at his craft through the interactions between Indian and mainstream American cultures and sensibilities. He has embraced this apparent dichotomy while nonetheless advancing an extended, barbed, and often humorous political critique of both Indian and non-Indian American cultures, as well as the genocidal history of American interaction with the Indians. Indeed, over the course of his career, Alexie has argued both that "good art is not universal. . . . Good art is tribal" (in Peterson 82) and that "my theory (and it's a betrayal/ of my tribe) is that art is colonial/ And the best art is imperialistic" (*Face* 98-99). In Alexie's estimation, "I wasn't saved by the separation of cultures; I was *reborn* inside the collision of cultures" (*Face* 80).

Sherman Alexie was born on October 7, 1966, in the town of Wellpinit in eastern Washington State, on the Spokane Indian reservation, a "Salmon people" devastated by the environmental impact of the Grand Coulee Dam in 1942, which destroyed "7000 miles of salmon spawning beds" (Grassian 1). Details of Spokane Indian reservation life that would recur in Alexie's works include the gossip and jokes at the Trading Post, endless games of basketball, house parties and alcoholic adults, commodity food and "government glasses," and working-class conditions often dipping into poverty and hunger. Alexie's father was a Coeur d'Alene Indian whose alcoholism made him somewhat unreliable for both financial and emotional support for the family, although Alexie has said: "Dad would never drink in the house. . . . He was always Mr. Mom. . . . Mom did most of the working. . . . Dad read to me a lot and gave me books and we played a lot" (in Peterson 77).

Alexie was born with hydrocephalus, or "water on the brain," a life-threatening condition that required dangerous surgery by the age of six months. He continued to be plagued by the side effects of the condition throughout his childhood, and he was bullied by his Spokane peers in school because of his enlarged skull.

Young Alexie became a voracious reader, attributing this to the fact that his hydrocephalus therapists "put books in front of me," and plowed through his father's own sizable collection of books as well as every book in the Wellpinit school library by age twelve (he notes dryly that it was a "small library") (in Peterson 162, 77). He also quickly turned to humor as a means of social self-defense against his less academically inclined peers. His mother was a strong advocate for education, including an emphasis on English as his primary language. Alexie was very aware of his limited prospects if he stayed on the reservation; after discovering that his "new" high school textbook for a class had his mother's name written in it, Alexie made the deliberate decision to commute off the reservation to attend a "white," academically superior high school in nearby Reardan, Washington. His experiences there as the only Indian and also as a high school basketball star shaped his perspective both on the "white" world and on reservation life, and would later be most clearly incorporated in his best-selling book to date, the young adult novel *The Absolutely True Diary of a Part-Time Indian* (2007). Although he was "pounded" by white students for being Indian, and by his Indian peers for daring to leave the reservation, he has stated, "I ended up getting very lucky: I ended up with a peer group of white kids who were obsessive, compulsive workaholics, who had their own dreams of leaving a little town. . . . we all were on our way to something bigger from our little towns. And whether it was Indian or white didn't matter as much as the desire to get out. All those smart, amazing white kids accepted me" (in Peterson 163).

After high school, Alexie, raised Catholic among the Coeur d'Alene, "the most Catholicized Indians in the country," briefly attended Gonzaga University, a Jesuit university in nearby Spokane, on a scholarship, but began binge drinking, although continuing to attend and pass his classes (*War Dances* 68). When a class with Professor Alex Kuo exposed him for the first time to poetry by American Indian writers, the experience was revelatory: "There's a line by a Paiute poet named Adrian Louis that says, 'Oh, Uncle Adrian, I'm in the reservation of my mind.' I thought, 'Oh my God, somebody understands me! At that moment I realized, 'I can do this!' That's when I started writing—in 1989" (in Peterson 25). Suddenly aware that he could write about his own life as an Indian in American culture in realistic terms, Alexie immediately began writing poetry at a prolific rate. When his first volume of poetry and some prose pieces, 1992's *The Business of Fancydancing*, was accepted for publication by Hanging Loose Press, including some poems written for Kuo's class, he decided to interpret that as a signal to stop drinking, and he has remained sober since. *The Business of Fancydancing* met with immediate critical acclaim. James R. Kincaid in a *New York Times* review judged Alexie's work in the book "so wide-ranging, dexterous and consistently capable of raising your neck hair that it enters at once into our ideas of who we are and how we might be, makes us speak and hear his words over and over, call others into the room or over the phone to repeat them" and called Alexie "one of the major lyric voices of our time." Other publishers immediately became interested, and Alexie quickly published two subsequent volumes of poetry, *I Would Steal Horses* in 1992 with Slipstream Publications, and *First Indian on the Moon* in 1993 with Hanging Loose Press.

Alexie's own life has always been reflected in his writing, and early volumes of poetry like *First Indian on the Moon* seem to incorporate not only his own feelings about his continuing moves away from his reservation (Alexie has noted that his mother teases him that he was "born with a suitcase") but also his love affairs, including love affairs with white women, sparking poems such as "Tiny Treaties" from that collection (in Peterson 162). He laments his older sister's death in a fire in several different books, and, across his entire career, explores his conflicted feelings about his father's life and death. By 1996's *The Summer of Black Widows*, his love poems are addressed to an Indian lover, and in "Drum as Love, Fear, and Prayer," he seems to suggest that he has chosen to love her in part because of her Indian ethnicity—as someone who can "share that crucial aspect of his being" (Grassian 138). Although Alexie has taken some pains to protect his family's privacy, his marriage to a woman of Hidatsa, Ho Chunk, and Pottawatomi descent and their lives with their two sons have also become recurring themes in his more recent work, both indirectly, as themes of marriage and parenthood in stories such as "The Ballad of Paul Nonetheless" from 2009's *War Dances*, and more directly and autobiographically, as in poems such as "A Comic Interlude" and "Chicken" from 2009's *Faces*.

Although Alexie considers himself first and foremost a poet and prefers to write poetry and short stories, he has been a prolific artist in a variety of genres and areas, even to the extent of becoming an accomplished and comedic "slam poetry" champion and reader of his own work (Jaggi). In 1992 and 1993 alone, he produced five books: four volumes of poetry (with some stories)—*The Business of Fancydancing* (1992), *I Would Steal Horses* (1992), *First Indian on the Moon* (1993), and *Old Shirts and New Skins* (1993)—as well as a collection of short stories, *The Lone Ranger and Tonto Fistfight in Heaven* (1993), which proved to be his breakthrough book, bringing him to widespread popular attention. His first novel, *Reservation Blues*, appeared in 1995; his second, *Indian Killer*, in 1996; and two novels in 2007, *Flight* and the young adult *The Absolutely True Diary of a Part-Time Indian*. He has also published additional collections of short stories: *The Toughest Indian in the World* (2000), *Ten Little Indians* (2003), and *War Dances* (2009). He has continued to publish poetry in journals and magazines, as well as in the collections *Water Flowing Home* (1996), *The Summer of Black Widows* (1996), *The Man Who Loves Salmon* (1998), *One Stick Song* (2000), *Dangerous Astron-*

*omy* (2005), and *Face* (2009). Each of these works explores, among other things, reservation and urban Indian life, often in biographical or quasi-biographical ways, ranging across the centuries of American history in ways that often conflate past, present, and future to make clear the conflicted position of Indians in America and offer a pointed critique of racism and stereotypes, but almost always leavened with Alexie's sharp sense of humor: "There's nothing worse than *earnest emotion*" (in Peterson 70).

Alexie's work has met with a generally favorable critical and popular reception, although not without exceptions and qualifications. In an October 17, 1993, *New York Times* review of *The Lone Ranger and Tonto Fistfight in Heaven*, novelist Reynolds Price commented that given Alexie's "sparse hints [to the reader about setting, description, and characterization], the reader is expected to perform a number of jobs that are generally assumed by the writer. . . . the great surprise is that given such narrow bounds, Mr. Alexie's strength proves sufficient to compel clear attention through sizable lengths of first-person voice." Frederick Busch, in an otherwise quite positive review of *Reservation Blues*, observed that "though there is wonderful humor and profound sorrow in this novel, and brilliant renditions of each, there is not enough structure to carry the dreams and tales that Mr. Alexie needs to portray and that we need to read. His talent may be for the short form." Alexie himself seems to agree with this assessment: "I really have to struggle with novels. If I never had to write another novel again, I'd be happy" (Cline). Others have praised the seemingly improvisational nature of his comedic voice and his willingness to take chances with material both serious and humorous. In her May 26, 2003, *New York Times* review of *Ten Little Indians*, Janet Maslin called the work "warm, revealing, invitingly roundabout stories" and Alexie himself "impressively fearless." Writing in 2004, Richard Gray argued that Alexie's stories are "exhilaratingly ragged and freewheeling, with an immediacy, energy, rawness and sometimes downright clumsiness—clumsiness here seems almost a mark of authenticity—that contrasts with the measured tone of the work of [Navaho writer M. Scott] Momaday—or, for that matter, the minimalist cadences of [Blackfeet-Gros Ventre writer James] Welch" (815). Fellow Native American novelist Leslie Marmon Silko, whose novel *Ceremony* is considered one of the definitive works of modern Indian literature, has called Alexie "one of the best writers we have."

Alexie's popularity with readers seems due in large part to the remarkably personable and disarming narrative voice in much of his work; by turns (or indeed simultaneously) irreverently funny, irritated, wistful, confused, lovelorn, or angry, and at all times self-questioning and ironic, his is an authorial voice intensely contemporaneous in its sensibilities. Perhaps fittingly, then, his work may be usefully viewed within a number of historical and cultural contexts, reflecting the fluidity of postmodern identity. As Alexie himself has noted, in describing the evolving complexity of his authorial perspective, "I think we belong to a lot of tribes; culturally, ethnically, and racially" (in Peterson 143). Alexie himself has named the "five primary influences in my life" as being "my father, for his nontraditional Indian stories, my grandmother, for her traditional Indian stories, Stephen King, John Steinbeck, and *The Brady Bunch*. . . . I'm the first practitioner of the Brady Bunch school of Native American literature" (in Peterson 69, 82).

As his statement hints, Alexie's work may be seen as clearly centered within the cultural experience of Generation X, those people born between 1961 and 1981, and strongly focused on popular culture. His early characters in particular view themselves (or are trapped in being viewed) as "geeks" or "jocks" and center themselves amid the litter of pop-culture fragments that made up the lives of the early Gen Xers. In *First Indian on the Moon*, itself a reference to the iconic moon landings that most early Gen Xers remember watching as young children, Alexie incorporates the theme music from *Rocky*, pop icons such as Bruce Lee, Luke Skywalker, and Darth Vader, the sound of Freddy Fender crooning "Before the Next Teardrop Falls," jukeboxes and the radio, basketball, pizza, Neil Armstrong, Lee Harvey Oswald, Disneyland, Elvis, the Vietnam War, and comic books (as Alexie notes elsewhere, "I learned to read with a Superman comic book"), as well as older memories kept alive by the television age: the *Hindenburg* (in "A Reservation Table of the Elements," Crazy Horse blows up the zeppelin); Bing Crosby and *White Christmas* ("Superman and Me"). As Alexie's characters have aged and grown throughout the evolution of his work, married, started families, and divorced, their Boomer or G.I.-generation parents aging and dying, that Gen-X perspective has remained central to his writing, in a way that makes his works seem quite familiar to readers of that generation in particular. His popular and acclaimed 2007 young adult novel, *The Absolutely True Diary of a Part-Time Indian*, for example, neatly transposes many of his own experiences growing up in the 1970s and 1980s into an Internet-and-Ipod century and generation. As Alexie notes, pop-culture references are "the cultural currency. Superman means something different to me than it does to a white guy from Ames, Iowa or New York City or L.A. [but] it's a way for us to sit at the same table" (in Peterson 92).

Alexie has also consistently, and quite consciously, worked to expand his audience. Like many ethnic writers, he is well aware that his primary audience is both white and female, if only for demographic reasons: "The reading literary public are white, middle-class and upper-class college-educated women. That's who my readers are. I mean, I do a reading at a bookstore and 70 percent of the crowd will be white women" (in Peterson 109). Although appreciative of this audience, he feels a strong obligation to an Indian audience as well: "I have a huge Native audience in a way that other Native writers don't because my subject matter is very pop culture oriented and sort of middle-class, lower-class based" (in Peterson 158).

Alexie's sense of obligation to this latter audience has at times prompted him to make somewhat controversial statements about other American Indian writers and writing:

You throw in a couple of birds and four directions and corn pollen and it's Native American literature, when it has nothing to do with the day-to-day lives of Indians. I want my literature to concern the daily lives of Indians. . . . I think most Native American literature is unreadable by the vast majority of Native Americans. (in Peterson 87-88)

After Alexie argued in 1997 that Anishinaabe-Chippewa writer Gerald Vizenor's intensely postmodern work is "obscure prose, a lot of word play and word masturbation, essentially, that results in nothing" (in Peterson 42), Vizenor countered in 1999 that Alexie "seems to be obsessed with the politics of terminal identity" (150). In 2000 an interviewer noted that

one central goal [of Alexie's] is to get his books read by twelve-year-old reservation kids, who, like him, grew up either with heroes who had been created by the white media or no heroes at all. "In order for the Indian kid to read me," Alexie says, "pop culture is where I should be. Literary fiction is very elitist." (Spencer)

Alexie has more recently expanded this argument from a purely Indian audience, as he noted in 2009: "If a fifteen-year old doesn't want to read me, what good am I?" (Konigsberg). Perhaps then satisfyingly, his young adult novel, *The Absolutely True Diary of a Part-Time Indian*, a National Book Award winner, has been his most widespread literary success, with almost uniformly favorable reviews and more than 200,000 copies sold by March 2010 (Roback).

Alexie's largest single impact on both American and American Indian popular culture to date, however, has undoubtedly been through his 1999 screenplay for *Smoke Signals*, directed by Chris Eyre (Cheyenne-Arapaho), the first major motion picture written and directed by Indians as well as featuring an Indian cast to receive major distribution. Alexie's interest in filmmaking to some extent derived from his interest in reaching a wider Indian audience: "Generally speaking

Indians don't read books. It's not a book culture. That's why I'm trying to make movies. Indians go to movies" (in Peterson 88). For Alexie, venturing into films broadened that audience even for his Spokane Indian critics: "The funny thing is, people loved the movie. Even those who didn't like my books much loved the movie, so the power of film was certainly revealed in that" (in Peterson 97). Following his success with *Smoke Signals*, Alexie also wrote and directed the independently produced and distributed film *The Business of Fancydancing* (2000), a decidedly more improvisational and less conventional movie featuring a young gay Indian poet as its protagonist.

Although as early as 1993 Alexie was saying that "I want to make clear that I don't claim to be a spokesperson for all natives" (in Peterson 7), his prominence as a media-savvy American Indian writer has nonetheless contributed to his being cast as an "unofficial spokesman" for American Indians everywhere, even to the extent of being the "Indian" on a July 9, 1998, PBS *Newshour* roundtable discussion, "A Dialogue on Race with President Clinton." His prominence, his success, and the elements he emphasizes about the American Indian experience have met with some criticism from within his ethnic community, some members of which feel, broadly, that he emphasizes the negative elements of their lives in a way that serves to define them in terms of their weaknesses and flaws. A January 18, 1998, article in the *New York Times Magazine* sums up the position of some Spokane critics of Alexie by noting that "a woman who runs a program at the reservation cultural center is dismissive. 'I don't have anything good to say about him, so I better not say anything,' she says. 'It's like he has used the reservation for personal therapy, and in so doing, he's hurt a lot of people'" (Egan). To some extent, Spokane criticism of Alexie seems to reflect the common experience of writers exploring the lives of their peers, with the added issues created by the minority status of Indians themselves, as Alexie has observed:

You know, because as Indians we've been so stereotyped and maligned and oppressed and abused, in acts and deed, in action and word, we seek literature that cheers us in some way, that acts as some sort of antidote, rather than an examination of us, and an interrogation of us. . . . I think a lot of Indians want Indian artists to be cultural cheerleaders rather than cultural investigators. (in Peterson 122)

Spokane Indians do read his work and attend his readings, however, and his Indian audience outside the Spokane is both large and appreciative.

One of the great issues historically afflicting American Indians has been alcohol and alcoholism, and the consequences of those elements on American Indians, and reservation life in particular, deeply influence Alexie's early works. Alexie has noted that as a hydrocephalic child "I was on phenobarbital from age one," and "I grew up in a family of alcoholics—my mother, my father, my brother, sisters, aunts, uncles, cousins, family dog, spiders roaming around the house with whiskey" (in Peterson 161). In part, Alexie has attributed this emphasis on alcohol in particular to his own brief period as a binge drinker and alcoholic, noting:

When I first started writing I was still drinking, so *Lone Ranger and Tonto* and the first book of poems, *The Business of Fancydancing*, are really soaked in alcohol. As I've been in recovery over the years and stayed sober, you'll see the work gradually freeing itself of alcoholism and going much deeper, exploring the emotional, sociological, and psychological reasons for any kind of addiction or dysfunctions within the community. (in Peterson 66)

His exploration of this element of American Indian life has been one of the key focuses of criticism of his work among the Indian community. Alexie has responded by noting: "It's not a stereotype. Alcoholism among Native Americans is a cold, damp reality" (Smiley).

Central to Alexie's writing to date has been his exploration of the idea of American Indian identity and lives, and in particular his sense of the way in which modern Indian identity becomes a negotiated and often problematic issue for Indians themselves, embedded as they are in a history of colonial exploitation and oppression, centuries of popular media representation, relative poverty, and psychological stress and conflict:

> You can never measure up to a stereotype. You can never be as strong as a stereotypical warrior, as godly as a stereotypical shaman, or as drunk as a drunken Indian. You can never measure up to extremes. So you're always going to feel less than the image, whether it's positive or negative. One of the real dangers is that other Indians have taken many stereotypes as reality, as a way to measure each other and ourselves. . . . I think that many Indians have watched too much television! (in Peterson 148)

The narrator of "A Drug Called Tradition," from *The Lone Ranger and Tonto Fistfight in Heaven*, notes the way that this idea of a glorious Indian past becomes entangled with pop American culture for his young peers on the reservation:

> We ditched the party, decided to save the new drug for ourselves, and jumped into Junior's Camaro. The engine was completely shot but the exterior was good. You see, the car looked mean. Mostly we parked it in front of the Trading Post and tried to look like horsepowered warriors. Driving it was a whole other matter, though. It belched and farted its way down the road like an old man. That definitely wasn't cool. (13)

Highlighting Alexie's exploration of Indian past, present, and self-mythologizing is his use of historic figures. Lakota warrior Crazy Horse features repeatedly in Alexie's work, usually depicted in ways that vividly illustrate the complexity and contradictions of modern Indian identity as well as a common Indian experience of colonialism, as, for instance, when he shows up in *The Business of Fancydancing* as a pan-tribal Indian figure shifted through modern settings as a convenience-store worker, a Vietnam veteran, and even as the titular namesake for the "Crazy Horse Highway" and the "Crazy Horse basketball jump shot." In Alexie's first novel, *Reservation Blues*, early twentieth-century African American bluesman Robert Johnson arrives at the Spokane reservation to abandon his satanic guitar, and nineteenth-century Indian-fighting generals George Wright and Phil Sheridan show up as exploitative record executives from "Cavalry Records." Alexie has argued that for Indians, "the past is still here for us. . . . Generally speaking, I think Indians have a much longer memory than white Americans. Or maybe we Indians hold more passionate grudges!" (in Peterson 6, 138).

In his later work, Alexie has shifted his focus from reservation Indian to "urban Indian" lives. In part, this change in emphasis reflects his own life: "I live in a white collar Indian world now." Alexie also argues that these are stories not yet told: "You don't see representations of white collar Indians in any kind of media—journalism or movies or books or magazines" (in Peterson 107), although as of 2006 "something like 70 percent of native Americans live in urban areas" (in Peterson 159). His 2000 volume of short stories, *The Toughest Indian in the World*, for instance, centers almost exclusively on the lives of white-collar, urban Indians, who often struggle with their sense of Indian identity even more than the reservation Indian characters on whom Alexie focused previously. In several stories in the collection, "urban Indian" characters married to white spouses seek out Indian lovers, prostitutes, hitchhikers, or even bar fighters, seemingly as a way to test and reaffirm their own Indian identities, and in "One Good Man," the narrator repeatedly asks, "What is an Indian?" (217-38). His most controversial work, the 1996 mystery novel *Indian Killer*, condemned by *Time* reviewer John Skow as "septic with . . . unappeasable fury" and criticized by Alexie himself as a "a very fundamentalist, binary book, the product of [my] youthful rage," explores the psychological stress of urban Indians who were "'lost birds'—Indians adopted out to non-

Indian families," a practice later prevented by the 1974 Indian Child Welfare Act (Jaggi). In addition to numerous short stories depicting the lives of urban Indians in 2003's *Ten Little Indians* and 2009's *War Dances*, Alexie continued his depiction of "lost birds" with the half-Irish character Zits in his 2007 novel *Flight*.

Alexie's work, particularly his early work, has often focused on "outsiders," people who refuse or are unable to fit into social "norms" of white, mainstream American culture or, for that matter, into the non-white cultures to which they otherwise belong. His characters are thus often Indians or people of other ethnic minorities, sometimes multiracial, and occasionally homosexual (Alexie has notably featured gay and bisexual characters in his more recent writing, or characters who have gay experiences, like the protagonist of "The Toughest Indian in the World"), as well as the poor, "geeks" and "nerds," and others. Alexie's use of outsider characters and themes seems clearly evident across the full chronology of his work, from early books like 1992's *The Business of Fancydancing*, with the first appearance of his iconic, often bullied or shunned, compulsive storyteller Thomas Builds-the-Fire, to the shy, nerdy autobiographical protagonist Arnold Spirit, Jr., in 2007's *The Absolute True Diary of a Part-Time Indian*. Talking about the power of film in popular culture versus that of literature, Alexie has observed that

> Thomas Builds-the-Fire, the character, has become a huge cultural character in the Indian world. . . . I get photographs of Indian kids who dressed as him for Halloween. His lines in the movie have become pop-cultural phrases. In the Indian world, we just don't have that. Our heroes have always been guys with guns. And now, to have this cultural hero who is this androgynous little storytelling bookworm geek—I think that's wonderful. (Spencer)

As Frederick Busch noted in a 1995 review of *Reservation Blues*, Alexie "writes about characters who are squarely in the middle of reservation life but who report it to us from a point of view that is simultaneously tangential to the mainstream of that life as well as part of its sad, slow rhythms."

In much of Alexie's later work, his characters are or become "outsiders" as well, stranded outside the boundaries of "normal" behavior by their actions, impulses, or obsessions. Paul in "The Ballad of Paul Nonetheless" from *War Dances*, for instance, becomes obsessed by a woman he sees at an airport. Richard, a lawyer of both African American and Native American heritage in "Lawyer's League," from *Ten Little Indians*, carefully arranges even his potential lovers with an eye to political electability, and then finds himself punching a racist lawyer during a pickup basketball game, a punch that makes it impossible for him to pursue his political aspirations. The nameless Indian protagonist of "Can I Get a Witness" uses her presence at a café terrorist bombing to walk away from her husband and two teenage sons. Other characters step into "outsider" territory but then return, as Indian character Mary Lynn does in "Assimilation," from *The Toughest Indian in the World*, when she deliberately has sex with a random Indian man but then returns to her white husband and their mutual love at the end of the story.

The most marked evolution in Alexie's own conception of his writing may be his increasingly complex exploration of tribalism and identity, seemingly in some ways as a response to his experience of his own life moving into middle age as an "urban Indian" and in some ways as a response to national and world events. In 1999, Alexie argued that "when a white reviewer says *Smoke Signals* is universal, what he's saying is that *white* people can get this and that *white* people are the judges of all that is universal" (in Peterson 82, 80). By 2007, although still writing extensively about Indian characters, Alexie noted that

for many years, I've said that my two strongest tribal affiliations are not racially based. My strongest tribes are book nerds and basketball players, and those tribes are racially, culturally, economically, and spiritually diverse. And like Arnold [the protagonist of *The Absolutely True Diary of a Part-Time Indian*], I also belong to a hundred other tribes, based on the things I love to read, watch, do. (in Peterson 190)

Alexie attributes a large part of his changing sense of tribal identity to the terrorist attacks of September 11, 2001, and their resulting decade of war, and his belief that both the terrorist attack on 9/11 and the American national response to it were essentially tribal responses, an evolution in his perspective that also seems to reflect his own fiercely progressive, liberal political beliefs:

> Ever since 9/11, I have worked hard to be very public about my multi-tribal identity. I think fundamentalism is the mistaken belief that one belongs to only one tribe. . . . War is all about the idea of tribes and defending your country, so I've been trying to let go of the idea of basing my politics on the good of a small group. I've become less and less Indian-centric as the years have gone on. After September 11th, I barely talk about it. I talk about poor people; I talk about disadvantaged people, and that sort of covers everything I need to cover. (in Peterson 130, 190)

Alexie's writing viewed in its entirety presents the reader with an excellent example of the full evolution of a writer from youth to maturity, from a singular focus on self and individual ethnicity to a multi-faceted, compassionate, and often sharply comedic exploration of human nature building from that ethnic focus. His greatest legacy may be that in doing so he has given other American Indian writers a sense of the broad range of artistic possibilities open to them, as well as bringing his own perspective on the almost entirely ignored world of the modern American indigenous population entertainingly to life, and thus to the attention of the non-Indian world, with all the history and humor, tragedies and survivals, struggles, hopes, fears, failures, and successes of that world vividly depicted.

# Works Cited

Alexie, Sherman. *The Absolutely True Diary of a Part-Time Indian*. New York: Little, Brown, 2007.

_____. *Face*. New York: Hanging Loose Press, 2009.

_____. *First Indian on the Moon*. New York: Hanging Loose Press, 1993.

_____. *Indian Killer*. New York: Warner Books, 1996.

_____. *The Lone Ranger and Tonto Fistfight in Heaven*. New York: Grove Press, 1993.

_____. *Reservation Blues*. New York: Grove Press, 1995.

_____. *The Summer of Black Widows*. New York: Hanging Loose Press, 1996.

_____. "Superman and Me." *Los Angeles Times* 19 Apr. 1998. Web. 10 Aug. 2010.

_____. *Ten Little Indians*. New York: Grove Press, 2003.

_____. *The Toughest Indian in the World*. New York: Atlantic Monthly Press, 2000.

_____. *War Dances*. New York: Grove Press, 2009.

Busch, Frederick. "Longing for Magic." *New York Times* 16 July 1995. Web. 10 Aug. 2010.

Cline, Lynn. "About Sherman Alexie." *Ploughshares* 26.4 (Winter 2000/2001).

"A Dialogue on Race with President Clinton." PBS *Newshour* 9 July 1998. Web. 10 Aug. 2010.

Egan, Timothy. "An Indian Without Reservations." *New York Times Magazine* 18 Jan. 1998. Web. 10 Aug. 2010.

Grassian, Daniel. *Understanding Sherman Alexie*. Columbia: U of South Carolina P, 2005.

Gray, Richard. *A History of American Literature*. Malden, MA: Blackwell, 2004.

Jaggi, Maya. "All Rage and Heart." *The Guardian*. 3 May 2008. Web. 10 Aug. 2010.

Kincaid, James R. "Who Gets to Tell Their Stories?" Rev. of *The Business of Fancydancing*, by Sherman Alexie. *New York Times* 3 May 1992. Web. 10 Aug. 2010.

Konigsberg, Eric. "In His Own Literary World, a Native Son Without Borders." *New York Times* 20 Oct. 2009. Web. 10 Aug. 2010.

Maslin, Janet. "Where the Men Are Manly and the Indians Bemused." Rev. of *Ten Little Indians*, by Sherman Alexie. *New York Times* 26 May 2003, late ed.: E10.

Peterson, Nancy, ed. *Conversations with Sherman Alexie*. Jackson: UP of Mississippi, 2009.

Price, Reynolds. "One Indian Doesn't Tell the Other." *New York Times* 17 Oct. 1993. Web. 10 Aug. 2010.

"Questions for: Sherman Alexie." *New York Times* 5 Jan. 1997. Web. 10 Aug. 2010.

Roback, Diane. "The Reign Continues: YA Queen Stephenie Meyer Holds on to Top Spots." *Publishers Weekly* 22 Mar. 2010. Web. 10 Aug. 2010.

"Sherman Alexie: Interview." FailBetter.com. 21 Apr. 2009. Web. 10 Aug. 2010.

Silko, Leslie Marmon. "Big Bingo." *The Nation* 12 June 1996.

Skow, Tom. "Books: Lost Heritage." *Time* 21 Oct. 1996. Web. 10 Aug. 2010.

Smiley, Tavis. "Sherman Alexie." *Tavis Smiley*. PBS. 27 Apr. 2007. Web. 10 Aug. 2010.

Spencer, Russ. "What It Means to Be Sherman Alexie." *Book: The Magazine for the Reading Life* July/Aug. 2000. Web. 10 Aug. 2010.

Vizenor, Gerald, and A. Robert Lee. *Postindian Conversations*. Lincoln: U of Nebraska P, 1999.

# Articulations of Difference:
## Minority Existence in White America in Sherman Alexie's *Indian Killer* and Toni Morrison's *The Bluest Eye*_____

Constance Bracewell

The psychological and emotional pain experienced by survivors of disasters such as the BP *Deepwater Horizon* oil rig explosion in the Gulf of Mexico in 2010 or Hurricane Katrina in 2005 often fill the pages of American newspapers and magazines. The resultant stories and images of ordinary citizens who are directly affected by such disasters inevitably compel an outpouring of social responsibility in action on the part of others. This can be readily seen in the aftermath of the Hurricane Katrina disaster, when literally tens of thousands of ordinary American citizens took part in volunteer missions in the disaster zone, helping to rebuild homes and jump-start the revitalization of communities indiscriminately demolished by winds and devastating flood waters. Within these stories and images, citizens of all racial and social makeups stand shoulder to shoulder, working together to effect positive changes for the residents of particular communities, survivors of extreme human disaster. It seems at times like these that many ordinary Americans take a step back and reflect on the certain realization that they too could one day wrestle with just such a devastating human event.

Yet, for every heartwarming story of Americans from all backgrounds tirelessly working together for the common good, there are also countless stories without such happy endings, stories that are predicated on the persistent tendency of American society to divide along racial lines. In actuality, Americans have a long history of racial discord and social separation along ethnic lines, a very different sort of human disaster that belies feel-good stories of ordinary people of all racial and social classes coming together in an orderly camaraderie of human spirit. Historically, vast numbers of Americans of nonwhite backgrounds have instead lived the ugly side of the American experience—that of racial discord and social standards of human value and beauty that often demand "white" characteristics, both of the physical body and of the inner person. Contemporary ethnic American writers of fiction often explore this aspect of the American experience. This premise—that ethnic Americans must somehow live up to arbitrary physical and behavioral standards deemed common to white Americans—is central to the plot of Sherman Alexie's *Indian Killer* (1996). Novels such as *Indian Killer* and Nobel Prize-winning African American author Toni Morrison's *The Bluest Eye* (1970) map out the psychological, emotional, and experiential pain of being "different" in an American society that is dominated by white standards of human worth. At first glance, Alexie's *Indian Killer* and Morrison's *The Bluest Eye* would seem quite dissimilar; however, when read in conjunction the two novels reveal an extraordinary level of similarity in how the authors explore what it means to be "different" in a white-dominated world.

One of the more immediately noticeable similarities between the two novels can be found in the way each book emphasizes physical standards of human worth and the symbolic implications of having blue eyes, particularly if the blue eyes in question appear in the face of a brown-skinned person. In Alexie's *Indian Killer* the "blue, blue eyes" (76) of protagonist John Smith's adoptive mother, Olivia, are in contrast to the "startling blue eyes" (90) of half-white, half-Spokane Indian Reggie Polatkin. Olivia Smith is presented as a kind, well-intentioned woman who, despite her many unintended blunders in raising her adoptive Native American son, is nevertheless a fine figure of white American upper-middle-class womanhood. Well educated, open-minded, and open to love, Olivia appears to in some way *deserve* to have the blue, blue eyes and clear, beautiful, pale skin that are the mark of white America at its collective best. In contrast is Reggie Polatkin, the product of a painfully mismatched union between a Spokane mother and a brutally racist white father named Bird Lawrence.

Bird himself evidences some of the worst qualities of that segment of white America that deems persons of brown skin color and non-English-speaking ethnicity inherently inferior and undeserving of basic human consideration. In Bird's estimation, his son's brown skin marks his Indianness and renders him unworthy of human value—or, to put it another way, Bird views his son as an ugly physical manifestation of the utter inferiority of brown-skinned people in comparison to their white-skinned counterparts.

Bird flays Reggie's very existence on a sadistically regular basis, demanding that he somehow eliminate his physical and inner Indianness in order to be more like Bird himself. The father brutally confronts his son through countless challenges to Reggie's desire to be somehow more than an Indian, such as when he demands that Reggie answer whether he wants to be a "dirty" or "hostile" Indian all of his life. The object for Bird is not literally to change his son into someone else—even Bird must know this is an utter impossibility. Rather, Bird seeks to impress upon his son one essential fact: that, despite his beautiful blue Caucasian eyes, Reggie will always be just another dirty brown-skinned person who can only ever hopelessly aspire to meet standards of whiteness. In short, Reggie is "different" from white Americans, despite his biracial background, and Bird's brutal treatment of his son serves as a rhetorical device on the part of the author to impress upon readers the unhappy fact that, for many white Americans, people such as Reggie can never be of value in quite the same way that white-skinned persons can be. Although most characters in the novel, Indian and white alike, find Reggie's physical appearance to be strikingly handsome, his home situation tells him otherwise. Even though Reggie has possession of one key physical feature of white America, his bright blue eyes, and a handsome face in which to frame them, in the end he is still an Indian, which forever ties him to a category of "difference" in wider American society.

Similarly, the implication of having blue eyes is a prominent part of Pecola Breedlove's story in Morrison's *The Bluest Eye*. Faced with a home situation that from its earliest days is in many ways as brutal as that of Reggie Polatkin and that will become tragically compounded in brutality with the rape of Pecola by her father, the young girl fixates on blue eyes as the sum total of the highest level of human worth. This belief is brought home to her by all she sees around her. From the faces of baby dolls to the living doll that Mrs. Breedlove tends to in the home of her white employer, to the bright curls, dimples, and big blue eyes of Hollywood icon Shirley Temple, the world in which Pecola and other black girls like her live is dominated by white standards of human worth and beauty. Seeking to imagine her own plain, black, apparently unlovable features as something worthy of admiration, love, and respect, Pecola decides that the key to beauty must lie in having blue eyes. It becomes her mission in the raw, tragic life she leads to find a way to transform her eyes to a proper level of blueness—and, in the process, transform herself from a nobody into a somebody, from being unworthily "different" to a person who matters.

In the end, Pecola does indeed gain blue eyes of a sort, but only in her own now-broken mind, which has folded under the pressure of her desperate, unhappy life. When con artist Soaphead Church, a self-designated spiritual and life-matters adviser, is moved to compassion by her pitiful plea for blue eyes and so attempts to trick her into believing that God has answered her prayers to have blue eyes, Pecola is primed and ready to believe in a miracle for herself. However, beneath her seeming acceptance of God's miraculous change of her eyes to a beautiful Caucasian blue lies the inescapable truth that the only way Pecola can rise to standards of white beauty is by psychologically checking out of reality. Once Pecola turns away from the real world around her and instead sinks into the uncertain shelter of her own mind, she can pretend to herself that all has changed and she now has a beauty that transcends the labels of difference, unworthiness, and ugliness that dark-skinned black girls labor under in her community. In other words, there is no escaping her blackness except through an escape from reality itself. Left behind in the real world, in which standards of beauty remain based on Caucasian features, are Pecola's nominal friends, the sometimes-narrator Claudia and her sister Frieda, who—readers can assume—will continue to be held back by their own inability to escape physical and behavioral "difference" as nonwhites in American society.

Certainly both *Indian Killer* and *The Bluest Eye* use blue eyes as a rhetorical device to demonstrate the difficulty and almost certain inability of brown-skinned Americans to meet, much less surpass, white standards of human worth and beauty. However, there is yet another similarity between the texts in relation to blue eyes that is perhaps even more important for readers to note. There appears within each story, to one degree or another, a certain theme by which the very *idea* of blue-eyed, white-skinned standards of human worth is symbolically dismembered or broken apart through scenes in which blue eyes are literally targeted and physically damaged or destroyed. This takes place violently and with brutal finality in *Indian Killer*, in which the anonymous killer targets and fixates on blue-eyed victims, most of whom indeed wind up brutally murdered. The killer even goes so far as to savagely pluck out and swallow the blue eyes of his first victim, literally ingesting elements of acceptance. Although much could be made of this narrative detail and of the scene as a whole, there remains the noticeable fact that in many ways these actions on the part of the killer appear to be a physical representation of the killer's belief that white men must die in order to set something in the world right again. In this sense, the brutalizing of the white man's blue eyes is as much a symbolic destruction of whiteness itself (and all that it stands for) as it is a literal physical act of violence. Readers can also note that John Smith's conclusion that a white man must die to set his world right is yet another way in which the narrative in *Indian Killer* presents multiple avenues for symbolic destruction of whiteness and, by extension, white standards for valuation of human worth. Although the ambiguous final scene of *Indian Killer* does suggests the possibility for a literal destruction of white America and a return for American Indians to a condition of existence similar to the period prior to European incursion, readers are denied knowledge of whether this will ever take place. In the absence of definitive answers on the matter of a literal return to prior systems of Indian existence, Alexie instead leaves readers with the suggestion that some things can perhaps change for the better—if not literally, then at least on a symbolic level.

In the case of John Smith, the symbolic nature of his determination that he "needed to kill a white man" (25) may be symbolic not only in a global sense (that is, applying to making something right for all Indians or all nonwhite people) but also in a way that is very specific to his own circumstances. An Indian who has been raised by a white couple, John is deeply confused about both the ambiguous, unknowable nature of his Indian background and the equally confusing white world in which he has been raised. His confusion is compounded by his experiences with the Jesuit priest Father Duncan. As a very young child, John spends just enough time with Father Duncan to gain a disquieting awareness of the ambiguity between white and Indian worlds that Father Duncan himself feels. When Father Duncan vanishes without a word, the seven-year-old John is left on his own to sort out his emotional confusion about where he fits between Indian and white worlds. In this sense, John's decision to "kill a white man" may not represent a desire to literally, physically end the life of a random white man. Rather, the white man he believes he should kill may in actuality be the white man he sees inside himself. By killing the inner white man that so confuses his existence, John can also symbolically kill the white standards of human worth that he unfailingly falls short of meeting, freeing himself to discover his personal value on his own terms rather than on terms that are dictated by men and women who look nothing like people such as the John Smiths of the world.

Similarly, in *The Bluest Eye* there appears a notable scene in which symbols of blue-eyed white beauty are used to literally and symbolically attack not only blackness but also the idea that standards of white beauty could or should dominate in a dark-skinned world. This occurs in the scene in which Geraldine's cat is thrown onto the radiator by her sadistic, affection-starved, and emotionally damaged young son, Junior. After luring tattered Pecola into his dark, empty house with the promise of seeing nonexistent kittens, an act that seems to appeal to Junior purely as a means to relieve a day's boredom, he maliciously throws his mother's pampered, blue-eyed, black-furred cat into Pecola's face. When his act of household terrorism fails and he realizes that Pecola is responding as affectionately to the hated cat as does his cold and unaffectionate mother, Junior retaliates by swinging the cat by one leg and violently flinging the animal against the window above the hot radiator, onto which the mortally injured cat falls, "its blue eyes closed, leaving only an empty, black, and helpless face" (91).

It is not incidental that all of this takes place in the home of a woman who fits the pattern of young black women of elevated social standing who create a higher standard of living for themselves and their families, and who inevitably mimic the beauty standards of the white world they emulate with bittersweet accuracy within their homes and their beauty routines. The omniscient narrator in this section of the novel details the pains to which Geraldine goes to project a genteel sort of blackness in her household, one that sets her and her family apart from what she sees as the common, uncouth blackness of poorer black people. In short, Geraldine seeks to emulate white standards of value in the members and functions of her household, a process that is emphasized in the black-furred but blue-eyed cat into which she pours all of the attention and affection denied to her husband and child. When Junior kills his mother's cat, it is an act that undoubtedly affords him malicious but painful pleasure as he eliminates the apparent usurper of his mother's affections.

Readers realize, however, that the cat is merely the physical manifestation of a rejection on Geraldine's part that touches much more than her young son. Rather than a rejection of Junior himself, Geraldine's coldness and refusal to offer warmth to any but the black-and-blue cat represent her own inability to accept the blackness that makes it impossible for her ever to truly escape the stigma of being "different" in white-oriented American society. Similarly, the death of the blue-eyed cat not only forecasts the death of something in Pecola's life in the acquisition of such eyes for herself but also suggests that there is an unviable, unhealthy aspect to nonwhite people attempting to orient their identities from a framework of white standards of human worth. In short, trying to "be more white than black," so to speak, is perhaps doomed to failure. In the end, the novel appears to argue that such white standards of human worth should literally be destroyed, much as they are symbolically destroyed with the death of the cat and the eventual collapse of Pecola's mind when she can no longer deal with her inability to be beautiful, loved, or valued according to the white standards that she sees all around her.

Sociologist Allan G. Johnson has formulated much of his life's work around a search for understanding of the ways in which standards of privilege function in relation to the establishment of systems of "difference" in American culture. In *Privilege, Power, and Difference* Johnson observes that when a particular privileged group has center stage in a society, there is inevitably a coexisting tendency on the part of most people to take this same privileged sector as the standard of reference for "the best that society has to offer" (95). Johnson goes on to note:

> Because privileged groups are assumed to represent society as a whole, "American" is culturally defined as white, in spite of the diversity of the population. You can see this in a statement like, "Americans must learn to be more tolerant of other races." The "Americans" are assumed to be white, and the "other races" are assumed to be races *other* than white. *Other* is the key word in understanding how systems are identified with privileged groups. The privileged group is the assumed "we" in relation to "them." The "other" is the "you people" whom the "we" regard as problematic, unacceptable, unlikeable, or beneath "our" standards. (96)

As Johnson points out, American society is persistently cast in terms that privilege whiteness in general. One could add to this the further observation that the same holds true in relation to how American society in general has historically measured human worth and beauty in terms of white standards of such, valuations that are readily apparent in the characters and events within *Indian Killer* and *The Bluest Eye*. At heart, each novel attempts to provoke readers to question these standards and the ways in which such standards of human valuation necessarily separate Americans into numerous categories of privilege and lack thereof.

In addition to the numerous ways in which Alexie's and Morrison's stories rhetorically explore ways in which nonwhite characters view themselves and others, the novels share similar approaches to underscoring the *how* of this process, which serve as a reflexive commentary on the very real difficulty experienced by ethnic Americans when they attempt to answer the question of *why* certain experiences happen to people of nonwhite ethnicity in the United States. In the opening pages of *The Bluest Eye* can be found the following observation from Claudia MacTeer, one of the narrators of the novel. Speaking of the story she is about to relate, Claudia notes: "There is really nothing more to say— except why. But since *why* is difficult to handle, one must take refuge in *how*" (6). What is interesting to note here is that this insightful observation of the pain that is implicated in the ethnic American experience is provided not by the protagonist—in the case of Morrison's story, Pecola Breedlove—but by an observer of that protagonist. In similar fashion, the reader of *Indian Killer* encounters Reggie Polatkin primarily through the eyes of other characters, such as Clarence Mather, Bird Lawrence, and Jack Wilson. The observations of the characters are often filtered through their reactions to and beliefs about white Americans, rather than being presented in plain, unvarnished fashion through the perspective of the protagonist in the story. Pecola, the girl whose greatest desire is to have blue eyes, and Reggie, the mixed-blood man whose greatest desire is seemingly to vent his inner pain on other people, are emblematic of the difficulty of being "different" (that is, not white) in white-dominated American society.

This narrative strategy is itself a telling commentary on the complexity of desires and outcomes often experienced by nonwhite Americans. For one thing, this aspect of Alexie's and Morrison's narrative strategies highlights that, regardless of how compelling the story of a particular ethnic American may be, the stories in this country are typically told by the dominators, not the dominated, and thus are necessarily reflected against white standards of living and being. Similarly, this narrative structure creates a system whereby the stories of those who are "different" are allowed to be told, while at the same time these "different" (that is, nonwhite) characters are actually silenced by virtue of not telling their own stories, in their own words. This can be seen in the way that readers obtain the details of Reggie Polatkin's life experiences, which are related primarily through the voice of the narrator and through the perceptions of those around Reggie rather than in Reggie's own words. Similarly, readers get Pecola Breedlove's story, but almost entirely through the filter of valuation assigned by white America, despite an African American narrator. Granted, this narrator, Claudia MacTeer, is utterly sympathetic to the tragic events of Pecola's life. And by extension, it could be argued that Claudia in *The Bluest Eye* and the early, Reggie-friendly period in which readers encounter Dr. Clarence Mather in *Indian Killer* represent the ability of white America as a collective to be sympathetic to the plight of ethnic Americans in postslavery, post-Western-expansion eras. Yet this sympathy in no way detracts from the fact that, although some situations have improved for American Indians and African Americans, in many circumstances there still exists a tendency to frame such discussions in the public forum through the perspective of an overseeing white American viewpoint.

In the case of Pecola Breedlove, readers encounter her story primarily through the reminiscences of young Claudia MacTeer, herself a black girl of lower socioeconomic status, although to a lesser degree than the poverty of Pecola. However, many of Claudia's most poignant memories of Pecola are embedded with Claudia's perceptions of white standards of human value and beauty, valuations that seem also to permeate the mind-set of Pecola's mother, Polly. In fact, it could be argued that part of Claudia's empathy for Pecola derives from her own unsettled feelings about being black in a white-dominated world. In a way, concern for Pecola becomes a sort of substitute coping process born out of Claudia's inability to feel love or desire for the white baby dolls she is given at holidays or the white standards of beauty that she associates with the dolls. What Claudia cannot feel for the dolls she *can* feel for poor, plain Pecola. The affection that the dolls fail to elicit is cheerfully passed on to the unfortunate Pecola.

A somewhat related narrative structure is evident in Alexie's *Indian Killer*. For Reggie Polatkin, identity is painful and utterly unresolved—and likely will remain unresolvable. However, the narrative structure creates a framework whereby the reader encounters Reggie's circumstances through a sort of reflective pattern. That is, Reggie's experiences and his emotional reactions to those experiences are usually made evident to the reader through the medium of white characters and *their* impressions of Reggie and his situation. From the wannabe-Indian Wilson to Reggie's misogynistic father, Bird, to his onetime hero, Mather, Reggie's life is defined by his startlingly blue eyes and the ways in which his experiences are reflected back to him (and to readers) by the white characters who most define him as a person. And, as in the case of the observation made by Claudia at the opening of *The Bluest Eye*, Reggie's story evidences mostly an attempt to winnow out the *how* of it all, rather than the *why*. Here is what happened, and here is *how* it happened. Here is Reggie's situation, and here is *how* it became so. The implication at this point is that the *why* of it all is so complex as to be unknowable in its entirety—or, that the why of it all is too painful to be confronted directly. In this sense, the painful aspect of a life like Reggie's necessarily *must* be reflected through characters that represent a different stance than his own situation and culture. This sort of process, while offering plenty of detail about Reggie's situation and circumstances, nonetheless blunts the details, allowing readers a distancing from the painful reality of Reggie's life and, by extension, that of all American Indians.

In addition to these types of strategies, whereby ethnic identity is reflected through the impressions and valuations of white characters, it is possible to identify a contrasting sort of reflecting strategy in both narratives, in which American Indian and black characters in the two novels are also reflected through the ideas that other nonwhite characters have about whiteness and being "different" in a white world. One example of this can be traced in Pecola Breedlove's pitiful attempts to find a way to possess the coveted blue eyes that she undoubtedly feels will make her as worthy of love as the curly-haired, blue-eyed Shirley Temple and the pink-and-gold, doll-like Fisher girl who has displaced Pecola in her mother's affections. On one hand, Pecola's determination to obtain for herself one of the features most closely associated with white standards of female beauty is made believable by virtue of the impressions of her that are held by other black characters in the novel. Practically every description of Pecola—from Claudia to Geraldine, to Polly, to Pecola's own ideas about herself—reflects not only that Pecola is singularly lacking in physical beauty but also that in general there is little beautiful about black girls anyway. In other words, the novel suggests that practically everyone, black and white alike, is at least partly convinced either that (a) black girls are necessarily ugly in comparison to white girls or (b) most people in society who are beautiful, well-dressed, well-moneyed, or otherwise socially privileged (most often white people) would agree that black girls are unattractive in comparison to most white girls in ways that are simply a matter of genetic, physical inferiority and thus not open to being rectified in any way. The unspoken implication here is that, although it of course would be impossible for black girls to obtain the socially privileged features and characteristics of white girls, nevertheless they would be better off if they could do so.

Morrison herself has alluded to this conundrum of being "different" in a white-dominated world in describing her thought process while she was creating the character of Western Indian Soaphead Church, a man who is himself a nonwhite in a white world and so could be capable of understanding Pecola's desire for blue eyes. Soaphead could also understand that, although the giving of literal blue eyes would be an impossibility, Pecola's painfully burdened mind could be tricked into believing that God had indeed granted her the desperately wished-for blue eyes. Morrison has noted that it was necessary for Soaphead's character to be convinced of the preferability for a child like Pecola to have blue eyes and be more like white people in order for him even to come up with the idea in the first place of convincing her that her wish had come true:

> I had to have someone—her mother, of course, made her want it in the first place—who would give her the blue eyes. And there had to be somebody who *could*, who had the means; that kind of figure who dealt with fortune-telling, dream-telling and so on, who would also believe that she was right, that it was preferable for her to have blue eyes. (in Taylor-Guthrie 22)

Soaphead's apparent agreement with the desirability of looking more like white people in a white-dominated world and his compassion for what he sees as Pecola's readily evident lack of physical beauty combine to offer a painful commentary on the pressures in America for persons of nonwhite ethnicity to aspire to Caucasian standards of beauty.

In *Indian Killer*, this sort of focus on establishing standards of beauty and worth through a Caucasian frame of reference is also evident. However, in Alexie's piece "beauty" can perhaps be more correctly understood as a *general* representation of human worth and beauty in the context of the sum total of the individual—physical, intellectual, spiritual, vocational, and so on—rather than a purely *physical* representation of human worth and beauty. This is most dramatically presented through the character of Truck Schultz, a bigoted radio commentator whose blind hatred of American Indians is total and unrelenting. In Truck's estimation, there are quite simply *no* redeeming qualities of human worth and beauty to be found in any Indian, anywhere. In his weekly radio broadcasts, Truck sows rumor and misinformation about not only the Indian supposedly involved in the "Indian Killer" case, but all Indians as a collective. As he puts it, "We should have terminated Indian tribes from the very beginning. Indians should have been assimilated into normal society long ago" (209). Notice that Truck uses the word "normal" to describe white-dominant American society as a whole. The use of this word necessarily invokes the understanding that to be Indian is to be, by default, abnormal and unacceptably "different."

Truck's open disdain for all things Indian, from cultural practices to the very physical existence of Indian bodies, is reflected in the uneasy feelings that many Indian characters have about their own selves and their tribal cultures. This can be seen in Marie Polatkin's difficulty in reconciling her desire to make a different life for herself away from the reservation with her love for Indian people in general, her own tribe included. Although Marie herself is perhaps not fully aware of how intensely standards of human worth based on whiteness affect her outlook on self and life, readers have a more ready ability to evaluate Marie's complicated feelings about herself and the difficulties of being different, of being Indian, in a world in which she wants to succeed, but in which she nevertheless feels set apart from white people and Caucasian representations of those things deemed valuable in human beings.

As with Pecola Breedlove, much of what Indian characters such as Marie experience is influenced—sometimes subtly, yet often with little subtlety at all—by the pressures of a general American society that deems "difference" to be synonymous with lesser value on a human level. Interestingly, this aspect of "difference" is doubled and concentrated in the central character of John Smith, an adopted Indian man with profound cultural disconnection resulting not only from his adoption into a white world but also from his complete inability to identify which tribe he comes from. In this sense, John's identity reflects not only the importance of not being different in the white world but also the importance of not being "different" among your own people as a person of nonwhite ethnicity. In yet another strange parallel, wannabe-Indian writer Jack Wilson creates a false sense of Indian identity for himself when he decides that (a) Indians are romantic and interesting, and (b) since his distant relative has a similar name to a real Indian, he must himself be an Indian. However, Wilson's Indianness is scoffed at by both Indians and whites, making a mockery of his individual worth and also underscoring John Smith's own inability to construct a sense of identity even within the general Indian community in the absence of tribally specific connections.

In this sense, Caucasian standards of human worth and beauty demand white characteristics, both in physical form and in ways of living, while Indian standards of worth and beauty require knowledge of one's specific tribe. John's inability to meet the demands of either spectrum reflect the ultimate in ethnic "difference," which itself reflects the negative effects of European colonization of American Indian lands and people. In "Muting White Noise," James H. Cox observes that "John Smith, a young Native man who imagines his adoption by white parents as a nightmarish abduction, is the primary victim of a violent colonial world created and maintained by the storytelling traditions in which Schultz, Mather, and Wilson participate" (178). In other words, the story of what is valued in America is usually told by white people, too frequently those who are deeply misguided or devoted to narrow or bigoted points of view. And when the stories of who we are and who we should be are predicated on the assumption that white ways of being and living are necessarily of more value than any others, it follows that to be "different" is to be of less worth than those who fit the standardized, white Euro-American norm. Or, to return to the term used by Truck Schultz, to be different is to be not *normal*. Readers are reminded of this over and over again, by virtue of multiple characters emphasizing the need to meet Caucasian standards of beauty and human worth, of "normality."

In both Morrison's and Alexie's works, this sort of narrative cushioning effect found in the use of multiple character viewpoints to underscore the many difficulties experienced by ethnic Americans in meeting standards of human worth is of course effective in allowing readers insight into painful ethnic American circumstances while allowing them enough distance so that the details are relatively palatable. However, it is also a commentary on the tendency in American society to frame the cultural, ethnic, or racial outsider through the perspectives of white Americans and white America itself and to avoid suggesting solutions for such problems in favor of simply conceding that problems do exist. Or, to go back to Claudia MacTeer's observation concerning the telling of Pecola's story, "since *why* is difficult to handle, one must take refuge in *how*" (6). In the case of *Indian Killer* and *The Bluest Eye*, the narratives deliver no summative commentary on the *whys* of being "different" in white American society, or the *whys* of the establishment and persistence of Euro-American standards of human beauty and value on the part of not only white Americans but many ethnic Americans as well. Instead, the two stories focus most of their attention on the many *hows* by which such standards are perpetuated.

Readers of the two novels, however, have the advantage of the reader's relation to the story, in which the *why* of it all is often the dominant quest for understanding on the part of the reader. One could argue that it is neither necessary nor even desirable for Alexie's and Morrison's stories to take overt stances on why such standards of worth are established and why these standards persistently play a dominant role in the maintaining of pejorative categories of difference among the many peoples in American society. Instead, the powerful, complicated stories of ethnic "difference" in Alexie's and Morrison's novels offer readers equally powerful opportunities to interrogate and better understand the many ways in which categories of human difference continue to dominate and define standards of human worth in America. In *God Is Red*, leading Native American scholar Vine Deloria, Jr., makes the following observation about human behavior: "One can only conclude that while Christianity can describe what is considered as perfect human behavior, it cannot produce such behavior" (201). Although Deloria is of course speaking rather specifically of standards of human behavior in relation to Christian ideals, his observation also holds true if one omits the word "Christianity" in favor of something along the lines of "Euro-Americans" or "white America." As Deloria notes, just because one group of people demands that a particular standard be met does not mean that this will in fact be the case. And, although some persons of ethnic difference may become persuaded of the necessity to produce in themselves that which white standards of human value demand of them, such as in the cases of Reggie Polatkin and Pecola Breedlove, it is nevertheless within the power of readers of *Indian Killer* and *The Bluest Eye* to decide for themselves why such standards exist, why these standards continue to dominate how Americans think of themselves and others, and, finally, the ultimate *how*—how Americans of all ethnicities and cultures can move beyond restrictive valuations of human worth and create a future in which "difference" is simply an observation and not the sum total of the value of an individual human life.

## Works Cited

Alexie, Sherman. *Indian Killer*. New York: Warner Books, 1996.

Cox, James H. "Muting White Noise: The Popular Culture Invasion in Sherman Alexie's Fiction." *Muting White Noise: Native American and European American Novel Traditions*. Norman: U of Oklahoma P, 2006. 145-99.

Deloria, Vine, Jr. *God Is Red: A Native View of Religion*. 30th anniversary ed. Golden, CO: Fulcrum, 2003.

Johnson, Allan G. *Privilege, Power, and Difference*. 2d ed. New York: McGraw-Hill, 2006.

Morrison, Toni. *The Bluest Eye*. 1970. New York: Vintage, 2007.

Taylor-Guthrie, Danille, ed. *Conversations with Toni Morrison*. Jackson: UP of Mississippi, 1994.

# Postmodern Magic, Traditional Rage:
## The Critical Reception of
## Sherman Alexie's Work _____

Tammy Wahpeconiah

In 1992, James R. Kincaid said of a new Native American writer:

> In [forming new modes and generic possibilities], perhaps the most com-
> manding voice will belong to Sherman Alexie, a Spokane/Coeur d'Alene
> Indian, whose first publication, *The Business of Fancydancing*, is so wide-
> ranging, dexterous and consistently capable of raising your neck hair that
> it enters at once into our ideas of who we are and how we might be, makes
> us speak and hear his words over and over, call others into the room or
> over the phone to repeat them. Mr. Alexie's is one of the major lyric voices
> of our time. He is also one of the most forgiving of those who see far-
> thest. (5)

From his earliest publications, Alexie has earned praise from reviewers and critics alike. He has won numerous awards for both his poetry and his fiction, marking him as an important voice in contemporary Native American literature. His work is widely taught in high
schools and universities, and one can locate him on reading lists in Native American literature classes as well as in classes that focus on contemporary American poetry, short stories, and novels. One might argue
that Sherman Alexie is the most prominent and well-known writer
working in the Native American genre today.

Scholarship focusing on Alexie covers the variety of issues he himself tackles in his writing. Issues of identity, the use (and subversion) of
stereotypes, the influence of popular culture and the media, the importance of orality in Native American tradition, and the significance of
humor as a method of survival for Indian people are all addressed in the
multiplicity of analyses of Alexie's work.

Sherman J. Alexie was born to Sherman Sr. (Coeur d'Alene) and

Lillian Alexie (Spokane) in October 7, 1966. He grew up on the Spokane Indian reservation in Wellpinit, Washington, which lies some fifty miles northwest of Spokane. According to Alexie, there are approximately 2,500 Spokane, of which about 1,100 live on the reservation. He calls the Spokane "Salmon people" who were devastated by the construction of the Grand Coulee Dam, which "took away 7,000 miles of salmon spawning beds from the interior Indians in Washington, Idaho and Montana" (Highway). Alexie was born hydrocephalic and had to undergo brain surgery when he was six months old. Doctors were concerned about his survival, so much so that his father had a Catholic priest administer last rites and his mother "snuck in a Protestant minister . . . to say a final prayer for me" (Blewster 76). He recovered and learned to read when he was three years old, allaying yet another fear of his doctors, that he would have permanent brain damage. His love of books isolated him from his peers, making him "a total geek" and an "outcast" (Marx 17). He read *Grapes of Wrath* when he was five years old and was so impressed with John Steinbeck that he went on to read *Cannery Row*, *Of Mice and Men*, *The Pearl*, and *The Red Pony* (Bellante and Bellante 12-13). He cites his early literary influences as "99 percent white. Steinbeck, Faulkner, Hemingway, Emily Dickinson, Stephen King, Walt Whitman" (Campbell 114). This statement, unfortunately, has displeased several Native critics. At Washington State University, Alexie enrolled in a poetry writing workshop, where his professor gave him a copy of the anthology *Songs from This Earth on Turtle's Back*. He read poems by Native American writers Simon J. Ortiz, Joy Harjo, Linda Hogan, Adrian C. Louis, and James Welch and realized that he could write about his own life experiences. He began writing in 1989.

Alexie published his first collection of poetry, *The Business of Fancydancing*, in 1992 with Hanging Loose Press. Slipstream Press published the chapbook *I Would Steal Horses* in the same year and *First Indian on the Moon* in 1993. After receiving numerous requests from literary agents and publishers, Alexie published *The Lone*

*Ranger and Tonto Fistfight in Heaven*, his first collection of short stories, which was a finalist for the PEN/Hemingway Award. Alexie's first novel, *Reservation Blues* (1995), won the Before Columbus Foundation's American Book Award. He followed with his second novel, *Indian Killer*, and another book of poetry, *The Summer of Black Widows*, both in 1996. Also in 1996, *Granta* named Alexie one of the twenty best American novelists under the age of forty. Alexie then switched gears and wrote a screenplay based on his short story "This Is What It Means to Say, Phoenix, Arizona." The film, *Smoke Signals*, directed by Chris Eyre and released in 1998, featured an entirely Native American cast and crew; it garnered several awards, including the prestigious Sundance Film Festival's Audience Award as well as a nomination for the festival's Grand Jury Prize. Alexie returned to poetry and fiction, publishing *The Man Who Loves Salmon* (1998), *The Toughest Indian in the World* (2000), and *One Stick Song* (2000). Alexie then wrote and directed the film *The Business of Fancydancing*, which was released in 2002. Dennis Harvey, in a review for *Variety*, said that the film "makes some fascinating points about identity politics, history, loyalty and the price of success—not a bad payoff for a first-time filmmaker."

Alexie's next collection of short stories, *Ten Little Indians*, was published in 2003. Quattro Venti, an Italian publishing company, published parallel translations in English and Italian of poetry selections from *The Business of Fancydancing* and *The Summer of Black Widows* titled *Il powwow della fine del mondo* in 2005. Alexie turned his attention to the young adult genre in 2007 with the publication of *Flight* and *The Absolutely True Diary of a Part-Time Indian*, which won the National Book Award for young people's literature. In 2009, Alexie returned to poetry with the publication of *Face*. He also published a collection of short stories interspersed with poetry, *War Dances*, which won the PEN/Faulkner Award for Fiction.

Reviews of Alexie's work have been, for the most part, positive. As quoted above, James R. Kincaid called Alexie "one of the major lyric voices of our time" in one of the earliest reviews of Alexie's work. Susan Olcott, in her review of *The Business of Fancydancing*, states that "Alexie writes affectingly about life on a reservation in eastern Washington state. His work displays tremendous pain and anger, but there is also love, humor and plenty of irony" (86). The themes of pain and anger have surfaced several times in other reviews. "Alexie uses the 'magic and loss' of song and story to forge an 'entire identity' out of anger and the nightmare of racism. Despite pain, the moving work celebrates something that can't be killed by cavalry swords, Thunderbird wine, 'fake ceremonies,' or 'continuous lies,'" Robert Allen writes in his review of *First Indian on the Moon* (77). Reviewers have noted the rage and pain even in Alexie's young adult fiction. Tom Barbash calls *Flight* "a narrative stripped to its core, all rage and heart. . . . It's raw and vital, often raucously funny, and there isn't a false word in it" (13).

Narrative technique is yet another focus of Alexie's work. Denise Low discusses the postmodern aspects of Alexie's writing, especially in *The Lone Ranger and Tonto Fistfight in Heaven*. She argues that these stories "could not have been written during any other period in history. The twenty-two short tales read like a casebook of postmodernist theory—beyond surrealism and absurdity, and certainly beyond classicism" (123-24). In yet another aspect of postmodern writing, "Alexie ruptures narrative, confuses human and fictitious people, pastiches images, and plays with illusion. . . . The aggregative technique of writing uses may vignettes that add up to a new kind of written storytelling that comes—often—too close to the truth" (124).

Alexie has received mixed reviews for some of his work, however, particularly *Indian Killer* and *Ten Little Indians*. *New York Times* reviewer Richard E. Nicholls agrees that any discussion of *Indian Killer* can make it sound

unrelievedly grim. It is leavened repeatedly, however, by flashes of sardonic wit, the humor that Indians use to assuage pain. . . . It's also difficult not to make the novel seem more angry than reflective. But Sherman

Alexie is too good a writer, too devoted to the complexities of the story, to settle for a diatribe. His vigorous prose, his haunted, surprising characters and his meditative exploration of the sources of human identity transform into a resonant tragedy what might have been a melodrama in less assured hands. (34)

John Skow, writing for *Time*, disagrees: "Alexie's tale is septic with what clearly seems to be his own unappeasable fury. . . . But the world is so oversupplied with justified hatred, righteously inflaming every continent and tribe, that it is hard to respond to *Indian Killer* with anything more openhearted than, 'Right. Understood. Take a number. Get in line'" (90). Although Alexie originally defended the novel, he has since changed his views. He calls *Indian Killer* "a pile of crap novel" (Weich 173) and views the violence with "overwhelming disgust" (Jaggi 11). He claims the novel "is a very fundamentalist, binary book, the product of youthful rage" (Jaggi 11).

Alexie's views on *Ten Little Indians*, especially "What You Pawn I Will Redeem," are markedly different from his views on *Indian Killer*. As he told one interviewer, when he reads the story, he thinks, "*This is really good*" (Weich 172). Janet Maslin agrees in her *New York Times* review of the collection: "In [Alexie's] warm, revealing, invitingly roundabout stories, the central figures come in all shapes and sizes, sharing only their wry perspective on Indian life off the reservation"; she calls the stories "affectionate tales of dealings between men and women" (E10). Lee Maracle could not disagree more. Alexie's portrayals of women in the collection disturb her; she expects him "to avoid the conventional images of Indian women that are prevalent in stories by non-native writers" (PT9). Moreover, in the story "The Search Engine," Maracle finds the main character, Corliss, to be no more than a stereotype of the "savage squaw," whose only options are to hate white men or to have sex with them. Maracle finds such characterizations "disappointing and plain lazy."

The scholarship on Sherman Alexie deals with many of the same issues, subjects, and themes touched on in the reviews, but in greater detail. Two book-length works provide thorough overviews of most of Alexie's work. Daniel Grassian's *Understanding Sherman Alexie* covers *The Business of Fancydancing* (1992) through *Ten Little Indians* (2003). Grassian offers insightful analyses of Alexie's poetry, short fiction, and novels, discussing Alexie's concern with reservation life and how that life is "held together by what destroys it (alcohol and poverty) and what helps it survive (humor and television)" (21). The epigraph in Alexie's poetry collection *Old Shirts and New Skins* (1993), "Poetry = Anger × Imagination," illustrates the importance of art, especially art fueled by rage. Grassian points out that although Alexie believes in the importance of Native literature, he is not idealistic enough to believe it can fix the problems that exist in contemporary Indian society. The other themes that Grassian addresses include the distances between Native American and mainstream culture, the ambivalent impact of popular culture, ethnic hybridity as both creative and destructive, and the sustaining value of cultural traditions.

Meredith K. James discusses Alexie's use of the reservation as metaphor in eight of his works, including the films *Smoke Signals* and *The Business of Fancydancing*. She provides a thorough overview of the historical beginnings of the reservation and includes works by other Native writers, such as N. Scott Momaday and Louise Erdrich, to compare their "reservations of the mind" to Alexie's own reservation of his mind. James notes that Alexie "does not merely depict his reservation as a physical location, but instead his literary reservation is an emotional destination, a place that transcends geographic boundaries, a place that characters can travel to without physically moving" (87).

Many scholars have addressed Indian identity, especially contemporary Indian identity, at length. Characters in Native-authored texts often struggle with maintaining both individual and tribal identities. Complications arise because these characters exist within and around a dominant culture that values the individual. In contrast, many Native cultures value the communal, focusing on the individual only as a member of the community. To understand how Native characters develop a sense of self with the communal, many scholars turn to the architectonic model of the human psyche developed by philosopher and literary critic Mikhail Bakhtin. According to Bakhtin, an individual's sense of identity is developed through a combination of others' perceptions of the individual and the individual's perceptions of his or her own self. In addition, because each person is influenced by others, no one voice exists in isolation. Bakhtin's theories are well suited to an examination of Native American concepts of self, community, and identity.

Jerome DeNuccio argues that Alexie establishes Indian subjectivity through a Bakhtinian dialogic, creating identity through the connections of past and present, the historical and the contemporary. Focusing on *The Lone Ranger and Tonto Fistfight in Heaven*, DeNuccio describes how Alexie's characters struggle to create identities that move beyond the "official discourse" of the dominant culture (92). Realizing that a particular "traditional tribal past . . . no longer exists," characters such as Junior struggle to find a viable tribal identity that encompasses past, present, and future but is not overly determined by one or the other (94). The false images of the Indian and "Indianness" that Hollywood and American history portray are internalized by the characters, so much so that they are unable to define what "Indian" means to them. Victor, Junior, and many others have thus become "finalized" selves. To become so is to become stagnant, to "slow dance with skeletons" and "risk being caught," as Thomas says, "'in the in-between, between touching and becoming'" (87). Bakhtin argues that the self cannot be finalized without threatening "the essence of selfhood" (Morson and Emerson 91). The historical and mass-media images of the Indian create monologism, reducing Indian identity "to the circumstances that produced them, without seeing their genuine freedom to remake themselves and take responsibility for the action" (92). Victor and Junior find themselves "both inside and outside [their] own experience," which results in self-abnegation. The characters must learn to accommodate and negotiate the "memories, dreams, and voices [that] form a network of social signification" (DeNuccio 87). Accommodation and negotiation manifest themselves in a character's embrace of a "viable traditional practice" (94), which Thomas Builds-the-Fire calls the "one determination" (73). For Victor, fancydancing is that viable traditional practice, that one determination. For Junior, it is coming to terms with and taking responsibility for his actions, especially the negative ones, symbolized by his failure to acknowledge the similarity between him and an inner-city basketball player. For Thomas, it is storytelling. Thomas's stories allow characters to bridge past and present, to connect the historical with the contemporary.

In contrast to *The Lone Ranger and Tonto Fistfight in Heaven*, which is mostly set on the Spokane reservation, *Ten Little Indians* takes place in Seattle. Jennifer K. Ladino discusses how Alexie's characters negotiate identity in urban spaces. Ladino argues that *Ten Little Indians* portrays problems that exist in a multicultural city such as Seattle "while simultaneously imagining a polycultural world" (38). Using Vijay Prashad's critique of multiculturalism, Ladino shows how Alexie addresses the problems that exist in the multicultural urban space. Alexie acknowledges, in his description of Seattle, the "reifying notions of cultural and racial purity and authenticity" present in theories of multiculturalism (37). Such notions "[reinforce] hegemonic power dynamics" and prevent people from engaging in truthful discussions about social and racial injustice (37).

While acknowledging such problematic issues, Alexie's *Ten Little Indians* focuses on polyculturalism—human interaction that transcends racial lines without eliding racial differences. The various characters reenact ceremonies that are not fixed and bounded by reservation parameters, allowing them to form communities within a space that is often defined as individualistic to the extreme. Aligning herself with Bakhtin's concept of unfinalizability, albeit through implication, Ladino demonstrates how the characters' motions and movement through the city symbolize how identity is always in flux. Furthermore, this movement allows communities to form in unexpected places, which is crucial to Indian identity. Ladino states, "Alexie's urban identity is like all identity: performative, cobbled together from a web of lineages, and at once self-generated and constructed by and within fraught social forces" (44). We are once again reminded of Bakhtin's architectonic model of the human psyche and how identity is developed through the dialogic.

Furthering and expanding the approaches taken by DeNuccio and Ladino, Kathleen L. Carroll argues for a performance-based approach to reading Native American texts. In a performance-based approach, we must first familiarize ourselves with the oral tradition so that we can understand how writers such as Alexie use those traditions in their texts. We then engage with the text in a dialogic process to remake Indian identity. Readers are able to identify damaging stereotypes not only held by whites but also internalized by Indians themselves. Moreover, recognition of these stereotypes allows both reader and character to "reimagine and recreate a modern identity that insures communal survival" (75). As Carroll states:

> Overlaying stories about heroic Native Americans of the past (diachronic moments) onto stories where Native Americans are trapped within modern stereotypes (the synchronic moment) characterizes Alexie's written strategy. By drawing the past into the present, Alexie brings the subordinate and the dominant cultures into conversations with each other. . . . Alexie experiments with form and theme to lead readers into the unlearning of these dominant definitions as he affirms the imaginative power of the oral traditions to refashion native culture. (75)

Alexie's focus on storytelling perpetuates the idea that it is through this particular ceremony that Indians can create individual and tribal identity. Alexie's storytellers, as well as the reader, engage in the subversion of stereotypes, particularly the Tonto stereotype of the silent, impassive ally of the white man. Carroll describes Alexie's narrators as illustrating W. E. B. Du Bois's theory of double consciousness, "always looking at one's self through the eyes of others" (qtd. in Carroll 76). Although I agree that these characters do have that sense of double consciousness, I would argue that, more important, they are engaging in the Bakhtinian "I-for-the-other" component of identity (Emerson and Morson para. 9). Thus identity becomes a constant act of negotiation between the fictionalized and historic past as well as between the contemporary Indian and white societies.

Another critical focus is Alexie's use of stereotypes and how he does or does not subvert them. Jhon Warren Gilroy uses the film *Smoke Signals* to illustrate how Alexie subverts common stereotypes of Indians. Presenting itself as a typical road/buddy movie, *Smoke Signals* comforts and familiarizes viewers through its connection to a well-known genre. However, the Otherness of the film immediately undermines viewers' expectations. The movie opens on an Indian reservation and introduces us to characters with whom we are unfamiliar. More important, as Gilroy notes, the male protagonist is an American Indian rather than a white man. To undermine expectations further, the film's narration does "not adhere to [the protagonist's] point of view," and the viewer "[obtains] some self-knowledge through a character that is decidedly Other" (26). Interestingly, the way the viewer obtains this knowledge is through the "internalized racist self-image" that Victor adopts (28). As Gilroy states:

> The empathetic relationship created by the realization that the characters have fallen victim to the same misguided conceptions—albeit in a much more insidious fashion—is essential to the viewers' recognition of the power of stereotypes. From the position of the viewers, this leads to the possibility of an awareness of their own preconceptions, ideas based largely on previous filmic representations of Indians; for the characters, it displays the depth of the medium's potential for enculturation and the internalization of racist self-images. (28)

Because of his subjection to filmic and literary stereotypes of the Indian, especially the stoic warrior, Victor believes that certain behavior is expected of him and depends on it for psychic protection. As viewers, we too are implicated in our ideal of what a "real Indian" should be, and as Victor begins to realize his own complicity in his racist self-image, we begin to understand ours as well.

Yet another subversive element of the film, according to Gilroy, is its commentary on the Western binary of truth and lies (37). Thomas's listeners are constantly questioning the veracity of his stories: Victor tells others that Thomas is "full of shit"; after hearing a story, Suzy Song asks, "Is that true?"; and Thomas asks Suzy for a story that is both truth and lies. As viewers, we closely identify with Thomas's listeners, especially Victor. Gilroy notes that "Victor's inability to see beyond his own internalized stereotypical perceptions of Thomas, himself, and his father keeps him from seeing the greater truths of Thomas' stories" (37). As Victor's perceptions change, he comes to understand Thomas's stories. Victor's understanding leads the viewer to value and accept the need for Indian self-representation.

Not all scholars view Alexie's work in such a positive light. Some see his characters and subject matter as reinforcing many of the negative stereotypes held by non-Indians. Gloria Bird, in an essay on *Reservation Blues*, argues that Alexie "contribute[s] to a portrait of an exaggerated version of reservation life, one that perpetuates many of the stereotypes of native people" (47). Alexie's use of popular culture does not serve to question the dominant ideology but rather to move "the story from one subject to another" (47). Bird questions the colonialist influence on *Reservation Blues* and how that influence implicitly shapes the novel for a mainstream audience. Instead of Alexie using stereotypes in order to undermine them, Bird posits that they "return an image of the 'generic' Indian back to the original producers of that image" (49). Furthermore, Indian culture in the novel is unspecified, reinforcing the idea of pan-Indianism and disallowing anything uniquely Spokane to come through. Alexie's description of the reservation reduces it to nothing more than a prop, "vacant of any emotional invest-ment"; the characters are inconsistent and unreliable, undermining "*native* aesthetic values" (50).

Bird does credit Alexie with addressing important Native issues such as assimilation and alcoholism, but she asserts that his representa-tions of Indians dealing with these problems in no way disturb the non-Native reader because the characters are presented in the way America likes to see them: tragic and desperate. Bird acknowledges the diffi-culty in presenting the rampant alcoholism that has ravaged Indian cul-tures and understands the struggle that any Native writer undergoes in attempting to "accurately represent our communities without exploit-ing them" (51). However, Bird argues, Alexie sensationalizes alcohol-ism instead of addressing the issues that lead to this damaging disease: poverty, lack of economic stability, and loss of culture. According to Bird, Alexie's work shows a dangerous lack of responsibility to Native culture.

In contrast, Stephen F. Evans argues that critics who see Alexie's work as reinforcing stereotypes are missing his purpose. Evans labels Alexie a moral satirist who constructs "a satiric mirror that reflects the painful reality of lives that have become distorted, disrupted, de-stroyed, and doomed by their counterimpulses to embrace or deny tra-ditional Indian culture, to become assimilated to or resist absorption into white civilization—or both" (49). Evans finds Bird's analysis of Alexie, especially her criticism of his stereotyping, a misreading, con-sidering that earlier Indian fiction depended on "stereotypes and for-mulaic constructions" as well (50). Furthermore, Evans argues, Bird's argument that colonialist influence is always negative and Native cul-ture is always positive "actually may foster or promote the replication of stereotypes, good and bad" (51). Alexie's use of the drunken Indian illustrates how white culture has repressed and exploited Native peo-ples, and he shows not only the historical reasons but also the "cultur-ally embedded patterns of modern Indian defeat" (55). Evans argues that Alexie's representation of the reservation and its inhabitants is intended "not to destroy [it], but rather . . . to [refashion] it and its members" (64). Evans sees Alexie's use of stereotypes as innovative and morally based, demanding that both Native and non-Native readers create new meanings from old structures.

In contemporary America, film and television are the most consumed forms of media and, as such, are where mainstream society gets its perceptions of Native Americans and Native American culture. The pervasiveness of these false images demands that Native writers respond to and assess how such perceptions affect their culture and their interactions with the dominant society. James H. Cox argues that Alexie's "characters . . . struggle for self-definition and self-representation against the oppressive technological narratives that define Native Americans as a conquered people" (56). The "white noise" they hear at the end of the television broadcast day symbolizes twentieth-century colonialism and its constant effort to destroy Native agency. In order to combat the destructive effects of visual media, the characters must envision an alternative. For Alexie, that alternative is Thomas Builds-the-Fire's stories, which "mute the white noise that infects the reservation" (61). According to Cox, Alexie revises colonialist narratives in order to expose" their destructive cultural biases and ideologies" and thus tells "new tales of Native American resistance" (66).

Stephanie Gordon's assessment of popular-culture references in Alexie's work differs slightly from Cox's. Whereas Cox sees only subversion and resistance, Gordon sees Alexie engaging in a dialogical exchange that is "as inclusive as it divisive" (29). She argues that Alexie engages in a dialogue that combines traditional and contemporary popular culture with high culture to create an Indian identity that differs vastly from what mainstream American society believes about Indian identity. Although television and film can hold Alexie's characters captive, Gordon points out, at times these media references "repair breaches between Indian and Indian and Indian and whites" (30). Alexie's characters are able to create community and new traditions out of both past and present, Native and Euro-American.

Alexie's use of popular culture takes an interesting turn in his novel *Reservation Blues*. Douglas Ford sees Alexie using this trope to illustrate a crossroads, or cultural intersection, where the oral tradition now exists in a hybrid form, "informed by the other discursive forms that have crossed its path" (198). Following Ralph Ellison's definition of the blues as a lyrical expression of one's "autobiographical chronicle of personal catastrophe" (qtd. in Ford 197), Alexie uses the blues to describe those catastrophes through a collective tribal voice and allows his characters to record previously unrecorded history, such as the U.S. Cavalry's slaughter of Indian horses, which Big Mom preserves in song. Thus the memory of such incidents is sustained in a hybrid form that contains elements of indigenous oral tradition and African American blues. Ford argues that Alexie uses the blues trope to complicate issues of identity. For example, characters name specific white celebrities as honorary Spokane and, in doing so, "[seek] out representations that go beyond an absolute, determined form" (202). Aside from identity issues, Alexie uses the blues to reinvent new possibilities for ritual and ceremony, specifically the oral tradition. Since the blues are, as Houston Baker defines them, "a point of ceaseless input and output, a web of intersecting, crisscrossing impulses always in productive transit" (qtd. in Ford 203), they help to redefine and re-create the oral tradition, which can no longer be maintained in a pure state. Thus *Reservation Blues* allows Alexie to reinvigorate the oral tradition, using the blues as a blueprint.

Scott Andrews, however, does not agree with Ford's view as to what *Reservation Blues* actually achieves. Andrews commends Alexie for his use of the trope of blues music as a path that could connect Native American and African American cultures. Like Ford, Andrews turns to Houston Baker's work on the blues. Andrews notes that Big Mom and Thomas act as "blues detectives," with their ability to "break away from traditional concepts and to supply new and creative possibilities" (Baker qtd. in Andrews 140). Big Mom uses her guitar to remember historical tragedies, while the guitar itself is "a celebration of the symbol of the American Dream" (141). Since Thomas uses both Native American and African American traditions in his music to create a hybrid orality, both Big Mom and Thomas should provide new possibilities and new identifications, but this does not happen in the novel. Rather than offering a hopeful ending, using the blues as a way out, the novel ends in silence and despair. Andrews posits that Alexie is unable to imagine success for Coyote Springs, the band Thomas forms, because of the essentialist, separatist notions contained within the novel. In other words, "the novel ultimately re-enacts the colonial dynamics it otherwise exposes" (151).

Similar to scholars who discuss Alexie's fiction, those who focus on his poetry see many of the same issues surface over and over again. John Newton claims that Alexie's poetry illustrates "his own easy affiliation with urban mass culture and the contemporary reservation" (414). Newton labels Alexie's poetry "autoethnographic," arguing that as a colonized subject Alexie "undertakes to represent [himself] in ways that *engage with* the colonizer's own terms" (Pratt qtd. in Newton 416). Alexie chooses romantic relationships as a way to engage colonialism and its effects. The object of the speaker's desire in "Indian Boy Love Songs" and "Tiny Treaties" is a white lover. These relationships, according to Newton, "memorialize that history of colonial conflict which is the lovers' differential legacy" (418). What Alexie attempts to do is to "change the story" by allowing his speakers and characters to acknowledge constructed identities, both their own and those of others.

Because Alexie writes in an autoethnographic vein, Ron McFarland labels Alexie's poetry "polemical" (252). McFarland does not use "polemical" in a negative sense; rather, he uses the word in its original meaning, which is derived from the Greek word for war. Calling Alexie a polemicist is calling him a warrior. McFarland sees Alexie's power as rhetoric "that reflects pain and anger" but refuses to fall into bitterness because of the humor that exists in his poetry (263).

Laura Arnold Leibman focuses on Alexie's poetry collection *The*

*Summer of Black Widows* to discuss the poet as both an agent of death and a creator of the world. Alexie uses Western poetic forms to "combat the white world and the death [his] people face" (545). For example, when a poet uses the elegiac form, both speaker and reader are able to mourn as a community. Since Alexie's readers are not necessarily part of the same community as the speaker, they may not be able to mourn together. However, Alexie attempts to bridge the distance between speaker and reader through an acknowledgment of that very difference. Alexie, as he does in his fiction, requires the reader to participate and "enact closure for the grief and loss the poems describe" (544). He wants readers to acknowledge the power of language to heal as well as to kill and to participate in the making of the poem and the renewal that will come out of that production.

Other Western forms that Alexie uses are the villanelle and the sestina. Alexie uses the villanelle, which consists of nineteen lines of five tercets and one quatrain, to deal with obsession and loss, a well-suited form because of its use of repetition. The sestina, a poetic form consisting of six six-line stanzas and a tercet, Alexie employs to "arouse anxiety with consolation" (553). His application of Western poetic forms permits him to revise and reorder both Spokane and Euro-American traditions.

Carrie Etter expands on Leibman's analysis sonnets. However, the way Alexie employs the sonnet form differs from the traditional European sonnet in that it resists resolution. Usually, the sonnet consists of three quatrains and a couplet that resolves the issue raised in the preceding quatrains. Etter argues that this lack of resolution is a metaphor for the resolution denied to Indians. Alexie's speakers deal with issues of identity and the lack of agency within Indian identity. In aligning themselves with their American Indian identity, the speakers find themselves "locked into its historical lack of agency" (146). Interestingly, such a move authenticates the speaker while at the same time denying him agency, because to claim "Indianness" is to "reinforce the traditional Anglo-Indian hierarchy" that leaves the speaker disabled

(146). Although the speaker never finds resolution, the sonnets point to an imagined place where identity is more than a construction created in a hierarchical environment.

Jennifer Gillan argues that Alexie's poetry deals with clichés surrounding Indians and Indian life. His speakers long for a return to a traditional life while knowing that such a life does not exist. Alexie does not engage in nostalgic writing because to do so would be a dangerous return to a view of Native Americans as stoic and strong without acknowledging their anguish. Alexie's speakers desire the American Dream given to them through television and filmic images, but they realize those images only provide and exist in a negation of Indian culture. Alexie "recognizes that the structural elements of the representation of Indianness—the Indian as savage or child—are central to the narrative of the United States as a nation. It is not just one image but a whole structure of domination that needs to be challenged" (103-4).

Alexie's work continues to challenge the destructive structure that threatens to destroy Native culture, while at the same time providing new rituals and ceremonies through which the culture can continue to grow. In addition, scholars will continue to address how Native American authors such as Alexie provide a new and important trajectory for American literature.

## Works Cited

Allen, Frank. Rev. of *First Indian on the Moon*. *Library Journal* 118.19 (15 Nov. 1993): 77.

Andrews, Scott. "A New Road and a Dead End in Sherman Alexie's *Reservation Blues*." *American Quarterly* 63.2 (2007): 137-52.

Barbash, Tom. "Native Son." Rev. of *Flight*, by Sherman Alexie. *New York Times* 27 May 2007, late ed.: 7.13.

Bellante, John, and Carl Bellante. "Sherman Alexie, Literary Rebel." *Conversations with Sherman Alexie*. Ed. Nancy J. Peterson. Jackson: UP of Mississippi, 2009. 3-15.

Bird, Gloria. "The Exaggeration of Despair in Sherman Alexie's *Reservation Blues*." *Wicazo Sa Review* 11.2 (1995): 47-52.

Blewster, Kelly. "Tribal Visions." *Conversations with Sherman Alexie*. Ed. Nancy J. Peterson. Jackson: UP of Mississippi, 2009. 71-82.

Campbell, Duncan. "Voice of the New Tribes." *Conversations with Sherman Alexie*. Ed. Nancy J. Peterson. Jackson: UP of Mississippi, 2009. 113-20.

Carroll, Kathleen L. "Ceremonial Tradition as Form and Theme in Sherman Alexie's *The Lone Ranger and Tonto Fistfight in Heaven*: A Performance-Based Approach to Native American Literature." *Journal of the Midwest Modern Language Association* 38.1 (2005): 74-84.

Cox, James H. "Muting White Noise: The Subversion of Popular Culture Narratives of Conquest in Sherman Alexie's Fiction." *Studies in American Indian Literatures* 9.4 (1997): 52-69.

DeNuccio, Jerome. "Slow Dancing with Skeletons: Sherman Alexie's *The Lone Ranger and Tonto Fistfight in Heaven*." *Critique* 44.1 (2002): 86-96.

Emerson, Caryl, and Gary Saul Morson. "Mikhail Bakhtin." *The Johns Hopkins Guide to Literary Theory and Criticism*. Ed. Michael Groden et al. 2d ed. Baltimore: Johns Hopkins UP, 2005.

Etter, Carrie. "Dialectic to Dialogic: Negotiating Bicultural Heritage in Sherman Alexie's Sonnets." *Telling the Stories: Essays on American Indian Literatures and Cultures*. Ed. Elizabeth Hoffman Nelson and Malcolm A. Nelson. New York: Peter Lang, 2001. 143-51.

Evans, Stephen F. "'Open Containers': Sherman Alexie's Drunken Indians." *American Indian Quarterly* 25.1 (2001): 46-72.

Ford, Douglas. "Sherman Alexie's Indigenous Blues." *MELUS* 27.3 (2002): 197-215.

Gillan, Jennifer. "Reservation Home Movies: Sherman Alexie's Poetry." *American Literature* 68.1 (1996): 91-110.

Gilroy, Jhon Warren. "Another Fine Example of the Oral Tradition? Identification and Subversion in Sherman Alexie's *Smoke Signals*." *Studies in American Indian Literatures* 13.1 (2001): 23-36.

Gordon, Stephanie. "'The 7-11 of My Dreams': Pop Culture in Sherman Alexie's Short Fiction." *Studies in American Culture* 24.2 (2001): 29-36.

Grassian, Daniel. *Understanding Sherman Alexie*. Columbia: U of South Carolina P, 2005.

Harvey, Dennis. Rev. of *The Business of Fancydancing*, Sherman Alexie, dir. *Variety* 22 Jan. 2002. Web. 17 June 2010.

Highway, Tomson. "Spokane Words: Tomson Highway Raps with Sherman Alexie." *Aboriginal Voices* Jan.-Mar. 1997: 36-41.

Jaggi, Maya. "A Life in Writing: All Rage and Heart." *The Guardian* 3 May 2008, final ed.: 11.

James, Meredith K. *Literary and Cinematic Reservation in Selected Works of Native American Author Sherman Alexie*. Lewiston, NY: Edwin Mellen Press, 2005.

Kincaid, James R. "Who Gets to Tell Their Stories?" Rev. of *The Business of Fancydancing*, by Sherman Alexie. *New York Times* 3 May 1992. Web. 3 June 2010.

Ladino, Jennifer K. "'A Limited Range of Motion?': Multiculturalism, 'Human Questions,' and Urban Identity in Sherman Alexie's *Ten Little Indians*." *Studies in American Indian Literatures* 21.3 (2009): 36-57.

Leibman, Laura Arnold. "A Bridge of Difference: Sherman Alexie and the Politics of Mourning." *American Literature* 77.3 (2005): 541-61.

Low, Denise. Rev. of *The Lone Ranger and Tonto Fistfight in Heaven*, by Sherman Alexie. *American Indian Quarterly* 20.1 (1996): 123-25.

McFarland, Ron. "'Another Kind of Violence': Sherman Alexie's Poems." *American Indian Quarterly* 21.2 (1997): 251-64.

Maracle, Lee. "Alexie Can Tell a Story, but Misses the Mark with Women." Rev. of *Ten Little Indians*, by Sherman Alexie. *National Post* [Toronto]. 28 June 2003, Saturday Toronto ed.: PT9.

Marx, Doug. "Sherman Alexie: A Reservation of the Mind" (1996). *Conversations with Sherman Alexie*. Ed. Nancy J. Peterson. Jackson: UP of Mississippi, 2009. 16-20.

Maslin, Janet. "Where the Men Are Manly and the Indians Bemused." Rev. of *Ten Little Indians*, by Sherman Alexie. *New York Times* 26 May 2003, late ed.: E10.

Morson, Gary Saul, and Caryl Emerson. *Mikhail Bakhtin: Creation of Prosaics*. Stanford, CA: Stanford UP, 1990.

Newton, John. "Sherman Alexie's Autoethnography." *Contemporary Literature* 42.2 (2001): 413-28.

Nicholls, Richard E. "Skin Games." Rev. of *Indian Killer*, by Sherman Alexie. *New York Times* 24 Nov. 1996, late ed.: 7.34.

Olcott, Susan. Rev. of *The Business of Fancydancing*, by Sherman Alexie. *Library Journal* 117.16 (1 Oct. 1992): 86.

Skow, John. Rev. of *Indian Killer*, by Sherman Alexie. *Time* 21 Oct. 1996: 90.

Weich, Dave. "Revising Sherman Alexie." *Conversations with Sherman Alexie*. Ed. Nancy J. Peterson. Jackson: Mississippi Press, 2009. 169-79.

# Half Child/Half Adult:
## Sherman Alexie's Hybrid Young Adult Fiction_____
Mark Vogel

When an established *adult* writer—Joyce Carol Oates, Francine Prose, or Sherman Alexie—deliberately enters the young adult genre, steeped in adult literary expectations, he or she is expected to add new realism, complex characterization, maybe even new themes. The current eagerness by adult writers to write for an adolescent audience reflects a thinning of the line between young adult and adult fiction, and also a maturing of the genre. A forty-year YA "golden age" shrugging off didacticism and restrictive taboos sets the stage for Sherman Alexie's two young adult novels, *Flight* and *The Absolutely True Diary of a Part-Time Indian*. His illustrations of hard truths confronting American Indian youth bring largely invisible viewpoints into the light. Couched in humor and insight, both books are invaluable contributions to writing for young adults.

Long before Alexie chose to write for young adults, his short stories and novels were being read by adolescents. A border crosser and multitribal spokesman, Alexie has long reached out to teachers, students, and librarians. Since his emergence as a writer, he has written many vibrant portrayals of young adults. He is a natural for young adult readers because beneath a dark and sometimes bleak exterior, his books are inherently positive and future-directed. Because young adult experience is by definition limited, YA fiction must be forward-looking—with more hope and possibility than illustrations of past history. Young adults desperately need Alexie's honesty without didactic preaching. Alexie's blend of humor and insight give survival skills to American Indian adolescents and others facing a lack of opportunities.

Nancy J. Peterson, in her summary of Alexie's National Book Award acceptance speech for *Part-Time Indian*, argues that his writing conveys "a strong commitment to communicating Native realities . . . ; an embracing of multiple and multifarious lines of influence . . . ; a desire to spread encouragement and hope to young people of all backgrounds; as well as an insistence that books and literature are not mere entertainment or luxuries, but essential to survival and understanding" (ix). Both *Part-Time Indian* and *Flight* appeared in 2007, at a time when few American Indian novels for young adults were widely read in schools, when selections too often were limited to *House Made of Dawn*, *The Education of Little Tree*, and works of Louise Erdrich and selected others, and when few contemporary portrayals of American Indian young adults existed.

This essay explores the relevance of Alexie's novels *Flight* and *Part-Time Indian* within the history of young adult literature. Of particular help to this task is Seth Lerer's perceptive work *Children's Literature: A Reader's History, from Aesop to Harry Potter*. Lerer notes that as early as 1692, John Locke (borrowing from Aristotle) argued that education, both formal and informal, should focus on instruction and delight—that mentors and models, both actual and in literature, are essential for young learners (104). Locke's writing encouraged a growing body of children's literature and prepared the way for Alexie, who has long understood the power of storytelling for educating the young and the crucial need for fiction accessible to youth. Alexie has asked, "If Indian literature can't be read by the average twelve-year-old kid living on the reservation, what the hell good is it?" (Purdy 42).

Both *Flight* and *Part-Time Indian* confront alienation and isolation and lack of an identity with insight unfiltered by romanticism. While the adversity Alexie's characters face is sometimes culturally specific, all young adults benefit from seeing perseverance blended with humor, and all can use additional survival skills. Because adolescence means pushing beyond "childish" boundaries in concrete physical ways (with parallel emotional and intellectual growth), young adults struggling against cultural restraints need examples of success. Because adults are often reluctant to relinquish control, young adults look for insight everywhere—especially in music, film, and literature. They do so to discover new rules for a new world.

In both novels the central characters, Junior (Arnold) and Zits, are "uglies," with no signs they will soon be made beautiful. Mired in physical and intellectual evolution, they are not fixed in their ugliness, but the possibility for turning out bad exists as easily as the possibility for turning out good. Junior's early fixation on his large head, his grotesque eyeglasses, his clumsiness, and his hopeless stammer sets the stage for significant change later in the story. Self-consciousness about physical attributes, combined with his intelligence and love of literacy, make him stand out among peers. In a similar way, Zits's acne is a seemingly permanent condition that mirrors his "ugly" lack of self-identity. Neither character sees his own strengths, and neither considers the possibility of attaining physical beauty. Their physical oddity soon becomes a metaphor for larger cultural "deformities." Because Zits is deprived of a stable family and is split between Indian and white cultures, he fights authority and actively alienates himself from others.

Transformative change has long been a staple theme in children's literature. Lerer's most potent examples come from Hans Christian Andersen's fairy tales (*The Ugly Duckling, The Emperor's New Clothes, The Little Mermaid, The Nightingale*) in which "physical appearance does not always show artistic virtue [and great] things may come in ugly packages" (218). Lerer notes that awkward physical appearance often functions as a complex reflection of social power, a reflection of choice and possibility, of seeing the authentic "in public verbiage" (218). When outward physical ugliness is mired in an oppressive environment, breaking free sometimes means the emergence of beauty in a new form, and this possibility resonates for young adults, who rarely are capable of predicting their mature form. The removal of ugliness (in fiction) often is synonymous with becoming comfortable within one's own skin.

The history of YA literature has been a toppling of persistent taboos, and readers expect realistic stories to take on raw needs with a frankness that sometimes makes adult readers uncomfortable. Alexie joins a long tradition of writers who delight in showing awkward characters redefining needs for a new generation. His YA novels cultivate an attitude of feisty rebellion, a willingness to unearth uncomfortable truths. Both *Flight* and *Part-Time Indian* present twisted and "bent" stories reflecting a world turned upside down, where urgency exists to find a self-identity and move toward a future.

In similar fashion, Lerer notes, Shel Silverstein, Edward Lear, and others portray protagonists in absurd environments, where "the speaker longs to be part of everyday society and yet is constantly aware that he can never fit in" (207). In a world where no Darwinian order exists and experience does not fit neatly into categories, protagonists stumble upon an adult world filled with bizarre sights, more weird than anything a child could produce. As they seek guidance, they observe in elders "patterns of behavior so unique or obsessive that it makes their own mischief small by comparison" (Lerer 199). Both Junior and Zits live in such a world, where possibilities are limited and unacceptable. Their stories are couched in the guise of realism, where few adults exist as helpful mentors, where survival is not a given, and where protagonists must routinely cross established boundaries to discover new possibilities. Alexie joins a long list of authors, from Edward Lear to the present, who take on an existing order with protagonists who are *immensely sane* in demanding that perception be "turned upside down."

Young adults, disempowered, are astute observers within the constraints of families and institutions. They watch peers and adults and try to make sense of what they see. Often they are the first to notice, like Junior, the "weirdness" of teachers and other adults. Yet, even as they dissect the adult world, they crave mentor figures. While "normal" kids have help as they deal with sometimes shocking adult knowledge, in the form of mentors who counsel, both Junior and Zits must cultivate a stubborn protective autonomy to make up for a lack of mentors. (It is almost a joke among readers of YA fiction how often parents and other significant adults are "removed" from the plot.) Both Junior and Zits face this condition. Though Junior has loving parents and a tolerant, loving grandmother, he lives in a household where his dog is shot because his family cannot afford a vet. Daily he encounters racism, homophobia, despair, drunkenness. In almost a parody of an adolescent-adult relationship, his mentor becomes Mr. P, the weirdest of his teachers, who often wears a bathrobe to class. Junior's breakthrough decision to attend an all-white school occurs after he is given an ancient textbook his mother once used. He heaves the book into the face of Mr. P—who later advises Junior to leave the reservation to find new opportunities. Zits, through much of his story, encounters largely violent amoral killers who become role models.

In *Flight*, Zits's Indian father has deserted his family; his mother died when he was six. In his fourteen years, Zits has lived in twenty foster homes. Knowing little of his Indian or white heritage, and uprooted without stability or community, the thought of a formal education meeting his immediate needs is absurd. Alexie's style is edgy and gritty, yet also surreal in its Dalí-like juxtaposition of the realistic with the dream. For Zits, making sense of an incomprehensible world is not easy, for early on he begins abrupt jumps through time and space in a postmodern disconnect where it is impossible to know what is real. Zits says, "I used to dream that I could run fast enough to burn up like a meteor and drop little pieces of me all over the world" (16). Literally, as his story progresses, he drops like a meteor into the historical past. He begins his hallucinations by imagining possibilities during a bank robbery. He thinks: "What if I have become that bank guard's bullet? What if I'm the bullet that blasted through my brain?" (59).

The nonlinear plot structure in *Flight* contrasts with the straightforward narrative in *Part-Time Indian*. Junior begins by asking, "What do you do when the world has declared nuclear war on you?" (31). This statement could appear in a thousand YA novels in which a first-person protagonist describes impossible adversity, but Junior's story is unique in that his difficulties are directly linked to the persistent reach of colonization, neglect, and racism. Already he has witnessed too many tragic premature deaths, and his school is so poor he uses textbooks his mother once used. Like Zits, he must deal with more than the "normal" YA adversity. Yet Alexie makes it clear that Junior's story is not merely an exposé of social evils. Instead, the focus remains on Junior's creating a coherent self-identity despite the limitations he faces. For both Junior and Zits, schizoid jumps from persona to persona will be the norm—sometimes in awkward and convoluted struggle—until a coherent self is formed.

Despite the bleak possibilities, for both characters humor and attitude show that hope exists. In both books Alexie's humor is not just about laughs and entertainment; it is necessary in explaining challenges, both personal and those interwoven with cultural history. Like young Dadaists, both Junior and Zits use the twisted humor of daily survival as a defining aesthetic. Their necessary rebellion against the status quo must find outlets. For Junior, this comes in the form of self-deprecating ironic humor and comic strips. For Zits, unconscious role playing and sarcasm help his lurching frenetic moves toward self-identity.

In both books, biting insight reflects a breaking away from violence and poverty, and suggests that Junior and Zits could be exceptional. Despite persistent adversity, a positive outcome still feels possible, simply because neither hides from unpleasant truths such as American Indian invisibility and how cold attitudes toward Indians can be (even from other Indians). With characteristic bluntness, Zits says: "The rich and educated Indians don't give a shit about me. They pretend I don't exist" (7). He knows that drunken Indians on the street are seen as "just a racist cartoon" and that a broken adult Indian is often ignored as "just a ghost in a ghost story" (7).

Junior takes his knowledge where he can find it—from his grandmother, who sells beaded key chains on eBay, from his best friend Rowdy's blunt in-your-face counsel—about girls and cartoons and sports—that cuts to the essential. Thus he learns first from Rowdy how others in his community will react to his decision to shift schools. Junior also learns from experience—on Halloween he goes trick-ortreating to raise money for poor people and is beaten and robbed by the poor, his own kind. He learns from his nerdy white friend, Gordy, who connects learning to having a "boner" (97). Throughout his story his sense of humor reflects a playful willingness to look at layers of twisted truth. On Thanksgiving, his father says with a smile, "We should give thanks that they didn't kill all of us" (102). For both Zits and Junior, humor is a consistent visible voice that talks back to what they face.

For Alexie in his daily life, "being funny breaks down barriers between people. If I make them laugh first I can say almost anything to them" (Nygren 149). He sees laughter as a "ceremony, it's the way people cope" (Marx 19). In his fiction, humor, linked with pain and violence, helps give perspective to a harsh world. Kelly Blewster suggests that Alexie's levity "has always been the weapon of choice: the best defense during an at-times embattled childhood and now a way both in person and on paper to discharge his message" (76). Wrenching poverty and senseless tragedy can make readers uncomfortable, and Alexie utilizes humor to manage the painful. He has noted: "If I were saying the things I'm saying without a sense of humor, people would turn off right away. I mean I'm saying things people don't like for me to say" (Blewster 77). Humor is the balancing act that keeps the possible alive.

Like a rhythmic drumbeat, harsh, unnecessary deaths occur throughout both books, and the details are not hidden from the protagonists. Junior's father's best friend is killed in a drunken shooting; his sister is killed in a trailer fire; his grandmother is run over by a drunk driver. Alexie uses the phrase "reservation realism" in his introduction to the 2005 edition of *The Lone Ranger and Tonto Fistfight in Heaven* to depict hard truths that cannot be avoided (xxi). The young protagonist, Victor Joseph, speaks of the difficulty coping with what he sees: "It's hard to be optimistic on the reservation. . . . it's almost like Indians can easily survive the big stuff. Mass murder, loss of language and land rights. It's the small things that hurt the most. The white waitress who wouldn't take an order, Tonto, the Washington Redskins" (49). Both Zits and Junior must learn to transcend anger and discover survival skills to live through the "small things" Victor mentions.

For both, the initial anger and outrage lead to surprising insights. In Zits's involuntary plunge into eye-opening history, shuffled through hallucinogenic scenes filled with pervasive and sometimes vengeful violence, he is perplexed by the underlying hurt that humans inflict on each other. As an FBI agent in the 1970s dealing with Indian activists, he sees both sides involved in brutal murderous acts. In a 2007 interview with James Mellis, Alexie suggested that Zits learns from this that "whatever our politics, we always find ways to justify violence" (181). Later, transformed into the son of a chief at the Little Bighorn, Zits sees an Indian grandmother cutting off a soldier's penis to humiliate him in the afterlife. He then is asked by his father to slash the throat of a young white soldier (77). Later—as an aging U.S. Cavalry scout— he sees the soldiers as "children" sent to kill for adults (84). Investigating a massacre perpetrated by Indians, he discovers "the body of a little girl, blond, blue-eyed, pretty even in death" (86). Alexie dramatizes the difficult moral truths that Zits confronts as the first step away from the fever of retaliation and endless bloodshed. Because, as Alexie notes, Indians "did plenty of killing on our own," Zits must see all sides of this killing habit (Mellis 181).

In both books the violence and tragedy are not gratuitous; rather, they are necessary truths that also reflect Alexie's personal experience. He has stated: "It's what I saw. . . . It's still ingrained in me" (Weich 170). Through Alexie's eyes the scenes of violence experienced by Zits and Junior are directly linked to a history of colonization and genocide. Alexie explains: "Think of your birth parent being your original culture. In a sense, Native Americans, anybody who's been colonized, they're in the position of an orphan. . . . here, after so many generations of being colonized, it's not about actual murder anymore. It's about the symbolic murder and the legacy of murder" (Weich 171).

In the 1970s and early 1980s, YA "problem novels" introduced readers to formerly taboo issues such as child abuse, sexuality, and drug and alcohol use. In some cases, showing the sociology of problems became the plots. In both *Flight* and *Part-Time Indian* the serious issues add realism to core themes, but the focus remains on adolescent growth rather than on documenting problems of American Indian culture. Both Junior and Zits are resilient in seeking solutions, knowing that if they do not find answers, they will succumb to a cycle of self-destruction. Both use language to push back—as a weapon, an establishment of power, a means of coping with new knowledge. Zits knows "how curse words frighten and disgust some people," and he uses his knowledge to shock and defy a political correctness that refuses to see "lived" truths (14).

Blunt humor and shocking language are survival skills practiced by young adults because, as Lerer notes, the "modern . . . world, even in West Virginia or New England, lives its rituals as unbelieved and ironized" (314). To deflect limiting truths, many boys become "one-up ironists of imagination" (315). According to Lerer, Artemis Fowl, the Time Warp boys, Stanley Yelnats in Louis Sachar's *Holes*—all are masters of these language skills (315). He argues that these abilities may mark "the difference between child and adult" (316-17).

Alexie's use of language that conveys an attitude can be seen when Junior asks Rowdy how he can make a beautiful white girl fall in love with him. Rowdy answers: "The first thing you have to do is change the way you look, the way you talk, and the way you walk. And then she'll think you're her fricking Prince Charming" (81). When Junior tells Gordy, his new acquaintance, that he wants to be his friend, Gordy responds without hesitation: "I am not a homosexual" (94). Recognizing rebellious language as a "creative option," Zits uses it to talk his way out of situations and to hide truths from others. This can be seen when he responds with "what . . . ever" to an order from his new foster father. He says it "slow and hard and mean, like each letter was a cuss word" (14). Without this skill his autonomy would be significantly diminished. For Zits and Junior, irony, cursing, and wry humor provide "a knowing detachment from experience, a kind of above-it-all imagination of a world in which you would rather live" (Lerer 317). These are necessary language skills in an age when "irony and bullshit are defining modes of culture and expression" (Lerer 318). Thus Junior and Zits manipulate skeptical audiences and deal with social expectation "in ways that preserve the inner self while at the same time keeping on the mask of conformity" (Lerer 318).

Adolescence is a move toward independence. In the process, young adults often experience a love-hate relationship with the world they seek to leave, seeing with disdain family, community, and even the landscape of home. Analyzing several centuries of literary history, Lerer summarizes what children face as they move into necessary new experience: "Childhood . . . is a time of exploration, an arena of adventure. . . . [But] childhood is, as well, a prison. How many of us sought to run away, to escape those confederacies of parents who made us toil at chores, who limited our freedom, who took us far away from friendships?" (150). Reflecting these discordant emotions, Junior experiences both pain and newfound pleasure when he attends his new school. On the basketball court he is rejected and booed by old friends and acclaimed by new white supporters. Like many other adolescents, he must learn to balance these emotions amid dramatic change.

As Junior observes the adult world, he makes sweeping, sometimes stereotypical, assertions about Indians and drinking, white attitudes toward Indians, teachers and schools. These adolescent pronouncements are a reflection that Junior exists in two cultures simultaneously (and is comfortable in neither). His generalizations are reliable only to the extent his limited knowledge and experience are taken into account. For example, when his father reminds him that white people are not better than him, Junior thinks: "But he was so wrong. . . . He was the loser Indian father of a loser Indian son living in a world built for winners" (55). He believes this before he enters the white world, before he can admit that he might be a winner. Soon after, when he characterizes a white kid in his new school as "magnificent" and Indian kids as without hope, his thinking begins to change as he discovers his white "perfect" girlfriend is an anorexic with a racist father and his new teachers are no smarter than those on the reservation (50).

Junior's bold pronouncements, too, are evidence of an attitude, a stance that may be essential in the midst of crucial change. What he knows is that accepting entrenched cultural and civic values and beliefs may not be healthy. What else could provoke a life-changing decision like changing schools and leaving behind friends? Similar "drastic" decisions made with too little information follow most adolescents. Junior's "healthy" precocious attitude marks him as different from his sister, who after high school began to "fade" and hide in the basement. Early in his story he states, "My sister is running away to get lost, but I am running away because I want to find *something*" (46).

For readers, the truth is that almost any fictional young adult is an unreliable, though not necessarily insincere, narrator, simply because the focus is always on a protagonist *in process*—with sharp, sometimes amazingly accurate, insights juxtaposed with returns to childish beliefs. Because most YA authors refuse to step beyond the exhilarating immediacy of experience, most adolescent novels end with the protagonists still adolescents, whereas adult stories about adolescence often carry the protagonists into adulthood. Because rapid change, both physical and intellectual, is a given, and inner turmoil is often mirrored in plot structure, what protagonists say matters less than their actions. Despite what the characters say, both Alexie books, like most YA fiction, are more about shifting hopes than about sociological reality. The truth of Junior's critique of his reservation world lies beyond, and around, his pronouncements. So when he says, "I don't know if hope is white. But I do know that hope for me is like some mythical creature," he voices his reliance on possibility (50). His goals are urgent, for even his lifelong friend, Rowdy, is in danger of losing his dreams, of fading. Junior knows that Rowdy's drunken and illiterate father will stand in the way of his son's further education. As Junior's teacher Mr. P says, "All these kids have given up" (40).

In *Part-Time Indian*, and in the movie *The Business of Fancydancing*, when the protagonist leaves the immediacy of his culture, he becomes acutely aware of what it means to be Indian. In *Fancydancing*, Seymour, the college poet, is not Junior, yet his outsider status both on the reservation and in an urban outside world could well be Junior, given a few more years. Both look beyond the reservation while remaining entangled in Indian culture. Both battle with alter egos (old friends) who stay on the reservation. Both mirror Alexie's growth and confusion as a young writer.

What separates *Flight* from Junior's story is that plot elements in *Part-Time Indian* come directly from events in Alexie's life. No one could read *Part-Time Indian* alongside Alexie's biography and not argue, as Tanita Davis and Sarah Stevenson do, that "in that respect, the story is absolutely true. And it's that ring of truth that gives it such power and makes Arnold [Junior] the character so fully realized" (187). Though *Part-Time Indian* is labeled fiction, and not memoir, an Alexie-lived life underlies Junior's suffering from seizures, his problem drinking, his sister's death in a mobile home fire, his white high school experiences and playing basketball, and the death of his beloved grandmother. The many autobiographical connections add energy to themes crisscrossing each work and situate protagonists in concrete worlds. Like Alexie himself, both Junior and Zits straddle two (or more) worlds, redefining how a contemporary Indian can be, or should be. In both books the clumsy moves from insider to outsider viewpoints mirror Alexie's experiences in high school and college. Alexie, too, faced ostracism from peers, loss of friendship, and confusion over conflicting Indian/white rules for living. In discussing his experiences in college, he has stated, "I didn't see myself in them [whites], so I felt like I was doing anthropology, like I was studying white people" (Marx 17).

Both Zits and Junior possess a unique style yoked with attitude and imagination. Applied to a literary character, style functions as a form of behavior, an attitude for survival, a representation of personality.

Lerer notes that by "the mid-twentieth century, children's literature was addressing the need for expression in the face of social expectation" (301). He illustrates how style influences theme by looking at two classics of children's literature, E. B. White's *Stuart Little* and Dr. Seuss's *The Cat in the Hat*. *Stuart Little* "seeks a clarity of vision in the muddiness of life" and helps children fit into a stable adult world, while in *The Cat in the Hat* resistance to an established adult order is seen as the proper intelligent response (294). Lerer links this subversive attitude with Allen Ginsberg's *Howl* and Elvis Presley's first television appearance, where protagonists resist doing what others want them to do. When subversion becomes a style in itself, this is revealed in language, in exaggerated forms of clothing, in action. In *The Cat in the Hat*, even the illustrations break from tradition and bring wild "color into a children's monochrome world" (295). Lerer suggests that Dr. Seuss's books teach that "the child can have a colorful life; that style is something we put on or invite into the house" (300).

Lerer links this ironic attitude to characters in Jon Scieszka's Time Warp Trio books and to Francesca Lia Block's *Weetzie Bat*, where the intelligent young cannot ignore the "bent" truths they encounter (307). Because contemporary children "live in communities of false belief and mistrust" where "their own beliefs may not be shared by others," many children "cultivate a kind of knowing distance from experience: a sense of humor, a witty detachment, a blasé unflappability in the face of deceit or disappointment" (307). Junior and Zits both utilize such "attitudes" to push back a history threatening to overwhelm, using wry humor as way of dealing with truth filled with pain. This is a defensive survival skill often seen in YA literature. Both struggle to discover moral and physical blueprints, learning quickly that seemingly hard-and-fast convictions can dissolve. As Junior encounters adversity in his new high school, he states with conviction, "In any fight, the loser is the first one who cries" (62). Yet he soon learns this rule does not apply with his new peers. When he responds to an insult by punching a white classmate, the football player refuses to hit him back. Instead of animosity, Junior encounters a surprising new respect.

Zits, too, desperately needs these survival skills as he zips through time. Because in each strange and discordant leap Zits is always "within" trying to make sense of an adult's point of view, his jumps function as a metaphor for a young adult's understanding of history—as piecemeal, linked more to individual moral decisions than to broad principles. Existing simultaneously as both his new character and his old self makes him "crazy"—for until he is one realized self, he will be unstable. Alexie summarizes succinctly the similarities and differences between Junior and Zits:

> Zits (more than Arnold) is utterly disconnected and lost, unmoored in identity and in time. This is very much unlike Arnold, who certainly struggles through life, and has many identity questions, but is not unmoored. . . . I'd say that Arnold is struggling to reconcile two identities (rez Indian and off-rez Indian) while Zits first has to learn how to be human, rather than a feral orphan. (Davis and Stevenson 188)

For much of *Flight* and, to a lesser extent, *Part-Time Indian*, a horrible inevitability exists not only for Zits but also for many other Indians immersed in American culture. Zits describes his bleak future: "All of them are going to drink booze. And their children will drink booze . . . and one of those grandchildren will grow up to be my real father, the one who decided that drinking booze was more important than being my father. The one who abandoned my mother and me" (67). As Zits and Junior fight against dark possibilities, both learn that seeing the past (and present) from multiple points of view is an essential part of the maturing process. Thus Junior learns about himself by seeing the flawed lives of others. As Alexie suggests, it is essential that both protagonists see "that, for lack of a better term, everybody's screwed" (Mellis 185).

By looking at what Lerer calls "absorption and theatricality" (229), one can better understand the balance that Zits and Junior seek. Absorption is the degree to which a character or author "ignores the audience" and follows an inner voice, while, in contrast, "theatricality means how someone plays to the viewer" or reacts according to pressure from outside (229-30). For Junior and Zits, the tension between absorption and theatricality lies in negotiating between individual autonomy and the sometimes rigid rules of new and old "tribes." Even when Zits is adrift in his fantasy world, he questions both his inner desires and the moral actions of others. Alexie summarizes his essential dilemma:

> I think he has a problem with having no identity. Like he says, being Indian and Irish would be the coolest thing in the world. I think he has a problem with nobody teaching him to value either culture, so I think that Native American kids' problem is not being a hybrid—not being two things at the same time—I think the problem is when people tell them they have to be one thing or the other. (Mellis 180)

Zits's story ends with a confrontation of the comfortable mythology of an Indian world inhabited largely by shamans and warriors. Alexie refuses the noble romantic portrait, as well as the deep well of justified revenge, as Zits experiences the vicious horror of war. Even an unsettled "half Indian" like Zits lives with the historical myth of Indian culture. He must become comfortable as a hybrid, both white and Indian, both child and adult. In a miraculous transforming moment, as Zits observes one young soldier saving a small Indian boy from slaughter, he understands that the endless cycle of violence can end. Zits learns that choice is possible, that one soldier's rejection can be the message for all. Somehow "that one white boy, that small saint, has held on to a good and kind heart" (93). The book's title, *Flight*, has come to represent a symbolic flight from Zits's broken past and from this lasting culture of anger, revenge, and violence.

Though in the end many questions remain about his uncertain future, he has faced war, violence, brutality and genocide. When Zits returns to his ugly present, he has empathy for others and awareness that others are linked by the brutal world in which they live. His respect for the police officer who wishes to adopt him has been tempered by his experience of living his father's futile attempt to gain respect. Ultimately, he and the police replay the video of the bank robbery. They notice a flicker (a blank space) at the moment Zits began his journeys through time. Though the flicker makes Zits wonder about what is real and what is not, there is no doubt that others care enough to take him into their world. Zits, the angry and depraved and burnt street kid, ends in a loving family life where mothers tousle hair and smile while presenting breakfast.

Near the end of *Part-Time Indian* Junior hears his basketball coach say, "You can do it," and he realizes how much he needs others. Knowing he now loves, and is loved by, many of his peers, he is now comfortable as a member of multiple tribes—including bookworms, beloved sons, small-town kids, and cartoonists. Though he remains in his Spokane tribe, he recognizes that few of his other tribes are racially or ethnically based. This acceptance of new labels is typical as young adults expand the circle from neighborhood and family to the larger world. Junior's powerful and life-changing awareness reflects Alexie's own growth, as he explains: "For many years, I've said that my two strongest tribal affiliations are not racially based. My strongest tribes are book nerds and basketball players, and those tribes are as racially, culturally, economically, and spiritually diverse. And, like Arnold, I also belong to a hundred other tribes" (Davis and Stevenson 190). At the end Junior knows entryways into new communities (basketball and academics and cartoons) and understands the power that one individual has to change lives. Knowing that switching tribes does not mean the rejection of previous allegiances, he is happily a hybrid, as he has been from the beginning.

It is fitting that *Part-Time Indian* is itself a hybrid book, with cartoons supplementing narrative. Lerer notes that "for many modern readers, the phrase [children's book] . . . connotes a volume in which pictures take precedence over text" (320). In contrast, in Junior's story the text takes precedence over the cartoons, but the illustrations serve as a bridge between his child/adult awareness and add to Alexie's sense of a book as a valued thing. The collaboration between Alexie and cartoonist Ellen Forney makes *Part-Time Indian* not a graphic novel, not a children's book, but, like much of young adult fiction, something in between.

A hybrid story is appropriate for both Junior and Zits, who grew up with Tonto and the Lone Ranger and movie westerns—portraits that serve as imprisoning walls. Yet immersion in popular culture also ensures that Zits and Junior are not "only" Indians but also members of a postmodern literacy absorbed by other young adults. As Alexie notes, he too, is a hybrid—living in multiple worlds with multiple identities. He states, "I suppose, as an Indian living in the U.S., I'm used to crossing real and imaginary boundaries" (Thiel 135).

It is telling that Alexie ends both books with hope, with demonstrations of the power of love. He is unapologetic about where he leaves Zits and Junior: "You know, because as Indians we've been so stereotyped and maligned and oppressed and abused, in acts and deed, in action and word, we seek literature that cheers us in some way, that acts as some sort of antidote, rather than an examination of us, and an interrogation of us" (Dellinger 122). This balancing between clinical examination and possibility fits well with the needs of adolescents, who crave hope mixed with a dose of realism.

Increasingly aware of reactions to his books, Alexie is conscious of his roles as spokesman, filmmaker, and writer. Though he is now a public figure, he has not forgotten where he came from: "I still get phone calls in the middle of the night—about deaths and car wrecks. . . . I'm incredibly privileged when I'm sitting at a typewriter, but once I get up and out of that role, I'm an Indian" (Fraser 95). Because of these ties, he continues to write for those who feel trapped. He states emphatically: "I think Arnold, by leaving the rez, is escaping a slow-motion death trap. But I would also love my readers to recognize that a small white 'mainstream' town can be a kind of death trap, too. . . . Metaphorically speaking, we all grow up on reservations, don't we?" (Davis and Stevenson 189). He continues with this goal in another interview: "I'm really hoping [*Part-Time Indian*] reaches a lot of native kids certainly, but also poor kids of any variety who feel trapped by circumstances, by low expectations, I'm hoping it helps them get out" (Mellis 183).

As a border-straddling writer who focuses more on the present than on a myth-driven past, Alexie has resisted pressures to write nostalgic depictions of traditional Indian life, what he calls the "corn pollen, eagle feathers, Mother Earth, Father Sky" kind of Indian literature (Peterson xii). He knows that as an American Indian author he has a certain responsibility, since his novels may be the only "Indian" books read by young readers, and because most of Indian literature "is written by people whose lives are nothing like the Indians they're writing about" (Purdy 43). Yet, like Zits and Junior, Alexie is adamant in rejecting the prescribed path: "I want my literature to concern the daily lives of Indians" (Fraser 87). As such, he insists in both books that Zits and Junior are not unique in facing adversity—that many American Indian young adults face similar challenges.

Alexie knows now his "little books about one little reservation in Washington State" have come to represent all Indians everywhere, though he remains perplexed by his influence. "Nobody ever asked Raymond Carver to speak for every white guy," he says. "I end up having to be a spokesperson for Indian people" (Himmelsbach 34). With this attention, questions follow: What of Indian culture and history must be explored? How to address readers with little knowledge of American Indian culture? He has learned from experience to be sensitive when writing about Indian traditions and spiritual practices, for "it's going to be taken and used in ways that you never intended for it to be" (Purdy 50), but he refuses to hide from problems. He states with emphasis: "A lot of people are so dysfunctional,

to the point they believe that any Indian striving for success becomes white, that failure is an American Indian attribute" (Blewster 77).

As a newly mature writer Alexie knows that because of "my ethnicity, my age, the times we live in, I have power" (Campbell 117). This
power means a duty to correct persistent misunderstanding of his culture. In both *Flight* and *Part-Time Indian* he provides a service by
showing how Indian young adults can find a self with a grace that reflects a future. Because their stories are linked to troubling history,
both books are more than simple stories of teens finding their identities. There is joy in both stories, and a sense of possibility. These two
precocious and entertaining young adults closely resemble Alexie's
definition of his country: "The one general statement you can make
about America is it's young, and wildly immature, and incredibly tal-
ented" (Chapel 99). Maybe the country can learn from Zits and Junior,
who end up well along the road to maturity.

## Works Cited

Alexie, Sherman. *The Absolutely True Diary of a Part-Time Indian*. Boston: Little,
Brown, 2007.
_____. *Flight*. New York: Black Cat-Grove, 2007.
_____. *The Lone Ranger and Tonto Fistfight in Heaven*. Expanded ed.
New York: Grove Press, 2005.
Blewster, Kelly. "Tribal Visions." *Conversations with Sherman Alexie* (1999). Ed.
Nancy J. Peterson. Jackson: UP of Mississippi, 2009. 71-82.
*The Business of Fancydancing*. Dir. Sherman Alexie. Perf. Evan Adams, Michelle
St. John, and Gene Tagaban. 2002. DVD. Wellspring Media, 2003.
Campbell, Duncan. "Voice of the New Tribes" (2003). *Conversations with Sher-
man Alexie*. Ed. Nancy J. Peterson. Jackson: UP of Mississippi, 2009. 113-20.
Chapel, Jessica. "American Literature: Interview with Sherman Alexie" (2000).
*Conversations with Sherman Alexie*. Ed. Nancy J. Peterson. Jackson: UP of
Mississippi, 2009. 96-99.
Davis, Tanita, and Sarah Stevenson. "Sherman Alexie" (2007). *Conversations
with Sherman Alexie*. Ed. Nancy J. Peterson. Jackson: UP of Mississippi, 2009.
187-91.
Dellinger, Matt. "Redeemers" (2003). *Conversations with Sherman Alexie*. Ed.
Nancy J. Peterson. Jackson: UP of Mississippi, 2009. 121-27.

Fraser, Joelle. "An Interview with Sherman Alexie" (2000). *Conversations with Sherman Alexie*. Ed. Nancy J. Peterson. Jackson: UP of Mississippi, 2009. 83-95.

Himmelsbach, Erik. "The Reluctant Spokesman" (1996). *Conversations with Sherman Alexie*. Ed. Nancy J. Peterson. Jackson: UP of Mississippi, 2009. 32-35.

Lerer, Seth. *Children's Literature: A Reader's History, from Aesop to Harry Potter*. Chicago: U of Chicago P, 2009.

Marx, Doug. "Sherman Alexie: A Reservation of the Mind" (1996). *Conversations with Sherman Alexie*. Ed. Nancy J. Peterson. Jackson: UP of Mississippi, 2009. 16-20.

Mellis, James. "Interview with Sherman Alexie" (2007). *Conversations with Sherman Alexie*. Ed. Nancy J. Peterson. Jackson: UP of Mississippi, 2009. 180-86.

Nygren, Åse. "A World of Story-Smoke: A Conversation with Sherman Alexie" (2005). *Conversations with Sherman Alexie*. Ed. Nancy J. Peterson. Jackson: UP of Mississippi, 2009. 141-56.

Peterson, Nancy J. "Introduction." *Conversations with Sherman Alexie*. Ed. Nancy J. Peterson. Jackson: UP of Mississippi, 2009. ix-xviii.

Purdy, John. "Crossroads: A Conversation with Sherman Alexie" (1997). *Conversations with Sherman Alexie*. Ed. Nancy J. Peterson. Jackson: UP of Mississippi, 2009. 36-52.

Thiel, Diane. "A Conversation with Sherman Alexie" (2004). *Conversations with Sherman Alexie*. Ed. Nancy J. Peterson. Jackson: UP of Mississippi, 2009. 135-40.

Weich, Dave. "Revising Sherman Alexie" (2007). *Conversations with Sherman Alexie*. Ed. Nancy J. Peterson. Jackson: Mississippi Press, 2009. 169-79.

# The Rhetorical, Performative Poetics of Sherman Alexie:
## Critical Reflections on Affect, Memory, and Subjectivity

Cindy M. Spurlock

> I was a smart Indian kid, a Native American kid. And smart Indian kids are supposed to be tribal saviors. We're supposed to be Jesus.
>
> —Sherman Alexie, University of Washington
> commencement speech, 2003

Historically speaking, rhetoric and poetics continue to be united by their complementary—and contested—relationships to language and emotion. From the ancient Greeks to contemporary scholars, rhetoric and poetics alike offer a wealth of possibility for considering both the conditions of possibility and the constraints of language as a vehicle for human expression. Indeed, philosophers and philologists alike have grappled with problematics of the expectations that audiences, readers, and authors/orators alike bring to bear upon the word. Concepts such as "democracy," "identity," "justice," "beauty," "evil," and "equality," for instance, seem to spill out of their symbolic containers into a swirling abyss of contextuality and ambiguity. Of course, it is tempting for some critics to suggest that this is a consequence of modernity: both Hobbes and Rousseau took issue with the notion that the plurality of voices, perspectives, and forms of self-expression in public should be granted as a right of the people.

Such views, as Bryan Garsten suggests, were considered problematic at the time because they undermined the privileged relationship between the governed and the sovereign. Fortunately for us, such views were challenged by others who viewed the right to self-expression as an a priori, constitutive quality of human freedom. Here, Enlightenment philosophers such as Immanuel Kant approached language as a tool for managing public reason and, in turn, for managing dissent. If, as Kant argues in his writings about the sovereignty of scholars, the interpretation of language and politics was simply left to those who would approach it "reasonably," then political harmony and good governance would surely follow. In this way, Garsten argues, Kant attempts to cleanse human expression of its emotion. Writing against these suppositions, Søren Kierkegaard, Friedrich Nietzsche, J. L. Austin, and Michel Foucault offer alternative perspectives that continue to leave readers with more questions than answers. If one accepts, as Austin suggests, that we are able to "do things with words" and call new truths into being through speech acts (such as "I now pronounce you husband and wife"), and if discourse provides frames through which we interpret and subject ourselves to regimes of truth, as Foucault argues, then language games may be perceived as inherently dangerous to political stability and the maintenance of power. They may provide a rich rhetorical arsenal for those who endeavor to question and/or challenge—or resist—those articulations of "common sense" to everyday practices and cultural norms that function as ideological apparatuses or assemblages in a given political-historical moment. Indeed, while many attempt to harness that power to move the social toward more inclusive, progressive ends, others encourage governments and private citizens alike to curtail or even preempt that power in the name of security or decorum. In these rhetorical moments, the personal and the political become intertwined.

Ultimately, one could argue that those forms of expression that suture political critique and personal narrative are ripe with considerable possibility for disrupting the ways in which the past is remembered, the future is imagined, and each is invoked to justify the present moment. While some might consider this problematic and attempt to advance standards of objectivity in public culture as a superior (that is, rational) form of communication best suited for logical engagement with controversial issues, others continue to advance the claim that emotional engagement with controversial issues plays a more significant role because of its ability to move the social by fostering and maintaining emotional identification or affect. But perhaps, as this essay suggests, there is a third or interstitial space that harnesses emotional disidentification in ways that trouble and disrupt cultural logic by demonstrating (often through humor or disgust) that its first principles are based not on objective, logical grounds but, instead, on regimes of truth that have roots in social and economic injustice.

It is here, in this precarious space, that Sherman Alexie's discourse makes claims upon—and contests—contemporary American experience. Thus this essay argues that Alexie's discourse is powerful *not* because of what it "means" but, instead, because of what it "does" rhetorically and performatively as it invites and demands (American) audiences to reconsider and rethink issues of deep significance in late modernity: embodiment, subjectivity, affect, and cultural memory. Indeed, when "we" laugh at or recoil from Alexie's words, the constitutive power of identification with the "we" of privilege and/or of Otherness is made visible and visceral in ways that may well trouble its grip on subjectivity. Although it is unlikely that a single essay is capable of critically engaging all of Alexie's oeuvre, this essay proceeds from a methodological and pragmatic approach to rhetorical inquiry established by Michael Calvin McGee more than twenty-five years ago that enables us to consider how particular fragments or extracts contribute to Alexie's re/vision of American life.

## Beyond Aesthetics: Reading Alexie's Discourses Rhetorically and Performatively

Ask (nearly) any English major under the age of thirty-five worth his or her salt who Sherman Alexie is, and most will be able to recount the basics: he is a contemporary Native American poet who has written about his struggles with poverty and addiction. Some may be familiar with the story of his survival against the odds as a child born with a rare medical condition, but few are likely to be familiar with his public advocacy—his speeches, editorials, and media interviews. Nevertheless, Alexie has continued to gain prominence as a public figure or celebrity during the past decade, and the artifacts that emerge as a result of his participation in public life complement his writing in ways that invite a rhetorical reading of his collected works as neither literary artifacts nor traditional forms of public address.

Rather, we should perhaps instead consider the myriad ways in which Alexie's discourses *address publics*. In other words, these poems, short stories, interviews, films, commencement addresses, and editorials constitute an archive of the present that attempts to intervene against its own cultural and political history. In a word, they press upon collective memory by favoring neither nostalgia nor melancholia in their recollection of everyday events. And, like the coyote in search of his eyes in Gates's apocryphal tale, even bizarre, tragic, and traumatic events (such as the accidental murder of Elder Briggs in *War Dances*) are recounted in ways that refuse to resolve conflict or traumatic loss through an appeal to authenticity. As Tina Chen argues about another of Alexie's short stories, "*Indian Killer* refuses to allow its readers the comfort of identification, asserting through multiple formal and thematic strategies the limited nature of identification as an effective ethical model for reading about and engaging with racial and cultural difference" (164). Furthermore, as Norman K. Denzin suggests, such interventions encapsulate a "performative cultural studies" wherein performance is defined "as an act of intervention, a method of resistance, a form of criticism, [and/or] a way of revealing agency" (9). Put another way, to read Alexie's poetry acontextually is to participate in an act of colonial violence that relegates it to the margins of the aesthetic instead of the pulse of the political. Or, as Alexie has it with a characteristic comic slant in the poem "Nudity" (from *Face*, his deeply personal and intensely energized collection from 2009),[1] when his wife asks, "What kind of movie did you just see?" he replies, "Honey, it was a farce about colonial discovery."

If performance is "sensuous and contingent," then performativity, writes Denzin citing Della Pollock, "becomes the everyday practice of doing what's done . . . [it is] what happens when history/textuality sees itself in the mirror—and suddenly sees double; it is the disorienting, [the] disruptive" (10). This matters as a rhetorical practice, to extend Pollock's argument, because performance may "bring imagined worlds into *being* and *becoming*, moving performers and audiences alike into palpable recognition of possibilities for change" (1). Moreover, the articulation of performance with auto/ethnographic or autobiographical storytelling invokes the specters of both witnessing and memory. Pollock continues, drawing heavily from Kelly Oliver's important work on witnessing as a philosophical, ethical act that unites experience, affective engagement, and social change, to suggest that "no one person 'owns' a story." Any one story is embedded in layers of remembering and storying. This is a central element of Alexie's credo as a writer, and it forms the foundation for his vehement response to the critique of Elizabeth Cook-Lynn, "the Sioux Indian writer and scholar" (as he describes her), who

> Has written, with venomous wit,
> That skins shouldn't write autobiography.
> She believes that "tribal sovereignty"
> Should be our ethos. But I call bullshit!

Alexie continues (in the poem "Tuxedo with Eagle Feathers") to indicate how his concept of performance has developed as an individual journey of discovery through multiple sources:

> If you study what separates me,
> The survivor, from the dead and car-wrecked,
> Then you'll learn that my literacy
> Saved my ass. It was all those goddamn texts
>
> By all those dead white male and female writers
> That first taught me how to be a fighter.

Pollock states, "Remembering is necessarily a public act whose politics are bound up with the refusal to be isolated, insulated, inoculated against both complicity with and contest over claims to ownership" (5). As J. Robert Cox argues, this endeavor requires a significant engagement with the performativity and materiality of rhetoric.

## Addressing Publics, Cultivating Subjectivity: Figuring (Out) the World with Sherman Alexie

Look around you, and you will see graduates from dozens of countries. Look at the color of the people around you. We're in some gigantic Crayola box right now. You've got the beige section over there, and the mauve section over here, and the siennas over there in the back. I can guarantee you, graduates, for most of you, your lives will never be this diverse again. You will never experience this diversity of race and religion, of politics and identity, of geography and spirit, of vocations and avocations. (Alexie, commencement speech 166)

In his 2003 commencement address at the University of Washington, Alexie invited the audience to reflect on the ways in which institutions of higher education provide an important site/sight for personal growth. As far as commencement speeches go, this claim seems to fit the occasion. In passing, it appears to articulate a positive image of the university as a needed place where diversity and equality are deliberately cultivated as civic virtues; the university, then, appears as a kind of idyllic haven that fosters diversity in ways that graduates will likely miss once they depart for other destinations. Yet in the same breath, Alexie's speech subtly gestures toward visible inequalities and toward problematic patterns of inclusion and exclusion that are rehearsed and performed even as diversity is celebrated: note his reference to the different "sections" and their spatial locations within the "Crayola box." Colors remain clustered together and ordered or sorted hierarchically in his line of sight from beige (closest to him) to sienna (in the back). While it is impossible to determine whether Alexie deliberately references the civil rights struggles of the 1960s by calling attention to the "siennas over there in the back," a careful auditor will catch this reference and reflect on its relevance to the present moment. In this and myriad other examples, Alexie's discourse invokes the specter of collective memory in ways that interrupt an interpretation of his rhetoric as a Pollyannaish celebration of a postracial moment. One may perhaps better understand these layered moments by turning to the interplay between identity and subjectivity as they contribute to the cultivation of particular kinds of citizens in late modernity. As Dorothy C. Holland, William S. Lachicotte, and Debra Skinner suggest, "Identity is one way of naming the dense interconnections between the intimate and public venues of social practice" (270). They argue that

> the first context of identity is the figured world . . . the frames of meaning in which interpretations of human actions are negotiated . . . figures that carry dispositions, social identification, and even personification just as surely as they carry meaning. Thinking, speaking, gesturing, cultural exchange are forms of social as well as cultural work. When we do these things we not only send messages (to ourselves and others) but also place "ourselves" in social fields, in degrees of relation to—affiliation with, opposition to, and distance from—identifiable others. (271)

Working outward from this definition, it is possible to reconsider "identity" as a term fraught with intellectual and political baggage that nevertheless remains *located* and *locatable* within the specificities and contingencies of a particular cultural context or a "figured world"— and, as Holland et al. note, a figured world that is construed, that is made and unmade and remade differently, through shared practices, vocabularies, and other material and discursive commonalities. However, power and status do not form a horizontal ontology within figured worlds; instead, they articulate divergent and conflicting positionalities both within the figured world and at the "borderlands" where figured worlds collide and, in turn, where meanings and practices are contested. Alexie resists the simplification of any single way of seeing, concluding the poem "Mystery Train":

> And she smiled and waved. I walked home,
> Chanted the first lines of this poem,
> And committed them to memory.
> And if a few strangers thought me crazy
>
> For writing poetry, aloud, in public,
> Like just another homeless schizophrenic,
> Then fuck them for wanting clarity
> And fuck them for fearing mystery.

As Holland et al. note, "The second context of identity, then, is positionality" (271). Positionality may be understood as always capable of being both fixed and in flux, depending on a range of factors (such as whether one "accepts" one's positionality, whether one's positionality in this particular figured world is constrained by one's positionality in another figured world, and so on). Here, a rhetorical approach to Alexie's work proves useful because it provides us with a set of tools for understanding how his discourse *works*. In other words, how do his stories, poems, and other modes of public intervention attempt to move the social by addressing the public as both the agent and scene of contextual, temporal, spatial, and performative contingencies that trouble "authentic" claims to identity? What do these discourses *do*?

At this point, tracing the ways in which shifts in the scholarly conversation during the past two decades have rendered most claims to a politics rooted in identity as deeply suspect is instructive. Arguably, the 1990s witnessed the deconstruction of essentialized categories such as race and gender; these notions were gradually stripped of the constitutive and material political gains that were made under their signs during the 1960s and 1970s and understood, instead, as bio-political markers—as performed. Holland et al. argue that this matters because the "the third context of identity is the space of authoring" (272), although the language of authoring locates the individual as an active agent in the processes of becoming—the quest for being—that are always already processual. Here, a rhetorical approach to Alexie's discourses enables us to focus on the imbrications of text and context, on performativity and performance of "self" as always already located within both dialogic tension with the performances of "self" offered by others, but also through the limits of interpretation and hermeneutics. The *post*-turn, then, is reflected in rhetorical studies' refusal to accept any singularity of meaning or meaning-making practices; and so, com-munication and identification (following Kenneth Burke, but drawing from Paul Ricoeur and others) are always incomplete, incommensura-ble, and acts of negotiation. This is not to say that "identity" is not a useful heuristic, but it is to suggest that "subjectivity" seems to do the heavy lifting that addresses significant lacunae and silences in identity theory. Alexie addresses this issue in many poems, using a familiar term, "the oral tradition"—which has been stuffed so full of meaning that it lacks precision—as the title of a poem in which he observes:

> But it is also when I first realized
> (And please forgive my naïve surprise)
>
> That poets will give you affection
> As they steal the audience's attention.
>
> Of course I'm no better than the rest.
> I turn each reading into a test.

Significantly influenced by Jacques Derrida, Gilles Deleuze and Félix Guattari, Judith Butler, Giorgio Agamben, Michel de Certeau,

Pierre Bourdieu, and postcolonial theorists such as Homi K. Bhabha, contemporary critical rhetorical studies is, to be fair, rather anxious when it comes to claiming that "the space of authorship" can be identified as singular, locatable, or author-driven. Instead, the dominant interpretive framework for thinking through this context is to radically pluralize and deterritorialize it. In this case, we are all coauthors, partially conscripted (to extend David Scott's analogy in *Conscripts of Modernity*) to power, processes, and, following Marx, conditions not of our own making. Without being reductive and ignoring the human capacity for creative resistances and appropriations, a rhetorical approach to these discourses refuses to focus on Alexie's interpretations and analyses of his intentions or motives. Here, instead, rhetorical approaches to public discourses labor to map the affective logics that permeate a given intervention and, in turn, to trace how those logics attempt to rewrite subjectivity. Alexie has been consistent in his acceptance of the "subjectivity" of his poetic persona, declaring in section 3, "Seattle, Washington, 2005," from the poem "Size Matters":

But it was Confucius who said, "Before you embark on a journey
Of revenge, dig two graves." I have spent my life in the dirt.
I own a well-worn shovel. My hands are big and bloody.
And I've used them to dig graves and write poems—to hurt and be hurt.

Indeed, following the largely polarizing effects of "identity politics" in the 1990s and early 2000s, several scholars and activists (Lawrence Grossberg, Stuart Hall, Todd Gitlin, and others) have explicitly called for a rethinking of the tactics and strategies that social agitators have deployed, in large part because a politics of multiplicity has, they argue, enabled the cultural and political right to regain dominance in the realm of public policy and electoral politics. As argued by João Biehl, Byron Good, and Arthur Kleinman, a reconsideration of the subject must entail "inquiries into the continuity and diversity of personhood across greatly diverse societies, including the ways in which inner processes are reshaped amid economic and political reforms, violence, and social suffering" (1). Subjectivity, Biehl et al. argue, is a way of engaging the "particularities of affect, cognition, moral responsibility, and action" (1). For Alexie, the singular is crucial, even as he continually addresses his complex relationship to his tribal heritage. As he insists in "Cryptozoology," a meditation on the distinctive features of a rare mutant crow, which is (akin to the speaker), "a crow that is the only one of its kind—/ A bird that is the only member of its tribe," a phenomenon that he wants to celebrate as "this odd glory."

Although Biehl et al. are clear in articulating the necessity of a post-Geertzian theoretical orientation toward "culture" that takes the body seriously, they contend that "research is showing that only through explicating the logic of key emotional and intersubjective constructs do major social dramas become intelligible; likewise, only amid such contemporary social enactments can we understand particular domains of affect and agency" (10). To be fair, Biehl et al. are sensitive to the fact that, in the words of Evelyn Fox Keller,

> poststructuralist analyses that have focused on the subject and subjectivity rather than on the self and experience have suggested that "subjects are epiphenomena, constructed by culturally specific discursive regimes (marked by race, gender, sexual orientation, and so on), and subjectivity itself is more properly viewed as the consequence of actions, behavior, or 'performativity' than as their source . . . selves are multiple and fractured rather than unitary, mobile rather than stable, porous rather than enclosed, externally constituted rather than internal or 'inner' natural essences." (13)

These lacunae, they argue, are often the result of oversimplification (13). Thus they conclude that sensitive, reflexive scholarship *must* attend to "the ways in which persons are constituted through social experience; the oft-invisible operation, in between institutions and within intimate relationships, of machineries that make people live and die; and the shaping of psychological processes through social encounters"

(13-14). And so subjectivity is figured (always already) as a plural, fragmented, complication of identity that addresses its theoretical and political uses as well as its limitations:

> The subject is at once a product and agent of history; the site of experience, memory, storytelling and aesthetic judgment; an agent of knowing as much as of action; and the conflicted site for moral acts and gestures amid impossibly immoral societies and institutions. Modes of subjectivation are indeed determined by the vagaries of the state, family and community hierarchies, memories of colonial interventions and unresolvable traumas, and medicoscientific experiments and markets. Yet subjectivity is not just the outcome of social control or the unconscious; it also provides the ground for subjects to think through their circumstances and to feel through their contradictions and, in doing so, to inwardly endure experiences that would otherwise be outwardly unbearable. Subjectivity is the means of shaping sensibility. (14)

With respect to his responsibility to speak "as an agent of history," Alexie offers in his poems many examples of his struggles with what he understands as an obligation to a history that has been largely unwritten, if not actively surpressed. In "Vilify," he ponders the faces on Mount Rushmore, a national monument located in "indian country," where he wonders why those particular presidents were selected, and then moves on to a typical imaginative excursion:

> And yes, I know there's a rival sculpture of Crazy Horse, but the
>     sight of that one is ball-shrinking
> Because Crazy Horse never allowed his image to be captured, so
>     which sculptor do you think he'd now attack?

While it appears as if Alexie is delivering an attack on the veneration of political leaders and the effects of "colonial intervention," his position, as ever, is much more qualified. In the third footnote to the poem (among fourteen that are much longer than the "poem" itself, and that are a gleeful testament to Alexie's amusement toward and delight with academic practices), he recounts an anecdote reflecting his proclivity for the interpositon of narrative fiction amid all of his other modes—another strategy to "think through [his] circumstances and feel through [his] contradictions":

> Native Americans are notoriously and ironically patriotic. During college, while drinking with a few Nez Perce Indian buddies—all of us loudly and drunkenly ranting and raving about broken treaties—a white guy walked up to us and said, "Man, I hate what our country did to you Indians. I hate being American. I hate the United States. It's evil, man, it's evil." One of the Nez Perce guys, the oldest one, jumped up from the table and slugged the white guy in the face and knocked him out. As we dragged our violent friend out of the bar, he shouted, "Nobody gets to talk shit about my country except me! You hear me? Nobody gets to talk shit about my country except me!"

The footnote follows the line "Who's on that damn T-shirt anyway? Is it both Roosevelts, Jefferson, and Lincoln?"

Here, in a move that might resonate in a complementary way with the rather divergent articulations of politics and movements by Sidney Tarrow and Michael Hardt and Antonio Negri, subjectivity and the modalities of experience that are created in the enactments of "the everyday" are (perhaps painfully visible as) political. As Tarrow notes, "It is in the struggle that people discover which values they share, as well as what divides them, and learn to frame their appeals around the former and paper over the latter" (122). In response, one of the ways in which advocates have worked to move the social in recent years has focused less on social movements, even less so on identification with a biopolitical category (race, sex, ethnicity, age, class, and so on), and more upon the reframing of trenchant critiques of policy and public opinion. Here, rhetors focus primarily on the unificatory possibilities that are made possible by identification with *shared experience—of figuring (out) the world*. It is here, where Alexie's discourses work to undo and rescript shared experience through humor and discomfort, that we must begin to reconsider how and why such modes of public address work to provoke, challenge, and unsettle private belief, but also how they affect public performances of self and the ways in which language constitutes and challenges community in everyday life. Indeed, thinking about Alexie's work in this manner requires "us" to rethink the role of collective memory as a rhetorical and performative strategy. Alexie's work offers us an ethical choice—if not a new categorical imperative—to question what is at stake when "we" are invited to share an experience of disgust, of laughter, or of self-recognition. In the poem "When Asked What I think About Indian Reservations, I Remember a Deer Story," Alexie directly confronts the audience:

> Children, have you ever heard a deer scream
> After its back legs and spine have been crushed
> Beneath the wheels of a logging truck?
> The scream is the sound of our grief
>
> After our failed fathers have been crushed.

The poem is an unflinching litany of loss and pain, concluding with the powerful injunction:

> So scream and bleed your way along the road,
> Until lungs, heart, and veins are empty
> Of grief, and deny your father's ghost
> His last chance to be your warrior-chief.

And if this were the common concern and voice of Alexie's work, the disgust might overwhelm the recognition, which is why the force of his grief is, if not balanced, at least ameliorated by his interposition of humor in startling and unexpected places. The concluding poem of *Face*, a multisection conglomerate called "Thrash" (Alexie's working title for the collection, which he changed when it was constantly misheard and misread as "Trash"), blends high-spirited hilarity with the most serious concerns of his life, musing in section 13:

> My lovely sons are uncircumcised.

> When I first wrote the sentence, I mistyped "songs" instead of "sons." So I had to circumsize a letter in order to correct my error. Do you think that's a coincidence?

> My lovely songs are uncircumcised.

This fusion of the serious and the seriocomic, a strain running through the poem, permits Alexie to blend the bawdy with the semisacred, enabling him to establish a comfortable conversational relationship with the reader/listener that also allows him to go beyond what is generally considered the delineations of decorum. This is his way to utilize a "unifactory experience" while maintaining the singularity of his outlook and, at the same time, acknowledging the singularity of the reader's responses.

The profusion of his poems in multiple forms and designs (such as his inventive personalization of an early rock lyric in "Ode to My Sharona" and his haunting homage to Dolly Parton in "Ode to Jolene," which appear in the winter 2010 issue of *Contrary Magazine*) since the publication of *Face* are an indication of how extensive Alexie's range and ambition have become as he returns to the genre that is at the origins of his writing life. His plunge into a rampage of poetic production continues to reveal how he construes his aesthetic agenda as a performative negotiation fusing the conditions of possibility with the constraints of language, and how this parallels his fusion of traditional form with his distinctly American Indian experience. As he has written in the conclusion of "Tuxedo with Eagle Feathers":

> The sonnet, like my reservation, keeps
> Its secrets hidden behind boundaries
> That are simple and legal at first read
> (Fourteen lines that rhyme, two rivers that meet,
>
> Poem and water joined at our confluence),
> But colonialism's influence
> Is fluid and solid, measurable
> And mad. If I find it pleasurable
>
> To (imperfectly) mimic white masters,
> Then what tribal elders have I betrayed?
> If I quote from Frost from memory faster
> Then I recall powwow songs, then what blank
>
> Or free or formal verse should I call mine?
> I claim it all; Hunger is my crime.

## Note

1. All of the poems quoted in this essay are from Alexie's collection *Face*.

## Works Cited

Alexie, Sherman. *Face*. Brooklyn, NY: Hanging Loose Press, 2009.
_____. "2003 University of Washington Commencement Speech." *Take This Advice: The Most Nakedly Honest Graduation Speeches Ever Given*. Ed. Sandra Bark. New York: Simon Spotlight Entertainment, 2005. 162-68.
_____. *War Dances*. New York: Grove Press, 2009.
Biehl, João, Byron Good, and Arthur Kleinman. "Introduction: Rethinking Subjectivity." *Subjectivity: Ethnographic Investigations*. Ed. João Biehl, Byron Good, and Arthur Kleinman. Berkeley: U of California P, 2007. 1-23.

Chen, Tina. "Towards an Ethics of Knowledge." *MELUS* 30.2 (2005): 157-73.

Cox, J. Robert. "On 'Interpreting' Public Discourse in Post-Modernity." *Western Journal of Speech Communication* 54.3 (1990): 317-29.

Denzin, Norman K. *Performance Ethnography: Critical Pedagogy and the Politics of Culture*. Thousand Oaks, CA: Sage, 2003.

Garsten, Bryan. *Saving Persuasion: A Defense of Rhetoric and Judgment*. Cambridge, MA: Harvard UP, 2006.

Holland, Dorothy C., William S. Lachicotte, and Debra Skinner. *Identity and Agency in Cultural Worlds*. Cambridge, MA: Harvard UP, 1998.

McGee, Michael Calvin. "Text, Context, and the Fragmentation of Contemporary Culture." *Western Journal of Speech Communication* 54.3 (1990): 274-89.

Pollock, Della. "Introduction: Remembering." *Remembering: Oral History Performance*. Ed. Della Pollock. New York: Palgrave Macmillan, 2005.

Scott, David. *Conscripts of Modernity: The Tragedy of Colonial Enlightenment*. Durham, NC: Duke UP, 2004.

Tarrow, Sidney. *Power in Movement: Social Movements and Contentious Politics*. 2d ed. Cambridge: Cambridge UP, 1998.

# A Rez Kid Gone Urban:
## Sherman Alexie's Recent Short Fiction_____

Richard Sax

Although Sherman Alexie most strongly self-identifies as a poet, and although he may be better known as the guiding genius—as author and screenwriter, then as author, screenwriter, and director—of two of the more acclaimed art-house films of recent years (*Smoke Signals*, 1998, and *The Business of Fancydancing*, 2002) than for his short fiction, he first achieved critical acclaim and respect in literary and intellectual circles with the five stories (and forty poems) of his initial book publication, *The Business of Fancydancing* (1992), followed soon by the twenty-two stories of his short-story collection *The Lone Ranger and Tonto Fistfight in Heaven* (1993). Alexie has continued to create significant works of art in an impressive variety of subgenres, from young adult novels to poetry to films to short stories, and each of his most recent short-story collections—*The Toughest Indian in the World* (2000), *Ten Little Indians* (2003), and *War Dances* (2009)—continue to reflect on recurrent Alexie concerns.

Perhaps most notable among these concerns are Crazy Horse as icon and role model for the contemporary Indian male, "John Wayne mythology" (*Toughest Indian* 191), and the theme of Indian spirituality and identity in contemporary popular culture. As Alexie has become comfortable with his changed identity as a "rez kid who's gone urban" (Teters 35), he has endeavored to describe new (for the Alexie corpus) phenomena that his various characters experience in the first decade of the twenty-first century, including the personal anguish of the frequent-flyer class of business traveler, female as well as male in the contemporary world, who leaves a spouse and children at home, as well as sympathetic renderings of various strains of Seattle and Pacific Northwest creative-class professionals.

Alexie's interest in Crazy Horse dates to his earliest published collection, the stories and poems that constitute the text of *The Busi-*

*ness of Fancydancing*, especially the third and concluding segment of that volume, which is titled "Crazy Horse Dreams," stipulatively defined intertextually as "the kind that don't come true" (72). Although Alexie's Interior Salish heritage in the Spokane and Coeur d'Alene tribes is geographically and culturally distinct from the Northern Plains traditions and practices of Crazy Horse's Oglala Lakota, Alexie's continuing usage of Crazy Horse in the first two decades of his career as a professional writer is one of the characteristic features of his frame of reference, even though it has not received its deserved critical attention. In the story "Class," Edgar Eagle Runner visits Chuck's, a dive Indian bar, as he reflects on his life, his marriage to blonde Susan McDermott, her infidelity, and the death of their newborn son. Drinking tap water at a bar where cheap beer and strong liquor are the norm, wearing clothes that make him look "like a Gap ad" (*Toughest Indian* 50), Edgar does not take the sage advice of Sissy, the profane but sympathetic bartender, to avoid a physical confrontation with the resident saloon bully and instead heads into the alley where "Junior" has gone. Edgar thinks to himself, "Deep in the heart of every Indian man's heart, he believes he is Crazy Horse" (53). Edgar then proceeds to take a swing at Junior, miss, and get knocked out, awaking later in Sissy's arms as she comments with dismay, "All of you Indian guys think you're Crazy Horse" (55). Although Edgar has failed miserably in his Crazy Horse-inspired attack on the bar bully, his urban-warrior behavior seems to serve some sort of expiating function, since he soon thereafter completes his slumming-with-poor-Indians escapade and returns to his wife, his marriage—flawed though it may be—and his upper-middle-class affluence. The invocation of Crazy Horse has resulted only in Edgar's new understanding that, regardless of his state of mind, he is hardly Crazy Horse—except momentarily and only in his most estimable sense of self-worth.

A more extended and crafted use of the Crazy Horse allusion occurs in "Indian Country" as Coeur d'Alene poet Low Man Smith travels to

Missoula, Montana, expecting to fulfill his professional obligations to Flathead Indian College even as he becomes more personally acquainted with Carlotta, a Navajo poet who teaches English at the college. However, any hope for an amorous visit ends as the story begins with the explanation that Carlotta has married and eloped to Arizona. A recovering alcoholic ten years from his last drink, Low Man drowns his sorrows in airport soda pop and realizes ruefully that one of his biggest challenges is the pain of repetitive typing on his computer keyboard: "There it was, the central dilemma of his warrior life: repetitive stress. In his day, Crazy Horse had to worry about Custer and the patriotic sociopaths of the Seventh Cavalry" (*Toughest Indian* 124). Low Man is, to some degree, an older and more literate, yet no more heroic, contemporary Indian warrior than the younger, "horsepowered warriors" (*Lone Ranger* 13) who populate Alexie's earlier short stories. Low Man accepts the limitations of his present existence and thinks wistfully concerning how he is focused on the sales of his latest book or his possibilities for intimacy after a speaking engagement, both individualized and selfish concerns, while Crazy Horse was a culture hero who generally, with one signal exception, acted on behalf of his Oglala Lakota people.

When two Missoula police officers locate Low Man to return to him his suitcase, which he attempted to trade to a convenience-store clerk for a ride to a used bookstore, one officer seeks to identify Low Man to make certain that the suitcase is being returned to its rightful owner. To the query concerning whether he is, in fact, Mr. Low Man Smith, he replies: "No, no . . . you must be mistaken. My name is Crazy Horse" (134). Alexie has commented on his use of Crazy Horse as an allusion, acknowledging that Crazy Horse was "an Oglala Sioux, which makes him from a different tribe and culture entirely. But I use him as a spiritual figure, a savior whose example we need to aspire to" (Bellante and Bellante 15).

Although the invocation of Crazy Horse seems to imply an overwhelming sense of Indian heroism and self-determination, Low Man seems to know Crazy Horse's biography well enough to realize that he was not only a spiritual leader and sometime war chief but also part of one of the most poignant and tragic Indian stories of love and loss, thereby suggesting a complex matrix of possible significances when his name is invoked. As the evening continues, and Low Man is released from police custody to his college friend Tracy, he accompanies her to dinner with her partner, Sara, a Spokane Indian, and Sara's parents, visiting from the rez, who are coming face-to-face with the prospect of their daughter's choices in sexuality and personal partners. Rife with worry for his old friend, Low Man remembers "how Crazy Horse—that great Indian warrior, that savior, that Christ figure—was shot in the face by his lover's husband" (138).

Low Man is accurately recalling how Crazy Horse from childhood was attracted to Black Buffalo Woman, a niece of Red Cloud; the attraction was mutual. In 1861, Crazy Horse went on one of his periodic vision quests, during which Black Buffalo Woman was married against her will to No Water. Over the next seven years, they had three children, and Crazy Horse refused a number of possible wives. In 1868, Crazy Horse and the married Black Buffalo Woman eloped and lived together for ten days. No Water tracked them down and shot Crazy Horse in the face. Crazy Horse recovered but with a significant scar; he lost forever his tribal status as a Shirt-Wearer and was apparently forced to marry Black Shawl. The following year, Black Buffalo Woman gave birth to her fourth and final child, a daughter with curly hair that reminded people of Crazy Horse's hair as a child. Black Shawl soon gave birth to a daughter as well, to whom Crazy Horse was devoted, but the daughter died of tuberculosis at the age of four (Sandoz 225-49; Sajna 221-30).

Low Man's identification here with Crazy Horse, however, seems not to be the operative referent concerning a case of star-crossed love. Low Man's amorous intentions are thwarted even before the story begins with Carlotta's marriage and elopement with Chuck, even as he flirts with both Tracy, his college friend and a lesbian, and Eryn, the clerk at the local Barnes & Noble, also a lesbian. Low Man is, given his heterosexuality, irrelevant to those women as a lover, even as he is a seemingly irrelevant fifth wheel at the dinner between the recently outed lesbian couple, Tracy and Sara, and Sara's socially conservative Spokane Indian parents. Low Man, despite his recollection of Crazy Horse's thwarted love, will not be the one scarred at dinner. When Sid, Sara's father, slaps his daughter, Low Man assesses the situation in generic terms: "One Indian man raised his hand to slap an Indian woman, but a third Indian stepped between them" (148). Low Man's intervention gets him a punch in the chest from the surprisingly strong Sid, who is in turn felled by a hard slap from Tracy. Tracy and Sara leave together, Sid and his wife Estelle leave together, and Low Man remains on the floor. If anything, it seems that Tracy and Sara deserve the Crazy Horse allusion more than Low Man: they have indeed been scarred by the verbal and physical abuse of Sara's father, and their ostracization from Sara's family and tribe is parallel in certain respects to the social cost that Crazy Horse endured after his ten-day elopement with Black Buffalo Woman.

Alexie again invokes Crazy Horse in another story in *The Toughest Indian in the World*, "Saint Junior." Roman Gabriel Fury, despite a mediocre reservation education and with no transportation to the private high school where the symbolically named Colonial Aptitude Test (CAT) is being administered, scores a nearly perfect score on the test. Interrogated concerning how he could have achieved such a superior score, Gabriel explains that he dressed in a grass-dance outfit for "a little extra power to do my best" (170), since a drum group, singing honor songs, might have disturbed the other test takers. Gabriel then asserts that as he opened the test booklet, he was "thinking, I am Crazy Horse, I am Geronimo, I am Sitting Bull, and I'm thinking the required number-two pencil is a bow and arrow, that every math question is Columbus, that every essay question is Custer, and I'm going to kill them dead" (171). Gabriel has successfully waged intellectual war on the culturally biased, "colonial" test, invoking the three greatest Indian leaders of the nineteenth century, with Crazy Horse foremost, as his inspiring muses for a twenty-first-century standardized examination. Alexie would reprise this passage with exactly the same diction and syntax two years later in his film *The Business of Fancydancing*, giving these lines to Aristotle Joseph as he responds to the condescending and insinuating queries of the identically named "Mr. Williams" (61). Alexie's recurrent themes and issues clearly cross genres from short story to screenplay to produced film, since, as he has stated, for him "it's all the same. It's just telling stories. It's not like I think about it separately" (Fraser 65).

Alexie continues to develop the possibilities of significance for Crazy Horse in the *Ten Little Indians* collection when Corliss, in "The Search Engine," wonders, "Were Crazy Horse and Geronimo supportive of their wives?" (16). In the case of Crazy Horse, he seems to have been a dutiful, if not perhaps a loving, husband to Black Shawl and father for the four years that he had a daughter. As Corliss views multiple examples of selfish and self-centered men in and around the student-center café, Crazy Horse again is invoked as an icon, this time symbolizing the possibility of a supportive husband. In "Flight Patterns," William wants to be able to access all elements of American culture; he disdains having to choose "between Mia Hamm and Crazy Horse" (*Ten Little Indians* 102)—that is, between a mass-marketed Caucasian American female athlete and perhaps the premier example of American Indian male agency and possibility. William wants the right to access all culture heroes, regardless of their—or his—racial or ethnic identity.

Unlike the Crazy Horse allusions, Alexie's treatment of movie star John Wayne is understandably more cynical and circumspect. In one of the more memorable scenes from *Smoke Signals,* Victor Joseph is suspicious about the fact that John Wayne's teeth cannot be seen in the Westerns in which Wayne generally plays a reticent tough guy: "I think there's something wrong when you don't see a guy's teeth" (66). Victor and Thomas proceed to sing extemporaneously an original song, or drum chant, "John Wayne's Teeth," performed in the film by the Eagle Bear Singers.[1] Alexie has stated that the song is "a combination of English lyrics and Western musical rhythms along with Indian vocables and Indian traditional drums" (West and West 63). The acerbic comedy of the humor situates the Indian-killing cowboy-movie hero in the almost clichéd position of a white man who cannot be trusted.

Therefore, the supposed audio transcript that constitutes "Dear John Wayne" in *The Toughest Indian in the World* undeniably breaks new ground in the place and legacy of John Wayne in American popular history. Etta Joseph, who as an eighteen-year-old Spokane Indian ingénue playing a Navajo as an extra on the film *The Searchers* in 1952 interacts briefly with Wayne in his screen role as Ethan Edwards, then recounts the incident a full century later, speaking from her nursing home. Ms. Joseph is quite aware of the "John Wayne mythology" and its "role in the shaping of twentieth-century American and Native American culture" (191). With "the Duke" passed on to his eternal reward more than seven decades before the supposed 2052 date of the interview, Etta Joseph's revelations are not a "kiss-and-tell" salacious story; rather, they provide qualities of depth and breadth to the intrepid but pasteboard cowboys that Wayne portrayed on-screen. She reveals to the younger interviewer that John Wayne, consummate movie cowboy, was afraid of horses because he had been kicked in the head by a horse at the age of seven, and that he was so sensitive that he cried every time they made love (201). When Wayne comes upon his sons applying lipstick and mascara in the film company's makeup trailer on location, he allows that this behavior seems to be simple experimentation and says that "I try to embrace the feminine in myself," as well as that "gender is mostly a social construction" (203).

Such revisionist views in the biography of John Wayne would contradict many popular notions of his character, but Alexie implies that he is showing the true John Wayne, the actual person behind the movie icon, who repeatedly asks Etta to call him by his *real* name, Marion, not his commonly recognized stage name. His comment that he views gender as a social construction puts his attitude and diction years ahead of the era in which he lived. Finally, as the story nears conclusion, Wayne calls off the affair, and Etta notes that he is a family man, that she did not expect him to leave his wife or children. Wayne supposedly qualifies his decision, though, telling her: "Yes, my family needs me. . . . But more than that, my country needs me. They need me to be John Wayne" (205). This concluding passage allows Alexie's character study of John Wayne to resonate with seeming authenticity, as he once again places duty and supposed honor above the needs of himself and his family. John Wayne seems to know and respect the position he has in contemporary popular culture, and he seeks to fulfill the public trust that he claims to possess.

As the twenty-first century began and Alexie was the only American Indian named on *The New Yorker*'s list of the best American fiction writers under the age of forty, he continued in effect to define for contemporary audiences issues of Indian identity and spirituality, even as he rejected the notion of being any sort of spokesperson for a pan-Indian perspective. What he certainly continues to articulate, however, is his understanding that "the way of being Indian now is vastly different than it was a hundred years ago" (Teters 35). In *The Toughest Indian in the World*, the first-person narrator in "One Good Man" describes how he has returned to the Spokane reservation in order to minister to his father, who is suffering from the long-term side effects of being a diabetic, including the loss of his gangrenous feet. As the wheelchair ramp is built for his father, the narrator finds his father's stashes of forbidden and life-threatening, highly sugared food: "two boxes of donuts buried beneath Pendleton blankets on the top shelf of the closet; a quart of chocolate milk laying flat in the refrigerator's vegetable drawer; a six-pack of soda pop submerged in the lukewarm water of the toilet tank; hard candy stuffed deeply into the pockets of every coat he owned" (213). The dutiful son has become the caretaker for his father, with parent-child roles now reversed. Throughout the story, the italicized question, *"What is an Indian?"* is asked no less than ten times in the thirty pages of the story, and the variety of answers, proximate and susbsequent, are eloquent and provide a stipulative definition of contemporary Indian identity. An Indian is "a child who can stroll unannounced through the front doors of seventeen different houses" (217); "a boy who can sing the body electric [allusive reference to Walt Whitman] or a woman who could not stop for death [allusive reference to Emily Dickinson]" (218); "the lead actor in a miracle or the witness who remembers the miracle" (221); "a son who can stand in a doorway and watch his father sleep" (222)—among other stipulative definitions, some of them story-specific, others crossing family, tribal, and racial boundaries.

Even as Alexie's literary reputation is itself a cause for celebration, he still shares with other so-called minority writers the burden and the dilemma of being the token ethnic, the exotic Other, in the literary marketplace. In *Ten Little Indians*, Corliss in "The Search Engine" succinctly defines a contemporary dilemma for the Indian, and indeed other minority, writers: "No matter what I write, a bunch of other Indians will hate it because it isn't Indian enough, and a bunch of white people will like it because it's Indian" (41). Alexie writes from his experiences and his imagination; although his experiences are as limited as the experiences of any single human being or literary artist, he also understands that he is "not limited by writing about Spokane Indians. Every theme, every story, every tragedy that exists in literature takes place in my little community. *Hamlet* takes place on my reservation daily. *King Lear* takes place on my reservation daily" (Highway 41). That is, tragic stories of human endeavor that are perhaps Shakespearean, in impact as well as quality, occur daily on the rez, so while the venue is specific and discrete, it is not limited in terms of describing the human condition. This does not, however, qualify the literature as "universal," a label that Alexie denies, saying that he seeks only to describe genuine and authentic human relationships. Alexie has asserted: "Good art is not universal. Good art is tribal" (Blewster 82). The stories have their own authenticity, and Alexie cynically notes that "when people say universal they mean white people get it" (Fraser 68). Alexie is not interested in being the token ethnic or the token Indian who writes with "universal" themes; his purposes are, it seems, didactic in part, showing the joy as well as the sorrows that constitute the identities of so many contemporary Indians. In the story "The Life and Times of Estelle Walks Above," the son of the title character (who, like his mother, is a community college instructor and therefore a cultural arbiter to the masses) notes that despite his own achievements, he feels diminished with respect to, or in awe of, legendary leaders in the past: "I don't speak my tribal language, and I'm allergic to the earth. If it grows, it makes me sneeze. . . . If I spend too much time outside, I get a nasty rash. I doubt Crazy Horse needed talcum powder to get through a hot summer day" (*Ten Little Indians* 134). Although Instructor Walks Above realizes that he is diminutive and mundane compared to the broad strokes of Crazy Horse's heroism, he is proud to be Indian and male, even if he is flawed with allergic reactions to nature that are never part of the stories and legends. He asserts: "I love the way Indian men often wear their hair long, cry too easily, wear florid clothes—all reds and pinks and lavenders and turquoises—and sing and dance most every day of their lives" (135). In classic Alexie style and form, he is proud of holding on to what is best in his culture—"1. The cheerful acceptance of eccentricity 2. The loving embrace of artistic expression 3. The communistic sense of community"—even as he seeks to "let go" of what he perceives as the worst elements of his culture: "1. Low self-esteem 2. Alcoholism 3. Misogyny 4. Lateral violence" (135). Individuals are part of communities, but they have the sentient and self-determining choice to be selective about their behaviors in the development of their discrete identities that are part of a greater whole. Indeed, Instructor Walks Above concludes these reflections with a statement of personal identity: "On the long list of things that I am, I'd put Indian at number three, behind 'bitterly funny' at number two and 'horny bastard' at number one for the last twenty-seven years running" (135). Although he may visually appear to others as a "Red Indian" (115), his race and ethnicity are not necessarily, perhaps not always, the defining elements of his identity. Most Indians today, like William in "Flight Patterns," "only ordered salmon from menus and saw deer on television" (116). As Alexie's own period of being a resident of the Spokane rez fades into the past, his stories and his fictional characters continue to metamorphose to describe the experiences of reservation Indians who have been drawn to larger population centers. As early as 1997, Alexie admitted, "I'm a rez kid who's gone urban, and that's what I write about" (Teters 35). Indeed, his short fiction especially shows this transition, and his most recent short fiction depicts new settings and dilemmas for his characters whose traditions and backgrounds do not always provide answers or succor to the challenges and dilemmas of contemporary life.

As a young writer in his mid-20s in the early 1990s, Alexie drove an old Ford van and rarely flew on airplanes. The Sherman Alexie of recent years, who has entered the canon of college literature classes throughout the English-speaking world, who has been named a writer of note by *The New Yorker* and has published short stories in that and other premier literary publications, is indeed the sort of frequent flyer who could write from personal experience stories such as "Flight Patterns" in *Ten Little Indians* and, even more recently and more disturbingly, "The Ballad of Paul Nonetheless" in *War Dances*. "Flight Patterns" never gets its protagonist on the plane; instead, Alexie simply describes the cab ride that frequent flyer and indigenous traveling businessman William takes from his home in Seattle to the Sea-Tac Airport. As country music plays on the clock radio that has awakened him for his early-morning departure, he realizes that, as proud as he is of his own Spokane Indian identity and that of his wife and daughter, he acknowledges as well that he is also intimately connected with poignant touch points of American popular culture that often trump his racial and ethnic identity and whatever responsibilities might accrue with that identity: "Who cares about fishing and hunting rights? Who cares about uranium mines and nuclear-waste-dump sites on sacred land? Who cares about the recovery of tribal languages? Give me Freddy Fender singing 'Before the Next Teardrop Falls' in English and Spanish to 206 Spokane Indians, William thought, and I will be a happy man" (103). William remains respectful of his traditions, but he very much lives in the present, popular-culture world of North America, which seems more proximate to him than the traditions of his or any other subculture of the United States.

Throughout the short story, each of William's observations or emotions are cataloged by the popular song whose lyrics are most apt for the moment. As William quietly dresses and prepares for his cab ride and air flight, he thinks of how his wife's seductive suggestions to cancel the trip and return to bed "sounded like she was writing a Top 40 hit in the Brill Building, circa 1962" (106). Of course, the Brill Building, still standing at Broadway and 49th Street in Manhattan, just north of Times Square and steps away from what used to be called Tin Pan Alley, was the building with offices that produced many of the pop-music radio hits of the middle decades of the twentieth century. When William resists the enticement, his wife, Marie, throws a *Death of a Salesman* reference at her husband: "Willy Loman, you must pay attention to me" (106). This attempt also fails, but it is significant that Top 40 music and a major work of twentieth-century American drama are the frames of reference here, nothing particularly Indian or Spokane beyond the racial identities of the characters. As William sits on the front porch with his garment bag and briefcase, waiting for the cab to arrive, he smells the salt water of Elliott Bay and the fresh water of Lake Washington. He muses: "Surrounded by gray water and gray fog and gray skies and gray mountains and a gray sun, he'd lived with his family in Seattle for three years and loved it. He couldn't imagine living anywhere else, with any other wife or child, in any other time" (108). Although William is sad to leave his wife and daughter, he calls them as soon as he arrives at the airport, and he seems to have come to terms with being a frequent flyer in order to provide for his family and to maintain a professional identity that he enjoys and will likely continue in.

At first glance, "The Ballad of Paul Nonetheless" seems to be a parallel story. It begins in medias res with Paul on a moving sidewalk at Chicago's O'Hare Airport, but instead of worrying about a wife and daughter at home, he seems obsessed with attempting to pick up a buff woman who is wearing Pumas. Again, Top 40 tunes provide the background music for his endeavors, beginning with Hall and Oates's "She's Gone," since the woman in question is indeed headed in the opposite direction and initially disappears into the crowd (117). As narrative commentary provides background on Paul, the popular culture references abound: he owns five vintage-clothing stores in the Pacific Northwest and is wearing a three-piece suit once owned by Gene Kelly (119). Indeed, he is traveling to North Carolina to bid on vintage Levi's jeans that have been found in a church attic. Alexie makes clear that Paul is eminently successful, even noting his income for the previous year at $325,000 (121). Paul catches up with the woman and flirts with her, referring to her by the name of another Hall and Oates song, "Sara Smile" (123). She thanks him for the attention but mentions that she is married, and they part.

When Paul sees her three months later at Los Angeles International Airport, he greets her as "Sara Smile," and she greets him as "Nonetheless," a word he used during their previous encounter (128-29). During this second and final conversation, he admits to being married but separated, and "Sara"'s interest in him clearly wanes, as she notes, "Grading on a curve, your loneliness is completely average" (131). As Paul tries to convince her that they should seize the serendipitous moment of a second chance meeting, she says simply, "We saw each other twice because we are traveling salespeople in a capitalistic country" (133), and they part again. Three years later, and with his divorce finalized, two of his daughters in college and the other having disowned him, Paul thinks he sees the woman in the Detroit airport, but after initial conversation he realizes that this stranger only resembles the previous woman. However, and with devastating results, Paul cannot let go of what he thinks she represents for him. He follows her throughout the airport as she tries to walk away from him, uninterested in his protestations that he is now divorced and therefore available to her, though this new woman believes, understandably, that he is simply a kook and perhaps a dangerous one at that. The story concludes with Paul in an interrogation room, presumably at a police station. With Marvin Gaye's "What's Going On?" racing through his head (a more than rhetorical question for which he has no answer at that point), Paul admits only to being very tired and possessing the hope that he not be forgotten—by his ex-wife, by his daughters, by Sara Smile, whoever she was. With "Flight Patterns," Alexie describes the possibility of a loving husband and father who must travel often to support the family; in "The Ballad of Paul Nonetheless," the title character is not able to handle the options and choices with which frequent flyers are presented, and the denouement of the story depicts a character without love, without a sense of purpose beyond the inane jargon of Top 40 music, and perhaps without the remnants of sanity that once made him a good businessman, a good husband, and a tolerable father.

As Alexie approaches the second decade of the twenty-first century and his own impending middle age, he continues to use with periodic regularity the short story subgenre to document his insightful observations on contemporary life that illustrate the quotidian poignancies of a life lived as a Seattle/Pacific Northwest American Indian creative-class professional. His characters and crafted plots are replete with a complex yet complementary frame of reference that is Native as well as classical, that alludes to Whitman and Dickinson as easily as to Crazy Horse and Geronimo. Alexie claims, "I think we belong to a lot of tribes" (Nygren 143), as he continues to identify and investigate how cultural and racial boundaries and understandings of "tribe" intertwine, respecting his tribal affiliation with book nerds and basketball players as well as with the Spokane and Coeur d'Alene tribes.

# Note

1. The "John Wayne's Teeth" chant appears as follows in the screenplay:

> Oh, John Wayne's teeth, John Wayne's teeth, hey, hey,
> Hey, hey, ye! Oh, John Wayne's teeth, John Wayne's teeth,
> Hey, hey, hey, hey, hey, ye! Are they false, are they real?
> Are they plastic, are they steel? Hey, hey, hey, hey, yeeeee!
> Oh, John Wayne's teeth, John Wayne's teeth, hey, hey,
> Hey, hey, ye! Oh, John Wayne's teeth, John Wayne's teeth,
> Hey, hey, hey, hey, hey, ye! Have you seen them? Have
> You seen them? Are they false, are they real? Are they
> Plastic, are they steel? Hey, hey, hey, hey, yeeeee!
>
> (*Smoke Signals* 66)

# Works Cited

Alexie, Sherman. *The Business of Fancydancing: Stories and Poems*. Brooklyn, NY: Hanging Loose Press, 1992.

_____. *The Business of Fancydancing: The Screenplay*. Brooklyn, NY: Hanging Loose Press, 2003.

_____. *The Lone Ranger and Tonto Fistfight in Heaven*. New York: HarperPerennial, 1993.

_____. *Smoke Signals: A Screenplay*. New York: Hyperion, 1998.

_____. *Ten Little Indians*. New York: Grove Press, 2003.

_____. *The Toughest Indian in the World*. New York: Atlantic Monthly Press, 2000.

_____. *War Dances*. New York: Grove Press, 2009.

Bellante, John, and Carl Bellante. "Sherman Alexie, Literary Rebel." *Bloomsbury Review* May-June 1994: 14-15, 26.

Blewster, Kelly. "Tribal Visions." *Conversations with Sherman Alexie*. Ed. Nancy J. Peterson. Jackson: UP of Mississippi, 2009. 71-82.

Fraser, Joelle. "An Interview with Sherman Alexie." *Iowa Review* 30.3 (2000): 59-70.

Highway, Tomson. "Spokane Words: Tomson Highway Raps with Sherman Alexie." *Aboriginal Voices* Jan.-Mar. 1997: 36-41.

Nygren, Åse. "A World of Story-Smoke: A Conversation with Sherman Alexie." *Conversations with Sherman Alexie*. Ed. Nancy J. Peterson. Jackson: UP of Mississippi, 2009. 141-56.

Sajna. Mike. *Crazy Horse: The Life Behind the Legend*. New York: John Wiley & Sons, 2000.

Sandoz, Mari. *Crazy Horse: The Strange Man of the Oglalas*. 1942. Lincoln: U of Nebraska P, 1961.

Teters, Charlotte. "Sherman Alexie: Poet, Novelist, Filmmaker." *Indian Artist* (Spring 1998): 30-35.

West, Dennis, and Joan M. West. "Sending Cinematic Smoke Signals: An Interview with Sherman Alexie." *Conversations with Sherman Alexie*. Ed. Nancy J. Peterson. Jackson: UP of Mississippi, 2009. 59-70.

# CRITICAL
# READINGS

# Dialectic to Dialogic:
## Negotiating Bicultural Heritage in
## Sherman Alexie's Sonnets_____

Carrie Etter

As James Clifford notes in *The Predicament of Culture*, cultural contact has consistently been portrayed as either "absorption by the other *or* resistance to the other," a dichotomizing event (344). However, is it ever so absolute? What do we make of Sherman Alexie's sonnets? Because they lack rhyme and meter, hence avoiding the strictures of Western form, do we interpret them as acts of resistance? Or does Alexie's willingness to undertake Western forms, among them the sonnet and the villanelle, suggest his absorption? Clifford goes on to ask, ". . . what identity is conceived not as a boundary to be maintained but as a nexus of relations and transactions actively engaging a subject?" (344). Through his sonnets, Alexie negotiates between his cultural inheritances, Coeur d'Alene/Spokane and Anglo American, a negotiation that enables the speaker of his poems to move from the stance of a passive observer to an active participant. Simultaneously, Alexie's restructuring of the sonnet enables him to upset the reader's expectation of resolution and thus promote the idea that the Indian dilemma is never a matter that can be easily or hastily solved.

From his first book, *The Business of Fancydancing*, Alexie modifies the English sonnet to handle its traditional themes—death and romantic love—as well as a different concern, familial relations. These sonnets utilize the traditional grouping of elements of a problem, and yet rather than employ the English three quatrains and a couplet, Alexie uses three tercets and one quatrain, making each thirteen lines. In *The Business of Fancydancing* and *Old Shirts & New Skins*, Alexie rejects the couplet, and more importantly, its function of resolving the preceding progression. Barbara Herrnstein Smith, in *Poetic Closure: A Study of How Poems End*, notes the widely held belief that the terminal couplet of the English sonnet makes for "striking resolution," yet qualifies this by saying it derives its force from the formal structure that precedes it. Even so, I argue that the English sonnet's presentation and development of an apparent dilemma also lead to an expectation of resolution. Thus, each of the sonnets works against resolution, urging that every Indian dilemma resists the pat denouement of the English sonnet.

Even so, the agency such action seems to offer eludes the speaker within the poems themselves. In "Indian Boy Love Song (#4)," the speaker reflects on his father's alcoholism and at the end waits at his window, "dreaming/ bottles/ familiar in [his] hands, not [his] father's, always/ empty." "Sudden Death" ends similarly; the speaker describes his father's memory of a football game in which he missed the field goal and his father's consequent desire to relive and revise that moment. Watching football on TV over twenty years later, his father,

> roaring past the fourth quarter like a train
>
> leaving a lover behind, stands eagle-armed
> on the platform, whistling for God and 1956
> to pick him up, carry him on their shoulders.

All of the speakers in *The Business of Fancydancing*'s eight sonnets present observers who only watch and record, ending in ambivalence and yearning for change.

This passivity results from a dialectic positioning. In these sonnets, Alexie divides his world into an American Indian us and an Anglo American them. The pervasiveness of this division evinces itself most vividly in "Indian Boy Love Song (#3)."

> I remember when I told
> my cousin
> she was more beautiful

than any white girl
I had ever seen.
She kissed me then
with both lips, a tongue

that tasted clean and un-
clean at the same time
like the river which divides

the heart of my heart, all
the beautiful white girls on one side,
my beautiful cousin on the other.

By naming the river with both its Indian and its Anglo sides "the heart of [his] heart," Alexie acknowledges his bicultural inheritance, and both the white girls and the cousin appear similarly beautiful at the end as opposed to the distinguishing compliment he gives his cousin earlier in the poem. He feels compelled to align himself with the American Indian side despite his realization of a bicultural identity. Similarly, in "November 22, 1983," the father "for twenty years [whispers]" to his wife "'ain't no Indian loves Marilyn Monroe.'" The title of the poem dates the twentieth anniversary of former president John F. Kennedy's death, suggesting that since Kennedy's death the father has claimed and reclaimed an identity opposed to the Anglo American Kennedy who presumably "loves Marilyn Monroe." Apparently the son learns from his father's model of an identity defined, in part, by difference. This reluctance to claim a bicultural identity arises, in part, from the speaker's self-identification as other; as Leslie Ullman recognizes in her review of *The Business of Fancydancing*, Alexie's characters "are free to leave and often do, only to find themselves facing another kind of boundary, a sense of being foreigners, bound more than they realized by a sense of where they came from and who they are" (187). As American Indians in an Anglo culture, Alexie's characters cling to their Indianness, at least partially, by announcing their differences from whites; any acknowledgment of an Anglo inheritance is not voiced aloud.

Yet claiming, even embracing, one's American Indian identity is not enabling in Alexie's 13-line sonnet. That identity comes with a historicity of inability to determine one's own fate, as it is limited again and again by the changing regulations and policies of the U.S. government. How does one claim that historically bound identity and yet forge the empowerment of agency that has been so long curtailed or denied? Ullman continues, "Many characters in this book are shown in a no-win situation at the end of a scene or poem, simply waiting 'for something to change' or to 'happen,' like the group of Indian boys on their way home from a basketball tournament, out of food, their car out of gas in the middle of the night on a cold highway in 'Traveling' (15). Other characters are caught in a kind of no-man's-land between dreams that will never be realized and memories of past glory . . ." (187). Alexie's speaker aligns himself with his American Indian identity and finds himself locked into its historical lack of agency, despite the sonnets' irresolution and consequent insistence on an alternate vision.

In part, the lack of agency results from Alexie's insistence on a dialectic. David L. Moore explains, "A dialogic . . . makes visible the possibility of exchange without dominance or co-optation, whereas the dialectic is haunted by the hierarchies of dominance inherent in dualism" (18). To claim Indianness in and of itself is to reinforce the traditional Anglo-Indian hierarchy, and that reinforcement ultimately disables the speaker, rendering him a passive recorder. This is the one ability that remains: to record the experience without romanticization. As Jennifer Gillan notes, "Rejecting both nostalgia for Indian life as it was and a claim for his own authenticity as one who knows Indian experience, Alexie struggles against the tendency to romanticize the past that he sees in much Native American writing" (95-96); Alexie's use of the sonnet enables him to render American Indian experience with greater authenticity by denying resolution, even as his insistence on a dialectic disempowers the speaker's agency.

Even though agency eludes the speaker, it does not elude Alexie. While any reader might identify the sonnets' inherent irresolution, a reader trained in Western poetics would be more likely to follow the sonnet progression and expect the resolution Alexie denies. In *The Mirror and the Killer-Queen: Otherness in Literary Language*, Gabriele Schwab supports Wolfgang Iser's claim that "texts carry within themselves their own model according to which they attempt to shape their contact with readers." That is, the text possesses "strategies of communication, its 'guiding devices' that exert a certain control by inviting or privileging specific responses." These devices give rise to a "textual agency that actively confirms, interferes with, or disrupts a culture's familiar communicative patterns that are presumably inter-nalized by its readers" (19). Alexie's sonnets enact their irresolution most effectively with the reader most informed in Western/Anglo poetics, disrupting her expectations for resolution. The Anglo-Indian hierarchical dialectic remains, and yet Alexie finds a way, within that hierarchy, to communicate, even as his poems' speakers remain dis-abled by the focus on a dialectic split between cultures.

This dialectic becomes more entrenched in Alexie's next book, *Old Shirts & New Skins*, as the sonnets focus on American Indian identity and become much more ironic in tone. Discussing Franz Boas's *Race, Language, Culture* in *Ethnocriticism*, Arnold Krupat remarks, "[W]hat is true of irony thematically, as an 'attitude,' is true of irony structur-ally, as a form, as well: ironic structures achieve their effects by frus-trating conventional expectations for climax and closure" (94). Alexie has created an ironic structure in his sonnet, "frustrating conventional expectations for . . . closure"; he insists to an implied readership which includes American Indians and Anglo Americans that any Indian di-lemma cannot be hastily resolved. In "Architecture," the speaker be-comes speakers; the individual American Indian becomes all reserva-tion Indians in an inclusive "we" which implies a "they" who created this confining and defining "architecture" of the reservation. "Translated from the American" makes the dialectic relationship between whites and Indians both explicit and divisive. "[A]fter all the drive-in theaters have closed," the speaker plans to "make camp alone" and "replay westerns," "wait[ing] for white boys/ climbing fences to watch this Indian speak." While plural fences separate the races, suggesting a greater divide between them than race alone, the whites can climb over these fences to enter Indian territory—or so they think. One fence is race, another is language—one that, as the end of the poem indicates, the whites cannot surmount.

Nevertheless, despite this racial and cultural division, the imagined space becomes the place for action. The speaker concludes not with reflection but with a response: ". . . when they ask 'how'/ I'll give them exact directions." This gives rise to the two visionary sonnets of *First Indian on the Moon*. There, the form changes from the 13-line structure to a structure more closely paralleling the English sonnet form with three quatrains and an ostensible couplet at the end. Yet these couplets do not resolve the preceding dilemma. Even within a closer approximation to the Western form, Alexie retains the irresolution; these couplets reflect on the preceding dilemma summarily without resolving it—if anything, they work to lodge the irresolution more firmly.

These poems come to terms with a dual cultural inheritance by deriving their visions from a cultural dialogic. Even so, this does not diminish Alexie's or his speaker's claim to an American Indian identity. As Moore asserts, ". . . [D]ialogical survival . . . maintains difference within the dynamics of opposition" and "[n]on-oppositional dialogics does not mean 'harmony' or 'communication,' any more than it means conciliation or complicity" (17). In "I Would Steal Horses," the speaker imagines all that he would do for his lover and hence for himself; the lack of what he has to give results as much from his own weaknesses as from historical ramifications. The speaker finds the basis of his identity not in a divisive "us/them," but in an inclusive we—an enabling American Indian identity without a dialectic opposition. While the activity is imaginary, it does release the paralysis of the historical, hierarchical dialectic that persisted in the 13-line sonnets.

"The Game Between the Jews and the Indians Is Tied Going into the Bottom of the Ninth Inning" demonstrates this cultural dialogic most effectively. Alexie recognizes a similarity between the Jews and Indians—a history of suffering and injustice intertwined with a history of survival. The cultural contact is not between two hierarchically divided groups but between two groups engaged in a similar struggle for cultural survival. The very act of this imagined game—tied at the bottom of the ninth—goes beyond the memories of suffering to create a reminder of their joint survival, offering action (the reminding) in place of passive observation.

> So, now, when you touch me
> my skin, will you think
> of Sand Creek, Wounded Knee?
> And what will I remember
>
> when your skin is next to mine
> Auschwitz, Buchenwald?
> No, we will only think of the past
> as one second before
>
> where we are now, the future
> just one second ahead
> but every once in a while
> we can remind each other
> that we are both survivors and children
> and grandchildren of survivors.

As Schwab says, "As a medium of cultural contact, the experimental forms of poetic language are instruments in an aesthetic experience that may well form a countersocialization—as long as literature retains its subversive potential" (46). Through his sonnets, Alexie "counter-socializes" his reader to accept the irresolution inherent in American Indian experience, revising the Western belief that action solves. What imagination and irresolution together create is the potential for agency—not as a move toward a definitive solution but, through the imagined dialogic, a place where the hierarchical dialectic cannot impose its historically bound limitations, and thus, a place that enables agency for the native speaker.

From *Telling the Stories: Essays on American Indian Literatures and Cultures*, edited by Elizabeth Hoffman Nelson and Malcolm A. Nelson (2001), pp. 143-149. Copyright © 2001 by Peter Lang Publishing, Inc. Reprinted with permission of Peter Lang Publishing, Inc.

## Works Cited

Alexie, Sherman. *The Business of Fancydancing: Stories and Poems*. Brooklyn, NY: Hanging Loose P, 1992.

Alexie, Sherman. *First Indian on the Moon*. Brooklyn, NY: Hanging Loose P, 1993.

Alexie, Sherman. *Old Shirts & New Skins*. Los Angeles: American Indian Studies Center, UCLA, 1993.

Clifford, James. *The Predicament of Culture: Twentieth Century Ethnography, Literature, and Art*. Cambridge, MA: Harvard UP, 1988.

Gillan, Jennifer. "Reservation Home Movies: Sherman Alexie's Poetry." *American Literature* 68.1 (1996): 91-110.

Krupat, Arnold. *Ethnocriticism: Ethnography, History, Literature*. Berkeley: U of California P, 1992.

Moore, David L. "Decolonizing Criticism: Reading Dialectics and Dialogics in Native American Literatures." *Studies in American Indian Literatures* 6.4 (1994): 7-33.

Schwab, Gabriele. *The Mirror and the Killer-Queen: Otherness in Literary Language*. Bloomington: Indiana UP, 1996.

Smith, Barbara Herrnstein. *Poetic Closure: A Study of How Poems End*. Chicago: U of Chicago P, 1968.

Ullman, Leslie. "Review of *The Business of Fancydancing*." *Kenyon Review* 15.3 (1993): 182-97.

# Sherman Alexie's Indigenous Blues_____
Douglas Ford

The blues speak histories that, from the conventional perspective, originate in the experiences of Africans in America. But invariably the blues exceed distinct, rigid cultural boundaries. Ralph Ellison's famous definition of the blues suggests an expansive vista, one limited only by the speaker's capacity to "lyrically" express his or her "autobiographical chronicle of personal catastrophe" (78). As an idiom, the blues record histories, yet Ellison's definition privileges the "personal" and leaves uncertain the place of our national histories, the stories that speak our collective experiences. Locating the collective histories in the personal—and vice versa—has proven a pivotal problem in literary inscriptions of the blues from Ellison's own fiction to works by Toni Morrison and Gayl Jones.[1] However, in Sherman Alexie's 1995 novel, *Reservation Blues*, the issues become more problematic. Here, the blues speak not just an African American history and identity, but instead seem to generate from a Native American point of reference. More than simply transcribing a blues idiom to "fit" the experiences of his Spokane characters, Alexie looks deeper, teasing out traces of an indigenous American culture in an expressive medium generally thought to begin with the Atlantic slave trade.

Aboriginality consequently becomes an ever-changing state for Alexie since contact with cultures of other continents constantly transforms one's means of representing that aboriginality. Nobody remains untransformed by this contact, not displaced Native Americans, not enslaved Africans, and not even the apparent conquerors, the European colonists. In Alexie's novel, the blues constitute more than an expression of catastrophe rooted in African American experience; they also act as a trope for an entire process in which rhetorical forms shape and inform one another. The appearance of Robert Johnson, the near-mythical Mississippi-Delta blues singer, on the Spokane Indian Reservation helps clarify this process. He bridges two different American experiences, African and Indian, and, in so doing, also helps bridge discourses.

Alexie underscores the slavery metaphors in the bluesman's story, depicting how Johnson trades his "freedom" to a white stranger at the crossroads in exchange for his unearthly musical ability (264).[2] A prominent blues image, the crossroads maintains a constant presence in Alexie's novel, providing a distinct blues-tone, but also serving to facilitate the cultural intersection for which the blues serve as trope. The novel ultimately presents a series of crossroads, signifying a constant process of miscegenation and cultural intersection. This kind of intersection first occurs when Robert Johnson passes on his guitar to Thomas Builds-the-Fire, enabling the formation of the Spokane Indian blues band, Coyote Springs. In the process, Alexie sensitizes us to expressive possibilities that developed when Europeans, Africans, and Native Americans began sharing, if not peacefully, the same continent. In its very form, Alexie's novel inscribes a crossroads similar to those in the blues, a juncture where we can see an indigenous Native American oral tradition still at work, but now in a hybrid form, informed by the other discursive forms that have crossed its path.

He does so with Spokane Indian characters whose personal histories still offer the personal catastrophes that Ellison finds in traditional blues material. Chess and Checkers must live with the memory of their younger brother's death, a needless occurrence owing to the inadequate medical care often found on Indian reservations. Chess describes the kind of destitution that led to this tragedy: there "weren't no white doctors around. There weren't no Indian doctors at all yet. The traditional medicine women all died years before. Dad just walked into the storm like he was praying or something" (64). Later in the novel, Junior, a member of the Coyote Springs blues band, shoots himself while atop a water tower, overcome by the collective weight of many painful experiences from parental abandonment to a tragic affair with a white woman. Alexie begins this section, and every other section, with song lyrics, emphasizing the blues as the novel's chosen idiom. "One more gone, one more gone, and our world filled with all our dead," is Alexie's blues in "Small World" (246), underscoring how Junior's death makes up only a small part of a larger, more disturbing, pattern of eradication.

Throughout the novel, Alexie's blues function in this way, voicing the personal catastrophes his characters experience collectively. Thus, he gestures toward the blues as an idiom that exceeds the boundaries of the personal, one that shapes a tragic history shared by many at once. Hence the absurdity of a question constantly posed to Coyote Springs. "Who's the lead singer?," a stranger asks before their first gig, beginning a pattern of questioning that continues throughout the novel, always involving an inquiry as to who sings lead (50). Alexie undercuts the validity of this question by frequently referring to Coyote Springs as a collective body as if the band's name signifies a character in itself. Even after Junior's death, we learn that "Coyote Springs didn't have the energy to sing or mourn properly," pointing toward the necessity for a voice that no single lead singer can provide on her or his own, but rather which requires group participation (277).

The desire to meet a collective need helps steer Alexie's version of the blues, a version that both inscribes and extends beyond traditional definitions. For Alexie, the blues spill over all boundaries, effectively blurring distinctions between the personal and the collective, even Native American and African American categories. In fact, Alexie comes to see the blues as encompassing a range of expressive possibilities that look further than any single, rigidly-defined cultural sphere or label. By focusing on the scene of play and interchange between such spheres, Alexie conceptualizes the blues in a way that encourages us to reconsider Houston Baker's seminal study of the blues in literature.

In *Blues, Ideology, and Afro-American Literature*, Baker envisions a "blues matrix," one providing African American culture its "proper figuration" (3). For Baker, this matrix enables the syncretism of multiple disparate practices and forms, creating what we now understand as African American culture. "Combining work songs, group seculars, field hollers, sacred harmonies, proverbial wisdom, folk philosophy, political commentary, ribald humor, elegiac lament, and much more," Baker writes, the blues "constitute an amalgam that seems always to have been in motion in America—always becoming, shaping, transforming, displacing the peculiar experiences of Africans in the New World" (5). Alexie moves further down this path, re-figuring the blues into a network that draws upon even more disparate sources, including a Native American oral tradition that, in turn, embodies a Native American history. Indeed, Alexie taps the blues in part to disseminate a history that frequently goes unrecorded or forgotten, and some of the more otherworldly and fantastic scenes in *Reservation Blues* have referents in actual events.

For example, Big Mom's memories go back to the horrific slaughter of Indian horses by US calvary soldiers, an event that continues to overshadow the contemporary events of the novel. The horses' screams follow the band members through traumatic events, usually perpetrated by the same soldiers who re-enter the text as record producers. But Alexie's otherworldly imagery actually illuminates a generally overlooked historical event that took place during the military campaigns waged against the Spokane Indians by Colonel George Wright, the basis for Alexie's Wright, the record producer/calvary soldier. In 1858, Wright's soldiers rounded up 800 to 900 horses apparently belonging to Tilcoax, a Palouse leader. Consequently, according to Robert H. Ruby and John A. Brown's history of the Spokane peoples,

> Wright had a problem on his hands. He decided to kill the horses. Although killing horses on the frontier was a crime, this was war, and all was fair in it. Wright feared that to keep the animals would be to invite raids from the Indians. In retrieving the horses, the Indians might scatter those of the command as well. The horses were too wild to be herded as the command moved east, and should they be permitted to fall back into Indian hands, their riders would have regained mobility to continue resistance and retali-

ation. Not to be overlooked as a motive for the horse slaughter was Wright's desire to punish the Indians for their resistance. A few simple words explained the thinking of the board convened by Wright to decide the animals' fate: "Without horses the Indians are powerless." (136)

The resulting scene of slaughter became known as "Wright's bone-yard," an image that Alexie uses as a motif throughout his novel (137). As Ruby and Brown point out, military records often differed from Spokane versions, which generally assumed an oral, rather than written, form.[3] Accordingly, when Alexie writes about the bone-yard, he does so in a way that emphasizes this oral tradition.

But the oral tradition in this case contains not just the Spokane story forms one would expect, but it also assumes a blues form. Not only does Big Mom preserve this event in the form of a song, but her impulse to record history indicates a rootedness in the deepest recesses of the blues tradition, and not solely in a Native American history and tradition. According to Ted Gioia, some versions of the blues' lineage go back to West African societies and *griot* music, involving songs that "figured not as an outpouring of *personal* expression . . . but as a way of preserving historical and folkloric stories for the larger tribal unit" (16). If this lineage holds true, then Alexie's way of using the blues to inscribe a collective history, even a Native American history, returns us to the blues' murkier possible origins in West Africa. In so doing, Alexie's cultural signifiers straddle many different borders and thus become increasingly difficult to separate from one another. West African, Spokane, and African American traditions intersect at innumerable points, framed by the European tradition of the novel in which Alexie writes. In other words, Alexie's blues may ultimately point back to West African origins as well as his own immediate Spokane traditions.

To some ears, Alexie's figuration of the blues could sound like an act of appropriation. During an interview, Thomas says that "an Indian woman invented the blues a day before Columbus landed, and rock 'n' roll the next day" (157-58). Additionally, after the healing he receives through Big Mom, the Spokane figure who provided similar help for Janis Joplin and Jimi Hendrix, Robert Johnson plays a form of the blues that resonates with the entire Spokane reservation. "Those blues created memories for the Spokanes," Alexie writes, "but they refused to claim them. Those blues lit up a new road, but the Spokanes pulled out their old maps. Those blues churned up generations of anger and pain: car wrecks, suicides, murders. Those blues were ancient, aboriginal, indigenous" (174). On the surface, words like *indigenous* indicate a decidedly Native American character for the blues, as opposed, it would seem, to Baker's notion that the blues developed out of the African American Diaspora.

Rather than seek out narrowly-determined origins, however, Alexie's novel instead highlights hybridity as an essential ingredient in the blues as well as in American culture in general. Despite P. Jane Hafen's claims that the novel denigrates hybridity, Alexie's aims in *Reservation Blues* lead us directly into the complexities of mixed heritages, both in people and in expressive forms. Hafen argues that "Alexie offers little compassion for mixed bloods like my children and grotesquely simplifies their interactions with their heritage" (76). While his characters agonize over their own feelings concerning white/Indian mixing, the remarkable miscegenation taking place at the level of the novel's discourse complicates the often staunch opinions that these characters voice. For example, Hafen identifies a passage in which Chess expresses her concern over the "quarter-blood and eighth-blood grandchildren [who] will find out they're Indian and torment the rest of us real Indians. . . . [They] will get all the Indian jobs, all the Indian chances, because they look white" (Alexie 283, also qtd. in Hafen 76-77).

Although the belief that mixed-bloods would not count as *real* Indians should concern us and provoke debate, Alexie also undercuts Chess's beliefs with references to Native American traditions that find figuration in such "white" figures as Lucille Ball and Janis Joplin. At one point, Alexie describes a gig at which the members of Coyote Springs create a "tribal music that scared and excited the white people in the audience. That music might have chased away the pilgrims five hundred years ago. But if they were forced, Indians would have adopted the ancestors of a few whites, like Janis Joplin's great-great-great-great-grandparents, and let them stay in the Americas" (79-80). Elsewhere, we hear about how Big Mom designated Jimi Hendrix, Janis Joplin, and Elvis Presley "honorary members of the Spokane Tribe" because of their self-destructive tendencies (201). Likewise, with an "indigenous" blues built into its form and title, *Reservation Blues* rejects oversimplified heritages and seeks out representations of identity that go beyond an absolute, determined form.

With his images, Alexie draws up an American identity where aboriginality appears in a constant state of becoming, where any claim to authenticity must contend with a continual process of miscegenation. In *Playing Indian*, Philip J. Deloria speaks of the formation of this American identity when, in the early republic, Indians provided figuration for a selfhood separate from England. By "playing Indian," Americans created "a new identity—American—that was both aboriginal and European and yet was also neither" (36). For Alexie, the blues function as a trope for this process, which continues to stay in motion well into postcolonial eras, with Joplin and Hendrix and Johnson still shaping the very notion of an indigenous American identity. Alexie's blues count for more than the music Coyote Springs plays; it points toward the dynamic interchange taking place at the level of rhetorical forms.

Hence, it becomes important to keep in mind Baker's notion of a blues matrix. In its very workings, Alexie's novel simulates Baker's idea of "a point of ceaseless input and output, a web of intersecting, crisscrossing impulses always in productive transit" (3) that ultimately generates the blues, and by extension, American culture as a whole. Such an idea appears behind the fascination with network images in the novel as when Father Arnold, the reservation's Catholic priest, reflects upon the dreamcatcher he received as a gift: "Other priests would have dismissed the dreamcatcher as Indian mysticism or mythological arts and crafts, but Father Arnold was genuinely thrilled by its intricate system of threads and beads. He had laughed out loud when he noticed the dreamcatcher was actually decorated with rosary beads" (250). The dreamcatcher's traditional function, to protect the sleeper by snaring unpleasant dreams in its webbing, takes secondary importance to the configuration of the webbing itself. This webbing functions as a metaphor for the processes of cultural interchange and combination that helps generate Alexie's version of the blues, a version not limited to any separate sphere, like a Catholic or Native American belief system, but instead working across such distinctions.

With Catholicism and traditional Spokane worldviews typically coming to a head throughout the novel, Alexie offers the rosary-beaded dreamcatcher as a signifier of a more complex relationship, pointing to an improbable hybrid between the two often-opposing worldviews. A bishop speaks of how "it's never easy ministering to such a people as the Indians. They are a lost people, God knows" (267). At another point, Thomas questions Chess's allegiance to a church "that killed so many Indians" (166). Elsewhere, Father Arnold experiences a troubling vision involving the Whitmans, missionaries who used the fear of small pox to convert the Indians to Christianity. Traces of these colonial relationships still exist in contemporary situations, Alexie suggests, and even the otherwise sympathetic Father Arnold can experience a troubling pleasure in his "newfound power" (164).

But even with these tensions, Alexie shows how the two distinct worldviews can interact and inform one another in his blues mixture. He strategically places the Catholic church at the reservation crossroads, not only a recognizable blues image, but also a place of intersection in the network of relationships traced by Alexie, creating opportunity for interchange as well as interference and obstruction in his webbing of discourses. A bishop hints something to this effect when he tells Father Arnold that for "better or worse, you and those Indians are stuck together" (268). While Alexie underscores the residual colonial-ism in such relationships, he also gestures toward the need to form something new through the interaction between Spokane tradition and Catholicism, something that makes the old equation of dominance and submission unsustainable. Big Mom once again facilitates the kind of border crossing that creates this possibility. After Junior's suicide, she takes Father Arnold in tow, explaining that nothing less than a fusion of Catholicism and Spokane tradition will complete the memorial ser-vice for Junior. "[You] cover all the Christian stuff," she tells Father Arnold, and "I'll do the traditional Indian stuff. We'll make a great team" (280). Alexie risks sounding merely conciliatory, or eager to placate the feelings aroused by his characters' more inflammatory re-marks about mixed relationships. Yet the interaction between Father Arnold and Big Mom speaks to a desire for miscegenation between disparate elements, elements still at odds, but paradoxically containing one another.

Similar contradictions drive Alexie's version of a blues matrix, a network that spans otherwise distinct cultures and facilitates combina-tions of different and often opposing forms and practices. To signify this process, Alexie gives Coyote Springs a repertoire that amounts to a cross-section of Americana, making its classification as a band nearly impossible. During one of the band's earlier gigs, Thomas sere-nades Chess with an improvised song that moves through "blues, country, and punk versions, [and he] even recited it like a poem. Once, he closed his eyes and told it like a story" (58). By falling back on a story form at the end of this cycle, Thomas reaffirms the place of a Spokane oral tradition among these other genres and practices, in ef-fect giving the band's performance an *indigenous* American dimen-sion. Throughout the novel, in fact, Thomas practices a traditional Spokane form of storytelling, preserving it despite the indifference, and sometimes even hostility, of those around him. It is his idea to make the name *Coyote*, drawn from the recurring figure of Native American trickster stories, part of the band's name. The reaction of

Victor and Junior to the name proves typical of the reservation's general hostility to traditional story-forms: "'That's too damn Indian,' Junior said. 'It's always Coyote this, Coyote that. I'm sick of Coyote'" (45).

The place of a pure, unadulterated Native American oral tradition is the crucial issue here: Thomas embraces it, Junior and Victor reject it, and the meaning it should still hold for a "real Indian" (the idea of such authenticity always a tenuous subject in this novel) becomes uncertain at best. In fact, the dissent among Alexie's characters reflects a larger, unresolved ambivalence toward "pure" tradition communicated by the novel as a whole. Alexie has further problematized this relationship in interviews. For instance, in his conversation with John Purdy, Alexie caustically asserts his own weariness with questions about connections between his work and the oral tradition. "I type it!" he says, adding that "I'm really, really quiet when I'm doing it. The only time when I'm essentially really a storyteller is when I'm up in front of a crowd. Growing up with traditional and non-traditional storytellers, and they're always riffin' and improvvin'" (6). But one can see signs of Alexie's own "riffin' and improvvin'" in *Reservation Blues*, with the oral tradition composing one set of materials at his disposal, along with innumerable other western and non-western forms, all in constant movement. Alexie's ultimate position to traditional oral forms, as well as to non-traditional forms, develops into an insider/outsider relationship. Simultaneously, Thomas becomes both parody and model for Alexie's own fiction-making voice, with the novel itself increasingly bearing a double-sided relationship to the oral tradition, both a part and apart.[4]

This double-sided relationship to the oral tradition becomes most evident in the follow-up scene to the argument about the Coyote name. Here, the novel's narrative voice assumes the textures, tones, and rhythms that Thomas uses in his own stories, describing how Coyote actually materializes only to disassemble Junior's truck and reassemble it inside a dance hall. In making this "traditional" story part of the novel's own webbing of discourses, Alexie presents a Native American tradition of narrative as both a presence and non-presence, at once canceled out by the written form of the Western novel, but nevertheless savvy enough like Coyote to slip in between the breaks and assert its presence when doubted the most. Ultimately, by having the Coyote story reveal itself through the Western form of the novel, *Reservation Blues* comes to draw upon the syncretism associated with the blues in its very form, making any single label, such as "Western" or "Native American," appear inadequate. Instead, Alexie's novel operates in the pathways between these labels, much like the criss-crossing patterns (read: crossroads) that, according to Houston Baker, give the blues their form.

As a matrix open to these patterns, the blues have the capacity to draw upon a seemingly distant and disparate discourse like the Spokane Indian oral tradition. The prospects of maintaining this oral tradition alone and in "pure" state become impossible or at least difficult thanks to contemporary political and cultural circumstances, so Alexie shows us that we can see its outline in other areas, like the blues, in itself *another* oral tradition. While Alexie has publicly asserted that his work has no direct connection to Native American oral traditions (as he says, he *writes* his texts), he has nevertheless acknowledged that these traditions have infused his work in a less direct sense, for instance in his public readings. In an interview with Doug Marx, Alexie describes how he gets "drunk off of public readings. I'm good at it. It comes from being a debater in high school, but also, crucially, it comes from the oral tradition of my own culture. It's in performance that the two cultures become one" (39). This last statement could easily apply to Alexie's written work as well, where we see signs of an oral tradition not as a static, self-contained entity, but as something passing through a series of what blues singers call the crossroads, constantly intersecting with other traditions and ever mutating. By drawing our attention to this process, Alexie's work forms a response to a postmodern world that, according to Chicano critic and novelist Rudolfo Anaya, has erased "our rituals and ceremonies, [and] has forced us to enter a linear time, a time which promises no renewal, no rising from the ashes of a new awareness" (471).

Anaya's comments appear in "What Good Is Literature in Our Time?," an essay that laments a decentered postmodern era and encourages writing that recovers "our own, smaller communities" in the wake of a postindustrial, globalized community. Instead of wholeheartedly resisting the pull of postmodernity, however, Alexie looks at it as an opportunity for reinventing the traditions that Anaya would claim as lost. While Anaya mourns the loss of a cohesive "center," Alexie views new possibilities in the burgeoning centerless networks that intersect on multiple levels. For Alexie, the blues matrix functions as one such centerless network that allows multiple entry points, including Native American oral traditions. In turn, multiple destinations and results emerge. Not only does it provide an entry point, but the oral tradition itself also undergoes a form of revival and transformation *through* this blues network.

Illustrations of these possibilities occur in the performances of Coyote Springs, with their songs that traverse multiple forms and styles, from country to punk, all ultimately converging in the Spokane oral tradition practiced by Thomas. Alexie also highlights these possibilities when he speaks of the blues' "aboriginal, indigenous" nature, a reference not just to the tragedies that originate in America, but to the methods of giving form to those tragedies. When Big Mom sings her song for the horses slaughtered by Wright, she uses music to place the event in a Native American continuum, governed by a notion of time that eschews European linearity. For Big Mom, the murder of the horses has never stopped happening. Her blues not only preserve the event, but they help inscribe a cyclical notion of time characteristic of many Native American belief systems. She also introduces an important idea in the novel about the role music plays in the creation of the world. Using a flute made from the bones of one of the horses, "Big Mom played a new flute song every morning to remind everybody that music created and recreated the world daily" (10).

This section continues with references to others who have played a role in this constant process, but Alexie looks beyond traditional Native American subjects and instead lists figures in American popular culture who have directly or indirectly drawn from the blues: "With each successive generation, the horses arrived in different forms and with different songs, called themselves Janis Joplin, Jimi Hendrix, Marvin Gaye, and so many others" (10). With passages like these, the novel embodies an impulse to see not just the blues, but other aspects of American popular culture as extensions of Native American forms. In his journal, Thomas Builds-the-Fire even follows up his definition of Coyote, the recurring trickster in many Native American literatures, by listing Lucille Ball as an example (48). Placing Janis Joplin in the context of the Native American oral tradition or imagining Lucille Ball as a manifestation of Coyote go beyond simply making associations between disparate forms of culture. Rather, they serve to illustrate Alexie's point that the blues and even American popular culture in general bear traces of Native American cultural forms that many believe forgotten, or at least irrelevant. In reality, the novel suggests, we have merely forgotten how to recognize them in our midst.

As Philip J. Deloria points out, early American development of a revolutionary identity created an opportunity for Native Americans to help shape American culture. Whites had their own skewed notions of Indianness, but even with such (mis)representations, *real* Indians managed to stay "present at the margins, insinuating their way into Euro-American discourse, often attempting to nudge notions of Indianness in directions they found useful" (8). The difficulty in recognizing these forms comes from the proliferation of mass-produced Native American images culled from white fantasies, that is, images that serve to affirm the preconceptions that white consumers hold of the Indian *other*. When their deal with Coyote Springs falls apart, Sheridan and Wright, the calvarymen/record producers, determine that their hopes of marketing Indians have not completely evaporated. They decide they can use Betty and Veronica,[5] the two white roadies who attach themselves to Coyote Springs: "Can't you see the possibilities?" says Sheridan. "We dress them up a little. Get them into the tanning booth. Darken them up a bit. Maybe a little plastic surgery on those cheekbones. Get them a little higher, you know? Dye their hair black. Then we'd have Indians. People want to hear Indians" (269). In Sheridan's mass market planning, Betty and Veronica become living *simulacra*, or what Jean Baudrillard would describe as "myths of origin and signs of reality," as well as "second-hand truth, objectivity and authenticity" (197). For Alexie, these *simulacra* create a form of double-consciousness in the Native Americans who look for their own reflections within them. He writes of Big Mom's former students, Indian men like Michael White Hawk, once drawn to her blues-toned teaching but who "started to believe their own publicity and run around acting like the Indians in movies" (208).

Paradoxically, Alexie's strategy involves using popular culture to counter this proliferation of images confused as the *real*. In fact, Alexie's novel implies that no unadulterated form of the authentic truly exists. Instead, we can recover only traces of the *real*, tangled up in the figurations and images that circulate through American mass media and culture. The possibilities of untangling these figurations appear too remote, so Alexie consciously makes himself part of the process. He enters American popular culture, the matrix figured as the blues, to unpack its images and re-synthesize them, in effect creating a relationship to American popular culture that proves both critical *and* self-reflexive. When he describes pop culture entering the psyches of his characters (as when Junior wonders why he doesn't have visions like "the Indians on television" [18], or when Thomas dreams about Indians who "whooped like Indians always do in movies and dreams" [70]), the same infiltration inescapably happens at the level of the novel's discourse. Even with the novel's ongoing critique of how American popular culture has represented Indians, an undeniable cinematic quality enters Alexie's writing. This quality becomes especially evident in the final scene: Chess and Checkers reach out and hold "tightly to the manes of those shadow horses running alongside the blue van," a scene that has all the ear-marks of a Hollywood fade-out (306). But rather than read his cinematic quality as acquiescence, something in Alexie's manner suggests otherwise, implying that if Hollywood can infiltrate the consciousness of Indians, then the reverse process can also take place.[6]

In effect, Alexie finds his own novel and the representations of popular culture at another crossroads in a novel of crossroads, allowing for moments of interplay as well as obstruction. For all its denigrating images, mass media provides new materials for signifying the Indian, and Alexie knows that no representation, regardless of authorship, can remain wholly immune to its effects. Popular culture often creates our (mis)conceptions of race, even so, it also provides a storehouse of materials that lend themselves to generating counter-images and new figurations of race. In other words, American popular culture offers Alexie a channel into the race-making apparatuses of American culture, providing an opportunity for both disruption and refiguration.

Hence Alexie's reasons for focusing on the blues, which serve as both the subject and model for this process. When he calls the blues "ancient, aboriginal, indigenous" (174), he works not simply to mask the *blackness* of the blues so much as he strives to highlight America as a scene of miscegenation, an "aboriginal, indigenous" site of interplay that has enabled the formation of the blues. By highlighting this constant interplay, Alexie renders blackness a mutable category, something which can even blur into other ethnic identities, including Native American, making them subject to an ever shifting ground. Needless to say, readers sensitive to the historical plight of Native American societies, as well as other groups plundered of land and identity throughout United States history, will find such mutability unsettling, something which promises more erosion of self-hood. But Alexie does not make it easy for us to find a message affirming the kind of nationalism or tribalism we might see in other Native American writers. Even tribal affiliations appear unfixed and mutable, as The-man-who-was-probably-

Lakota, an otherwise minor character, serves to emphasize with his vague background. Similarly, when Thomas tells Chess that they were at Wounded Knee even though "there were whole different tribes there, no Spokanes or Flatheads" (167), rigid notions of tribal identity give way to something more fluid, less certain.

With this uncertainty, cultural boundaries begin to blur, allowing the kind of cultural interchange both produced by and signified by the blues. It becomes tempting to view Alexie as the kind of writer Elizabeth Cook-Lynn identifies as cosmopolitan, those who counter nationalist desires by "serving as translators of materials into an already existing mode," striving to "legitimize 'hybridity,'" "transcend national affiliations," and "serve as 'exotica'" (29). In a recent essay, Cook-Lynn underscores the tensions between Cosmopolitanism and Nationalism in Native American writing, and she raises concerns over how the dismissal of "blood and ancestral ties and lineage" (34) can lead to the kind of insensitivity we see in the "'becoming Indian' fad so offensive to Indian populations" (35). But even if Alexie's writing contains some characteristics of Cosmopolitanism, he does so with a critical eye toward its effects. Note his treatment of Betty and Veronica, the two New Age band groupies who want to become Indian because they think, according to Checkers, that "Indians got all the answers" (158). Yet even as Alexie critiques the denigrating notions of Betty and Veronica, he also hints that *some* transformations can take place, that a subject-position *can* shift between Indian and non-Indian. Alexie describes a transformation of this sort with Robert Johnson, who by the conclusion wears "a traditional Indian ribbon shirt made of highly traditional silk and polyester" (303). The categories that appear so closed to Betty and Veronica suddenly seem more open to Johnson, even if the "tradition" in his clothes appears entangled with Westernized materials, much like the rosary-beaded dreamcatcher given to Father Arnold.

But Alexie implies that as a blues musician, Johnson knows the finer workings of crossroads, the transit system that allows the complex interchange we see most vividly in song and discourse, but experience most profoundly at the level of selfhood. Make no mistake that Alexie is merely showing us the obsolete and flawed notion of the American melting pot. Instead, he shows us something far more unruly, a system of routes and links between cultures, creating not homogeneity but endless combinations and entanglements, fraught with tension. We can find such tension and interchange throughout American improvised music, like the blues, jazz, and r 'n' b that Alexie constantly uses as reference points. Consider Ralph Ellison's description of the "cruel contradiction implicit" in a jazz performance, which might also apply to Alexie's own blues-toned improvisations: "For true jazz is an art of individual assertion within and against the group. Each true jazz moment . . . springs from a contest in which each artist challenges the rest" (234). Alexie takes what Ellison imagines as artistic tension and extends it into other dimensions of his work. We find that creative tension in the way Alexie manipulates and improvises his materials, such as when he riffs on the Coyote tale his characters mock. We also find that tension in the apparent oppositional nature his materials hold to one another, yet Alexie shows that these materials inevitably contain traces of one another.

Hence, Alexie asks us to see the Indian in places we might least expect: in the blues, rock 'n' roll, TV sitcoms, not to mention the Western form of the novel synthesized with sizable portions of the Spokane oral tradition. The difficulty lies in how to *see* the Indian, a problem that Alexie highlights with the skewed perceptions that follow Coyote Springs. An airport crowd sees the band and thinks they could be "hijackers" (218). A fry cook and a waitress in a New York bar disagree over whether or not Chess and Thomas's appearance verifies their Indian identity. "They look Puerto Rican to me," says the fry cook (239). The authentic in our midst becomes harder to recognize. "If any New Yorkers had stopped to look," Alexie says elsewhere during Coyote Springs' trip to the city, "they would have seen three Indians slow dancing, their hair swirling in the wind. . . . It could have been on the cover of the *New York Times Sunday Magazine*" (230).

As this passage suggests, Alexie calls our attention to the Indian around us, the Indian who emerges unexpectedly out of forms considered securely defined and thus outside his or her sphere. Yet Alexie delights in unsettling those secure definitions. The blues in his novel do not solely reveal themselves through black signifiers. Unpacked, they reveal a new way of signifying the Indian, as well as a self-reflexive metaphor for cultural miscegenation. Alexie's novel finds a place at the crossroads, extending a Native American oral tradition into dissimilar forms. For this process to occur we must look at songs and stories as organic things, a quality the novel reveals in the way discourses can combine with one another, morph into new forms, merge with human beings, and even repair vans. Thomas' stories, we learn, can climb "into your clothes like sand" and give "you itches that would never be scratched. If you repeated even a sentence from one of those stories, your throat [is] never the same again" (15). Likewise, the arrival of Robert Johnson's guitar results in music with the ability to work "its way into [the] skins" of Victor and Junior (23). Nothing in the events of *Reservation Blues* exists outside the realm of discourse, with stories and songs having the ability to penetrate people, machines, and other forms of discourse.

Ultimately, this quality of storytelling in itself calls us back to an indigenous American experience, that is, a Native American oral tradition that considered storytelling as a source of creation. This quality of language enables what Paula Gunn Allen calls "the sacred power of the utterance" that allows the Indian people to "shape and mold, to direct and determine, the forces that surround and govern human life and the related lives all things" (242). Alexie affirms his place in this tradition by writing a blues that calls the world into being when Big Mom sings for the fallen horses, reminding us of the way "music created and recreated the world daily" (10). By participating in this process, Alexie engages in an act of recovery, excavating the traditions we would presume lost in a tide of postmodernity, the age Rudolfo Anaya sees as bringing a "loss of the center, a loss of harmony with nature, a desperate consumerism that seems to find hope only by consuming more and more" (473). Remarkably, Alexie not only finds his Native American traditions salvageable, but he also finds them in a transformed state—one that allows him to do such an "unIndian" thing as play the blues.

This essay first appeared in *MELUS: Journal of the Society for the Study of Multi-Ethnic Literature of the United States*, issue 27.3 (Fall 2002), pages 197-215, and is reprinted by permission of the journal. Copyright © 2002 by *MELUS*.

## Notes

1. See, for instance, Jones' *Corregidora*, where the author imagines the blues as a container for history, or even a mechanism for overcoming the more painful aspects of a slave family narrative spanning generations. The novel's protagonist, a blues singer and a descendant of slaves, struggles with her family's collective memory of a ruthless slave master who is also one of her ancestors. The blues function as a vehicle for maintaining this memory and for transcending it.

2. Alexie's decision to make the "stranger" *white* becomes interesting in light of other versions of the Robert Johnson myth where the figure he meets, understood to be the devil, is often black. Alexie's revision of the myth suggests a desire to depict the white exploitation of African Americans that one finds throughout the history of American music.

3. As an example, Ruby and Brown cite the story of an interpreter sent to the US soldiers by a Spokane group. Despite the white flag carried by the approaching interpreter, the "soldiers shot him dead" (136). According to the authors, this event does not exist in the military reports "because the event, if true, would have looked poor in the record" (136).

4. We can also see this type of relationship at work in *Smoke Signals*, Alexie's own adaptation of stories from *Lone Ranger and Tonto Fistfight in Heaven*. When Thomas and Victor bum a ride to the bus station, Thomas offers as payment a story about Victor's father's experience with the 1960s counter-culture movement. At the end of the story, Victor tells Thomas that he's "full of shit," but another listener gives her cheeky approval: "I think it's a *fine* example of the oral tradition." As viewers, we do not receive clear signals on how to receive the joke: film can present us with the image and voice of the storyteller, but it *still mediates* our position to that storyteller. Both Thomas's story and the film as a whole come to occupy a liminal place in relationship to the oral tradition, appearing closer to it than print, but still filtered through a non-traditional medium. In effect, the film extends the way in which Alexie plays *through* and *around* traditional Native American materials, exhibiting both closeness and distance.

5. Alexie's critique of American popular culture further deepens with his choice of names for the roadies, which, of course, come from old *Archie* comic books.

6. See Cox for a reading of Alexie's work that focuses on the complex relationship Alexie has to popular culture. Cox makes a particularly revealing point when he writes, "Alexie does more than allude to popular culture productions: his narrative strategy is to revise and subvert the misrepresentations in popular culture narratives while concomitantly emphasizing how the misrepresentations have a destructive influence on his characters' self-perceptions" (64-65).

## Works Cited

Allen, Paula Gunn. "The Sacred Hoop: A Contemporary Perspective." *The Ecocriticism Reader: Landmarks in Literary Ecology.* Ed. Cheryll Glotfelty and Harold Fromm. Athens: U of Georgia P, 1996. 241-63.

Alexie, Sherman. Interview. "Crossroads: A Conversation with Sherman Alexie." By John Purdy. *Studies in American Indian Literatures* 9.4 (1997): 1-18.

_____. Interview. "Sherman Alexie: A Reservation of the Mind." By Doug Marx. *Publishers Weekly.* 243.38 (1996): 39-40.

_____. *The Lone Ranger and Tonto Fistfight in Heaven.* 1993. New York: HarperCollins, 1994.

_____. *Reservation Blues.* 1995. New York: Warner, 1996.

Anaya, Rudolfo. "What Good Is Literature in Our Time?" *American Literary History* 10.3 (1998): 471-77.

Baker, Houston A., Jr. *Blues, Ideology, and Afro-American Literature: A Vernacular Theory.* Chicago: U of Chicago P, 1984.

Baudrillard, Jean. "The Evil Demon of Images and the Precession of Simulacra." *Postmodernism: A Reader.* Ed. Thomas Docherty. New York: Columbia UP, 1993. 194-99.

Cook-Lynn, Elizabeth. "The American Indian Fiction Writer: Cosmopolitanism, Nationalism, the Third World, and First Nation Sovereignty." *Wicazo Sa Review* 9.2 (1993): 26-36.

Cox, James. "Muting White Noise: the Subversion of Popular Culture Narratives of Conquest in Sherman Alexie's Fiction." *Studies in American Indian Literatures* 9.4 (1997): 52-70.

Deloria, Philip J. *Playing Indian.* New Haven: Yale UP, 1998.

Ellison, Ralph. *Shadow and Act.* 1953. New York: Random House, 1972.

Gioia, Ted. *The History of Jazz.* New York: Oxford UP, 1997.

Hafen, P. Jane. "Rock and Roll, Redskins, and Blues in Sherman Alexie's Work." *Studies in American Indian Literatures* 9.4 (1997): 71-78.

Jones, Gayl. *Corregidora.* Boston: Beacon P, 1975.

Ruby, Robert H. and John A. Brown. *The Spokane Indians: Children of the Sun.* Norman: U of Oklahoma P, 1970.

*Smoke Signals.* Dir. Chris Eyre. Written for the Screen and Co-Produced by Sherman Alexie. Perf. Adam Beach, Evan Adams, Irene Bedard, and Gary Farmer. Shadow Catcher Entertainment, 1998.

# The Exaggeration of Despair in
# Sherman Alexie's *Reservation Blues*_____

Gloria Bird

A prolific writer, Sherman Alexie (Spokane/Coeur d'Alene) has become an enigma on the literary scene in only a few years' time. Most reviewers—as far from the rural reservation setting as they come— have heaped praise upon Alexie's work as representative of contemporary reservation life. Philip Patrick, "who works and writes in New York," and whose commentary otherwise on the absence of music in a novel about music is perceptive, makes the characteristic claims: "With what can only be described as a deep understanding of the hell and joys that must be reservation life, Alexie soars in *Reservation Blues*," "Alexie brings to the page the life of the Spokanes," and, "Alexie's reservation is as evocative as James Baldwin's Harlem or Dorothy Allison's backwater Carolinas."

This review questions the assumption that because someone is Indian what they produce is automatically an accurate representation. It addresses specific problems with the construed, generic "Indian" qualities that are attributed to diverse tribal peoples. It attempts to discuss the elements of Alexie's latest work *Reservation Blues* (Atlantic Monthly Press, 1995) that, in the spirit of an Indian Spike Lee, contribute to a portrait of an exaggerated version of reservation life, one that perpetuates many of the stereotypes of native people and presents problems for native and non-native readers alike.

The resemblance to other script-minded novels, and the cultural (mis)representation in Spike Lee films should be examined in relation to how native culture is modified in *Reservation Blues*. In film, Spike Lee selectively exposes little known aspects of African American culture and life, and has been credited with having successfully interpreted that experience from an insider's perspective to the mainstream audience. The mixed-messages generated by Lee in film are analogous to the effect of *Reservation Blues* upon the mainstream in interpreting the representations of Indian. Examples from the novel will be examined in detail later. I would like to begin by comparing how *Reservation Blues* resembles script.

In *Reservation Blues*, the cinematic style is apparent from the start. Like script, on page one, the cast of characters from Sherman Alexie's earlier work appear, as well as the newcomer to the reservation, Robert Johnson, the legendary bluesman. Before we are off the first page, we pan in to a "close-up" of Robert Johnson: "a small man with very dark skin and huge hands, he wore a brown suit that looked good from a distance but grew more ragged, frayed at the cuffs, *as he came into focus*" (3) [Italics mine]. The script-like prose is comparable to Fanny Flagg's "novel," *Fried Green Tomatoes at the Whistle Stop Cafe*, where if you've read the book, you've basically experienced the storyline of the film on which it is based. "Chapters" are arranged in "scenes" that are followed in order in the film.

The traps of popular culture inform *Reservation Blues* to the extent that discussion of pop culture and postmodern sensibilities need be called upon. I begin with a generalization: In *Reservation Blues*, alluding to popular culture as a literary strategy does not serve as either a parody or as a serious interrogation of popular culture. It is a way of carrying the story from one subject to another.

Pop culture is a self-referencing medium. Audiences need to be informed and pop-culture-sophisticated to 'get' the messages that flood the TV and movie screens. In the same way, the following dialogue between Victor and Thomas exemplifies how the novel relies on readership exposure to film: "You sound like we're in some goddamn reservation coming-of-age movie. Who the fuck you think you are? Billy Jack? Who's writing your dialogue" (211)? Again, toward the conclusion of the novel, Victor is visited by the ghost of Junior Polatkin. "'Happy reservation fucking Halloween,' Junior said, and Victor screamed, which made Junior scream, too. They traded screams for awhile" (288). In case you didn't catch the allusion, Alexie fills you in. Victor addresses Junior, "What do you think this is? An American

Werewolf in London" (288). The comic entry of the visitation—a scene that is stolen directly from the film *An American Werewolf in London*—overrides the seriousness of Victor's questioning as to *why* Junior committed suicide. The scene self-consciously makes references both to itself and the film on which it is based. Allusion is a device through which *Reservation Blues* becomes self-conscious of its own constructions.

In what is termed cosmopolitan or postmodern literature—in my understanding of its manifestations—*Reservation Blues* might find a limited context if we are speaking of its connection to literary and media productions where the images that have been produced from a period are mirrored back to the original producers. A colleague has pointed out that referring to pop culture is not the problem; it becomes problematic, however, when this is the only exposure to native literature to which mainstream readers are exposed.

In thinking about the purposes of native literary production, the temptation to use western theories to inform one's reading is not the type of engagement with the literature I find most useful. But I do have questions about how we might productively discuss *Reservation Blues* in its connection to postmodern sensibilities, if only to speculate. Foucault, in questioning "What Is an Author?" in his essay of the same title, speaks about the disappearance of the author as a development "in the effacement of the writing subject's individual characteristics," where "the writing subject cancels out the signs of his particular individuality" (102). The end result, so he writes, is that "the writer is reduced to nothing more than the singularity of his absence." His ideas on the "disappearance—or death—of the author" are taken to the extreme by Italo Calvino. Calvino, for instance, has taken the dissolution of the author to a new level, the dissolution of the narrator as well. Lacking the identity of a protagonist, a reader is forced to enter the "void" to identify with the narrator. When we begin to search for the sense of such self-referencing (in the postmodern sense) in *Reservation Blues*, the motive for its literary strategy begins to blur. Self-referencing here is author-intrusive; the author does not want to be forgotten as he constructs the story, and continually reminds us of the singularity of his presence.

In the end, at least for this writer, reading *Reservation Blues* as a postmodern novel does not work, except in limited ways. *Reservation Blues* is certainly a product of postmodern film. For my purposes, my reading is informed by a post-colonial dialogue on literary production in colonial contexts that, as far as I can tell, exist everywhere in Third/ New World discussions, with the exception of this country. When we change our focus to a native readership and what is being represented *to* us and *about* us, a very different set of relationships must be examined. As a native reader, my concern is with the colonialist influence on the native novel, and how that influence shapes the representation of native culture to a mainstream audience. It also cannot help but shape the native reader's relationship to the native novel.

In his book *Decolonizing the Mind*, the African writer Ngugi Wa Thiong'o discusses African writers who 'prey' upon their culture to produce works written in colonial tongues, and then claim to invest the colonizer's language with an *Africanness*. There is a parallel with Alexie's *Reservation Blues* in that it attempts to invest his novel with *Indianness*, but ultimately 'preys' upon a variety of native cultures along the way. The examples are numerous, and include for instance, the use of the greeting, "ya-hey," which is a contrived expression. One can only speculate that it is based upon the Diné greeting, *ya'át'ééh* (ya-tey). Mainstream readers who do not have access to native language usage, either Salish or Diné, will not have a way to make an accurate assessment of its appearance in the novel and will rely solely upon what they *read* as being representationally accurate. When we examine how stereotypes of Indian are returned to the source of their original production and the dynamics that come into play in *Reservation Blues*, the impress of colonial influence become more apparent.

There is the nameless character who is described as having "cheek-bones so big that he knocked people over when he moved his head from side to side" (11), a feature that signals his Siouan descendance. Exaggerated high cheekbones plays upon an unquestioned characterization of native people; and the most prominent "Indian" is, of course, the Plains Sioux. This character is referred to as "the-man-who-was-probably-Lakota," a Bible-thumping "crazy old Indian man" (11) prophesying the end of the world. Sioux culture is disparaged in the personage of this "man who-was-probably-Lakota." The character is never humanized because Alexie neglected to attribute to him a name. Yet, Thomas appropriates the Siouan address "all my relations" in his dream of a sweat*lodge* (instead of the Northwest sweat*house*) scene. The insensitivity of native people who exploit and 'prey' upon Indian cultures is another uncomfortable example of appropriation. Stereotyping native peoples does not supply a native readership with soluble ways of undermining stereotypes, but becomes a part of the problem, and returns an image of a generic "Indian" back to the original producers of that image.

The danger is with the gross representation becoming implicit. That is, when people (who haven't grown up on an Indian reservation) decide this representation is accurate and, like Philip Patrick, reinforce that assumption back to a general readership, who, in turn, have no empirical knowledge as a basis for comparison. Mainstream readers trust the "native" novel mistaking it for complete representation. *Reservation Blues* as the representative "native" novel, in actuality, omits the core of native community, and exists solely in the marginal realm of its characters who are all misfits: social and cultural anomalies. It is a partial portrait of a community wherein there is no evidence of Spokane culture or traditions, or anything uniquely Spokane. There are no signs of elders, with the exception of Big Mom whose figure is exalted to mythical disproportions. Pan-Indianism becomes the axiom for *Indianness*, a borrowing from various native cultures and traditions that, in the end, misconstrue what is Indian, or specifically Spokane, to the general public.

The idea of 'preying' on one's culture is disturbing. Like Spike Lee, who has attempted to take on interracial romance as the subject of film, along with the tensions and the controversy surrounding such an alliance, Alexie, too attempts to explain and vindicate, and at the same time to discredit, Victor's attraction to white women. To Junior's question, "Why you like white women so much?" Victor's scatological, "Don't you know? Bucks prefer white tail" (233), is basically a non-answer.

It is the Indian woman's voice *via* Chess who speaks for Indian women and, we are told, takes the "traditional" stance. Chess thinks men like "Junior and Victor are traitors" who are "betraying their DNA" (82). Her argument runs the gamut from "preservation," as in survival of the race, to the apologetic, "as traditional as it sounds, I think Indian men need Indian women. I think only Indian women can take care of Indian men. Jeez, we give birth to Indian men. We feed them. We hold them when they cry. Then they run off with white women" (81). She seems to imply that only "traditional" Indians are concerned with self-preservation (in terms of blood quantum) and are the only ones to express racist sentiments regarding interracial mixing. It is an odd perspective, given that we are told early in the novel that the Spokane "were mostly a light-skinned tribe" (4) which implies that the Spokanes are the products of interracial mixing. Given that background, it's unlikely that Thomas, Junior, and Victor are all "fullbloods," as is claimed.

Calling Chess's attitudes "traditional" does not ring true. Most tribes traditionally intermarried with neighboring bands and tribes as a way of strengthening the blood lines, and frequently adopted new blood into the tribe.[1] Earlier, Chess summarizes the bleak outlook for Indian women in choosing a partner:

When Indian women begin the search for an Indian man, they carry a huge list of qualifications. He has to have a job. He has to be kind, intelligent, and funny. He has to dance and sing. He should know how to iron his own clothes. Braids would be nice. But as the screwed-up Indian men stagger through their lives, Indian men need only to have their own teeth to get snagged. (74-5)

On the one hand, we have the "traditional" view; on the other, the bleak "reality" for Indian women in their selection of men. Which is it that guides women in their choices then, blood quantum or choppers? The options are ridiculous, and in the end the relationships between Indian men and women are not invested with any seriousness.

The male characters, too, have their own thoughts on the subject: "Junior knew that white women were trophies for Indian boys. He always figured getting a white woman was like [the Plains tribes' practice] of counting coup or stealing horses, like the best kind of revenge against white men" (233). Then there is the naivete of Thomas, who "agreed with Chess, but he also knew about the shortage of love in the world. He wondered if people should celebrate love wherever it's found, since it is so rare. He worried about the children of mixed-blood marriages. The half-breed kids at the reservation school suffered through worse beatings than Thomas ever did" (82). His logic is skewed, and simple self-preservation guides his motive for empathy. His view that there is a shortage of love in the world is almost New Age and, if true, still evades the issue.

In terms of its relationship to script, 'effect' and 'prop' seem key to any discussion of the novel beginning with the stereotypical employ of the names of the characters: Thomas Builds-the-Fire, the Warm Water sisters, and Lester Falls Apart. The community of Wellpinit and its surroundings are intimate props, familiar scenery that is vacant of any emotional investment. There is none of the sweeping, lyrical prose of Momaday's *House Made of Dawn*, whose lines like "The canyon is a ladder to the plain" stay in the mind for years. Neither is there the detail of Silko's *Ceremony*, wherein description of the New Mexican landscape is dense with meaning:

> He stood on the edge of the rimrock and looked down below: the canyons and valleys were thick powdery black; their variations of height and depth were marked by a thinner black color. . . . He took a deep breath of cold mountain air: there were no boundaries; the world below and the sand

paintings inside became the same that night. The mountains from all the directions had been gathered there that night. (145)

Instead, we are told matter-of-factly how, "Benjamin Pond used to be called Benjamin Lake, but then a white man named Benjamin Lake moved to the reservation to teach biology at the Tribal High School. All the Indians liked the teacher so much that they turned the lake into a pond to avoid confusion" (26). Given the intrusive, omnipresence of the narrator, it is odd here that Alexie's narrator distances himself from "the Indians," as if he were a non-native observer. This, of course, could be attributed to Alexie's third-person narration that automatically distances the narrator.

Character development is inconsistent and, while I want to say that it is a human foible to be inconsistent, in this novel the danger is in the contradictory sentiments of the characters who then become unreliable. It's Chess, again, who, while acceding that "everybody wants to be an Indian," appears to sympathize when she says that, "Not every white person wants to kill Indians. You know most any white who joins up with Indians never wants to leave. It's always been that way" (168). In the same argument only a page later says, "But not everybody is an Indian. It's an exclusive club . . . Why do all these white people think they can be Indian all of a sudden" (169)? Thomas, who never seems to quite manage to make distinctions, answers, "I've always had a theory that you ain't really Indian unless, at some point in your life, you didn't want to be Indian." Contradicting sentiments ooze from the mouths of the characters, and as readers, we can never be sure where anybody stands. Postmodern irony rules. The characters, in the end, contradict both themselves and one another. The effect is a leveling of values and weakening of emotional investment, in particular, *native* aesthetic values are undermined. If this is the predicament of uncertainties posited by postmodernism, it contributes to the weak link in the production of the native novels that rely on these tendencies. Too, as a parody, the novel operates to reinforce that native people are incapable of self-analysis or thoughtful commentary on contemporary social dilemmas.

In *Reservation Blues*, the introduction of elements for "affect," likewise become stripped of emotional investment. It is a literary strategy that is consistent throughout the novel. For instance, the historical event (in which over 700 horses of the Spokane Tribe were slaughtered by the U.S. cavalry) is introduced through the character Big Mom. However, it is introduced less for its significance and more for the convenient metaphor of the horses whose scream appears throughout as a refrain. The refrain, "the Indian horses screamed," repeats so many times so as to draw attention to itself and begins to serve as a background musical score.

The horses, and Big Mom's relationship to them, are rendered, again, matter-of-factly, and from the position of an observer who stands outside of the events with no connection to them. No explanation is given for the killing of the horses. But the horses are assigned more weight a little later as we become witness to the killing of a single remaining colt in "close up":

> The colt shivered as the officer put his pistol between its eyes and pulled the trigger. *That colt fell to the grass of the clearing, to the sidewalk outside a reservation tavern, to the cold, hard coroner's table in a Veterans Hospital.* (10) [Italics, mine]

The horses take on a new metaphorical significance, that of the Indians themselves who fall victim outside of bars or as unrecognized veterans of war. The reduction of Indian existence to defeat reads as internalized oppression, of buying into a vision of ourselves as dying/vanishing and simply returns the representation of Indians as they are produced in American literature and in the media back to itself. The central metaphor of the novel associates Indians to the slaughtered horses as fallen victims of the bottle and a country that does not love us. This image, in turn, is remade only two paragraphs later, as the "horses" reincarnate as a multitude of famous musicians including Janis Joplin, Jimi Hendrix, Elvis and Marvin Gaye. The quick fix allusion to pop culture sets up Big Mom as the teacher of all good (and troubled) musicians and savior of Robert Johnson. The larger-than-life character of Big Mom is not just a teacher, but is also a catalyst for all major American musical forms (jazz, rockabilly, rock 'n' roll).

Intermittently sprinkled throughout the novel like bait are sage-smudging, stickgame, sweetgrass enough to titillate the curiosity of non-native readers—while simultaneously mishmashing Indian cultures to create a pan-Indian, non-specific representation of an Indian community that is flawed because of its exaggerated "Indian" qualities. Thus, commodity food appears every time the characters return to their HUD house, and the characters overuse (sometimes incorrectly) the Red English term "enit." Exaggeration seems to be the rule (a symptom of postmodern literature); it is the exaggeration of despair without context that doesn't offer enough substance to be anything more than a "spoof" of contemporary reservation life.

Yet, despite its flaws, there are some aspects of the novel that ring true and are plausible as real lived experience. The dilemmas of being an Indian on the reservation are many; take for example the assessment of assimilation and amalgamation in contemporary native societies:

> Those quarter-blood and eighth blood grandchildren will find out they're Indian and torment the rest of us real Indians. They'll come to our pow-wows, in their nice clothes and nice cars, and remind us how much we don't have. Those quarter-bloods and eighth-bloods will get all the Indian jobs, all the Indian chances, because they look white. *Because they're safe.* (283) [Italics, mine]

The distance from tribal memories and bonds does have its perceived rewards both monetarily and psychically.[2] Alexie's narrator, however, doesn't appear to recognize that the representations of Indian he presents to a non-native audience are also "safer," because they are dressed in America's favorite subjects when it comes to Indians: tragedy and despair. In denying Indians a full-fledged humanity and in presenting only superficial markers for the representations of Indian, he ends up with the only other acceptable possibility (for mainstream readers): the drunken Indian.

The portrayal of alcoholism that has been rampant through the generations cannot be denied and presents a paradox with which native writers must grapple. The pathetic city drunks, and the pitiful alcoholic parents of the Warm Water sisters, Junior, Thomas, and Victor ring like wake-up calls to the social problems facing Indian people. Yet, the representation of alcoholism in *Reservation Blues*, however accurate, still capitalizes upon the stereotypical image of the "drunken Indian." It's not the kind of 'mirroring,' portraying colonial impact, that non-native people want to accept—and is a sore subject for Indians because it is all too familiar for most of us. This is the dilemma for not only Alexie, but native writers in general: to accurately represent our communities without exploiting them. The buffer in *Reservation Blues* is to sugarcoat the picture with enough side-tracks and comic scenes to tone down the real issues. Despite the verisimilitude of Alexie's portrayal of alcoholism and its impact upon individual lives, he does not attempt to put the social problems of economic instability, poverty, or cultural oppression into perspective. Instead, alcoholism and drinking are sensationalized: Lester is "the most accomplished drunk on the Spokane Reservation" (151), a notoriety that wins him "tribal hero" (151) status. Victor, incapable of coping with rejection, turns to the bottle for solace, the tragic failed artist.

Victor's demise brings to mind a comment from Paula Gunn Allen, who in *The Sacred Hoop* has said that, "conflict-based plots require a tragic outcome if the relationships between Indian and white are represented with historical accuracy" (1986), an idea, by the way I do not want to support, but which seems an accurate assessment of much recent native literary output. Not all of the characters in *Reservation Blues* are tragic though. Robert Johnson, the stranger to the reservation who comes for redemption, finds it, at the expense of both Victor and Junior.

Betty and Veronica, Beaver and Wally, the American Werewolf and Billy Jack, Janis Joplin, Jimi Hendrix, Marvin Gaye and Robert Johnson, along with the ingredients borrowed from many native cultures, all contribute to the cut-and-paste of *Reservation Blues*. In the end, I am reminded again of Spike Lee, African American filmmaker, who I want to cheer for being able to create movies about African Americans that star African American actors. What is missing from his films, and from *Reservation Blues*, is a sense of responsibility to the cultures they are attempting to represent. *Reservation Blues* is fiction that relies on the strategies of film. It is more specifically a product, and reflection, of the techno-generation, clever at times, but not the serious literature it's cracked up to be. To derive *meaning* from the novel for the native audience is to become lost in its ambiguity of purpose, its terminal dysfunction as a native novel. But then, it's quite possible that we're not supposed to think about it all that hard.

From *Wicazo Sa Review* 11, no. 2 (Fall 1995): 47-52. Copyright © 1995 by the University of Minnesota Press. Reprinted with permission of the University of Minnesota Press.

## Notes

A condensed version of this review appeared in *Indian Artist*.

1. After contact, the practice was continued with runaway slaves and captured whites. In the case of the Spokane, it is documented in the tribal records that a number of white families were adopted into the tribe.

2. Compare, for instance, Sidner Larson's autobiographical *Catch Colt* to the pain inflicted through bigotry as experienced by Janet Campbell-Hale in her autobiography *Bloodlines: Odyssey of a Native Daughter*.

# Bibliography

Alexie, Sherman. *Reservation Blues*. New York: The Atlantic Monthly Press, 1995.

_____. *The Lone Ranger and Tonto Fistfight in Heaven*. New York: HarperPerennial, 1994.

Bird, Gloria. "An Indian Spike Lee." *Indian Artist*, Fall 1995.

Calvino, Italo. *If on a Winter's Night a Traveler*. New York: Harcourt, 1979.

Campbell-Hale, Janet. Bloodlines: *Odyssey of a Native Daughter*. New York: Random House, 1993.

Flagg, Fannie. *Fried Green Tomatoes at the Whistle Stop Cafe*. New York: McGraw-Hill, 1987.

Gunn-Allen, Paula. *The Sacred Hoop: Recovering the Feminine in American Indian Traditions*. "Whose Dream Is This Anyway?," Boston: Beacon, 1986, pp. 76-101.

Larson, Sidner. *Catch Colt*. Lincoln, NE: University of Nebraska Press, 1995.

Momaday, N. Scott. *House Made of Dawn*. New York: Harper, 1968.

Patrick, Philip. "Missed Riffs on Big Mom's Mountain," *Hungry Mind Review*, Summer 1995: 24, 26.

Rabinow, Paul, editor. *Foucault Reader*. "What Is an Author?" New York: Pantheon, 1984, pp. 101-120.

Silko, Leslie Marmon. *Ceremony*. New York: Penguin Books, 1977.

Wa Thiong'o, Ngugi. *Decolonizing the Mind: The Politics of Language in African Literature*. Portsmouth, England: Heinemann Educational Books, Inc., 1986.

# Reservation Home Movies:
## Sherman Alexie's Poetry _____

Jennifer Gillan

When David Bell, the protagonist in Don DeLillo's *Americana*, leaves New York, he heads north on a long journey into the "gut of America."[1] He arrives in a small Maine town resembling a sound stage and stays overnight in an old house, "the place where everyone's grandmother lives in television commercials." He is told a story about a Sioux holy man, Black Knife, who prophesies that only a trip into what Bell earlier calls the swamp of our being would cure America and allow it to become, finally, "the America that fulfills all of its possibilities" (128-29). The story reassures David that he needs to travel to the "great golden West" filled with Indians to find the "big outdoor soul of America" (123, 25). Although, like many before him, he sets off on a road trip west hoping to find America in the heart of Indian country, he never makes it to his destination. Instead, he finds himself in a small Midwestern town, unable to piece together the "fragments of the exploded dream" (137) of his life and of America.

Sherman Alexie, a Spokane/Coeur d'Alene Indian from Washington State, is even more distraught than David Bell that the authentic American landscape eludes him. He reiterates David's concern, "What simple splendors had I missed to have been born so late" (*Americana*, 220), but with a difference. From a tribe neither Plains nor Pueblo, which few would associate with the Hollywood version of American Indians, Alexie wonders whether his people ever had access to the authenticity all America seems to associate with Indians. Alienated from their American Indian culture as well as from America, the characters in Alexie's poetry and prose collections want to believe in the wisdom of old Indian prophets, want to return to the "old ways," but know that doing so will just trap them inside another clichéd Hollywood narrative.

Alexie's poems and stories often careen toward these clichés, as the reader waits in stupefied patience for the inevitable impact of the meeting between the Lone Ranger and Tonto, the warring factions that have often marked the poles of his life. A self-described *Brady Bunch* Indian, Alexie was born in 1966 on the Spokane reservation and grew up in the 1970s in the glare of the kaleidoscopic colors of a "mod" TV sitcom. His first poems appeared in *Hanging Loose* in 1989, and the press of the same name published his first full-length manuscript, *The Business of Fancydancing*, in 1992 when Alexie was just twenty-five.[2] Between 1993 and 1995 Alexie published another poetry collection, *Old Shirts and New Skins* (1993); a poetry and prose compilation, *First Indian on the Moon* (1993); a book of short stories, *The Lone Ranger and Tonto Fistfight in Heaven* (1993); and a novel, *Reservation Blues* (1995).[3]

Critical reception of his books has been positive, if limited. Some reviewers have been perplexed by Alexie's youth and productivity. Reynolds Price wondered in a review of the *Lone Ranger and Tonto Fistfight in Heaven* if Alexie might be too prolific, publishing "too fast for his present strength."[4] Complaining that Alexie "has plumbed a number of obsessive themes and relationships as deeply as they permit," Price suggested that Alexie should slow down and "discover a new and merciful rhythm that [would] help him find new eyes, new sights and patterns in a wider world, and a battery of keener voices for launching his urgent knowledge toward us."[5] It is this urgency that fuels Alexie's writing. Always aware that the average Indian male dies at fifty, Alexie seems determined to fashion poetry out of his experiences while he can. Given the poverty level on most reservations and the fact that American Indians have the highest suicide and alcoholism rates in the country, perhaps this urgency is justified.[6] Often, it is his manic pace that makes Alexie's work so wondrous, even if it is marked, as Price observed, by "moments of unrevealing monotony."

Perhaps these moments of monotony can be attributed to Alexie's flat poetic style, which relies heavily on ordinary prose to illuminate its vision. In fact, the prose-like quality of Alexie's writing often makes it difficult to differentiate between his stories and poems. The stories in

*The Lone Ranger and Tonto Fistfight in Heaven* are crafted in this same flat style as his poems. Adopting a minimalist approach to character and setting, Alexie writes in vignettes which often begin with a fragmentary characterization and end with a flash of revelation. One of these stories, "Jesus Christ's Half-Brother Is Alive and Well on the Spokane Indian Reservation," is organized into a series of short sketches, each about a paragraph in length. Because these vignettes are so fractured and the events they detail almost surreal, it is impossible to describe them in terms of plot. They seem instead to be organized around a series of epiphanies through which each narrator comes to accept his own past. In one sketch in which the narrator saves a baby from a fire and decides to adopt him, the vignette format is especially powerful: "I pick James up from the cold and the grass that waits for spring and the sun to change its world but I can only walk home through the cold with another future on my back and James's future tucked in my pocket like an empty wallet or a newspaper that feeds the fire and never gets read. Sometimes all of this is home" (*LR*, 114). And home, as we learn in Alexie's poetry, is a HUD house and commodity cheese, a Seven-Eleven and a twelve-inch T.V., a powwow and an All-Indian basketball tournament. These mundane aspects of reservation life are pieced together in Alexie's poetry into a pattern of twentieth-century survival.

Donald Hall might have had these eclectic poetic recombinations in mind when he said, "poems embody the coexistence of opposites that together form an identity" and quoted the Roman poet Catullus to demonstrate his point: "*odi et amo*: I hate and I love."[7] That Alexie both loves and hates his bicultural inheritance is evidenced in the *Lone Ranger and Tonto Fistfight in Heaven* by an epigraph from musician-poets Lou Reed and Joy Harjo. From Reed Alexie takes the poignancy of the blues: "There's a little bit of magic in everything/ and then some loss to even things out." And from Harjo he summons the wondrous survival of Indians who, as Harjo says elsewhere, were not meant to survive: "I listen to the gunfire we cannot hear, and begin/ this journey with the light of knowing/ the root of my own furious love."[8] Alexie complements these voices with his own ambivalent song:

Vision (2)

No money for lunch so I rode an elevator to the top of the ONB Building, highest elevation in Spokane, where I stood at a window and witnessed 500 years of America: *Over 1 Billion Illusions Served.*

There is so much of this country I love, its supermarkets and bad television, the insane demands of a dollar bill in my pocket, fireworks celebrating the smallest occasions.

I am happy I can find a cup of hot coffee 24 hours a day.

But, America, in *my* country, there are no supermarkets and television is a way of never opening the front door. The fields here are green and there are no monuments celebrating the invasion of Christopher Columbus.

Here, I imagine 1492 and 1992 are two snakes entwined, climbing up the pole some call good medicine, while others name it progress or Manifest Destiny. Maybe it's economics or an extra-inning baseball game. Maybe it's Cotton Mather and Andrew Jackson looking for rescue. Maybe it's a small-pox blanket wrapped around our shoulders in the coldest winter.

Then again, who am I to talk? In the local newspaper I read this morning that my tribe escaped many of the hardships other Native Americans suffered. By the time the 20th century reached this far west, the war was over. Crazy Horse was gone and the Ghost Dancers were only ghosts. Christopher Columbus was 500 years and 3,000 miles away, fresh from a starring role in the Great American Movie.

I've seen that film at the reservation drive-in. If you look closely, you can see an Indian leaning against the back wall. You won't find his name among the end credits; you can't hear his voice or his song.

Extras, we're all extras. (*OSNS*, 27)

Like "Vision (2)," most of Alexie's poems are concerned with the entwined experiences and identities that position him within cultures with different demands. Not willing simply to retreat into nostalgia for a precontact world, he wonders how to characterize the marks that the European arrival in the New World has left on his life: "I imagine 1492 and 1992 are two snakes entwined, climbing up the pole some call good medicine, while others name it progress or Manifest Destiny." Early in the poem, Alexie declares his "furious love" for American culture. But his tone changes with the lines, "But, America, in *my* country, there are no supermarkets and television is a way of never opening the front door." He still claims America as his own, but he recognizes the disparity between his reality and that represented on the screen. This discrepancy resurfaces in his later poem, "A Reservation Table of Elements":

> When the pipes froze
> last winter
>
> on the reservation
> I crawled beneath
>
> the HUD house
> with a blowtorch
>
> and discovered
> America.
>
> (*FI*, 40)

By locating America in the foundation of his reservation house, Alexie demonstrates that it has always been the Indian who is at the heart of America's definition of itself. When he declares, "Maybe it's Cotton Mather and Andrew Jackson looking for rescue," he pinpoints the ironic reversal in American history that transformed these leaders into saviors. History demonstrates that Indians actually saved them, by showing them planting techniques to survive in the New World and by having land and resources which could be exploited. Still later, Indians became a mythological safety valve, a life preserver for an American culture slowly sinking under the weight of its own industrial and technological present.

Indeed, it is consumer culture and its mediated forms of communication that DeLillo's David Bell heads west to avoid. Assuming that there is a more authentic America buried beneath all of these television images, buried perhaps somewhere on reservation land, he hopes that somehow American Indians can cure his "soul sickness" (*Americana*, 123). Writing about Bell's contemporary heirs, the white gurus who preside over the men's movement, Alexie wonders about this search for lost authenticity: "Much of the men's movement focuses on finding things that are lost. I fail to understand how Native American traditions can help in that search, especially considering how much we have lost ourselves."[9] Because his culture always has been outside the frame of the movie version of American history, Alexie has to cure his own "soul sickness" by recreating a relationship to his complex inheritance. Rejecting both nostalgia for Indian life as it was and a claim for his own authenticity as one who knows Indian experience, Alexie struggles against the tendency to romanticize the past that he sees in much Native American writing. This nostalgia is dangerous, he suggests, because it allows Native Americans "to admire the predictable spiritual strength of Native Americans while conveniently omitting the incredible pain and suffering endured by those very same people."[10] Thus, although he needs to create a vision of this past, he wants it to be an imaginative space not populated solely by shamans, warriors, and doe-eyed Indian maidens.

Applying his imaginative powers to an understanding of his history, Alexie approaches poetry as a modern day vision quest. As "Vision (2)" suggests, Alexie has left the tribe and ventured into the city in search of an enhanced understanding of his life and culture. This experience is a disconcerting one that changes him irrevocably; like the narrator in his story "Somebody Kept Saying Powwow," he is left stranded in a bad dream: "Sometimes I still feel like half of me is lost in the city, with its foot wedged into a steam grate or something. Stuck in one of those revolving doors, going round and round while the white people are laughing. . . . Stuck in an elevator that will not move with a woman who keeps wanting to touch my hair" (*LR*, 207). Before he can return to the tribe he must do battle with what Gerald Vizenor has characterized as the "tragic simulations" of Indian identity, which in Alexie's life usually take the form of images of Indians from Hollywood westerns.[11] The line with which "Vision (2)" ends—"Extras, we're all extras"—is repeated several times throughout Alexie's other collections, as if this peripheral position in American culture is the one against which he is constantly struggling. He realizes, however, that it may be this marginality that allows him to negotiate a tenuous survival in both worlds. Whether or not this is the case, Alexie is concerned with how to extricate himself from the scalp-lock American culture has placed him in: "How can we imagine a new language when the language of the enemy keeps our dismembered tongues tied to his belt? How can we imagine a new alphabet when the old jumps off billboards down into our stomachs?" (*LR*, 152). The image of the "dismembered tongues" reminds us that despite all those savage war parties depicted in westerns, Indians were more often the hunted than the hunters in the Indian Wars. And when the government required American Indian children to attend federal boarding schools, white culture tightened its hold even further, depriving Indians of their right even to speak their own language. Tongue-tied by this history, Alexie struggles to find the words to articulate his pain.

This articulation is no easy feat for the twenty-seven-year-old narrator of "My Heroes Have Never Been Cowboys." Surrounded by the dazzling transmissions that bounce off the walls of his poorly constructed HUD house and enthralled by the promises of consumer happiness he hears on TV, he has no idea how to displace the Euro-American codes and gain access to his Spokane heritage: "Twenty years ago, television was our way of finding heroes and spirit animals. Twenty years ago, we never knew we'd spend the rest of our lives in the reservation of our minds, never knew we'd stand outside the gates of the Spokane Indian Reservation without a key to let ourselves back inside" (*FI*, 104). Trapped in the "reservation of his mind," he always experiences himself and his culture mediated through these television images. Through this mediation he has learned to see himself as an actor in an elaborately scripted drama, "the same old story whispered on the television in every HUD house on the reservation" (*FI*, 103).

"My Heroes Have Never Been Cowboys" juxtaposes the representations of American history, particularly the "winning of the West," with the American Indian interpretation of that history: "In the reservation textbooks, we learned Indians were invented in 1492 by a crazy mixed-blood named Columbus. Immediately after class dismissal, the Indian children traded in those American stories and songs for a pair of tribal shoes" (*FI*, 102). When the children walk out on this version of America, the reader is reminded of the powerful alternative history that tribal culture represents. In "A Good Story" Alexie employs a similar image of children who, through their continued contact with the alternate stories available to them on the reservation, still have the power to dream: "these were the children who carried dreams in the back pockets of their blue jeans, pulled them out easily, traded back and forth" (*LR*, 142). Continuing these reversals of standard formulations of American culture, the narrator of "My Heroes Have Never Been Cowboys" describes the way "cowboys and Indians" is played on the reservation: "all of us little Skins fought on the same side against the cowboys in our minds" (*FI*, 102). Yet, the strength they gain from this unified front cannot change the fact that in the West that exists on the wall of televisions in the Sears Entertainment Department, the cowboys always win. While this West with its cowboys who can fire fifty bullets and never have to reload is obviously fake, it has come to be accepted as "real" by American culture:

Outside it's cold and a confused snow falls in May. I'm watching some western on TBS, colorized, but the story remains the same. Three cowboys string telegraph wire across the plains until they are confronted by the entire Sioux nation. The cowboys, 19th century geniuses, talk the Indians into touching the wire, holding it in their hands and mouths. After a dozen or so have hold of the wire, the cowboys crank the portable generator and electrocute some of the Indians with a European flame and chase the rest of them away, bareback and burned. All these years later, the message tapped across my skin remains the same. (*FI*, 103)

Because the reservation is saturated with these debilitating images, the poem ends on a despairing note, reiterating the final lines of "Vision (2)": "I have no words which can save our lives, no words approaching forgiveness, no words flashed across the screen at the reservation drive-in, no words promising either of us top billing. Extras, Arthur, we're all extras" (*FI*, 104).

Even on the reservation, it always is John Wayne or some other Anglo-American cowboy who receives top billing. Describing Wayne's omnipresence in American fantasies, Joan Didion attributes a similar experience to all American children: "when John Wayne rode through my childhood, and perhaps through yours, he determined forever the shape of certain of our dreams." In her fantasy world, Wayne represents "a place where a man could move free, could make his own code, and live by it."[12] But, for Alexie's characters, Wayne cannot be this heroic figure because the establishment of his code often means the destruction of an Indian culture. A larger-than-life figure, Wayne—and the white American paternal ideology he comes to represent—dominates the waking dreams of Alexie's characters, their relationship to his mythic status, unlike Didion's, conflicted because of their Spokane heritage. Wayne's power over their lives is so strong that in "My Heroes Have Never Been Cowboys" he even becomes God the judge, God the paternal overseer who measures human significance: "I asked my brother what he thought God looked like and he said, 'God probably looks like John Wayne'" (*FI*, 103).

Although most of Alexie's characters are too young to have watched first-run John Wayne movies, endless looping reels of Anglo cowboys defeating Indian villains are replayed at drive-ins and on TV. As these heroes subdue dark Indians hour after hour, they convey the message of Indian inferiority, which gains strength and legitimacy with time, repetition, and syndication. By encapsulating American history into two hours of cowboy-heroes defeating Indian-villains, these movies represent the American past as an ahistorical encounter between character types acting in one continuous narrative—what Alexie calls the Great American Movie starring Christopher Columbus, Cotton Mather, and Andrew Jackson—in which those who represent colonial interests become symbolically Americanized, even if, like Columbus, they lived long before the existence of the United States as a nation. Moreover, the replication of nineteenth-century battle scenes in twentieth-century western films, the refiguring of those film scripts in TV dramas, and the reruns of both that air continuously on cable television justify American Indian dispossession and imply that Indians are unworthy and incapable of correctly using the land or of representing themselves. Other films that play at the drive-in confirm their insignificance. Overtly present in westerns, American Indian characters are absent in melodramas or TV sitcoms, erased from the site of American normalcy—the single-family suburban home. Because Anglo America is perceived as the American national norm, the Indian does not even appear absent—except, of course, to American Indian spectators.

The ambivalence of the American Indian spectators at the *Star Wars* film in "Reservation Drive-In" indicates how difficult it is for the Indian members of the audience to position themselves in terms of these texts. While they often do desire the version of America that is marketed on television, they realize that to accept it would be like entering into a treaty and surrendering their right to self-determination: "Every frame of the black and white western is a treaty; every scene in this elaborate serial is a promise. But what about the reservation home movies? What about the reservation heroes?" (*FI*, 104). A similar concern about the lack of "reservation home movies" is expressed by the speaker in "Introduction to Native American Literature":

> Somewhere in America a Television explodes
>
> & here you are again (again)
> asking me to explain broken glass.
>
> You scour the reservation landfill
> through the debris of so many lives:
> old guitar, basketball on fire, pair of shoes.
> All you bring me is an empty bottle.
>
> (OSNS, 3)

While Alexie certainly does not deny the rich variety of American Indian literature, as evidenced by his inclusion of epigraphs from Joy Harjo, Linda Hogan, and Adrian Louis, he doubts the impact of this literature on the daily lives of reservation Indians. He describes a reservation saturated with Hollywood, Motown, and Nashville icons, not with characters from Erdrich, Silko, or Vizenor. When the TV detonates and only silence remains, the speaker asks if there is indeed an authentic Native American system of representation to replace the distorted TV sounds and figures.

Although Alexie recognizes the emptiness of these images, he still wants to believe in the world that cinema offers Americans. While surrounded by these movie images, he wants to pretend that the land of opportunity is his country. He reminds the reader, "There are so many illusions I still need to believe" (*OSNS*, 74). In order to maintain these illusions, he has to deny the historical relations between American Indians and white Americans. By doing so he accepts the message of Indian insignificance and the representations of Indians that have been ingrained in his consciousness, recalling these lines from "My Heroes

Have Never Been Cowboys": "All these years later, the message tapped across my skin remains the same." Like Morse code, cinema does not portray actual Indian people but only a series of codes associated with "red-skin." Thus, the message broadcast across his skin is one readable in cinematic terms of Indianness. In the American popular lexicon, the Indian has been reduced to a simple caricature of the bare-chested savage who greets the mysterious white man with the monosyllabic "How."

But not all of Alexie's characters are simply passive audience members; often they reject their implied positioning in these representations and are not completely consumed by the images on the screen. They learn to negotiate between their desire to be the image on the screen and the recognition of their implied exclusion from that image. Their ambivalent position is related to a complex process of identification. In *Black Skin, White Masks*, Frantz Fanon explains the way natives living in a colonized state react to the colonizer's culture. He describes a group of men from the Antilles at two showings of a Tarzan movie, one at home and one in Europe. Their reaction to the representation of black characters is mediated by how they are defined in the culture and situation in which they are viewing the film, as well as by the composition of the theater's audience. Fanon challenges the idea that a spectator's identification is singular, that one will simply identify with the character closest to one's own background. Thus, when the Antilleans watch a documentary about Africa at home, they laugh at the actions of the tribesmen and try to distance themselves from the representations; Fanon implies, however, that the intensity of their laughter may betray a "hint of recognition." Yet, when they watch the same documentary in France, they cannot separate themselves from the characters in the film because those seated around them equate the figures on the screen with any black person in the audience, regardless of cultural affiliation and background. According to Fanon, these spectators become "at once Antillean, Bushman, and Zulu" because they are associated with the codes of blackness as established by the film.[13]

Similarly, for white spectators at the North Cedar drive-in the American Indian audience members become at once Spokane, Sioux, and Pueblo, expected to conform to the codes of generic Indianness as established by the cinema, even if these codes are inaccurate or far removed from the particular experience of Spokane or Coeur d'Alene Indians. While Alexie and his characters are American Indians who live in the western part of the United States, they are not associated with the images of the Wild West and the Plains or Pueblo Indians. The only way the white American audience can deal with the existence of these non-Indian Indians is to translate them into the film images and erase their cultural difference.

More complicated, though, is the way the American Indian audience responds to their recognition of their own difference from the characters portrayed on the screen. The process of identification Fanon describes is precisely the dynamic at work for the Chippewa spectators in Louise Erdrich's poem "Dear John Wayne." Wayne's blue eye fills the screen, his profile looming over a bunch of Indian boys at a drive-in. Erdrich's image refers not simply to a single shot but rather indicates that the film is seen from the blue-eyed perspective. Wayne is a figure who becomes what Ella Shohat calls a "center of consciousness" because he comes to represent a set of specific Anglo-American community discourses which mediate the cinematic narrative.[14] Film can disseminate codes of American identity and culture and establish what is un-American. The blue-eyed gaze is political, intended to create and fix a narrative of unworthiness to justify Indian dispossession. When American Indian spectators in Erdrich's poem interiorize the western movie soundtrack and the implications of Wayne's "American" gaze, they learn to judge Indians and their own skin as inferior:

> How can we help but keep hearing his voice,
> The flip side of the sound-track still playing:
> *Come on, boys, we've got them*

---

*where we want them, drunk, running.*
*They will give us what we want, what we need:*
*The heart is a strange wood inside of everything*
*we see, burning, doubling, splitting out of its skin.*[15]

When the movie voice in Sherman Alexie's poem "My Heroes Have Never Been Cowboys" proclaims, "win their hearts and minds and we win the war," it recalls the voice that Erdrich's Indian moviegoers hear and internalize. Both poems indicate the pain of this splitting of the Indian self in spectatorship. Like Alexie's specific history as Coeur d'Alene/Spokane and Erdrich's as Chippewa, the teenagers' Indian heritage cannot allow them to have the same relationship to the John Wayne myth as other viewers; while the western narrative encourages them to identify with the hero, they also recognize themselves in the Indian villains. Thus when they cheer for the white heroes they are confused and angry:

> Sometimes, it is too much to ask for: survival. There are too many dangers, a fresh set of villains waiting for us in the next half-hour, and then in the next, and the next. They murder us, too, these heroes we find in the reservation drive-in. The boy, Luke Skywalker, rises up against his dark father and the Indian boys cheer, rise up and fall out of car windows, honk horns, flash headlights, all half-anger until the movie ends and leaves us with the white noise of an empty screen. (*FI*, 17)

Although Alexie's characters can reject the film's assumed spectator position and refuse to cheer for Skywalker, they will pay the price for this rejection. When the movie ends, they discover that the white noise of the empty screen is scarier than the barrage of sound and light that preceded it.

Written against this white noise, Alexie's broad caricatures of reservation figures like Lester Falls Apart and Seymour match the larger-than-life quality of omnipresent icons like Elvis or John Wayne. In his farcical narrative poem "Rediscovering America," Alexie creates a stage play in which Christopher Columbus is hit by a flying beer glass accidently hurled in his direction by an irate bartender. Columbus is rushed to the Indian health clinic, where "all the Native American employees shout in unison, 'Christopher Columbus, you've found us'" (*FI*, 95). They leave Columbus alone with Lester Falls Apart, who takes the opportunity to practice his method acting and begins to perform the codes of Indianness: "Lester opens his mouth wide and lets out a silent war cry." Lester is then transported to the Plains in 1876, where he "is dressed in full traditional wardance outfit, with the addition of mirrored sunglasses and high-top basketball shoes" (96). The audience members' reactions to this tableau differ depending on their race; the whites are terrified, while the lone Indian in the back row—wearing mirrored sunglasses—smiles. Even in this humorous jibe at the construction of American history and identity, there is a recognition that many Anglo-Americans envision Indians only as historical artifacts or humorous spectacles. At the end of the poem, when Lester appears as a stand-up comic on *The Tonight Show* hosted by Christopher Columbus, he rejects this caricature when he "kicks the microphone over, stands half in and half out of the spotlight . . . clears his throat loudly and opens his mouth to speak" (*FI*, 97). Lester and the other Spokane characters in Alexie's poems must struggle to articulate the complexities of their circumstances as they confront legal, educational, and cinematic systems that attempt to define their experience for them.

Alexie's poems indicate the difficulty of negotiating the various systems of categorization that attempt to fix and determine American Indian identity. One method of intervention is suggested in bell hooks's *Black Looks: Race and Representation*. Hooks claims that African Americans need to decolonize their minds and learn to unsee the way they have been represented in cinematic discourses. This decolonization involves not only resisting images but also creating new ways to reimagine and remake the future.[16] Unlike hooks, Alexie is unsure that this decolonization can be achieved. He recognizes that the structural elements of the representation of Indianness—the Indian as savage or child—are central to the narrative of the United States as a nation. It is not just one image but a whole structure of domination that needs to be challenged.

Through his ability to unsettle media versions of both Americans and Indians, Alexie intervenes in these debates about authenticity and identity. Referring to the federal government's "blood-quantum" measurement of American Indian heritage in "Reservation Mathematics," Alexie confronts the burden of his mixed blood:

> Mixed-up and mixed-blood
> I sometimes hate
> the white in me
> when I see their cruelty
> and I sometimes hate
> the Indian in me
> when I see their weakness

because I understand the cruelty and weakness in me. I belong to both tribes. It's my personal Wounded Knee, my own Little Big Horn. On the telephone, my friend from New York told me I drifted back into a reservation accent only when I talked about pain. How could I tell her

> that the reservation is more
> than pain?
> It's double happiness, too
> when I watch the fancydancers
> or
> the basketball players
> or
> the comic book collectors
> all dreaming

of a life larger than this one, constructed by walls everywhere. It doesn't matter if it's square, rectangle, or triangle, they all mean the same thing. They're all the direct opposite of a circle. It doesn't matter if it's a triangle, rectangle, or square. They're all the direct opposite of a circle. I've been dreaming of a life.

with a new shape, somewhere
in the in-between
between tipi and HUD house
between magic and loss.
I'm always dreaming
of a life between
the 3/16 that names me white
and the 13/16
that names me Indian.
That's what has happened to us.
Indians have learned

to love by measuring cup. I can count up all my cousins. I can count every can of commodities in the cupboard. I can count every piece of broken glass on my reservation and I still wouldn't have enough of anything, neither answers nor love. But I can stand up in front of you and recite formulas; my voice will tremble and my hands will shake. I can stand up, like Lucille said, through your destruction. I can stand up, like Lucille said, through my destruction. I can stand up, like Lucille said, through our destruction, through

every little war, every
little hurricane.
I'll take my Indian thumb
and my white fingers
on my strong right hand
and I'll take my white thumb

and my Indian fingers
on my clumsy left hand
and I'll make fists,
furious.

(*FI*, 43-44)

Alexie still struggles inside the reservation of his mind in an attempt to come to terms with this complex heritage. While at times he seems to move toward reconciliation or even what he calls "forgiveness," most often he struggles with a deepening sense of ambivalence about his position as a Spokane/Coeur d'Alene Indian in the United States of America.

In two poems with the same name, Alexie confronts the impact of "500 years of that same screaming song, translated from American" (*FI*, 103). The speaker in the poem "Translated from the American" in Alexie's second collection attempts to displace this song. He is sitting in the North Cedar drive-in replaying westerns. His presence is juxtaposed with the image of Indians grunting on the screen:

I'll wrap myself
in old blankets    wait    for white boys
climbing fences  to watch this Indian
speak

in subtitles    they'll surround me
and when they ask    "how"
I'll give them exact directions.
(*OSNS*, 35)

While he cannot translate the supposedly authentic Indian language of the film, he is a living translation of what "Indian" means in the twentieth century. Yet, this hopefulness that he can articulate his Indianness is ambiguous in his poem of the same name in *The Business of*

*Fancydancing*. This "Translated from the American" is set on the road to the reservation and focuses on a Spokane man who can speak only the English and German he learned in Catholic schools. His girlfriend talks to him in Salish, which she cannot translate effectively into English. The speaker is an outsider to the Indian world, trying to reconcile with his past and traditions. He is far removed from any sense of collective history or a shared past and travels to the All-Indian powwow specifically because of his need to reestablish these connections. The end of the poem conveys hope for the possibilities of the powwow as a communal event yet still seems ambivalent about the ability of the speaker to translate himself, recognizing that he does not have easy access to a past that has been so distorted by time and by his Euro-American education.

The title of Alexie's first collection, *The Business of Fancydancing*, confronts the problematic legacy of the powwow and describes it alternately as a mode of cultural resistance or of conformity. On the negative side, the powwow makes the Indian the object of the tourist's gaze. Menominee poet Chrystos recognizes that Hollywood Indians, bedecked in feathers and dancing at a powwow, are represented as real Indians. In "The Real Indian Leans Against," she declares her frustrated rejection of cardboard cultural reproductions:

> I want to bury these Indians dressed like cartoons of our long dead
> I want
> to live
> somewhere
> where nobody is sold.[17]

Chrystos's concern about whether the powwow is a sell-out to the commercial conception of the Indian is continued in Alexie's poem "Powwow Polaroid." The speaker describes the impact of all those black and white photographs that fixed their Indian subjects forever in mock-ceremonial poses.[18] As these tourist images were commodified,

Indians were expected to embody them. The speaker in the poem describes the effect of being shot by one tourist's camera: "the flashbulb burned, and none of us could move. I was frozen between steps, my right foot three inches off the ground, my mouth open and waiting to finish the last sound" (*OSNS*, 43).

The tourist's position at the All-Indian Powwow is similar to the Anglo audience's at a western film. According to Ella Shohat, the audience experiences Indian culture as so uncomplicated that it can be easily understood by any passerby.[19] Yet, the simplicity of the powwow has been a performance; after the tourists leave, the atmosphere changes. The rush and noise of the festival is replaced by the even breathing of Indians. The speaker in "Snapping the Fringe" describes the peace of being surrounded by Indians whose breath is a calming song: "At three in the morning, there are no locked doors on the powwow grounds. I creep among the tipis, the breathing of so many Indians like a long and slow song" (*OSNS*, 58). This breathing song counteracts the soundtracks that blare from reservation televisions. The powwow brings into being shadows of a world seemingly lost to the narrator.

Even in a poem like "Powwow Polaroid," the tourist aspect of the fancydancing event is overshadowed by an affirmation of community. The poem ends with the following lines: "My four-hundred pound aunt wept into the public address system. My uncle held his great belly in his hands, walked among the fancydancers, said this: forgiveness" (*OSNS*, 43). These lines are significant not only because they indicate reconciliation with the Anglo world, but also because they suggest a reestablishment of the tribal ties between extended family through the evocation of the Aunts and Uncles. Still, the tone of the poem is tentative and evokes Alexie's ambivalence about his troubled peace with his conflicting cultural backgrounds.

Alexie's intense desire for fancydancing to be his source of redemption is most explicit in "Vision: From the Drum's Interior," in which the powwow drumming and music are connected with the reestablishment of the community. The poem describes twentieth-century fancy-dancing:

> Who said, "I figured drums was my best defense?" Who said, "I am in the reservation of my mind?" Was it Toni and Adrian who heard drums in words? I want to fancydance back into the reservation of my mind, fancydancing toward a vision, a 20th century measure of music, music of commodity cans and six-packs, music of stickgames: forgiveness hidden in the hands of old women who need you to choose the hand holding our future tight. "Is it the left or the right hand?" Both fancydance easily at the ends of the arms which held you as hard as they ever held this drum or any other drum. It's the drum, yes, the reservation is a drum, the music beyond *Love Me Tender*, the music just before *A Love Supreme*, drums pulling you fast from your skinny bed at 3 a.m. from dreams you barely remember, dreams echoing through the reservation night air, where you stood once at the window of the largest HUD house in the world, waiting for the music of the powwow to finish before you went back to sleep, knowing drums would button your shirt, tie your shoes, open the front door and throw you back onto the road, back into the river, changing the current as you stand in the middle of a new life, new music for the 20th century fancydancer fancydancing. *Fancydancing*. (*FI*, 73)

Through this drumming Alexie has returned to the gates of the res-ervation after his arduous vision quest. Commenting on the men's movement shamans' misunderstanding of the significance of the drum in native culture, Alexie remarked, "They fail to understand that a drum is more than a heartbeat. Sometimes it is the sound of thunder, and many times it just means some Indians want to dance" (30). The drum can sometimes just be a drum, an instrument which inspires dances, not visions. Other times a drum is a versatile instrument like the one in "House(fires)" that beats "itself over the head with big sticks, a drum called drum, a drum called *trumpet*, a drum that sits in the bar and lies about how often it sounds like a heartbeat" (*FI*, 46). It is this multiple characterization of drumming that captures the ambivalence at the heart of Alexie's poetry. These repeated references to drumming suggest that it is through music—not words—that Alexie can express himself:

> Music. Then, more music. Does it matter what kind? Let's say it is bagpipes. Or a grade school orchestra practicing *Roll on, Columbia, Roll on.* Or the blues. Or just a drum that sounds like the blues. I have heard that kind of drum at three in the morning when I pull myself from bed and my ordinary nightmares. Listen. (*OSNS*, 85)

These lines from "Red Blues" explore the possibilities of crosscultural articulation, of Alexie's adaptation of the blues to express his own joy and loss. As Ralph Ellison once described it: "The blues is an impulse to keep the painful details and episodes of a brutal experience alive in one's aching consciousness, to finger its jagged grain, and to transcend it, not by the consolation of philosophy but by squeezing from it a near-tragic, near-comic lyricism."[20] It is Alexie's ability to improvise out of the crosscultural materials that he has been allotted which gives him this "near-tragic, near-comic lyricism." The twentieth-century fancydancer makes music by fingering all the discordant strings of his life; his survival is entwined with fancydancing, the stickgame, even alcoholism, government dependence, and basketball. And it is by playing this music that Alexie tries to find his way home.

## Notes

1. Don DeLillo, *Americana* (Boston: Houghton Mifflin, 1971), 119-20. Subsequent page references are given in the text.

2. His chapbook, *I Would Steal Horses*, was published in 1992 by Slipstream Publications.

3. Sherman Alexie, *The Business of Fancydancing* (New York: Hanging Loose Press, 1992); *First Indian on the Moon* (New York: Hanging Loose Press, 1993); *The Lone Ranger and Tonto Fistfight in Heaven* (New York: Atlantic Monthly Press, 1993); *Old Shirts and New Skins* (Los Angeles: American Indian Studies Center, UCLA, 1993); *Reservation Blues* (New York: Atlantic Monthly Press, 1995). Throughout the essay page references to these books are given in the text using the following abbreviations: *BF, FI, LR, OSNS*, and *RB*, respectively.

4. Reynolds Price, "One Indian Doesn't Tell Another," a review of Sherman Alexie's *The Lone Ranger and Tonto Fistfight in Heaven, New York Times Book Review*, 17 October 1993, 15-16.

5. Price, 15-16.

6. See Ward Churchill, *Indians Are Us? Culture and Genocide in Native North America* (Monroe, Me.: Common Courage Press, 1994), for a discussion of these issues in contemporary native communities.

7. Donald Hall, *Poetry: The Unsayable Said* (New York: Copper Canyon Press: 1993), 7.

8. Joy Harjo, "Anchorage," *She Had Some Horses* (New York: Thunder's Mouth Press, 1983), 15.

9. Sherman Alexie, "White Men Can't Drum," *The New York Times Magazine*, 4 October 1992, 30.

10. Alexie, "White Men Can't Drum," 24.

11. See Gerald Vizenor, *Crossbloods, Bone Courts, and Other Reports* (Minneapolis: Univ. of Minnesota Press, 1990).

12. Joan Didion, *Slouching Toward Bethlehem* (New York: Simon and Schuster, 1961), 31.

13. Frantz Fanon, *Black Skin, White Masks*, trans. Charles Lam Markmann (New York: Grove Press, 1967), 153 n. 15. E. Ann Kaplan discussed the importance of this passage in an informal lecture at the Humanities Institute, State University of New York at Stony Brook on 14 March 1993.

14. Ella Shohat, "Ethnicities-in-Relation: Toward a Multicultural Reading of American Cinema," in *Unspeakable Images*, ed. Lester Friedman (Urbana and Chicago: Univ. of Illinois Press, 1991), 217-18. See also Shohat's "Imaging Terra Incognita: The Disciplinary Gaze of Empire," *Public Culture* 3 (1991): 41-70.

15. Louise Erdrich, *Jacklight* (New York: Henry Holt, 1984), 12-13.

16. bell hooks, *Black Looks: Race and Representation* (Boston: South End Press, 1992), 5.

17. Chrystos, "The Real Indian Leans Against," *Ms.*, September 1992, 28; reprinted in *Unsettling America: An Anthology of Contemporary Multicultural Poetry*, ed. Maria Mazziotti Gillan and Jennifer Gillan (New York: Viking, 1994), 305-06.

18. Edward Curtis specialized in these images. Between 1906 and 1930 he published a twenty-volume photographic collection, *The North American Indian*, to document tribal culture in the United States before it vanished.

19. Shohat, 225.

20. Ralph Ellison, *Shadow and Act* (New York: Vintage Books, 1972), 212.

# A New Road and a Dead End in
# Sherman Alexie's *Reservation Blues*_____

Scott Andrews

With the title of his first novel, *Reservation Blues*, and the presence of Delta blues legend Robert Johnson on the first page, Sherman Alexie quickly and clearly acknowledges similarities between the social and economic conditions of African Americans and American Indians. Concurrently, he signals the possibility of a cross-cultural exchange between these two groups of Americans that offers hope for emotional and material improvements in their lives. Early in the novel, its protagonist, Thomas Builds-the-Fire, says that blues music, combined with reservation stories, could offer his troubled community a "new road," a new way of seeing old problems and defeating them. However, despite the hopeful beginnings of Thomas's efforts to "save his little country" (16), the novel cuts short the possibilities of this "new road" and the music is silenced. Rather than exploring the exciting opportunities that cross-cultural exchanges can create for individuals and communities, the novel resorts to a puzzling sense of despair and settles for survival rather than imagining success for its protagonists. The novel bitingly and comically criticizes popular culture's consumption of American Indians and the influence these pop culture creations have on American Indians who use these images to build their identities. However, while *Reservation Blues* may criticize the "Vanishing race rhetoric" that permeates much pop culture productions, as James Cox has discussed (63), it also participates in that rhetoric when it silences Thomas's band and its message of hope. Alexie's novel depicts multiple, intriguing hybridities—mixed musical styles, mixed heritages, and mixed bloods—in ways that Douglas Ford says "makes the old equation of dominance and submission unsustainable" (204), but the failure of Thomas's band suggests that dominance and submission are still in place. This essay explores the possibilities of that cross-cultural exchange and the ambiguity of its failure.

If the living conditions of African Americans in the South helped generate the blues as a musical form, then that form could seem appropriate for those American Indians living with severely limited opportunities. Long after slavery's end, African Americans continued to be exploited—limited freedoms, governmental harassment, poverty, poor or nonexistent health care, etc. In *Looking Up at Down: The Emergence of Blues Culture*, William Barlow discusses the social and economic conditions that gave birth to the blues. He writes that the blues "have always been a collective expression of the ideology and character of black people situated at the bottom of the social order in America" (xii). The blues provided "critical assessment of the working conditions, living conditions, and the treatment of African Americans by the white-controlled criminal justice system in the South [that] helped to sharpen the contradictions between the black and white social orders" (Barlow 6). The blues artists were "the oracles of their generation, contrasting the promise of freedom with the reality of their harsh living conditions" (6).

Many of the living conditions and injustices that Barlow describes easily could apply to many American Indian communities in recent years. In *The Turn to the Native*, Arnold Krupat says it is tempting to label American Indian literature as post-colonial, since it frequently asserts its differences from the "imperial center," as do many of the accepted works of post-colonial literature. But Krupat points out that "there is not a 'post-' to the colonial status of Native Americans . . . a considerable number of Native people exist in conditions of politically sustained subalternity" (30). He then cites the material effects of this condition:

> Indians experience twelve times the U.S. national rate of malnutrition, nine times the rate of alcoholism, and seven times the rate of infant mortality; as of the early 1990s, the life of reservation-based men was just over forty-four years, with reservation-based women enjoying, on average, a life-expectancy of just under forty-seven years. (30-31)

Given these conditions, the appeal of an "Indian blues artist" seems evident. Many Indians, it seems, have earned the right to sing the blues.

Blues music was born in the South from the mediation of poverty and plenitude. The black musician married his poverty and his dreams of a better life to a rich musical art form. In his book *Blues, Ideology, and Afro-American Literature: A Vernacular Theory*, Houston A. Baker Jr. says the first blues artists took as their musical inspiration the train, which promised movement—representing the freedoms of physical and social/economic movement. In the midst of his poverty, the blues singer could dream of the things the railroad seemed to promise. Baker states, "Even as they speak of paralyzing absence and ineradicable desires, their instrumental rhythms suggest change, movement, action, continuance, unlimited and unending possibility" (8). Baker's description of the blues helps explain how Thomas might see the genre as "a new road" for his community.

*Reservation Blues* tells the story of Thomas Builds-the-Fire and his band, Coyote Springs. It is made up of Thomas, who writes the songs, Victor Joseph, who plays the guitar, and Junior Polatkin, on drums. They are joined by Chess and Checkers Warm Water, who sing and play the keyboards. Thomas forms the band after he is given a guitar by Robert Johnson, one of the fathers of the Delta Blues. All accounts of his life said he had died many years ago, but it turns out he has just been on the run from "The Gentleman." He had sold his soul to the Devil for his ability to play the guitar like no other. He winds up on the reservation, looking for a place to heal up and to get rid of his guitar, which seems to be possessed. Thomas gives the guitar to Victor and sets out to "save his little country" with the music that he has heard Robert Johnson play. After some initial successes, the band is invited to audition for a record contract in New York. But during the audition, the guitar refuses to cooperate with Victor and is finally destroyed—as are the band members' hopes for fame, fortune and the rescue of the Spokane Reservation.

When Thomas writes his first song, using Johnson's magical guitar, he is inspired by a disparity similar to the one Baker cites for the first blues artists: the gap between what society promises and what the artist has. But for Thomas the symbol of this disparity is not the railroad, as that would resonate with very different meanings for Indians of the American West. Thomas' symbol for this disparity is the television—and by association popular culture in general. Not long after the band's first performance, for which they play other artists' songs, Thomas goes to sleep and dreams about "television and hunger." In his dream, he sits "hungry and lonely," watching television "to watch white people live." The television "constantly reminded Thomas of all that he never owned" (70). He writes his first song, "Reservation Blues," after staring at his empty refrigerator—"his growling stomach provided the rhythm" (47). He tries to relieve that hunger by imitating popular culture, by writing a song similar to those that he has heard growing up on the poor yet media-saturated reservation.

In mixing musical styles and forms—that is, American Indian life with African American expression—Thomas is following the lead of Big Mom, the mystical, timeless mother figure who lives atop Wellpinit Mountain on the Spokane Indian Reservation and who is "a part of every tribe" (199). Thomas puts together a band, Coyote Springs, and Big Mom becomes their musical and spiritual counselor. Teaching them how to play rock 'n' roll, she plays on her own guitar, which is "made of a 1965 Malibu and the blood of a child killed at Wounded Knee in 1890" (206). Like Thomas's blend of native sentiment and African American musical styles, Big Mom's guitar is a blending of very different elements—the pleasure of a muscle car with the pain of genocide—into an exciting and invigorating invention.

Thomas and Big Mom each are a kind of "blues detective." According to Baker, the blues detective is a "creatively improvisational hero" who employs "whatever means come to hand" to solve the problem. Baker writes: "What is crucial to the work of the blues detective is his ability to break away from traditional concepts and to supply new and creative possibilities" (135). By depicting such a potentially exciting alliance between cultures, Alexie's novel echoes sentiments of Vine Deloria Jr., who in 1976 called for "a larger variety of cultural expression." In an interview, Deloria says, "I don't see why Indians can't be poets, engineers, songwriters, whatever. I don't see why we can't depart from traditional art forms and do new things" (Warrior 93). Nearly twenty years before the publication of *Reservation Blues*, Deloria seems to wish Thomas and his new blend of musical styles into being.

A condition necessary for the birth of the blues detective is his or her poverty or existence on the margins of society. It is that poverty or that lack of access to power that creates the need for the *blues* detective's improvisational abilities. Denied the tools for success available to the rest of society, the blues detective must fashion his or her own path to success or at least to survival. This same existence at the margins requires Big Mom to improvise her tools, as it does for Thomas. Big Mom's guitar is made up of the tools at hand for the American Indian—made from the memory of military oppression, genocidal government policies, and from a material plenitude made possible in part by that conquest and the empire it created; her guitar is a memorial to a tragedy in American Indian history, but it is also a celebration of the symbol of the American Dream, of power, excess, and freedom: the muscle car. Like Big Mom, Thomas is an improvisational artist, blending the cultural forms he has inherited with those he finds—in this case, the music of Robert Johnson's guitar with the sadness and beauty of the reservation. Thomas hopes that adapting the African American blues form to an American Indian context can create a "new road" for his community to escape its poverty and hopelessness. In his effort to combine native situations and modern traditions—the Indian with the African American and the mainstream—Thomas is trying to create new answers to old problems. Like Baker's blues detective, he is investigating "new and creative possibilities."

One of Thomas's improvisations, designed to gain acceptance of these new cultural forms among his people, is his claim that American Indians invented rock 'n' roll and the blues. During a radio interview, Thomas says, "But, hey, an Indian woman invented the blues a day before Columbus landed, and rock 'n' roll the next day" (157-58). The rock and blues that Coyote Springs performs are always-already Indian, he suggests and therefore not alien to the Spokane. However, Thomas's revisionist history is just another way in which he follows in the path of Big Mom; in this case, they are both participating in "retroactive prophecy." Jarold Ramsey defines retroactive prophecy as a tribal narrative "in which an event or deed in pre-Contact times is dramatized as being prophetic of some consequence of the coming of the whites." These narratives help native people "assert the traditional continuity of their disrupted and disordered lives" (153). These stories cannot undo the calamity, but they can restore a sense of continuity, as the calamity now is not an alien invasion of the tribe's world or understanding of that world; the calamity or its potential has always been present and makes sense within the tribe's culture. Big Mom can be seen as Alexie's attempt to create a continuity between pre-Contact traditions and modern traditions: buckskin dresses meet CNN. And although there is a constant sense of loss or pain about the events she witnesses or evokes—the murder of Indian horses, the bodies of children at Wounded Knee—not everything must be calamitous. She has participated in the creation of something wonderful and life-affirming: rock 'n' roll music.

Big Mom, we learn, has counseled, healed, and taught music to the biggest names of rock 'n' roll history, regardless of their ethnicity. Robert Johnson comes to Big Mom after dreaming of her, hoping she can fix the "bad deal" he made with the Devil. Elvis, Diana Ross and Chuck Berry hide thank-you's to Big Mom in their songs (200); she helps Les Paul with the designs for the original electric guitar; and she teaches the Andrews Sisters their dance steps (201). Big Mom's role reflects the apparent contradictions that inform the entire novel—the simultaneous resistance of and participation in mainstream American culture. She serves as critique and celebration of American culture; the sort of double-bind character that fills Alexie's fiction and poetry. Except in Big Mom's case, she not only participates in that mainstream culture, she is an originator of it, teaching the icons of popular culture the hallmarks of their fame: "She was the teacher of all those great musicians who shaped the twentieth century" (201).

If we return for a moment to Baker's source for the idea of the "blues detective," we will see an interesting element not included in blues ideology. Baker drew his basic ideas of the "blues detective" from Albert Murray's book *The Hero and the Blues*, published in 1973 from a series of lectures at the University of Missouri, Columbia. Although Murray discusses the "blues idiom" throughout his lecture series, and although he discusses Louis Armstrong in particular, he also discusses at length the works of Ernest Hemingway and Thomas Mann as examples of improvisation and stylistic innovation. Drawing parallels between "high art" (Hemingway and Mann) and "folk art" (blues), Murray claims that both are equally products of conscious observations of form and tradition. The blues and other elements of African American artistic production had been praised by many for their ability to express "raw" emotion—and Murray brackets raw in ironic quotation marks. But all artists, Murray says, must capture the stuff of "real life" into stylized forms, whether those forms are music or prose. He writes:

> What makes a blues idiom musician is not the ability to express raw emotion with primitive directness, as is so often implied, but rather the mastery of elements of esthetics peculiar to U.S. Negro music. (83)

In other words, the improvisation so important to African American musical forms, such as the blues or jazz, is not necessarily a sign of poverty—primitiveness being a poverty of civilization—but of wealth. Actual poverty may supply the content, but creative wealth supplies the style. Those expressions have a richness of form, methods, and techniques that the artist must master and arrange in ways peculiar to his or her own needs. In addition, other forms outside of those traditions are available. So we find elements of gospel music influencing the blues, and vice versa, according to Murray. So, when he quotes Hemingway asserting that the modern writer "robs and steals from everything he ever wrote or read or saw," Murray is emphasizing the wealth of material available to the artist and the artist's freedom—if not his obligation—to plunder that hoard (79).

Thomas follows this dictum when he boldly and bravely appropriates Robert Johnson's music for his own purposes, to "save his little country." Alexie signals his own boldness and bravery when, in the first pages of his novel, he tells us that Robert Johnson had not died so many years ago in the South, as history books had told us, but was alive, though not well, and walking through the Spokane Indian Reservation. Alexie quickly informs his reader that his novel will defy their expectations of the American Indian novel by robbing and stealing from what he has written, read, seen or heard: pop culture, Hollywood, Motown, etc. He will not limit his selection of material or forms from only that category recognized by others as the American Indian novel.

Seeing Alexie's novel through the perspective of Baker and Murray can help us see some of the parallels between the experiences and expressions of African Americans and American Indians. However, while Baker and Murray can help us see *Reservation Blues* more fully, they also help us detect some of its emptiness. One arena from which Alexie does not borrow, rob or steal from is Spokane traditional culture. *Reservation Blues* refers to an event from local history—the killing of hundreds of ponies by the U.S. Army—but there are few markers of indigenous song or narrative styles, family structures, mythology, etc. One cultural marker, though, is the novel itself. It fits into oral tradition by being part of an Alexie story cycle—characters and events return from previous short stories and poems, though they remain in many ways independent of each other; for instance, Thomas's adventures in the short stories do not directly influence his adventures in the novel, just as Coyote's exploits and lessons in one story do not influence his efforts and knowledge in the next. However, Big Mom, despite living at the heart of the reservation, has little to mark her as specifically Spokane. Instead, she is a pan-Indian mythical figure, "a part of every tribe." She and Thomas have rich cultural forms available to them, but they are nearly all the cultural forms of American popular culture in the twentieth century—Patsy Cline, Jimi Hendrix, Disneyland, Detroit muscle cars, etc. But their improvisational methods, unlike those described by Murray, are caused by their poverty. The seeming lack of tribal cultural forms available to Big Mom and Thomas requires that they build something to replace those missing forms from the materials they have at hand. In her discussion of Alexie's poetry and short prose, Jennifer Gillan has observed a similar lack of native cultural capital, which she characterizes as an anxiety about tradition and its accessibility. She suggests that "Alexie wonders whether his people ever had access to the authenticity all America seems to associate with Indians" (91).

When Thomas tries to create a new sense of Indian identity from the cultural tools at hand—his reservation life, his Hollywood-influenced imagination, African American blues traditions—he comes close to being what Gerald Vizenor calls the "postindian": "that sensation of a new tribal presence in the very ruins of the representation of the invented Indian" (3). When he attempts a new road, he comes close to joining what Vizenor calls the postindian warriors, "who bear the simulations of their time and counter the manifest manners of domination" and who create "the new stories of survivance over dominance" (4). With an Indian identity he has cobbled together from the remnants that surround him and from the images he has received from American popular culture, Thomas is working among those "very ruins," and in working to revive his community he is attempting to counter those "manifest manners of domination"—that is, the various consequences of colonization and conquest of the Spokane in the name of Manifest

Destiny. In his discussion of American Indians and popular culture, Cox suggests a similar project for Alexie's fiction: Alexie "suggests that imagining alternatives to the dominant culture's narratives of conquest . . . is a powerful weapon" (58).

Here we can turn again usefully to Murray. He describes a dynamic, which he claims spans all cultures, in which the epic hero and his or her foe are engaged in "antagonistic cooperation." That is, the hero's obstacle forces him to grow in his abilities and strengths—through improvisation many times—until he can overcome the obstacle. In this sense, the dragon that must be slain contains the key to its own defeat by the fact that the dragon inspires the hero to defeat him. Murray says this is true for the detective-story hero as well. The hero's "knowledge of strategy and his skill with such tools and weapons as happen to be available . . . enable him to turn his misfortunes into . . . benefits. . . . He proceeds as if each setback were really a recoil action for a greater leap forward" (58). Baker, in his discussion of blues ideology in African American literature and music, sees a similar heroic optimism: Despite the poverty or suffering that surrounds the blues artist, his or her expressions are driven by an undercurrent of "unlimited and unending possibility" (8).

In *Dangerous Crossroads*, George Lipsitz describes something similar to these "new stories of survivance" and this "unlimited and unending possibility" when he discusses the cross-cultural musical exchanges made possible today through technology and the world-wide marketplace: "the rapid movement of ideas, images, and expressions across the globe have created new networks of identification and affiliation that render obsolete some traditional political practices and identities while creating complicated and complex new cultural fusions with profound political implications" (13). Through Johnson's songs and Thomas's adaptation of African American art forms to an American Indian context, *Reservation Blues* suggests just such "new networks of identification and affiliation," but none of these possibilities are realized in the novel.

Coyote Springs has an audition in New York for Cavalry Records, the modern embodiment of a foe Thomas's people have faced for more than a hundred years. But the audition ends in disaster when the guitar that Robert Johnson gave them refuses to be played. Until this point, playing the guitar had hurt Victor's hands, but the guitar had simultaneously seduced Victor. It created within him a need for the guitar, and so Victor "had mastered the pain" until "he could have placed his calloused hands into any fire and never felt the burning." But now, at the audition, the guitar acts differently: "The guitar bucked in [Victor's] hands, twisted away from his body. He felt a razor slice across his palm" (225). Finally, it breaks free from his body and falls to the floor in a "flurry of feedback" (226), and the audition ends when the record company executives storm out.

The band members are labeled losers by some on the reservation, are rejected as traitors by others for their apparent cooperation with forces off the reservation, and they are damned as sinners by those in the tribe opposed to the supposedly satanic influences of rock 'n' roll. Thomas's hopes to "save his little country" end in defeat. The band breaks up. One member kills himself. Another becomes a derelict drunk. Thomas and his backup singers depart the reservation for Spokane, where Chess has a job lined up as a telephone operator. Ultimately, Coyote Springs does not act very trickster-like, despite its namesake. It does not outfox the evil record company executives. It does not revive the reservation through mechanisms of the very forces that have driven the reservation into poverty and hopelessness. The "powerful weapon" that Cox describes turns out to be powerless. No "antagonistic cooperation" exists in the novel. There is survival, yes, as Alexie emphasizes with the novel's closing lines and throughout his poetry. But the suffering of his subjects does not bring greater strength and ultimately triumph—just, perhaps, the greater strength to survive some more, but to survive only and not to succeed.

The band's failure to revive the reservation could be an indictment, or at least a criticism, of conservative forces found on some reserva-

tions. Vine Deloria Jr. knew that these Indians existed when he conducted the interview cited earlier. When he discussed the need for new
native artistic expressions, he knew some would resist, "horrified
when they learn that an Indian is not following the rigid forms and
styles of the old days" (Warrior 94). When the Spokane Reservation
residents reject Thomas's new road, despite the lack of opportunities
provided by their "old map," they enact what Vizenor calls "the terminal creed," static beliefs that, because of their unchanging nature, ensure the eventual emotional, cultural, or literal deaths of those who
hold them. The people of Thomas's reservation expose such terminal
creeds when they reject Thomas's attempt to redefine Indian culture by
mixing in rock 'n' roll and African American musical traditions. The
traditionals are guilty of projecting their terminal creeds when they reject Thomas's music because it is not Indian enough or looks too much
like cooperation with white America; the Christians reveal their terminal creed by rejecting this new music as sinful. When Coyote Springs
departs for New York, the reservation is characterized as waiting for
the band's failure, which could be added to a reservation stew of
"failed dreams and predictable tears" (220).

Much of the novel is a criticism of the unbalanced power dynamics
between marginalized people and the mainstream distributors of their
artistic productions. However, the nature of the band's failure does not
fully realize the potential of this criticism; it is not the result of the evil
machinations of the Cavalry Records executives. Alexie offers plenty
of criticism of mainstream media representations of Indians, but he
does not make that media responsible for the failure of Coyote Springs.
In fact, one could say that the band's failure saves it from exploitation
by Cavalry Records, but this is not an easy conclusion to maintain
since the band falls apart completely once it returns to the reservation.
The band is saved from one type of doom in order to fall victim to
another bleak fate.

It is the guitar's behavior during Coyote Springs' important audition
that troubles the novel's impact. One possible explanation for the gui-

tar's contradictory behavior is the presence of horses throughout the narrative. The spirits of the horses killed by the U.S. Army function like a Greek chorus, screaming at various moments, though unheard by the characters in the novel (Thomas thinks he hears them, but only in his dreams [47]). Their screams signal to the reader a commentary on the actions of Thomas and his friends or the forces that threaten them. For instance, when the record company executives celebrate their discovery of Coyote Springs, the narrative is interrupted by a single sentence, set off as its own paragraph: "The horses screamed" (193). The executives do not hear it, but the reader is alerted to something bad happening. Likewise, the horses scream when Thomas admits that he wants to be famous for the wrong reasons, as a result of the guitar's seduction: "But I want all kinds of strangers to love me" (213). During the audition, as the band counts down the start of its first song, the horses again scream. It could be argued that the guitar's bucking is a sign that the horses are doing more than screaming, that they are instead trying to wrest the guitar away from Victor. The imagery could suggest they have inhabited the guitar, but the razor cut on Victor's hand, consistent with the guitar's behavior earlier in the novel, is unlike the horses. Furthermore, the spirit horses scream and comment on various events, but they do not influence the narrative directly; with this sole possible exception, they do not have any material, physical influence on characters or events. Perhaps Alexie does intend this scene to be a rescue; perhaps he is just guilty of inconsistency in the execution of his story. If the band members are rescued, that leaves us with the problem of the ultimate result of this intervention—they are not rescued to a better fate. They escape the evil record company executives only to fall apart back at the reservation.

The reason for the band's silencing is difficult to unpack. If Alexie intends to emphasize the uneven power of the marketplace for ethnic music, would it not be the executives who destroy Coyote Springs? The studio, after all, replaces Coyote Springs with a pair of white women who mimic New Age versions of American Indian music—

just as Johnson and his colleagues were eventually appropriated by mainstream impersonators such as Elvis Presley. If the band was intended to discover that it was about to make the same bad deal that Johnson made—that is, about to sell its soul for material, mainstream success, which the screaming horses suggests—wouldn't the band back out of the bargain with the help of someone such as Big Mom? After all, she counsels them against going to New York for the audition. Helped by her, they would learn from the encounter. But this doesn't seem to be the case. My only conclusion is that the novel itself is too conflicted about the implications of the band's potential success; the studio scene is the novel's moment of narrative crisis—the band's success seems unimaginable for Alexie. Although Thomas is trying to be a postindian warrior of survivance, the novel will not allow the transformation.

The novel continually points to the ways in which the Indian and mainstream America are inextricably mixed, but at the same time it depicts the same separatist discourse that frequently marks nationalist literature. Chess Warm Water introduces this separatist notion in the novel when she complains of Victor and Junior sleeping with white women and when she says it is best for Indians to marry Indians. In the language of national loyalty, she says that Victor and Junior are "betraying their DNA" with non-Indian lovers (82). Later, she describes the child born of such a union in fatalistic terms: "He's always going to be half Indian . . . and that will make him half crazy. Half of him will always want to tear the other half apart. It's war" (283). Such a child will always be at war with himself, she says. She can imagine no resolution, no peace. The solution, for Chess at least, is to produce fewer of these mixed-blood children. She suggests that she and Thomas get married and have many children: "Lets have lots of brown babies. . . . I want my babies to look up and see two brown faces. That's the best thing we can give them, enit? Two brown faces?" (283). It is easy to agree with the position that Chess professes; biological continuity promotes the continuity of a community and its culture. But to insist that the mixed-blood person is forever fighting an internal war is to fail those millions of American Indians (and other ethnicities) who are mixed, biologically and culturally; do they face nothing but war every day, a war without ceasing because they will never be able to restructure their divided DNA? I doubt most view their lives with such little optimism.

In his discussion of cultural hybridity in the novel, Ford usefully reminds us to be leery of letting one character speak for the novel's politics. The mixed state of other elements in the novel (the characters themselves and the products of popular culture) undercuts Chess's exclusionary position; Ford states: "With his images, Alexie draws up an American identity where any claim to authenticity must contend with a continual process of miscegenation" (202). We must keep in mind, Ford continues, that Alexie's novel simulates Baker's "blues matrix," which is "a point of ceaseless input and output, a web of intersecting, crisscrossing impulses in productive transit" (Baker 3; Ford 203). However, if we consider Coyote Springs and its music one of those points on the "web of intersecting, crisscrossing impulses," we may locate the novel's final position on hybridity, for the band's journey is not ultimately an example of the "productive transit" that Baker describes. *Reservation Blues* does not function as Murray's blues detective, turning its obstacles into opportunities, re-imagining that culture or biological mixture as a boon rather than a curse. It gestures toward such opportunities with Thomas's mix of musical styles, but it cannot or will not realize their potential.

To allow Coyote Springs genuine success would be to accept fully that mixedness and the admittedly uneven terms on which it is based— and to imagine a resolution for the anxieties and dilemmas that mixture creates. To do that would perhaps require the abandonment of those separatist, essentializing notions. How can one press for the mixed qualities (whether racially or culturally) of the contemporary American Indian and at the same time insist upon demonizing that with which he or she is mixed? The word "demonizing" comes to mind not because I wish to exaggerate any intentions or actions, but because the novel makes a significant alteration in Johnson's legend. On the night Johnson sells his soul, we are told the devil is a "handsome white man" (Alexie 264). Most versions of Johnson's legend do not racialize Satan, though one, associated with another blues artist, identifies the devil as a "big black man" (Guralnick 18). However, Alexie's Johnson strikes his bad deal with a white devil, just as Thomas and Coyote Springs strike their deal with another white devil of sorts: the representatives of Cavalry Records, gentlemen named Wright and Sheridan, who work for a yellow-haired man named Armstrong (why give this one executive Custer's middle name and not the infamous last name, as the other executives are given?). Granted, such an alteration in the Johnson legend is easy to imagine, given the long history of race relations in the United States and the uneven balance of power in creating and marketing "ethnic" artistic production. However, imagining that "white devil" as insurmountable is not ultimately productive; in such a situation, there is little chance for genuine or beneficial cultural exchange to occur.

My thoughts concerning *Reservation Blues* are similar to Stuart Christie's argument concerning another Alexie novel, *Indian Killer* (1996). Among the criticisms he makes, Christie notes that Alexie ends *Indian Killer* with the suicide of its central character, John Smith, who embodies the mixed-blood child forever at war with himself described by Chess Warm Water in *Reservation Blues*. In John Smith's case, the mixed-blood also becomes insane and homeless because of his antagonistic heritages. *Indian Killer* "thus renders paradigmatic what was the merely provisional (if equally despairing) mandate" of James Welch's *The Death of Jim Loney*, a much earlier novel that also ends with the suicide of its protagonist. In *Reservation Blues*, we have the suicide of Junior, the lost loneliness of Victor, and the death of Coyote Springs and its music. Alexie's paradigmatic despair seems to have been in place before the publication of *Indian Killer*.

Ultimately, my remarks on Alexie's otherwise exciting, funny, and entertaining novel arise from a simple concern: How can I use this novel? Does it help me or others imagine solutions to real problems? Some of my readers might say that Alexie cannot be criticized for not catering to all of my needs. That is true, but Alexie himself has suggested that usefulness to the reader is a criterion by which a literary work can be judged. In *Mixedblood Messages*, Louis Owens quotes Alexie from a 1997 Internet exchange in which Alexie complains of his frustrations with Gerald Vizenor's writings: "Well, what would a twelve year old rez kid do with Vizenor's transgressive lit?" and, more importantly for my point, "And if a work of Nat Lit is unusable by a 12 year [*sic*] Indian kid living on the rez, then what's the purpose?" (Owens 79). What is the purpose for that twelve-year-old "rez kid" of seeing a mixed-blood identity that is conceived of only as internal and terminal war? What is the purpose of evoking Coyote's power but then resorting to stereotypically self-destructive Indians who absolve America of its guilt in their symbolic disappearance?

To conclude, let me turn to Kwame Anthony Appiah, whom Krupat uses to structure some of his comments on the nature of American Indian literature as either colonial or post-colonial. Appiah says that the postnationalist novels of Africa critique the Manichean logic of Africa vs. Europe, that the nationalist novels "fail to acknowledge the full significance of the fact that Africa is '*a multiple existence*'" (155). I would like to think that the message of *Reservation Blues* is to point out the limitations of this Manichean logic (red vs. white) for American Indian literature. Appiah's description of a postnationalist novel could fit my sentiment: "If you postulate an either-or choice between [Indian] and [white], there is no place for you in the real world" (155). But the novel's apparent inability to imagine success for the mixed-blood in a world not dominated by either-or thinking makes it hard for me to rest easy with this conclusion. The novel ultimately re-enacts the colonial dynamics it otherwise exposes.

*From Arizona Quarterly* 63, no. 2 (Summer 2007): 137-152. Copyright © 2007 by *Arizona Quarterly*. Reprinted with permission of *Arizona Quarterly* and Scott Andrews.

# Works Cited

Alexie, Sherman. *Reservation Blues*. New York: Warner, 1996.

Appiah, Kwame Anthony. *In My Father's House: Africa in the Philosophy of Culture*. New York: Oxford University Press, 1992.

Baker, Houston A., Jr. *Blues, Ideology, and Afro-American Literature: A Vernacular Theory*. Chicago: University of Chicago Press, 1984.

Barlow, William. *Looking Up at Down: The Emergence of Blues Culture*. Philadelphia: Temple University Press, 1989.

Christie, Stuart. "Renaissance Man: The Tribal 'Schizophrenic' in Sherman Alexie's *Indian Killer*." *American Indian Culture and Research Journal* 25.4 (2001): 1-19.

Cox, James. "Muting White Noise: The Subversion of Popular Culture Narratives of Conquest in Sherman Alexie's Fiction." *Studies in American Indian Literatures* 9.4 (1997): 52-70.

Ford, Douglas. "Sherman Alexie's Indigenous Blues." *MELUS* 27.3 (2002): 197-215.

Gillan, Jennifer. "Reservation Home Movies: Sherman Alexie's Poetry." *American Literature* 68 (1996): 91-110.

Guralnick, Peter. *Searching for Robert Johnson: The Life and Legend of the "King of the Delta Blues Singers."* New York: Plume, 1998.

Krupat, Arnold. *The Turn to the Native: Studies in Criticism & Culture*. Lincoln: University of Nebraska Press, 1996.

Lipsitz, George. *Dangerous Crossroads: Popular Music, Postmodernism and Poetics of Place*. New York: Verso, 1994.

Murray, Albert. *The Hero and the Blues*. Columbia: University of Missouri Press, 1973.

Owens, Louis. *Mixedblood Messages: Literature, Film, Family, Place*. Norman: University of Oklahoma Press, 1998.

Ramsey, Jarold. *Reading the Fire: Essays in the Traditional Indian Literatures of the Far West*. Lincoln: University of Nebraska Press, 1983.

Vizenor, Gerald. *Manifest Manners: Narratives on Postindian Survivance*. Lincoln: University of Nebraska Press, 1999.

Warrior, Robert Allen. *Tribal Secrets: Recovering American Indian Intellectual Traditions*. Minneapolis: University of Minnesota Press, 1995.

# "The res has missed you":
## The Fragmented Reservation of the Mind in *The Business of Fancydancing*

Meredith K. James

Alexie's directorial debut *The Business of Fancydancing* was released in 2002 to mixed reviews. Some critics referred to the film's style as pretentious. What they perceived as pretentious is Alexie's critique of himself and his place in the canon of American Indian literature. Alexie even anticipates his reviews by including blurbs at the beginning of the film. There is a positive review from a fictitious New York film critic, and the review from Indianz.com calls him "full of shit." It seems that Alexie predicted correctly. Critics such as Elvis Mitchell of the *New York Times* recognized that the "visual clunkiness becomes secondary to the eloquent emotional desolation,"[1] and more importantly, film critic Hazel-Dawn Dumpert makes the distinction that "it doesn't seem quite right to call it a film" with one of the reasons being that "the whole business is strangely noncinematic. The picture is tightly constructed, with an unflaggingly lyrical pace and moving performances."[2] Dumpert's observation of the "lyrical pace" is significant because unlike Alexie's *Smoke Signals*, *The Business of Fancydancing* is not based on a work of fiction with a fairly standard narrative structure; this is a film based on Alexie's poetry. Constructing a standard narrative would be an impossible feat.

In the "film," Alexie returns to issues that he has addressed in his other works such as the manipulation of Native images and stereotypes by non-Natives. However, here Alexie uses the semi-autobiographical character Seymour Polatkin as the one who fetishizes his own definitions of "Indianness" and his own identity as a Native person. He is the one who simultaneously criticizes non-Natives' erroneous perceptions of American Indians, and exploits these perceptions to his advantage. As well, the major conflict in the film is Seymour having to resolve his place in his homeland, and see the reservation as a place of recovery, rather than seeing it as a prison.

## *You talk and white people pay attention* (Agnes): Sherman Alexie's Sandbox

The character Seymour Polatkin is semi-autobiographical in that he uses literary talent to gain success in the world outside of the Wellpinit reservation. Alexie himself has enjoyed the same success which has caused some tension between him and the Indian community. In interviews, Alexie describes himself as a bookworm, and because of his love of literature, he was largely disdained by others on the reservation. In many of Alexie's other works, the character Thomas Builds-the-Fire takes on the role as the reservation outcast, the storyteller who is not heard.

At the beginning of the story, Mouse is shooting a home video of Seymour and Aristotle's graduation from Wellpinit High School. Seymour and Aristotle discuss how they are going to St. Jerome the Second University. This is autobiographical in that Alexie went to a Jesuit school in Spokane after he graduated from high school. This scene is poignant because Mouse proclaims that he is going to work in the uranium mines. This establishes the guilt that Seymour will feel later in the film about Mouse's death and his deteriorated friendships with Aristotle and Agnes. This "Indian survivor's guilt" comes to a head later in the film when Seymour is being interrogated by an interviewer about his success off of the reservation.

"Indian survivor's guilt" is nothing new in Native American literature. Many characters who leave the reservation to pursue the "American Dream" often feel as though they have abandoned family and friends. This is not uncommon among some of Alexie's other characters such as Marie Polatkin in *Indian Killer* who finds herself caught between traditional tribal roles and academia. Even Evan Adams who plays Seymour recognizes the difficulty in negotiating success with his

---

reservation life: "I thought facing my demons (my sister's death, my own departure from the rez, my own selfishness and goal-directed life) through the movie would make me a better person, and I think I was right."[3]

In the interview with Canadian playwright Tomson Highway, Alexie acknowledges his position: "All those qualities about me that made me an ugly duckling on the reservation—ambitious, competitive and individualistic—these are not necessarily good things to be when you're part of a tribe."[4] This biographical information about Alexie also comes out in the film's first interview/interrogation scene with an unnamed literary critic. This interview scene appears to be a culmination of all the interviews that Seymour has ever had and represents the pressure Seymour feels even though he tries to thwart the interviewer's forceful questions with glib replies. Seymour's sense of humor is often lost on the unrelenting interviewer and she often accuses him of giving "standard literary answers." The interview/interrogation throughout the film seems to represent the public and private questioning of how to balance success and community survival.

### *I feel like I'm dead* (Mouse): The Dangers of Being a Fixed Reality

At two points in the film, Seymour reads his poetry to largely white audiences, who nod their heads sympathetically. Seymour is the fetishized object, but it is not that he doesn't enjoy this position through most of the film. He seeks approval from white audiences which to him equals success. This is the great conflict. Although much of Seymour's poetry criticizes mainstream American notions of "Indianness," he enjoys being the center of attention in the literary world.

Seymour's poem "The Great American Indian Novel" clearly denounces the Hollywood image of "the Indian." This poem originally appeared in Alexie's *The Summer of Black Widows*. He writes that the "great American Indian novel" must be about a half-breed from a horse culture which is the accepted Hollywood view of what Indians should look like and act like. This hearkens back to Victor's "warrior training" in *Smoke Signals*, during which Victor tries to convince Thomas that being from a "fishing tribe" was not heroic and did not reflect the image of the Indian warrior. Alexie pushes this issue further in *The Business of Fancydancing* because Seymour gives his fans what they want. Ironically, his book of poetry is titled *All My Relations*, which is the way plains people, particularly Siouan peoples, begin and end their prayers. By pandering to the stereotypical notions that he avoids in his own work, Seymour fetishizes and exploits Native peoples, particularly the people on his reservation.

The film is punctuated with scenes which at first seem awkwardly juxtaposed. At the beginning of the film, there is a scene which shows Seymour making out with a statue of a stoic Indian warrior. As well, there are scenes which are edited together which make a stark contrast between Aristotle and Mouse drinking and huffing on the reservation and Seymour's upper middle class life in Seattle with his OB/GYN male partner. These brief scenes only add to the idea that Seymour loves what the Indian statue represents, frozen ideals of "Indianness." In the coffee house scene, Aristotle tells Seymour that he is leaving the university and asks Seymour to go back to the reservation with him. Seymour tells him no and Aristotle accuses him of enjoying "playing Indian":

> You like it out here, don't you? Playing Indian, putting on your feather and beads for the white folks? Out here, you're the Public Relations warrior, you're Super Indian, you're the expert and authority. But back home, man, you're just that tiny little Indian who cries too easy.[5]

Simultaneously, Seymour profits from ideals and images that hold Aristotle and Mouse hostage, frozen and unable to break free from the romantic and damaging notions of "Indianness." There is a quick scene of Mouse's home videos that shows people on the reservation playing freeze tag. In a poignant moment, Mouse "un-freezes" one of the children, symbolically freeing her from a static existence, even if only momentarily.

In order to gain control over the stories Seymour tells about the Wellpinit Reservation, Aristotle and Mouse make fun of his book and accuse Seymour of telling lies and using their stories in order to be famous and successful. Mouse says, "I feel like I'm dead." Instead of Seymour immortalizing Aristotle and Mouse, he has taken their stories and made them his own rather than allowing them to exist in the stories or to tell their own stories. They feel captured in words. Seymour makes excuses throughout the film that his memories are blended with Aristotle's in hopes of convincing himself that he has not stolen stories. Even though Aristotle makes fun of Seymour's work, he burns Seymour's book while repeating "Forgive him." Aristotle understands that Seymour does not realize what he has done.

In a confrontation with Seymour at Mouse's wake, Aristotle makes Seymour understand that without the Indian community, Seymour would have no stories and no art. At the end, it seems Seymour realizes that the stories are owned by the community not by the individual.

As well, Seymour projects his romanticism of Indians on Agnes when he finds out that she has been seeing Aristotle. He accuses her of seeing Aristotle as the "dreamy warrior boy around these parts."[6] However, he must come to terms with his own issues of exploitation. His justifications are rendered useless when he is again confronted by the interviewer/interrogator. She asks him about the despair of reservation life and how he overcame the horrible odds against an Indian man: "The average life span of a reservation Indian man is 49 years. The number one cause of death for reservation Indian men is suicide. And nearly 60% of reservation Indian men are alcoholics."[7] She implies the close connection between reservations and concentration camps as she cites Primo Levi about the Nazi death camps: "the best people did not survive. You must remember, he wrote, that it was the liars, cheaters, and thieves who survived."[8] In the film, though not in the published screenplay, Seymour replies that he is a whore. Seymour, again, justifies his actions by saying it is all right that he has essentially sold himself. He argues that it is his right to exploit himself, yet he doesn't consider that by exploiting himself and being part of a tribal community, he is by extension exploiting his people.[9]

## *You can always come back* (Agnes)

At the end of the film, after Seymour returns to the reservation to attend Mouse's wake, he and Agnes rekindle their friendship as they talk about the important role of the reservation in their lives. At first they imagine themselves as small commodities. In the screenplay, they imagine they are small, concentrated Indians and they decide if they ever need money they can hang off of rear view mirrors. In the film, they decide to be "Indian" products, a dreamcatcher and a burden basket. They laugh about the exploitation of "Indianness," but there is a truth to what they are saying. Seymour has had to come back to reconcile his profitable career as an Indian writer and his "reservation of the mind." He must realize the absurdity of commodifying his identity and realize that material ambition without a sense of home will lead to his destruction and the destruction of his people.

Agnes is pivotal in helping Seymour recover his place on the reservation. He calls the reservation a prison while Agnes points out that "it's your ambition that made the rez a prison."[10] As cited earlier in the interview with Tomson Highway, Alexie expresses the difficulty of being individualistic and ambitious while also being part of a tribal community. Agnes states the answer to Seymour's problem simply: "You can always come back." As well, during the wake, Agnes tells the others that Seymour has always stayed in touch through his poetry. Agnes holds the pieces together for the people on the reservation who resent Seymour and for Seymour who has grown to resent the reservation. Evan Adams recognizes that Agnes is the main character in this film: "I think this movie belongs to St. John's 'Agnes.' . . . I am proud to have been her foil, and reflect the integrity of an honest Indian woman. I guess I feel like I came in 'Miss Runner-up' this time around."[11] It is Seymour's conflict that needs resolution, yet Agnes is the only one who can help.


## How I built landscapes and imaginary saviors: Alexie as Filmmaker

In the behind-the-scenes feature of the DVD, Alexie concedes that there were definite time constraints on the editing of the film so that it would be ready in time for the Sundance Film Festival. He said he would like to go back and re-edit the film including many of the un-used scenes. However, I don't think it would change the film's poetic nature and I don't think things would be wrapped up in a nice package. There is no definite resolution; as the audience, we can only hope that Seymour will not stay away from the reservation, physically or emotionally. But Alexie isn't so interested in a neat resolution. As he writes in his essay "What I've Learned as a Filmmaker," "Fuck resolutions, fuck closure, fuck the idea of story arc."[12] Based on his theory of filmmaking, it is no wonder that Alexie in *The Business of Fancy-dancing* has created a postmodern pastiche of Indian identity.

### Notes

1. Elvis Mitchell, "A Poet Finds His Past Is Just Where He Left It," *New York Times*, 18 Oct. 2002: 25.

2. Hazel-Dawn Dumpert, "Stranded and Swept Aside: The Business of Fancydancing and the Pain of Letting Go" (*LA Weekly* October 25-31, 2002).

3. Sherman Alexie, *The Business of Fancydancing, The Screenplay* (New York: Hanging Loose, 2003), 121.

4. "Spokane Words: Tomson Highway Raps with Sherman Alexie," *Aboriginal Voices* Jan-March 1997. www.fallsapart.com.

5. Alexie, *The Business of Fancydancing, The Screenplay*, 52.

6. Alexie, *The Business of Fancydancing, The Screenplay*, 46.

7. Alexie, *The Business of Fancydancing, The Screenplay*, 21.

8. Alexie, *The Business of Fancydancing, The Screenplay*, 21.

9. Sherman Alexie, director, *The Business of Fancydancing*. Outrider Pictures, 2002.

10. Alexie, *The Business of Fancydancing, The Screenplay*, 73.

11. Alexie, *The Business of Fancydancing, The Screenplay*, 121.

12. Alexie, *The Business of Fancydancing, The Screenplay*, 7.

# A Bridge of Difference:
## Sherman Alexie and the
## Politics of Mourning_____

Laura Arnold Leibman

In Sherman Alexie's fourth poetry collection, *The Summer of Black Widows* (1996), the "abandoned uranium mine" on the Spokane reservation has created a modern Valley of the Shadow of Death,

. . . where the night
sky glows in a way that would have invoked songs and stories a few generations earlier, but now simply allows us to see better as we drive down the highway toward a different kind of moon.[1]

Having lost the ability to respond with "songs and stories" is almost as dire as the threat of poisoning and death. In American Indian oral tradition, storytellers are often represented as spiders. The volume's second poem recalls that spiders "appeared suddenly/ after that summer rainstorm," causing a controversy over who and what they were.[2] Some saw them as pests or threats and tried to poison them, but "[t]he elders knew the spiders/ carried stories in their stomachs" ("SBW," 12). Although the spiders eventually disappear, the people continue to find their small, white egg bundles up in the corners of their old houses, and "nothing, neither fire/ nor water, neither rock nor wind,/ [can] bring them down" ("SBW," 13). The spiders and the "bundles of stories" they "left behind" embody the power of oral tradition ("SBW," 13). They cannot be destroyed. The Spokane must learn not to resist the spiders but to use them and the power they contain.

Alexie presents the poet as a descendant of the spiders, a modern spinner. In the volume's first poem, the poet asks his beloved for "permission/ to weave a story/ from your hair" that will keep them "warm and safe."[3] But if stories are the offspring of black widows, then spiders are both creators and agents of death. The poet's ability to create or destroy perpetuates and recreates the world through song but also potentially offers death. The poems in *The Summer of Black Widows* serve as witness to the power of stories and show the Spokane community how to heal in the face of danger and tragedy.

To combat death, poetry—and the poet—must contain death's power. This potential helps explain the presence of both non-Indians and white poetics in Alexie's poetry. In spite of the history of American genocide, which has left the Spokane in mourning for their past as well as their future, Alexie uses what I call a bridge of difference to join diverse readers as allies in the cause of Spokane renewal. This bridge of difference and the community of mourning and renewal it enables represent an important shift in the politics of performance and in the use of formalism in Native American poetry.

## A Bridge of Difference

Conventional elegies create a dialogue between or within "solo plaints" and a chorus of mourners.[4] As these voices come together through an emotional bond of loss and concern, the elegy (re)forms them into a community. This is possible because, as Mark Strand has noted, "death constitutes a cultural event" but also because elegies serve to mediate the division between the personal and the public.[5] The conventional elegy moves the reader and the speaker through the mourning process to achieve consolation. But as Alexie asks in the opening poem for his third collection, *Old Shirts & New Skins* (1993), what happens when the speaker and reader are not from the same community? What if some of the readers are from the community responsible for the poet's loss? What then is the role of the reader's grief? "Often, you ask forgiveness," Alexie observes, but Native American literature will only give you a "10% discount."[6] It does not absolve all readers of their guilt in order to create a community of mourners capable of healing; indeed, such absolution might be at odds with the renewal of the Spokane that motivates Alexie's work.

Alexie's concerns about the politics of caring reflect a long-standing debate about American Indian cultural property rights. Activists and artists have defined cultural property as "both real Property, the land, the burials, the 'ruins,' etc., and intellectual property, the writings, the languages, the images, the culture itself."[7] Many American Indian writers have expressed concern about who should have access to their cultural property and how these materials should be approached.[8] Alexie's concern about the proper way to mourn is based on the notion that not only the literature he is writing but also the loss he is undergoing are part of American Indian cultural property, yet his poetry also reflects a change in the political climate. In the past some American Indian writers have insisted upon excluding all non-Indians from Indian renewal ceremonies, but Alexie encourages a wide range of readers to engage his work.

While writers such as Gary Snyder have argued that poetry provides a way to "cross barriers" because "[a]ll poetry is 'our' poetry" and therefore provides a common bridge between people, many Native writers have doubted the existence of such a bridge, either in the physical world or the imaginative realm of poetry.[9] While Alexie does not want non-Indians to mistake their emotions for those of Native Americans, he does allow for the possibility of a bridge; it must begin, however, with an acknowledgement of difference, not its erasure.

The poem "Introduction to Native American Literature" offers Alexie's most explicit explanation of this new bridge and its community of readers through an inventive use of the second-person "you." The poem's epigraph is a quotation from Alex Kuo, a Chinese American poet and novelist who lives and teaches near the Spokane reservation:

> *Isn't it enough that I give you my life*
> *to mess around with that I must give you*
> *the last words to the story too?*

> ("I," 3)

In Alexie's poem as well as its epigraph, antagonism defines the relationship between speaker and reader, with the reader characterized as greedily desiring what rightfully belongs to the speaker.[10] While second-person pronouns are often used in poems to bring the reader closer, here the accusations draw a line between the speaker and a directly addressed, non-ideal reader. The complaint against this "you" concerns unequal work: the writer must give more than his share while the reader merely takes. While the speaker has a life that interests the reader, who would like to "mess around" with it, it is the responsibility of the artist to prevent this casual appropriation. The speaker's refusal to provide "the last words to the story" indicate not so much a postmodern stance as a redefinition of the role of the Native American artist. In releasing the author from an obligation for closure, Alexie also requires that the ideal reader of Native American literature be a writerly reader, one who helps enact closure for the grief and loss the poems describe.

In the lines that follow, we learn that readers cannot take an empathetic role in the poem because they cannot—and should not try to—identify with the speaker. The relationship between the speaker and reader is based on distance and the reader's lack of knowledge about the speaker's life:

> Because you have seen the color of my bare skin
> does not mean you have memorized the shape of my ribcage.
>
> Because you have seen the spine of the mountain
> does not mean you made the climb.
>
> ("I," 4)

Just as seeing a mountain is not the same as climbing it, so reading about American Indians—visualizing them, describing them, imagining them—is not the same as understanding them. Alexie underscores the reader's role in the final stanza of the poem: "It [Native American

Literature] will read you the menu./ It will not pay your half of the bill" ("I," 5). In Alexie's ideal community, both the poet and the readers take part in the creation of the poem and in the renewal it will enact.

This relationship is crucial for understanding Alexie's innovative use of the elegy, a form that predominates in *The Summer of Black Widows*. Borrowing from oral tradition, elegiac conventions, and formal poetic structures, Alexie creates a performative poetry in which words enact deeds. Because this performance requires the work of both the writer and reader, Alexie's elegies, like "Introduction to Native American Literature," renounce readers who refuse to "pay their way." These elegies, however, take Alexie's poetics one step further. While they offer critiques of non-ideal readers and writers, they also provide models for how one can write and read Native American literature productively. All the poems in *The Summer of Black Widows* also ponder the responsibility of the poet to heal the community through storytelling as well as the new role of readers in that healing process.

## Weaving Consolation

Alexie's responsibility to the subject of his art and his fears about the dangerous power of the spoken word are paramount in the third sequence of poems in *The Summer of Black Widows*. As the speaker mourns his sister after her death in a house fire, he struggles not only with the relationship between sister and brother but also between fire and smoke—death and its signs. In this sequence, the danger of the spoken word comes partly from white people, who once destroyed the Spokane through cavalry raids and alcohol but who more recently built the uranium mines and taught the Spokane to say "cancer" as often as they say "oxygen" and "love."[11] Given the association of white people with destruction, it is not surprising that the speaker weaves into his mourning a fear about who will read the poems and how they will read them, as well as a concern about his own relationship to white society. Yet in large part the danger arises from poetry and the poet himself.

Like the spiders, the poet must reclaim death and its power as part of his domain, hence the presence of white poetics in the sequence. Here the problem of the non-Indian reader in "Introduction to Native American Literature" is expanded to address the problematic relationship of white culture to healing. For the oral tradition to combat the white world and the death Alexie's people face within it, poetry must include the strategies of the white world it fights—including its poetic forms.[12] Thus, as the poems become increasingly formal—moving from a prose poem ("Elegies") to multiform stanzas ("Fire as Verb and Noun") to a prose sonnet ("Sonnet: Tattoo Tears") to a villanelle ("Sister Fire, Brother Smoke")—the artist's strength increases.

The speaker's troubled relationship to death is the main subject of the sequence. Unlike the poet in "Elegies," who camps near an exploding volcano despite repeated warnings by experts, the speaker of this sequence must reject his fascination with death and embrace the poet's power to heal. Reclaiming death as part of his power, he must learn to reject the vision of the artist as "near death" even as he acknowledges his own power to destroy.

The sequence begins with "Elegies," a lament for those who succumb to death and its seductive lure. Organized as a list of people seeking and meeting death, the poem is written "for people who died in stupid ways" ("E," 49), from wealthy white people who risk their lives in search of cheap thrills to Alexie's own people, who ignore their enemies and hence are devoured by them. As the list lengthens, it becomes not only increasingly inclusive but also capable of maintaining oppositions:

> This is a poem for the cooks who prepared those enormous meals
>      and feel no guilt.
> This is a poem for the cooks who prepared those enormous meals
>      and feel guilty.
> . . . . . . . . . . . . . . . . . . . . . .
> This is a poem for people who jump off the Golden Gate Bridge
>      and change their minds halfway down.

> This is a poem for everybody who jumps off the Golden Gate
>> Bridge because they all change their minds halfway down. I have
>> faith that nobody wants to die for any time period longer than the
>> few seconds it actually takes to commit suicide.
>
> ("E," 50)

In a strategy he may have borrowed from Walt Whitman, Alexie uses the repetition of the opening phrase "this is a poem" to unite disparate and contradictory elements. A number of the poems in *Black Widows* involve the character of Walt Whitman or are written in a long-line style that might be seen as influenced by Whitman's poetry. Robin Fast has offered a persuasive analysis of dialogism in one of Alexie's other poems in the volume, "Defending Walt Whitman."[13] Although Fast is right to locate the use of repetition and parallelism in the poem as part of the inheritance of oral tradition, clearly another source for this poetics is Whitman's own verse, especially the parallelism and lists that link disparate elements into an all-encompassing democratic unity.[14] Whitman's brand of political poetics may be one possible source for the bridge of difference I am discussing in Alexie's work, but Alexie goes beyond Whitman's egocentric form of democracy, embedding a recognition of the poet's fallibility and limitations. In the Golden Gate Bridge pairings, for example, Alexie leaves room to correct his vision. This tendency toward complication and revision intensifies when the speaker turns to himself: "This is a poem for me. No. This is a poem for the me I used to be" ("E," 50). In the poem's psychological study of the lure of death, it moves from Napoleon's great-grandson and people of far-removed headlines to the poet himself, his family, and his tribe. In the beginning, the deaths are clearly absurd: Napoleon's great-grandson "snapped his neck when his ridiculously long scarf caught in the rear wheels of the convertible he was driving" ("E," 49). Alexie adds symbolic weight to this death by juxtaposing it immediately with the "stupid" death of General Custer. The poem is decidedly brief about this new would-be conqueror: "This is a poem for General George Armstrong Custer." Here the parallel structure asks the reader to do the work: how is Custer—the man who fought the Plains Indians and lost—like Napoleon's great-grandson? The linking of Custer to men who die in the pursuit of luxury and excess points to the ludicrousness of the Indian wars and to the futility of the loss and genocide they spawned.

The historical scale of the first section of the poem gently eases into a more personal reading of the lure of death for Spokane Indians such as the poet himself. According to the poem, the problem for many of the Spokane is not that death is inescapable but that they do not desire to escape it. As the poem continues, it resists seeing the speaker as distant from death's lure but instead implicates the artist along with the other death seekers. Here Alexie acknowledges that artists have often courted death and glorified those who live on the edge; while the poem leans toward a celebration of this perspective, ultimately it rejects it. We are told that the poem is "for the me I used to be"—the man who sought death by driving when drunk ("E," 50). Perilous road trips are a common motif in American Indian poetry, which is often crowded with images of broken-down vehicles and car accidents, symbolizing the antagonism between the American Indians' journey and the damaging influx of white culture and technology.[15] The poet in "Elegies," however, moves beyond the lure of death and the white technology that helps him pursue it by allowing his former self to embrace death and thus break free of it. In a blazing car wreck, he kills off "the me who kept driving" ("E," 51). In a sense, the poet's former self has become the non-ideal reader—the implicit "you" who is rejected and against whom the ideal community is defined. It is only after dissociation from the former self that the poet can move on to lament the way his family members court death—his brother, sister, father, and finally his tribe.

The death of the poet's former self allows the consolation to begin. For the elegist, death's lure presents a special problem. Narcissism and melancholia are constant dangers, because in the midst of this fixation on death, the poet can identify with the dead and thereby undermine his power to defeat death. This attachment to death leads to what Peter Sacks calls in his discussion of English elegies "regressive narcissism . . . an identification between the ego and the dead such that the melancholic tends toward self-destruction."[16] For the elegist to succeed, he must replace the dead with art; his own destruction would be counterproductive. By killing off the death-loving self, the true poet escapes both narcissism and melancholia. Although the end of Alexie's poem accomplishes this goal for the speaker, it raises a larger problem: the people of his tribe are not ready to end their own pursuit of death. How, then, can a community of healing be created? Moreover, since they have forgotten to turn to songs and stories, there is less hope that the poet's writings will be able to help. The poem then reiterates the tripartite problem the speaker faces: he must reject melancholia; he must build a community of healers by teaching his tribe to reject melancholia, offering song in its place; and he must come to terms with the dual power of song to heal and kill.

In the second poem of the sequence, "Fire as Verb and Noun," the poet attempts to build a community by overcoming the Spokane's melancholia and fixation on death through an emphasis on the power of language. A lack of faith in this power is what the Spokane have learned from white culture, it seems, given the epigraphs for the poem, a review from *Publishers Weekly* and a quotation responding to it from a "Donna Brook":

*Working from a carefully developed understanding of his place in an oppressed culture, [Alexie] focuses on the need to tear down obstacles before nature tears them down. Fire is therefore a central metaphor: a sister and brother-in-law killed, a burnt hand, cars aflame.*

—*Publishers Weekly*

*Sherman, I'm so sorry your sister was killed by a metaphor.*

—Donna Brook[17]

The problem the poet faces here is not unlike the one he faces with his tribe. For the writer of the review, words are just words; they are not alive and have no real power. The idea that fire is mere metaphor goes against the central premise of the book: stories are the offspring of black widows—real, alive, creative, and dangerous. Donna Brook's statement points to the ludicrousness of a reading that denies this power. One should not mistake art for artifice. Language, like fire, has the ability to destroy. The excerpts from *Publishers Weekly* force the poet to face another problem: *has* the metaphor killed his sister? In order to mourn successfully, the elegist must replace the beloved—here, the sister—with language. In this sense, the metaphor kills the memory of the sister as it replaces her. A central question Alexie faces throughout the sequence, then, is how the artist can weave stories to cure and shelter rather than kill or maim.

In the fourth and final poem, "Sister Fire, Brother Smoke," Alexie grapples not only with survivor's guilt but also with writer's guilt as the poem circles around the question of whether the creative process has distorted his sister's death. As the climactic poem of the sequence, it is also the most formal; as a villanelle, it brings a sort of uneasy resolution to the earlier problems raised by language's ability to create and destroy. Part of this resolution is provided in the structure itself, which pursues a traditional poetic form of insistent regularity, with few deviations. Twentieth-century poets who turned to the villanelle— W. H. Auden, Dylan Thomas, Sylvia Plath, Elizabeth Bishop, Anne Sexton—used it to explore the possibility of solace in a time of loss. Alexie invokes not only the villanelle's historical associations with loss but also its ability to heal the poet's present obsessiveness.[18]

The villanelle's ability to maneuver through and respond to loss makes it the perfect form for Alexie's purposes here, helping also to explain the villanelle's considerable presence in his oeuvre. Kenneth Burke has argued that all "[f]orm in literature is an arousing and fulfillment of desires. A work has form insofar as one part of it leads a reader to anticipate another part, to be gratified by the sequence."[19] The emotion aroused by the villanelle's structure is clearly obsession: the heavily repeated lines and rhymes circle around each other, never fully letting go of the problem plaguing the speaker. Ezra Pound has perhaps best characterized the villanelle's form in his prescription for fulfilling its potential: "The villanelle . . . can at its best achieve the closest intensity. . . . [T]he refrains are an emotional fact, which the intellect, in the various gyrations of the poem, tries in vain and in vain to escape."[20] For the modern elegist, the villanelle's emotional fact is death, and the intellectual "gyrations" are the poet's attempts to grapple with it.

For Alexie, the poem "gyrates" around two central concerns surrounding a sister's loss and a brother's writings about it:

> Have I become an accomplished liar
> if I see my sister in every fire?[21]

These two ideas, which originally seem to be one inseparable question—like the speaker and the sister he has lost—are pulled apart and examined individually in each stanza. Indeed, it is the nature of the villanelle that throughout the course of the poem the two initially connected issues raised in the two repeated lines are separated and explored in isolation. Alexie's concern over the loss that occurs when reality is fictionalized into art is an essential part of the elegiac process. As Walter Benjamin has suggested, the poet is plagued by "a conviction of guilt, or of being irredeemably fallen, [which] partly determine[s] the melancholy fear that language could be no more than a fabric of opaque and unfulfillable signs."[22] This survivor's guilt is translated into writer's guilt and becomes the main problem the poet faces.

But does the poem provide a model for escaping this obsession and loss? While Pound sees such escape as "in vain," the villanelle's form provides a potential relief from the poem's earlier "gyrations" through the unique final stanza. Whereas stanzas two through five separate and explore each of the two repeated lines in isolation, in the final stanza the two lines are reunited, having obtained new meaning through their separate forays. The relief of the reunion is reinforced by the change in the final stanza from the pattern of three lines to four. This change emphasizes the poem's closure and provides an end to the circling that occurs in the previous stanzas. In this sense, the form provides a model for dealing with loss. While contemporary poets such as Bishop and Sexton have undercut the resolution of loss by changing the structure of the final stanza, this undercutting is only possible because the educated reader of the villanelle expects closure. When the form is complete, such as in Thomas's "Do Not Go Gentle into That Good Night," the intensity of the emotion aroused by the repetition gives the poem a "ritualistic" and "incantatory" feel that is brought to a successful climax in the final stanza.[23]

The ritualistic aspect of the villanelle helps to make sense of Alexie's use of a European form to deal with deaths of Native Americans at the hands of European descendants.[24] The poet's fear that he has become "an accomplished liar" seems partially a result of his expertise, on display here, in Western poetic forms. Yet Alexie's use of the villanelle could also reflect a standard strategy in Native American poetics. Anthropologist and linguist Dell Hymes has pointed out that like Western poetry, Native American poetry tends to be

> organized in terms of lines, verses, and stanzas. The grouping of lines into verses, and of verses into stanzas, tends to follow, but not exclusively, the pattern numbers of the culture. . . . Verses appear always to be grouped in terms of a covert pattern of rhetorical cohesion. Such a pattern appears to be congruent with the pattern numbers of the culture, depending upon pairs and sets of pairs in cultures in which the pattern number is four, and upon threes and fives in cultures in which the pattern number is five.[25]

Since these pattern numbers play a significant role in the cosmology of Pacific Northwest tribes, the repetition of sounds or whole lines in Native American poetry has a religious significance and hence a performative power to bring about change. The villanelle mirrors these pattern numbers. Based on the number-pair of three and five, the form is composed of five three-line stanzas, with a concluding four-line stanza, for a total of six stanzas.[26] Hymes theorizes that just as in Western poetry, variation in Native American poetry is seen as highlighting the intensity of the utterance;[27] hence, the variation of the number of lines per stanza at the end of Alexie's poem would add to the gratification provided by the final stanza. The parallels between the poetic strategies of villanelles and of traditional Native American poetics may suggest the appeal of this repetitive form for Alexie.[28]

The intensity of the final stanza underscores the poem's paradox as it circles around both the desire for resolution and the persistence of questions. The entire sequence lacks resolution because it seeks to bring about engagement, not closure. (It is not the job of the poet to "provide the last words.")[29] The poem "Sister Fire, Brother Smoke" becomes like a ritualistic offering, albeit one fraught with tensions as the poet asks:

> Is she the whisper of ash floating high
> above me? I offer these charred questions.
> Have I become an accomplished liar
> if I see my sister in every fire?[30]

Having rejected the lure of death for himself and for the artist, the speaker mulls over the power he has gained. Here the resolution offered by the form pulls against the unanswered questions. The poet works through his own guilt at not being there when his sister died and then insists upon reliving her death now that he cannot stop it. In the third poem of the sequence, Alexie tells us: "[I]magination is the only weapon on the reservation."[31] It is the job of the poet to learn how to use this weapon without harming himself or the one he seeks to protect. The weapon Alexie wields is further explored in the final sequence of poems in the book, when the poems' speaker returns to the issues of responsibility, survivor's guilt, and genocide. Here Alexie refines his vision of the role of the artist and the role of the reader in the mourning process.


## Genocide and the Politics of Identification

In the seven-part poem "Inside Dachau," a Native American visitor to a Nazi concentration camp beholds the evidence of genocide and answers for what he sees, becoming a reader of the museum at Dachau.[32] At the site of cultural memory, this visitor, as spectator and witness, illustrates how to be empathetic but not parasitic in confronting tragedy. The seven parts of this poem also seek to heal the Spokane poet and his people through a performative act of poetry in which an engagement with healing occurs not through an erasure of ethnic boundaries but through a bridge of difference.

In the poem's first section, "1. *big lies, small lies*," we learn that this visitor to Dachau is neither part of the community being mourned nor a tourist or consumer of the tragedy. And whereas most visitors choose to see the camps during the spring and summer, it is now winter:

> Only a dozen visitors walked through the camp
> because we were months away from tourist season.
> The camp was austere. The museum was simple.[33]

In spring, the camp would offer a sense of renewal, the season implicitly belying the deaths that occurred with its suggestion of the inevitability of consolation and the promise of regeneration.[34] By visiting the camps during winter, and in fact by emphasizing the persistence of winter throughout the poem, the speaker refuses this easy source of consolation.

Distinguishing himself from a tourist, the speaker also lets go of his desire to identify with another kind of traditional sojourner in the camp—the Jewish inmates during World War II. As a poet, he had originally intended to deceive his readers, to

> . . . write poetry about how the season
> of winter found a perfect home in cold Dachau.
> I would be a Jewish man who died in the camp.
> I would be the ideal metaphor.

> ("ID," 117)

But the poet quickly realizes that his desire for identification is misguided. There is a gap between his reality and that of the inmates that cannot be bridged by metaphor or art. He had

> . . . thought it would all be simple
> but there were no easy answers inside the camp.
> The poems still took their forms, but my earlier plans
> seemed so selfish. What could I say about Dachau
> when I had never suffered through any season

> inside its walls? . . .

> ("ID," 117)

Art and emotion cannot replace experience. Although the speaker and his people have also suffered genocide, he has neither the knowledge nor the right to imagine himself as the camp's victim. The tragedy must remain individual, not universal. It is possible, however, to devise a poetry that is less "selfish" in dealing with other people's suffering, to create a poetry that does not erase difference.

Alexie's choice of a sestina for the poem's first section reveals the speaker's anxiety. Like the villanelle, a sestina is highly repetitive and traditionally considered one of the most difficult Western poetic forms to master. Built on multiples of three, its six six-line stanzas and final envoi of three lines circle obsessively around the same six end-words, like "a thin sheet of flame, folding and infolding upon itself," as Ezra Pound elegantly puts it.[35] While the envoi provides enough change to signify closure, it does not provide a respite from repetition; it intensifies its pacing by condensing the end-words into three lines rather than their usual six. The sestina, then, arouses anxiety without consolation. For the first six stanzas, as William Empson has explained, "[t]his form has no direction or momentum; it beats, however rich its orchestration, with a wailing and immovable monotony, for ever upon the same doors in vain." The final stanza does not alleviate but intensifies the wound that drives this "wailing."[36]

The poet's German hosts remind him that there were death camps in the United States too and that they have become perhaps even more insidious than Dachau because they remain unacknowledged, "ignored, season after season" ("ID," 118). Like the sestina, the memory remains caged, pacing back and forth in its close quarters. Such enfolding (in poetry or life) leads to hopelessness:

> Inside Dachau, you might believe winter will never end. You might
> lose faith in the change of seasons
> because some of the men who built the camps still live in Argentina,
> in Washington, in Munich.
> They live simple lives. They share bread with sons and daughters
> who have come to understand the master plan.
>
> ("ID," 118)

Throughout the rest of the first section, and indeed throughout the poem, Alexie encourages us to believe that winter will never end and that the regeneration we associate with the change of seasons will never reappear, but he suggests at the same time that this is not the only possible solution. Resolution and consolation require involvement in the healing process by a community larger than the immediate victims. Spectators outside this community must be re-formed into agents of mourning. For genocide to end, the men who built the Nazi death camps but still live in "Argentina, Washington, and Munich" must not be allowed to "share bread with [their] sons and daughters"—that is, they must not pass along their ideology. As Robert Pinsky suggests, the poetry of witness "may or may not involve advocacy, and the line between the two is rarely sharp; but the strange truth about witness is that . . . it involves the challenge of not flinching from the evidence."[37] The sestina's obsessive repetition and circling refuses to allow the reader to flinch or turn away. Just as the sestina cannot be resolved without a respite from the repetition, ideologies of genocide that are passed along routinely like bread bring the promise that death, not rebirth, will reappear.

The next three sections of the poem use the idea of memory to confront denial and its alternatives. All three sections play with repetitive poetic forms, thus continuing the pacing and circling in the first section.[38] In "2. *history as home movie*," Alexie argues against forgetting. The first step is to accept one's involvement in the crisis. Like the Germans who turned away from what happened in the camps, or the Americans who continue to deny American Indian genocide, the reader is accused of trying to disavow a relationship to the past, of trying to "ignor[e] the shared fires in our past" and of "eras[ing] our names from the list" ("ID," 118). Alexie's refrain line reminds us that such an attempt is futile: all "begins and ends with ash" ("ID," 118). Returning to the idea of the endless winter and the endless death, the cyclical nature of the seasons has been transformed from continual awakening to continual renewal of death. The poet finally insists that such denial will lead to our own obliteration:

> We ignore the war until we are the last
> standing, until we are the last to persist
> in denial, as we are shipped off to camps
>
> where we all are stripped, and our dark bodies lit
> by the cruel light of those antique Jew-skinned lamps.
>
> ("ID," 118)

The first stage in healing, then, is to recognize one's role in history—to make it a part of one's family history—a "home movie."

Alexie immediately proceeds to question the purpose of such a personalization. What is the relationship between the self and other, or between one's family history and genocide? For Alexie, being an alert visitor to the museum involves a series of "commonly asked questions":

> Why are we here? What have we come to see?
> What do we need to find behind the doors?
> Are we searching for an apology . . . ?
>
> ("ID," 119)

As a villanelle, the third section, "3. *commonly asked questions*," revolves insistently around these inquiries and around the rhyming word in the middle line of each stanza: "door." These doors are potential views into the world that was and the one that will be. Even as the word *door* emphasizes a future—alternatives, a way out—its repetition gives the poem an even more obsessive feel than the usual villanelle, where we expect the second line of each stanza to rhyme but not for the words to be all the same. As the poem repeats, weaves, and progresses, it interrogates us, asking what we expect from the various people involved in the camps, as well as those who refused involvement: the "ghosts of unrepentant Nazis," the actors on the "set," the Germans who "refused to see/ the ash falling," the citizens of other countries with similar yet more hidden pasts, and the men who have locked the doors to the past and keep the keys "hidden" ("ID," 119). The poem is searching for who and what will provide resolution, even as it questions the purpose of witness. Why do victims of genocide and their descendants visit the camps or write about them? "Are we searching," the poem asks four times, "for an apology?" Is an apology enough? Although the questions are not answered here, the poem later suggests that perhaps apologies are not the solution.

The visitor's questioning of the purpose of the camp leads him to hypothesize about what he, as an American Indian, wants from his own country. Thus, in "4. *the american indian holocaust museum*," he takes his own advice and uses the experience at Dachau to begin questioning himself and his relationship to death. A mutated villanelle, this section circles around three repeated lines, without resolution:

> What do we indigenous people want from our country?
> We stand over mass graves. Our collective grief makes us numb.
> We are waiting for the construction of our museum.
>
> ("ID," 119)

Rather than vicariously experiencing the pain of the camp's victims, the poet of witness views their suffering and reflects on his own condition. His loss is parallel but not the same. Moreover, he assigns the perpetrators of the violence a role in the recovery: they cannot feel his pain but they must acknowledge their guilt. In Germany, the collective amnesia and denial have given way to holocaust museums, yet in the United States, this transformation has not occurred. The veterans and descendants of the Indian wars are "still waiting for the construction of our museum." Just as the Germans have begun the process of recovery and renewal, the United States must escape its narcissism if American Indians are to be allowed to heal their "collective grief" and numbness. This fourth section outlines the requirements for mourning to occur and invites the reader into the process.

In the sixth section, "6. *after we are free*," Alexie continues this reenvisioning of the relationship between viewer and victim in parallel couplets. The first one asks a question about how Jewish survivors "mourn," "fall in love," or "sleep at night" after the Holocaust, and the second couplet answers with a Spokane Indian's response to the genocide of his own people:

> If I were Jewish, how would I find the joy to dance?
> I am Spokane. I drop a quarter into the jukebox.
>
> ("ID," 121)

---

Although the speaker cannot find answers for the Jewish people, the questions can lead him to confront his own history and suggest answers for the Spokane. This personal confrontation neither replaces nor obliterates the loss suffered by the victims of the Holocaust but exists parallel to it. This parallelism constitutes the bridge of difference.

Throughout the poem, the speaker beholds the evidence of Dachau and testifies to it, but he allows the victims their autonomy. The deaths are both known and unknown, alike and unlike. Rather than eliminate the role of the poet or reader, Alexie envisions new roles. For both the descendants of the victims and the descendants of the perpetrators, remembering is the first step toward healing. The second step, however, is to use the example he provides to unlock the door to a new future. The final section, "7. *below freezing*," hopes for renewal but insists that certain actions must take place before it occurs. The writer does not claim to have made any changes yet: "I am not a Jew," he tells us, and "I have nothing new to say about death" ("ID," 122). Indeed, the landscape rebukes the attempts at renewal: "Dachau was so cold I could see my breath." Yet while spring has not come and winter remains, the perfection of the villanelle and the seven steps outlined in the poem's seven sections provide a promise of the potential for resolution. While it has not come yet, it is possible. Alexie uses the sequence about visiting Dachau to forge a new identity for the mourner and a new mourning process—one that is active. Through this transformation of readers into agents in mourning, the poet seeks to bring about change.

## The Responsibility of the Poet

If we accept Pinsky's view, a poet has two social responsibilities: to continue the art and to change the terms of the art as given.[39] In this vision, poetry is by nature political. All too often, though, discussions of ethnic American poetry search for the politics in the poem while ignoring the artistry itself. Such a move is not only distorting but dangerous. Poetics is an important means by which culture is preserved and reinvigorated and through which politics are expressed. To ignore it is to ignore the heart of the message. Alexie's elegies in *The Summer of Black Widows* take preservation and renewal as their explicit goal for the artist who confronts loss: of family members, the purity of Spokane lands, and people through genocide. In the midst of abandoned uranium mines, alcoholism, and despair, he searches for a means by which he can restore himself and his culture. As I have suggested here, Alexie turns to the performative nature of poetry embedded in elegies and other traditional forms as the means by which he can heal the Spokane.

The performative nature of this work serves as a reenactment of Native American oral style—that is, a way of continuing the art he has been given. As the poet-singer, however, Alexie disorders and reorders poetic form by moving in and out of Western forms, melding them to Spokane traditions, and claiming them as his own. Throughout *The Summer of Black Widows*, the forms break down as Alexie writes perfect villanelles and sestinas, then mutates them and combines them with other poetic traditions. Nowhere is this clearer than in the fifth section of "Inside Dachau," "5. *songs from those who love the flames*," which is at once a mutated sestina; a pantoum; a twelve-bar blues poem; and a traditional American Indian lyric, the ghost dance song.[40] Alexie's ability to preserve and revise existing forms complements his political arguments about how the Spokane must reclaim power over encroaching Western culture. By claiming the ground others seek to take, art maintains its power, whether to heal or destroy. Moreover, rather than being merely content to defend the boundaries of Spokane cultural property, Alexie seems to insist on claiming as his own what was previously seen as Anglo-American, African American, or just American. The entire category *American* is challenged. Is the reclaiming of formal territory in his poems—whether they are sonnets, sestinas, villanelles, or free verse—a reappropriation? Who is to say who influenced whom? The categories have been renamed, reclaimed, and reassigned. The American landscape—cultural and otherwise—has once again become the inheritance of the Spokane and other tribes.

## Notes

I would like to thank Ellen Stauder, Rupert Stasch, Rishona Zimring, Chris Moses, and Laura Weiser for their helpful comments on drafts of this essay.

1. Sherman Alexie, "Elegies," *The Summer of Black Widows* (New York: Hanging Loose Press, 1996), 51. Further references to this poem will be cited parenthetically in the text as "E."

2. Alexie, "The Summer of Black Widows," *Black Widows*, 12. Further references to this poem will be cited parenthetically in the text as "SBW."

3. Alexie, "After the First Lightning," *Black Widows*, 11. Through the weaving metaphor, spiders are associated with texts and writing and hence serve as an important figuration of the poet, who bridges oral and written texts.

4. Peter Sacks, *The English Elegy* (Baltimore: Johns Hopkins Univ. Press, 1985), 34-35.

5. Mark Strand, "The Elegy," in *The Making of a Poem: A Norton Anthology of Poetic Forms*, ed. Mark Strand and Eavan Boland (New York: Norton, 2000), 167-68.

6. Sherman Alexie, "Introduction to Native American Literature," *Old Shirts & New Skins* (Los Angeles: American Indian Studies Center, University of California, 1993), 4. Further references to this poem will be cited parenthetically in the text as "I."

7. See Karen M. Strom, "A Line in the Sand," © 1996-2005, www.hanksville.org/sand/ (April 2005). Internet sites like this one constructed by David Cole, Jordan Dill, and Tara Prindle provide opportunities for American Indians and American Indian communities to distribute their writing when access to other publishing venues may not be possible.

8. For more on cultural property rights in American Indian culture and literature, see the special issue of *American Indian Quarterly* "Cultural Property in American Indian Literatures: Representation and Interpretation," ed. David L. Moore (fall 1997): 21. See also Bruce Ziff and Pratima V. Rao, eds., *Borrowed Power: Essays on Cultural Appropriation* (New Brunswick, N.J.: Rutgers Univ. Press, 1997); Phyllis Messenger, ed., *The Ethics of Collecting Cultural Property: Whose Culture? Whose Property?* (Albuquerque: Univ. of New Mexico Press, 1989); and Marjane Ambler, "Cultural Property Rights: What's Next after NAGPRA?" *Tribal College: Journal of American Indian Higher Education* (fall 1996): 8-11.

9. Gary Snyder, "The Politics of Ethnopoetics," *A Place in Space* (Washington, D.C.: Counterpoint, 1995), 130, 141.

10. Robin Fast has noted a similar use of an antagonistic second-person reader in the work of American Indian poets Chrystos and Wendy Rose; see *The Heart as a Drum: Continuance and Resistance in American Indian Poetry* (Ann Arbor: Univ. of Michigan Press, 1999), 51.

11. Alexie, "Halibun," *Black Widows*, 29-30.

---

12. Leslie Marmon Silko makes a similar suggestion in her novel *Ceremony* (1977), where the medicine man Betonie insists that in order to combat white witchery, the ceremonies must contain aspects of white culture.

13. See Robin Fast, *The Heart as a Drum*, 211-12; see also Alexie, "Defending Walt Whitman," *Black Widows*, 14-15.

14. Critics who have discussed Whitman's use of parallelism include Calvin Bedient, "Walt Whitman (1819-1892)," *Voices and Visions: The Poet in America*, ed. Helen Vendler (New York: Random House, 1987), 10-14; and Wai Chee Dimock, "Whitman, Syntax, and Political Theory," *Breaking Bounds: Whitman and American Cultural Studies*, ed. Betsy Erkkila and Jay Grossman (New York: Oxford Univ. Press, 1996), 69-78.

15. This trope is common throughout the work of Luci Tapahonso and Louise Erdrich but can be seen in particular in Erdrich's poems "Family Reunion," "Indian Boarding School: The Runaways," and "Walking in the Breakdown Lane," *Jacklight: Poems* (New York: Henry Holt, 1984), 9-10, 11. Tapahonso puts a new spin on the broken-car motif by using rundown cars and car accidents as sites for cultural misunderstanding in "I Remembered This One in Tucson" and "That Guy," *Blue Horses Rush In* (Tucson: Univ. of Arizona Press, 1997), 57-59, 93-94.

16. Sacks, *The English Elegy*, 17.

17. Alexie, "Fire as Verb and Noun," *Black Widows*," 52.

18. During the Renaissance, the villanelle was a rather frivolous mode of verse associated with popular songs and highly conventional lovers' laments; however, during the twentieth century, the villanelle has been more commonly used for dealing with weighty and metaphysical subjects such as loss and death.

19. Kenneth Burke, "The Nature of Form," *Discussions of Poetry: Form and Structure*, ed. Francis Murphy (Boston: Heath, 1964), 1.

20. Ezra Pound, "Lionel Johnson," in *Ezra Pound: Literary Essays* (New York: New Directions, 1968), 369 n; quoted in Ronald McFarland, *The Villanelle: The Evolution of a Poetic Form* (Moscow, Idaho: Univ. of Idaho Press, 1987), 83.

21. Alexie, "Sister Fire, Brother Smoke," *Black Widows*, 60.

22. Walter Benjamin, *The Origin of German Tragic Drama*, trans. John Osborne (London: New Left Books, 1977), 224; quoted in Peter Sacks, *The English Elegy*, 178.

23. David Holbrook, *Dylan Thomas: The Code of Night* (London: Athlone, 1972), 196; quoted in McFarland, *The Villanelle*, 89.

24. The equation of a sister's death by fire with deaths from genocide is made most clearly in the poem "Fire as Verb and Noun," where the sister's burning is compared to the burning of Jews in the ovens during World War II and to "an American/ Indian who had heated bayonets/ held against his hands/ until they blistered" (*Black Widows*, 54).

25. Dell Hymes, "Tonkawa Poetics: John Rush Buffalo's 'Coyote and Eagle's Daughter,'" in *Native American Discourse: Poetics and Rhetoric*, ed. Joel Sherzer and Anthony Woodbury (Cambridge, Eng.: Cambridge Univ. Press, 1987), 22. There has been controversy surrounding Hymes's proposal. Rodney Frey has affirmed the importance of Hymes's observations for Indian Peoples of the Inland Northwest, including the Coeur d'Alene (see *Stories That Make the World: Oral Literatures of the Indian Peoples of the Inland Northwest as Told by Lawrence Aripa, Tom Yellowtail, and Other*

---

*Elders*, ed. Rodney Frey [Norman: Univ. of Oklahoma Press, 1995], 151); but Dennis Tedlock complains that the practice of breaking down texts into lines when there is no metrical scheme is "wide open to gerrymandering, however clear the larger units—verses and stanzas—may sometimes be." Tedlock also argues that scholars should avoid generalizing Hymes's observations to the oral literatures of Native Americans outside the Northwest, such as the Zuni (*The Spoken Word and the Work of Interpretation* [Philadelphia: Univ. of Pennsylvania Press, 1983], 57).

26. Frey notes that for the Nez Perce, Klamath, and Klikitat (tribes in the area around Spokane and Coeur d'Alene), "three- and five-verse groupings are typically found," *Stories That Make the World*, 151.

27. See Hymes, "Tonkawa Poetics," 22.

28. The emotional work done by poetic forms is often subconscious, so the villanelle's appeal for Alexie may be hard to reduce solely to a deliberate choice.

29. Melissa Zeiger argues that the contemporary elegy is characterized by a resistance to closure (*Beyond Consolation: Death, Sexuality, and the Changing Shapes of Elegy* [Ithaca, N.Y.: Cornell Univ. Press, 1997]). I believe that the lack of resolution in Alexie's work differs from the poets Zeiger analyzes, however, because Alexie resists closure only temporarily. That is, even if closure is not achieved fully in the poems, he imagines a space in which closure would be desirable.

30. Alexie, "Sister Fire, Brother Smoke," *Black Widows*, 60.

31. Alexie, "Sonnet: Tattoo Tears," *Black Widows*, 58.

32. See Robert Pinsky's statement in "Responsibilities of the Poet": "[We must] use the art to behold the evidence before us. We must answer for what we see" (11). Pinsky is paraphrasing a statement by Carolyn Forché in "El Salvador: An Aide Memoire," *American Poetry Review* 109 (July-August 1981): 6.

33. Alexie, "Inside Dachau," *Black Widows*, 117. Further references to this poem will be cited parenthetically in the text as "ID."

34. On death and rebirth in the elegy, see Sacks, *The English Elegy*, 19-20, 27.

35. Ezra Pound, *The Spirit of Romance* (Norfolk, Conn.: J. Laughlin, 1952), 27; quoted in *The New Princeton Handbook of Poetic Terms*, ed. T. V. F. Brogan (Princeton, N.J.: Princeton Univ. Press, 1994), 271.

36. William Empson, "Sidney's Double Sestina," *Discussions of Poetry*, ed. Murphy, 80. Empson does not discuss the effect of the final stanza upon this monotony.

37. Robert Pinsky, "Responsibilities of the Poet," in *Politics and Poetic Value*, ed. Robert von Halber (Chicago: Univ. of Chicago Press, 1987), 11.

38. "2. *history as home movie*" is a mutated ballade envoi; "3. *commonly asked questions*" is a villanelle; and "4. *the american indian holocaust museum*" is a mutated villanelle.

39. Pinsky, "Responsibilities," 19.

40. I encountered this range of possibilities when I asked students to identify the poetic form of this section of Alexie's poem on a final exam for my course "Ethnic American Poetry," Reed College, fall 1997. I am grateful to the students for their insight.

---

# A World of Story-Smoke:
## A Conversation with Sherman Alexie _____

Åse Nygren

Songwriter, filmmaker, comedian, and writer of prose and poetry, Sherman Alexie grew up on the Spokane Indian Reservation in Wellpinit, Washington, about 50 miles northwest of Spokane. The reservation (approximately 1,100 Spokane Tribal members live there), where the effects of what Alexie chooses to call an "on-going colonialism" still asserts its painful presence, is central in Alexie's fiction, *The Lone Ranger and Tonto Fistfight in Heaven* (1993) and *Reservation Blues* (1995). Presented as a demarcated space of suffering, Alexie's fictional reservation is a place where his characters are tormented by collective memories of a genocidal past, of cavalry-approved hangings, massacres, and smallpox-infected blankets. It is a haunted place where "faint voices . . . echo[] all over" (*Reservation Blues* 46) and where "dreams . . . [a]re murdered . . . the bones buried quickly just inches below the surface, all waiting to break through the foundations of those government houses built by the Department of Housing and Urban Development" (*Reservation Blues* 7). Although some of Alexie's characters leave the reservation and enter the urban space in his second novel, *Indian Killer* (1996), the experience of growing up, as Alexie puts it in the interview, "firmly within borders," continues to affect the characters' lives, especially their emotional lives.

Inevitably when dealing with ethnic literature, it is impossible not to be self-conscious of one's own position. As a European white female scholar, I felt compelled to raise questions of perspective, including those of nationality, ethnicity, and gender. Within this context of self-reflection, the interview touches upon issues such as the desire for a "pure" or authentic American Indian identity and the critical demand for the genre "American Indian literature."

One of the most intriguing aspects of Alexie's fiction is his use of the comic. Although the subject matters in Alexie's fiction are morally and ethically engaging, the same texts are often ironic, satiric, and full of humor. As the characters in a caricature-like manner stagger across the reservation, between drinking the next beer and cracking the next joke, the reader is often invited to laugh along with them, even at them. Alexie's artistic vision thus mixes humor and suffering in a manner that for me resembles what Roberto Benigni does in his film *Life Is Beautiful* or Art Spiegelman in his graphic novels, *Maus: A Survivor's Tale*. Such a comparison becomes all the more justified in the light of one of Alexie's most provocative comments in the interview, his parallel between the Indian and the Jewish Holocausts.

Alexie's texts can be considered trauma narratives, and the interview explores his views on trauma and the thematization of suffering. Although trauma does silence, and suffering does exist without expression in language and without metaphysics, the moment pain is transformed into suffering, it is also transferred into language. This enables the traumatized person to remember, work through, and mourn the lost object. Given the inarticulateness of many of Alexie's characters, I also suggest that Alexie's narratives call attention to the inherent difficulties of representing suffering. The characters are muted by the traumas of hatred and chaos, loss and grief, danger and fear, and cannot—except in a few rare cases—articulate their suffering. Instead, they tend to resort to self-destructive behavior, including violence and substance abuse. Thus, while Alexie's narratives demonstrate the need to give suffering a language, they also call attention to the inherent unsharability of suffering. In the interview with Alexie, I was particularly interested in his views on trauma and his thematization of suffering.

While in Alexie's early fiction, the reservation is a geographical space of borders and confinement, in his more recent fiction, *The Toughest Indian in the World* (2000) and *Ten Little Indians* (2003), the reservation changes its ontology and becomes a mental and emotional territory. In the interview below, Alexie says that this ontological change is a result of his own "expanded world-view." During the course of his writing career, Alexie explains, he has moved from what he calls a "fundamental" world-view which earlier made him "so focused on Indian identity that [he] didn't look at the details," to what he hopes will be "the triumph of the ordinary." His writing has thus shifted in emphasis from angry protests to evocations of love and empathy.

\* \* \*

***Åse Nygren: What are some of the inspirations and motivations behind your writing? Are they autobiographical, political, or historical?***

**Sherman Alexie**: Like we were saying just before we turned the tape on, people in Scandinavia don't really know about Indian writers or know that there even are Indian writers. I didn't know either. Even though I was growing up on a reservation, and going to reservation schools, I had never really been shown Indian literature before. So it wasn't even a possibility growing up. I loved reading but I hadn't thought of a career as a writer. I hadn't thought about books as a career in any form. I took a class in creative writing because I couldn't handle human anatomy lab and it was the only class that fit my schedule. This was the first time anyone had shown me contemporary poetry. The most contemporary poem I had read before was "The Waste Land." I had no idea you could write about NOW. I read Allen Ginsberg's "Howl" for the first time. Even Langston Hughes felt new to me. And I fell in love with it immediately. Over night, I knew I was going to be a writer.

***ÅN: Were there any Indian writers on the reading list for the poetry class you took?***

**SA**: The poetry teacher gave me a book called *Songs from This Earth on Turtle's Back*, an anthology on Native literature by Joseph Bruchac. Before I read that book I had no idea that you could write about Indian life with powwows, ceremonies, broken down cars, cheap motels; all this stuff that was my life as I was growing up on the reservation. I remember in particular one line by Adrian Louis, a Paiute poet: "Adrian, I'm in the reservation of my mind!" It captured for me the way I felt about myself, at least then. It was nothing I'd ever had before. I thought to myself: I want to write like this! So that's where it began. The beginning was accidental. But I got very serious about it quickly. I went through the college library looking at poetry journals trying to figure out what was going on in the world, trying to catch up, essentially, for a lifetime of not reading.

**ÅN: Did you read all different kinds of poetry, or did you focus on works by American Indians?**

SA: Any poetry. Anything and everything. I pulled books off the shelves randomly because I liked the title, or the cover, or the author photo. I read hundreds of poems over a year or so to catch up. As I sat there in the poetry stacks in the library a whole new world opened to me. Before, I had always thought that I was a freak in the way I saw and felt about the world. As I started reading the works of all these poets I realized that I, at least, wasn't the only freak! [Laughs] I think we belong to a lot of tribes; culturally, ethnically, and racially. I'm a poet and this is the world in which I belong.

**ÅN: So your ambitions and motivations weren't political to begin with?**

SA: No. My writing was very personal and autobiographical. I was simply finding out who I was and who I wanted to be. As I started writing I became more political, much because of people's reactions to me. I was writing against so many ideas of what I was supposed to be writing. So even though much of my early work deals with alcohol and alcoholism because of personal experiences, I got a lot of criticism because alcoholism is such a loaded topic for Indians. People thought I was writing about stereotypes, but more than anything I was writing about my own life. As an Indian, you don't have the luxury of being called an autobiographical writer often. You end up writing for the whole race. At the beginning of my career I was 21 years old, and I didn't have any defense against that. So I became political because people viewed me politically. I got political to fight people's ideas about me. It is only in the last few years that my politics has found a way into my work that feels natural. Part of the reason is because you grow older. The way I think about it is that I used to spend more time looking inside myself, looking internally. Now I look at more of the world and a wider range of people.

*ÅN: Ethnic literatures have a powerful social role in shaping ethnic identity and in making ethnic groups visible, thus filling an important political function. With the rise of ethnic literatures, there has been in criticism a tendency to link literature written by writers of a certain ethnic descent with a specific group of people, and thus with a specific ethnic experience. Is this a classification that you are comfortable with?*

**SA**: I think it's lazy scholarship. For instance, Gerald Vizenor and I have nothing in common in terms of what we write about, how we write, and how we look at the world. There'd be no reason to link us other than our ethnicity. He has much more in common with experimental writing, like William Gass's *In the Heart of the Heart of the Country*.

I guess the problem is not that I'm labeled as a Native American writer, but that writers like John Updike and Jonathan Franzen aren't labeled as White American writers. They are simply assumed to be the norm, and everybody else is judged in reaction to them.

*ÅN: But even though the term "Indian" is a limitation in some ways, couldn't it work as a door opener in other ways?*

**SA**: Yes, it is good in some ways. The good thing is that there are so few of us that I'm automatically exotic. It makes me different automatically. We live in a capitalistic society and it's all about competition. In the world of writing, I have an edge because I'm an Indian. If I was a white guy writer I'd be just another white guy writer.

*ÅN: Do you think that these labels—African American literature, American Indian literature etc.—are useful in promoting a specific group of writers?*
SA: Economically, I think this type of labeling helps because it focuses the market. But in terms of criticism I don't think it does. Such labels are often used by critics to diminish the works, or by supporters to promote it. There are people who love Native literature, for instance, just because Indians write it. They don't really view it critically. On the other hand, some critics think that we have careers or success just because of our ethnicity. You end up being pushed by two sides: Loved only because you're an Indian, or hated because you're an Indian!

*ÅN: In discussions on American Indian literature, some critics claim that one of the characteristic features of American Indian literature is often a certain dose of sentimentality. What critics mean by this is that references to the Indian beliefs and spirituality—the four directions, Father Sky, Mother Earth, corn pollen, etc.—are somehow always already charged with sentimentality. In your fiction, you seem to refuse this sentimentality through various means, for example, through your use of irony. I would like to hear your reaction to such a categorizing of American Indian literature and how you work against it in your fiction.*
SA: I'm not sure if sentimentality is the right word. But I would agree that there is a lot of nostalgia. Like any colonized people, Indians look to the pre-colonial times as being better just because we weren't colonized. There is a certain tendency there of nostalgia as a disease. Because our identity has been so fractured, and because we've been subject to so much oppression and relocation—our tribes dissipated, many destroyed—the concept of a pure Indian

identity is really strong in Indian literature. For instance, very few of the top 30 or 40 Native writers publishing now grew up on the reservation, and yet most Native literature is about the reservation. So there is a nostalgia for purity: a time when we were all together and when our identity was sure, and when our lives were better.

*ÅN: It's an understandable nostalgia in one sense.*
SA: Yes. And there is great writing coming out of that nostalgia. I would say that bad Native writing is sentimental, and there is plenty of it. But writers like Scott Momaday, James Welch, and Simon Ortiz are not sentimental.

*ÅN: In an interview by Swiss scholar Hartwig Isernhagen, American Indian writers Gerald Vizenor and Scott Momaday, and First Nations writer Jeanette Armstrong were all asked the question, "How do you address the question of violence in your works?" Is there, in your opinion, a central narration of violence in Indian literature?*
SA: Well, yes, I think so. After all, we come out of genocide, and our entire history is filled with murder and war. Perhaps violence is not the right word, though. But there is definitely a lot of humiliation in Native literature. We write about being humiliated a lot. And that takes physical forms, emotional forms, and mental forms. I think Native literature is the literature of humiliation and shame.

*ÅN: How important is tribal specificity to your own writing? Is it the Spokane Tribe or a more generic concept of "Indianness" that is of interest to you?*
SA: To me, there are a few things going on. I'm very aware of my Spokaneness. I grew up on the Spokane Indian reservation, and my tribe heavily influences my personality and the ways in which I see the world. But there is also a strong Northwest identity. Because we spend so much time interacting now, I think Indian identity is more

regional than it is tribal. Navajos and Apaches are going to have a lot more in common with each other than they would have with the Spokane. I strongly identify with salmon people, and so I get along with the tribes on this side. The way in which they talk and act feels close to home.

*ÅN: One important concern among American Indian writers has been the question of how one deals with a painful past, such as the one shared by the Indian peoples of the United States, without falling into the trap of victimization. How important is this issue for you when you write your fiction?*

SA: I write autobiographically, so when you talk about surviving pain and trauma and getting out of it—I did, I have! But the people I know have not. So what do I do in my literature? Do I portray the Indian world as I see it? And I do see it as doomed, and that you have to get lucky to escape that. Should I write the literature of hope no matter how I feel? No! I'm not hopeful. So how do you avoid victimization? We can't. We are victims.

*ÅN: Vizenor is very adamant when it comes to this question. I spoke with him in 2002 and what he seems to want to avoid more than anything else is victimization, something which is reflected in terms that he uses in his literature, like, for instance, "survivance."*

SA: Survival is a low hope. I don't want just survival, or "survivance." I want triumph! But you don't get it. That's the thing. You don't get it. Also, our story is not worse than anybody else's.

*ÅN: How do you mean?*

SA: Pain is relative. For instance, in the last movie I made I worked with a woman who grew up very wealthy, very privileged economically, but she had lived through such hell in her family that it made my life seem sweet and gentle. So I try not to measure people's pain.

I mean, if I'd throw a rock randomly right now I'd hit someone whose life is worse than mine ever was. Nothing in my life can measure up to the kids in that school [in Beslan]. Nothing! Nothing! And nothing in my life can measure up to losing somebody in the World Trade towers. Everybody's pain is important.

*ÅN: I find the concept of "collective trauma" particularly useful concerning the suffering that many of your characters are experiencing. Many of them suffer from not only personal losses and grievances—absent fathers, poverty, unemployment, alcoholism, etc.—but also from a cultural loss and a collective trauma, which include experiences of racism and stereotyping. Their losses and grievances affect their behavior and their lives on many levels. In my view, your fiction explores how such trauma both damages and creates community and identity alike. Both identity and community are, of course, condemned to ongoing dysfunction. Do you think that suffering is part of what constitutes Indianness? Perhaps in a somewhat comparable way by which we have come to associate African American identity with slavery, or Jewish identity with the Holocaust? If so, how does this relation differ from, e.g., the relation between African Americans and suffering, or Jews and suffering?*

SA: Yes! The phrase I've also used is "blood memory." I think the strongest parallel in my mind has always been the Jewish people and the Holocaust. Certainly, their oppression has been constant for 1,900 years longer, but the fact is that you cannot separate our identity from our pain. At some point it becomes primarily our identity. The whole idea of authenticity—"How Indian are you?"—is the most direct result of the fact that we don't know what an American Indian identity is. There is no measure anymore. There is no way of knowing, except perhaps through our pain. And so, we're lost. We're always wandering.

*ÅN: Like the lost tribes of Israel?*

**SA**: Yes. It's so amazing that the indigenous people of the United States have become the most immigrant group. The process is slowly changing. My generation and the next generation—we are immigrants! I am an immigrant into the United States, and now my children are fully assimilated.

*ÅN: A scholar by the name of Kai Erikson has put a social dimension into the term "trauma." He talks about "traumatized communities" in the sense of damages to the tissues that hold human groups together as well as to the dominant spirit of a group, which is a fitting concept when we talk about "collective trauma" or "blood memory."*

**SA**: Yes it is. Some day they're going to find it, but I feel that it is true that pain is carried in the DNA. And because it is carried in the DNA, pain can mutate through generations. One of the most obvious proofs for that is child abuse. Kids who get abused so often grow up and become abusers.

*ÅN: Many of your characters—Victor and Junior in* **The Lone Ranger** *and* **Reservation Blues,** *John Smith in* **Indian Killer,** *Harlan in* **Ten Little Indians,** *to mention a few—are struggling with their experiences of what it means to be an Indian, and what they are told it means to be an Indian. At times, they seem at a loss as to what Indian identity really IS. Is their struggle linked with the fact that Indian identity has often been reduced to stereotype? In other words, do you think that the long-term reduction of the Indian to stereotype in American culture has resulted in a collective crisis of identity for many Indians today?*

**SA**: Yes, certainly, because you can never measure up to a stereotype. You can never be as strong as a stereotypical warrior, as godly as a stereotypical shaman, or as drunk as a drunken Indian. You can never measure up to extremes. So you're always going to feel less than the image, whether it's positive or negative. One of the real dangers is that other Indians have taken many stereotypes as a reality, as a way to measure each other and ourselves. Take Harlan Atwater, for instance. Because he was adopted out, and because he grew up this way or that way, he would be viewed by other Indians as not being Indian. White people wouldn't see him as Indian and now Indians don't see him as Indian. Indians have accepted stereotypes just as much as non-Indians have. We believe them too. I think that many Indians have watched too much television! [Laughs]

*ÅN: In a sense, of course, the search for identity is endemic for everyone, isn't it? Aren't we all searching for a sense of belonging?*
SA: Yes, I guess that's a good way to put it. The search for identity is not special.

*ÅN: But for Indians, that search has been complicated by, for instance, the stereotype?*
SA: Well, we have no economic, political, or social power. We have no power to change our lives. We are powerless.

*ÅN: Is that one of the reasons why, although images of Jews and Blacks displaying exaggerated ethnic features—such as big noses and lips—have been forbidden in the U.S. decades ago, racist images of Indians continue to flourish? The image of the Indian mascot is only one example here. Does the answer lie in what you have just touched upon, that Indians are powerlessness?*
SA: Yes. We have no power to change the stereotypes. We have no allies. No other group is joining with us to fight those things. The romantic idea is that if people are feeling a lot of pain you'd wish that people would empathize more. I wish that was true.

*ÅN: Of course feminism as a movement encounters similar prob-
lems.*

**SA**: Yes. It's the whole idea of the human range of empathy. Hon-
estly, I think that people who can't empathize with the mascot or
with feminism, for instance, are not so far removed from a criminal.
The inability to understand why something might be offensive is a
form of sociopathy.

*ÅN: Although the subject matters in your texts are morally and
ethically engaging, the same texts are often ironic, satiric, and
full of humor. I read your ironic and satiric re-thinking, even
defamiliarization, of a painful past, in alignment with writer Art
Spiegelman and film maker Roberto Benigni. Spiegelman's two
books in cartoon form, entitled* **Maus: A Survivor's Tale I and II,**
*and Benigni's film* **Life Is Beautiful** *both deal with the Jewish
Holocaust in the comic mode, and have, consequently, shocked
readers/viewers out of any lingering sense of familiarity with
the historic events described. Would you like your books to have a
similar effect on your readers? What are some of the gains? Dangers?*

**SA**: Well, I'm a big fan of graphic novels. I like their immediacy.
Automatically when you look at a graphic novel, or when you look
at a cartoon, there is always an ironical, satirical edge and an underlying humor. So yes, I aim to be funny, and I aim for my humor to be
very political. But I think more along the lines of political stand-up
comedians like Richard Pryor and Lenny Bruce than I do about
other writers.

*ÅN: What might be some of the gains and dangers?*

**SA**: Dangers? Playing to the audience. Reacting completely to the
audience rather than generating it from yourself, so that you're reflexive and you're performing rather than dealing with something
on an emotional level. I think I have a tendency in my work to lapse

into performance mode. Rather than something out of my heart, it ends up being something on the surface designed for effect. One of the great things is that through that immediacy of performance and humor you can reach people who otherwise might not be listening. I think being funny breaks down barriers between people. I can get up in front of any crowd, and if I make them laugh first I can say almost anything to them.

*ÅN: In "The Search Engine" (from* Ten Little Indians*), the Indian student Corliss is reading a book by (the somewhat amateurish) Indian writer Harlan Atwater. You write that "Harlan Atwater was making fun of being Indian, of the essential sadness of being Indian, and so maybe he was saying Indians aren't sad at all" (7). In "The Approximate Size of my Favorite Tumor" (from* The Lone Ranger and Tonto Fistfight in Heaven*), we can read about the Indian man who is dying of cancer, but who still manages to joke about his situation: "Still, you have to realize that laughter saved Norma and me from pain, too. Humor was an antiseptic that cleaned the deepest of personal wounds" (164). My third example is taken from your novel* Indian Killer, *where you write that among Indians "laughter [is] a ceremony used to drive away personal and collective demons" (21). What is the function of humor, then? Do you mean to suggest that humor can be transformative and liberating?*

SA: [Laughs] When I write it, I believe it! I don't know if it works in real life. Making fun of things or being satirical doesn't make me feel better about things. It's a tool that enables me to talk about anything. I don't know if it necessarily changes things, or changes anybody who is listening to me. It makes dialogue possible, but I don't think it makes change possible.

*ÅN: Are you ever afraid that the comical element will subvert attention from the gravitas of your writing?*

SA: Yes, it happens all the time. People assume that you're not being serious because you're being funny. By and large I figure that people who say those sort of things aren't funny. And being funny is just how I am. I can't just stop . . . [Laughs]. But it's also a personal defense, of course. When I don't want to talk about something, or when I'm uncomfortable. It's not all good, humor, but it's always serious.

*ÅN: Your parodic intertextuality and ironic re-thinking of historic events are commonly seen as markers of postmodernity. What do you think the term "postmodernism" promises, or does not promise, with respect to your fiction? Can we understand your works of fiction better by aligning them with postmodernist ideas?*

SA: Again, it's a generic label. I don't think the term "postmodernism" says anything more about my work than the term "Native American" does. It's just a label. My idea of postmodern will always be the language poets or Andy Warhol—that sort of more intellectual and less emotional work. That's how I look upon postmodernism, as more of an intellectual enterprise. And that's not me.

*ÅN: Alternate responses to a loss of the past and of a communal feeling among your characters are* **repeating** *or* **re-membering,** *in Toni Morrison's idea of the latter. This is particularly true about your first three works of fiction—* **The Lone Ranger, Reservation Blues,** *and* **Indian Killer.** *While re-membering is a painful process, which brings back personal and collective horrors, it may also have a healing and freeing effect once memory is properly revisited and worked-through. The character of Thomas Builds-the-Fire is actively, almost obsessively, re-membering a painful past, and is described as "the self-proclaimed storyteller of the Spokane tribe": "Thomas repeated stories constantly. All the other Indians* *on the reservation heard those stories so often that the words crept into dreams. . . . Thomas Builds-the-Fire's stories climbed into your clothes like sand, gave you itches that could not be scratched. If you repeated even a sentence from one of those stories, your throat was never the same again. Those stories hung in your clothes and hair like smoke, and no amount of laundry soap or shampoo washed them out. Victor and Junior often tried to beat those stories out of Thomas, tied him down and taped his mouth shut. . . . But none of that stopped Thomas, who talked and talked." Have you taken on a similar role of a storyteller? If so, for whom are you telling, and re-telling, your stories?*

SA: [Laughs] Do you mean I'm irritating? Well, demographically speaking, most of the fiction in this country is bought by middle class, college-educated white women. So that's who I'm writing for. That's who's getting my stories in their hair like smoke. If you go to my readings, that's who's there. At the beginning I had ambitions about a specific audience, but now I write for pretty much everybody. I want everybody! And I'm not waiting for people to come to my stories, I'm going to them. I want the whole world to smell like story-smoke, my story-smoke! So in that sense I'm like Thomas. Thomas is really obsessed about making sure that people hear him, but his world-view is tiny in terms of his audience. My world-view was small in the beginning, too. Now, it has expanded.

*ÅN: According to some, man is a fiction-making animal, one that is defined by fantasies and fiction. Peter Brooks, for instance, sees the narrative impulse as an attempt to cope with the human facts of our existence in the body and in time, that is, with death. Silence, as equivalent to death, is what must be avoided in order to "remain in the world." I am curious to hear some of your thoughts on such existential claims as to the function of literature.*

SA: That's a very serious way to put it, I guess. I think what that definition is missing is the element of play. Even animals play, even animals create fiction. Narrative is play and we all practice that. I think that's more of what it is.

*ÅN: That's a postmodern idea, narrative as play.*
SA: Is it? Well, I guess I am a postmodern writer then. [Laughs] But the play could be very serious. The thing is: I love telling stories. I'm not in agony when I'm telling stories. I'm not serious. Most of the time I'm pretty excited!

*ÅN: I suppose that Brooks's theorizing on the narrative drive doesn't exclude the question of play. What he is talking about is that narrative drive we have, the desire to create plots out of our lives.*
SA: Well, yes. I would agree with him on that. When I'm really in the groove, everything disappears. The whole world just fades away and it's just me and the story. I do know that that's when I feel closest to God, whatever God is. That's when I feel like I'm praying. I never feel spiritual anywhere, except in the presence of my own stories.

*ÅN: In trauma literature, the storytelling impulse is generally seen as an attempt not only to work-through a painful past but also a necessary means to break through the silence imposed by trauma. In my own work, I conceive of silent suffering as the endurance of pain over time, while complaint, or conscious suffering, should be understood as the beginning of narrative. If attended to by another's anticipation and empathy, the silence imposed by trauma can be broken through. In your view, could an imaginary reader—any reader that the writer has in mind when writing his/her text—fulfill the function of a "witness" who attends emphatically to the text's complaint (through an act of engagement and remembering)?*
SA: The ideal reader would do that. But as the reader takes the story

or witnesses it, doesn't he or she use it to witness their own lives? I don't think the readers jump across the text to the author very much, except in a very generic way. An ideal reader would, but real readers don't. I wish I had an ideal reader!

**ÅN: Do you have an ideal reader in mind when you write?**
**SA**: I gave up predicting what readers will do, or wanting a certain reaction. It's just impossible to know. That's a serious control issue if you think you know what your readers are going to do. I like to think of myself as the ideal reader. Not necessarily of any individual texts, but I love everything, and I approach everything with excitement and love. I'm a reading addict. I love books, comics, magazines—everything! So I guess an ideal reader for me would be less about a specific reaction to the work than a way in which they approach it. I just want passion!

**ÅN: In my own work, I contend that traumatic inarticulateness is typically accompanied by an inherent need to break the silence imposed on the traumatized victim. The silence of trauma, I argue, is broken out of necessity, since a trauma unrelieved will typically lead to neurosis or pathology, i.e., illness or violence. To witness, or to endure such suffering, would be deeply disturbing to say the least. Would you say that your characters in this sense simply suffer their pain in time? Or do some of them transform their pain into suffering? Does your fiction, in a sense, give them the right to suffer? Does it assign their suffering an ethical (metaphysical) value?**
**SA**: Oh, God. Huge question!

**ÅN: Because in your first three works of fiction in particular, there is a lot of suffering . . .**
**SA**: Oh, yes. It's terrible! I myself as a person have gotten out of that, and my characters have gotten out of it in a way. I was suffering

with the characters earlier when I was writing. What they felt, I felt. Because the work was so autobiographical, it was like reliving it again. In a therapeutic sense, I guess you could say that. That also happens in therapy. You talk about it, you say it!

*ÅN: Like Freud's idea of the "talking cure"?*
SA: Yes. I've done play-acting, reenacting, taking the voices of all the people. . . . The thing is, that when you're in therapy doing this crap you do the exact same crap you do as a writer. So I don't know that it helps writers. Because the thing that fucked you up in the first place is what you're doing again. As for the characters—I make them suffer! I specifically designed them to be suffering. John Smith, for instance, there's no redemption there; there's no healing, there's no talking cure. For a lot of the characters there's no cure. All there is, is suffering. The whole point of their identity is suffering. What keeps coming back to me is that when I think about Indians all I think about is suffering. My first measure on any Indian is pain.

*ÅN: In an earlier interview, you have stated that if there is one thing you would like to achieve as a writer it would be to contribute to the building of an American Indian Holocaust museum. In the poem, "The Game Between the Jews and the Indians Is Tied Going into the Bottom of the Ninth Inning," you draw a parallel between the experience of the Jewish people and the Indians: "Now, when you touch me, my skin/ will you think of Sand Creek, Wounded Knee/ What will I remember/ when your skin is next to mine/ Auschwitz, Buchenwald?" And in the poem, "Inside Dachau," you also draw a parallel between the Jewish Holocaust and the centuries of colonization that Indians in the present day U.S. have been subjected to: "We are the sons/ and daughters of the walking dead. We have lost everyone./ What do we indigenous people want from our country?/ We stand over mass graves. Our collective grief makes us numb./ We are waiting for the con-*

*struction of our museum." In your opinion, is the term "holo-caust" applicable when describing the effects of five centuries of colonization on the Indian peoples of what is today the U.S.? Are genocides comparable?*

**SA**: Yes, I think genocides are comparable. The difference is that this country did what they planned to do. Hitler didn't get to finish it. He didn't get to accomplish it.

*ÅN: What about the risk of de-historicizing unique experiences of oppression, then? There are, for instance, varying views in acade-mia as to whether you can use the term "holocaust" or not, with regards to other events than the Jewish Holocaust, which is con-sidered a unique event by many. Demographer Russell Thornton does, however, refer to what happened in this country as "The American Indian Holocaust."*

**SA**: I call it that. It's a political move to call it that. It's rebellious. I'm sure it could be interpreted as anti-Semitic in a way of claiming ownership of somebody else's word. But I call it that to draw direct parallels in a way that people don't want to. People outside of this country will tend to view what happened here as genocide. But you will not get people to admit that here. It's a very exclusivist view. People will not even own to the fact that they live in a colony. That it's still a colony. They won't even accept that term, let alone the idea of genocide. So it's very much a political move on my part to call it a Holocaust. I realize the term was generated to mean some-thing specific, but I want it to mean more. They had the same ambi-tions, and the end result is the same. So yes, I want what happened here to receive the same sort of sacred respect that what happened in Germany does. I want our dead to be honored.

*ÅN: Are genocides comparable?*

**SA**: It's not necessarily a comparison. I'm not measuring the size. One death is too many. But I think other people measure the value of lives differently. Some deaths are more important. And I think they're all important. I want them all to be acknowledged. I think we end up measuring them by their success rate rather than the philosophy that started it. We talk about the genocide itself rather than the genocidal impulse. And it's easy to become a Nazi.

*ÅN: The focus and mood has slightly shifted in your two latest books,* **The Toughest Indian in the World** *and* **Ten Little Indians.** *Rather than exploring the terrain of reservation life where anger times imagination is the ascribed method for survival, your characters have entered the urban scene where they continually negotiate between their Indian identity, their "American" identity (whatever that is), and other identities based on, for example, sexuality, class, and generation. While many of your characters in your earlier works seem to be denied subjectivity, or character, and have been assigned, as it were, to such mental reservations as stereotypes, it seems that your "new" characters are beginning to claim, and attain, subjectivity. In that capacity, many of them seem to be exploring the inner and intimate landscape of love—searching for love, holding on to love, falling in love, failing love, etc. There are portraits of loving fathers and husbands, ethnically mixed marriages, one of them lesbian, where your characters "lov[e] each other across the distance," and then there is, of course, Seymour who goes on a nonviolent killing spree in search of love. You have said that when you read the line "I'm in the reservation of my mind" from a poem by Paiute poet Adrian Louis you knew that you wanted to be a writer. How would you say that Louis's concept of "the reservation of my mind" relates to the characters I have referred to, let us call them love-seeking? Do your "new" characters so to speak alter how you relate to Louis's concept of a "mental reservation"?*

SA: As an Indian the idea of the reservation is always there. You grow up firmly within borders. As you grow up as an Indian, you know mathematically for certain your ethnicity. I'm 13/16 Indian. Everything is assigned and valued and placed. When I was born, I had a social security number and a tribal identification number. So I think my new characters carry that idea of borders into their love lives and into their new lives. Even if they can be successful, the idea of borders goes beyond their ethnicity and into their personal decisions, and they limit themselves in other ways. Love for me has always been political. It has always been informed by the reservation, and it still is. I guess some of my characters are trying to get away from that.

*ÅN: Love is very much in focus in your two last books,* **The Toughest Indian in the World** *and* **Ten Little Indians.**
**SA**: Yes. I've been married for ten years, more than a quarter of my life now. And the changes in my life have been dramatic. My house is 1,300 square feet. This [where we are sitting] is my floor. But I grew up poor! So to survive I had to assign a certain set of values for myself, when it came to measuring any emotion. I was so rigid that I had to set up a way of survival that was really mercenary, and narcissistic. My characters go through similar things. Once you get to a place where you have financial success or security, when you don't have to worry about the light bill or food, and you still have all those mercenary narcissistic feelings, what do you do? What do you do when survival is assured? Then it really gets complicated. Worrying about racism is easy! Easy! Dealing with racism is easy, compared with dealing with being in love.

*ÅN: Love is tough. It's hard work.*
**SA**: Yes, it is. And it's the stuff I go through, and that I see now. I couldn't see all this stuff before. I was fundamental. I was so focused on Indian identity I didn't look at the details. So having children, having friends, my life diversifying—all that has changed me. When you talk about love, part of what I write is simply fantasy ful-

fillment. Part of it is simply alternative worlds—taking an emotion and going somewhere with it. So back again to the play. I'm no longer a reservation Indian. I don't want to be extraordinary anymore, or exotic.

**ÅN: Just ordinary?**

**SA**: Yes, just ordinary. Low bar again. I want to be the triumph of the ordinary!

This interview first appeared in *MELUS: Journal of the Society for the Study of the Multi-Ethnic Literature of the United States*, issue 30.4 (Winter 2005), pages 149-169, and is reprinted by permission of the journal. Copyright © 2005 by *MELUS*.

## Works Cited

Alexie, Sherman. *First Indian on the Moon*. New York: Hanging Loose, 1993.
_____. *Indian Killer*. New York: Warner, 1996.
_____. *The Lone Ranger and Tonto Fistfight in Heaven*. New York: HarperPerennial, 1994.
_____. *Reservation Blues*. New York: Warner, 1995.
_____. *The Summer of Black Widows*. New York: Hanging Loose, 1996.
_____. *Ten Little Indians*. New York: Grove, 2003.
_____. *The Toughest Indian in the World*. New York: Atlantic Monthly, 2000.
Brooks, Peter. "Freud's Masterplot: A Model for Narrative." *Reading for the Plot*. New York: Knopf, 1984.
_____. *Psychoanalysis and Storytelling*. Oxford: Blackwell, 1994.
Erikson, Kai. "Notes on Trauma and Community." *Trauma: Explorations in Memory*. Ed. Cathy Caruth. Baltimore MD: Johns Hopkins UP, 1995.
LaCapra, Dominick. *Writing History, Writing Trauma*. Baltimore MD: Johns Hopkins UP, 2001.
*Life Is Beautiful*. Dir. Roberto Benigni. Miramax, 1998.
Spiegelman, Art. *Maus I: A Survivor's Tale: My Father Bleeds History*. London: Pantheon, 1986.
_____. *Maus II: A Survivor's Tale: And Here My Troubles Began*. London: Pantheon, 1992.
Thornton, Russell. *American Indian Holocaust and Survival: A Population History Since 1492*. Norman: U of Oklahoma P, 1987.

# Indian Killer

Daniel Grassian

Whereas *Reservation Blues* was in large part gentle in its social criticism, often presenting Indians as resilient survivors and utilizing comedy to diffuse anger, pain, and tragedy, Alexie's next novel, *Indian
Killer* (1996), is an uncompromising look at rage, anger, and violence
both in the Indian community and in the larger world. In *Reservation
Blues*, Alexie argues that ethnic hybridity can often be a space of productive creation, but in *Indian Killer* that same hybridity turns violent
and destructive. In an interview, Alexie explains the initial genesis of
the novel, dating back to when "I was sitting at Washington State [Uni-
versity] with frat guys in the back row who I wanted to kill. And I
would fantasize about murder."[1] Alexie further explains how his own
anger and dissatisfaction motivated the writing of *Indian Killer*: "It
was a response to the literary movement where a lot of non-Indian
writers are writing Indian books. Non-Indian authors enjoy a success
that is not determined or critiqued by American Indians. So I want to
make sure they're aware of an Indian critical response to their work."[2]
Indeed, through his criticism of Clarence Mather, a white professor of
Native American studies, and other pseudo-Indian fiction writers like
Jack Wilson, Alexie does exactly that.

Whereas Alexie's previous works met almost universal praise, reviews of *Indian Killer* were mixed, presumably because of the sometimes graphically violent subject matter. In a review of the book, *Time*
magazine called Alexie "septic with his own unappeasable anger."[3]
With his characteristic humor, Alexie shrugged off *Time*'s criticism,
telling an interviewer that, "I got a T-shirt with the quote on it. I loved
the reaction. In some masochistic way, I love the really violent reviews
more than the good reviews."[4] Still, Alexie claims that *Indian Killer*
"was the hardest to write" of his works to date and that it "troubled"
him the most, but it is also the book he "probably cares most about."[5]

More common were mixed reviews from critics such as John Skow, who describes the novel as "sad and eloquently written" but "also ugly," accusing Alexie of further polarizing ethnic groups.[6] However, such a viewpoint simplifies Alexie's novel, which may be pessimistic and vilify white society but also vilifies aspects of Indian culture and attitudes. While it is clear that Alexie's sympathies lie more with Indians, he does not excuse or endorse their actions and attitudes. Indeed, the ambiguity of the novel is apparent in the title, which can be read as an Indian who kills or an individual, presumably nonwhite, who kills Indians. In that, the title manifests a veritable circle of violence, which the novel itself plays out.

The protagonist of *Indian Killer* is John Smith,[7] an Indian who was adopted by a white couple, Daniel and Olivia Smith, themselves incapable of having children. For Alexie, a good deal of the novel's tragedy stems from the adoption. In an interview, he explains: "I've met a lot of people like him [John Smith]—'lost birds'—Indians adopted out by non-Indian families—we call them lost birds. . . . The social problems and dysfunctions of these Indians adopted are tremendous. Their suicide rates are off the chart, their drug and alcohol abuse rates are off the chart."[8] Indeed, the fictional protagonist, John Smith, was adopted at a time (in the 1960s) in which Indians were sometimes coerced into adoption since "until the passage of the Indian Child Welfare Act in 1978, many religious organizations actively recruited Native American parents to give up their children for adoption."[9]

Olivia and Daniel, John's white adoptive parents, represent the well-intentioned ignorance and obliviousness that Alexie perceives in the relationships of certain non-Natives with and toward Indians. Olivia and Daniel are far from malicious; rather, they are more like vapid pawns who subscribe to the ideas of the cultural majority without really thinking anything through. Olivia, a highly attractive white woman, is particularly narcissistic and oblivious, more a blank slate than an individual, who has never had any real ambition other than to be artistically cultured and wealthy. They decide to adopt a baby not because they are altruistic but because they cannot have one of their own and because they feel that at their age, it is socially proper to have a child. Daniel, the well-meaning but ultimately ineffectual father figure, tries his best to interest John in sports and in Indian culture, but Daniel lacks authority; he is unwilling to give up on John as a basketball player even though it turns out that John has no aptitude or even great interest in the sport. Furthermore, when John becomes a teenager and plays loud Native American music, which clearly disturbs Daniel, Daniel cannot confront John about it. In a way, Olivia and Daniel are products of a politically correct culture. Wanting to do the socially accepted right thing by exposing John to Native American culture, they both inundate John with all the information they learn about Indians and take him to Indian functions in order to expose him to "his culture." They even insist that an Indian Jesuit baptize John. However noble their intentions might be, Daniel and Olivia only serve to distance John from the Indian world, which in part excludes him because of his adopted white parents and because John, who does not know anything about his biological parents other than that his mother was fourteen when he was born, cannot claim heritage from any single Indian tribe.

All this leads John to misguided beliefs about Indians and whites. When Daniel and Olivia take John to an all-Indian basketball tournament, John misinterprets and romanticizes the various Indians of different tribes. He interprets their frequent laughter and joking to be evidence of their security and happiness when it is more like a self-defense mechanism to stave off despair. Along similar lines, as John gets older, he further romanticizes reservation and Indian life as well as his own feelings of ostracism. John's perception of Indians as noble savages may be informed by the overdramatic descriptions of Indians and their culture in the books that Daniel and Olivia give him, many of which were probably written by non-Natives without much or any direct knowledge of reservation life. *Indian Killer* begins with a chapter appropriately called "Mythology" in the sense that it is John's overly self-conscious elevation of his adoption into tragedy. John imagines being stolen by white people from his mother at birth, taken by a man in a jumpsuit into a helicopter, who randomly fires on people in the reservation, igniting a miniwar, while John is brought to his adopted white parents. No doubt the actual adoption process was significantly more innocuous than John would like to believe.

In other chapters of *Indian Killer*, Alexie identifies how John idealizes life on the reservation and imagines his biological family to be loving, strong and mutually supportive. In John's vision, everyone in the family eats well and as a unit; the children are taught Indian culture, and there is no conflict whatsoever between anyone. John's wizened grandfather tells stories while John dutifully prepares for college, planning to be a doctor and to later practice on the reservation. Missing from John's portrait, of course, is violence, alcoholism, rage, extreme poverty, and humor, all hallmarks of reservation life as Alexie details it in his previous works.

While it is undeniable that John is somewhat mentally unstable, at the very least, Alexie leaves it unresolved as to how much John's problems are genetically or socially based. That John often has trouble distinguishing between fantasy and reality indicates psychosis. In addition, his consuming paranoia toward virtually everyone and the imaginary voices he hears indicate possible schizophrenia. He even believes that there are several different Olivias and Daniels, all of whom are in some way out to get him. Further evidence of John's instability includes how, at twenty, John believed himself to be pregnant, a psychotic fantasy he takes to the point of buying birthing supplies. While Daniel and Olivia try to treat John's problems by getting him to take pills and threatening institutionalization, they are ultimately too weak as parents, in some ways probably fearing John. Despite evidence to the contrary, Daniel describes John's behavior as merely "little teenage rebellions."[10]

To be fair, John's mental problems may be exacerbated by his social milieu, such as being the only Indian teenager at a private school—which Alexie himself has experienced—leading John to feel ostracized from others. John's exclusion gradually develops into feelings of inferiority in contrast to the other white students, whom he deems to be more intelligent and complex than himself. To some extent, the attitudes of others cause John's feelings of inferiority. When John dates white girls, their parents view John with suspicion and subtly disapprove of their budding relationships. Like Daniel and Olivia, John's teachers are often overwhelmingly acquiescent of his frequently erratic behavior, never realizing that their response to John also makes him feel further isolated. When John gets into a fight, the principal lets John go without even a reprimand because of his ethnicity. To some extent, his teachers have good intentions in that they realize that, being an orphan and an Indian in a predominantly white school, John has a much more difficult time than most, but like Daniel and Olivia, John's teachers' seemingly good intentions actually evince a stereotypical and demeaning attitude toward Indians, whom they dehumanize in their generalized pity. What they don't realize or understand is that John, although adopted, comes from a wealthy family, and that one cause of his social problems are actions like those of his teachers that make him acutely aware of his ethnicity, which, because of his adopted status and his lack of knowledge about his biological parents, he has to deny.

In part motivated by how he is treated by people like his teachers, John attempts to find a sense of authenticity as an Indian. However, his attempts at authenticity are something of a masquerade, based on what John believes to be Indian role models, but whom John is drawn to because of their envied fearlessness: Mohawk Indian steelworkers who worked on the World Trade Center in New York City. Thereby, John becomes a construction worker, fully embracing anything deemed by the mainstream to be "Indian" because he has no real cultural identity, complicated by the fact that "tall and muscular, he looked like some cinematic warrior, and constantly intimidated people with his presence" (32). Ironically, John appears like a stereotypical image of an Indian, but culturally he is more Caucasian than Indian. Seeking power and acceptance from both the white and Native American worlds, John begins to lie to other people, telling whites that he is of Sioux origin "because that was what they wanted him to be," and telling Indians that he is Navajo "because that was what he wanted to be." John is not only aware of how intimidating he can be, he comes to believe that he could "rule the world" if he would dress as a stereotypical, savage, bellicose Indian (40). This is symptomatic of his delusions of grandeur. In fact, because he has lost his Indian heritage, John overdramatizes its power to the point of virtual omnipotence.

Complicating matters is that John appears in some ways traumatized by his Jesuit upbringing. Throughout the novel, he obsessively thinks of Father Duncan, a Spokane Indian Jesuit priest, who plays a significant role in John's childhood in adding to his vehemence against non-Natives by convincing him that white people killed most of the Indians but Indians did not kill all the white people because "they didn't have the heart for it" (14). Although Duncan vanishes after John turns seven, he remains an important mental fixture in John's life, whom John consults during his search for a stable community and for an otherworldly being like Bigfoot, whom he actively seeks and admires as a quintessential trickster figure.

John's reality is much different than his fantasy. The real-time narrative of *Indian Killer* in the present finds John, age twenty-seven, a reclusive, antisocial construction worker who avoids virtually all human contact. His ostracism is at least partially self-imposed, a product of his emotional instability, but also due to being Indian without having a definitive tribal identity in a predominantly white society. In part due to his internalization of the Indian archetype of men as warriors, John fantasizes about terrorizing the foreman of his construction company. Furthermore, his perception of Indians as having otherworldly power over nature (such as calling on the wind to strike at his perceived enemies) originates from Western stereotypes. In a deluded, possibly psychotic haze, John decides that he needs to kill a white man. Alexie thereby entices the reader to suspect that John himself is the Indian Killer, as he will with virtually every character in the novel. While

John believes he is capable of killing a white man, he also realizes the futility of doing so, even on a large scale. John rationalizes his murderous desire as retribution for crimes against Indians, but in truth he is mostly driven by anger due to personal feelings of isolation and powerlessness. John's rantings have some sense to them, however, such as his claim that "white people no longer feared Indians" (30). Indeed, to mainstream white America, there is more of a perceived threat from the larger African American community, especially evidenced by riots of the past forty years, than there is from Indians. Alexie depicts John wanting to achieve power by frightening whites. To some extent, this may be part of Alexie's purpose in the novel. That is, he may feel that through fear, Indians can achieve some progress in social equality. John, however, desires whites to fear him more for his own personal benefit.

Another major character whom Alexie gradually implicates as a possible suspect for being the Indian Killer is Marie Polatkin, an undergraduate at the University of Washington and radical leader of the Native American Students Alliance. According to Ron McFarland, Alexie chooses the surname Polatkin because it "associates [her] with Chief Polatki, one of whose daughters was married to Qualchan, who led the Spokane, Palouse, and Coeur d'Alene tribes in 1858 against Colonel Wright."[11] Marie, a hot-tempered Spokane Indian activist, organizes protests against university policies that discriminate against Indians, such as a prohibition against powwows. As with John, Marie's anger and isolation are products of both Native American and white society. As a gifted, motivated student who knows very little about Spokane culture, Marie was immediately ostracized on the reservation, deemed to be not wholly Indian. It is important to recognize that John is not the only Indian struggling with how to achieve a sense of individual authenticity. Not only is Marie involved in the same struggle, so are all Indians, Alexie suggests, by obsessively ranking each other on the basis of how authentically Indian each is, determined not only by ethnicity but by knowledge of cultural traditions and purposeful isolation from the white world. Marie becomes convinced that in order to be happier, she needs to find other Indians whom she determines to be less authentically Indian than herself. Indeed, this is what ultimately drives her to be a Native American student leader at the University of Washington.

Alexie first entices the reader to believe that John is the killer when he has a streetside confrontation with a white man he accidentally bumps into. The condescending, possibly racist white man calls John "Chief," and when John doesn't say anything, the white man calls him a drunk and patronizingly asks if he needs help. The white man's blatantly assertive behavior infuriates John, reminding him of the many times he has felt powerless in his life. Alexie ends the chapter, however, by telling the reader that John follows the young man but not that he kills him. Rather than tell the reader this, Alexie maintains the mystery of the killer with third-person omniscient chapters written about or from the perspective of "the killer."

When Alexie describes the murder itself, he makes it sufficiently ambiguous by describing the prelude of the murder through a third-person omniscient narration of the "killer" who has a streetside confrontation with a white man similar to the one John just had. Still, streetside confrontations are sufficiently common that the killer could certainly be someone other than John. Whether or not the killer is John or someone else, Alexie makes him or her have the same difficulties distinguishing between fantasy and reality that John has and the same desire for power and to inspire fear. While Alexie writes that "the killer had not necessarily meant for any of it to happen" (53), the killer also takes pride in the kill by scalping the man. Furthermore, the killer derives a sadistic joy from murder as well, one that seemingly cannot be satiated, concluding that "one dead man was not enough" (54). The killer then leaves what becomes a trademark signature: two owl feathers.

The killer aspires to act like an owl, and Alexie chooses the owl feathers for their symbolic significance. As Bobby Lake-Thom explains, "The Owl is considered a bad sign and a bad power by most Native American tribal groups. It is a messenger of evil, of sickness, or of a fatal accident. It is also considered a sign of death."[12] Along similar lines, Alexie explains that the killer begins to consider the murders to each be part of a larger "hunt" and the scalping to be "trophies" or proof of a perceived power over whites. However twisted the killer's logic might be, he or she is not fully deranged and there is some method to this killer's madness. Later in the novel, the killer decides to kidnap a young white boy, Mark Jones, which proves to be a relatively shrewd terror tactic as it frightens families throughout Seattle. In a way, the kidnapping of Mark Jones mirrors John Smith's own imagined kidnapping at the beginning of the novel, which does lend evidence to the theory that John Smith is the killer.

Ultimately, the killer desires attention and overdramatizes his or her actions by claiming that the murders, the scalping, and the kidnapping of Mark Jones are the beginning of "the first dance of a powerful ceremony that would change the world" (192). Ultimately, the killer plays a cat-and-mouse game with the authorities. That the killer is not fully insane or murderous is evident in the surreptitious return of Mark Jones to his mother, past the not very watchful eyes of the police. However, returning Mark Jones does not denote a real change in the attitude of the killer, who, not long afterward, proceeds to mercilessly kill a businessman, Edward Letterman, ignoring Letterman's pleas for his life, even "feasting on his heart" before scalping him (328).

While the killer is the obvious villain of the novel, he or she is not the only one. With the character of Clarence Mather, a white professor of Native American studies, Alexie creates a metaphorical murderer, one who destroys, twists, or appropriates Indian culture and tradition for his own selfish devices. To some extent, Alexie uses Marie, a student in Mather's Native American literature class, as a mouthpiece against the teaching of Native American studies by non-Natives and also as a critique against the many fraudulent works of Native American literature actually ghostwritten or written by whites. Alexie describes Mather as a "Wannabe Indian" and, through Marie's critical eye, lampoons his reading list for the course as derived from misguided Euro-American conceptions of Native Americans and primarily designed for non-Natives as evidenced by the fact that Marie is the only Indian student enrolled in the class (58). When looking at the syllabus, Marie criticizes Mather's inclusion of *The Education of Little Tree* (which she believes to be written by a former Ku Klux Klan grand wizard) as well as *Black Elk Speaks, Lame Deer: Seeker of Visions*, and *Lakota Woman*, which she believes to be either ghost- or co-written by whites.[13]

In response to Marie's frequent, heated objections, Mather tries to defend his choices and course as "viewing the Native American world from both the interior and exterior" (60). However, Marie continues to object to Mather's choices, claiming that "a non-Indian can't present an authentic and traditional view of the Indian world if he isn't authentic and traditional himself" (66). It is important not to mistake Marie's views for Alexie's views, although they may be similar. Alexie portrays Marie as somewhat of a victim of her own background, and thus she may not be a completely accurate mouthpiece for Alexie, especially considering that Alexie describes her motivations for objecting to Mather as being partially selfish, rooted in her own recurring personal struggles and her own need for conflict, which has become a nearly constant element in her life.

While Marie thrives on conflict, she also is at least partially altruistic, as evidenced by her volunteer work for homeless Indians in Seattle, many of whom call her "The Sandwich Lady" because of the food she provides for them. Still, Marie's rage is also directed toward Indians, many of whom she accuses of frittering their money, time, and energy away during powwows or other "celebrations," which she believes to be fraudulent and especially indulgent considering the many destitute and hungry Indians who could be helped with the time and money that other Indians devote to powwows. Alexie wants the reader to believe that, given Marie's rage, she also could be the Indian Killer, a possibility suggested by Marie's explosive reaction to a person, Boo, who helps her deliver food to the homeless. When he suggests that they use mayonnaise on the sandwiches, Marie has a near violent reaction due to a concern for money, and Boo tells her that she sounds like the Indian Killer. In addition, when Boo asks Marie, half in jest, whether she is the Indian Killer, she ducks the question, never answering it. Furthermore, Marie's growing obsessive disdain of Mather, which leads to stalking him on more than one occasion, appears borderline pathological or psychotic.

For Mather, the situation with Marie reaches a breaking point after weeks of confrontation. Mather's ignorance becomes increasingly apparent with such claims as "gambling casinos on Indian reservations are very much an act of fiscal rebellion," which Marie convincingly refutes by calling them "a financial necessity" (83). While Mather insists that, through his course and his research, he attempts to provide an uplifting account of Indians, he is obviously blinded by his own conception of Indians (even if it is positive) and, at one point, sternly slams his office door in Marie's face during one of their after-class confrontations. Alexie further entices the reader to consider Marie as the Indian Killer with a description of how infuriated she feels after Mather shuts the door in her face—to the point of wanting all whites to "disappear," wanting "to burn them all down to ash and feast on their smoke" (85). Even if Marie is not the Indian Killer, Alexie's intention is to show how Indians commonly experience violent rage and anger due to marginalization, discrimination, and unequal power struggles. This, for Alexie, is much more of an accurate generalization than depicting Indians as benevolent and nature-loving or warrior/savages.

Another character who is more of a probable suspect as the Indian Killer, given his violent tendencies, is Marie's cousin, Reggie Polatkin, at one time a close friend of Mather's. With Reggie, Alexie shows how being of mixed ethnicity can be as trying, if not more so, as having no biological parents (John Smith) or being full-blooded but ostracized (Marie). Again vilifying whites, Alexie describes Reggie's white father, Bird Lawrence, as violently racist toward Indians, whom he believes to be ignorant savages. He forces Reggie to use his Indian mother's surname and refuses to let him use the surname Lawrence until Reggie displays sufficient docility toward him. Bird's abusive behavior, demonstrated by calling Reggie a "stupid, dirty Indian" when Reggie does poorly in school (94), leads Reggie to harbor feelings of anger and inferiority. Consequently, over time Reggie comes to prize his white ancestry, considering it to be responsible for his successes, while he vilifies his Indian ancestry, holding it responsible for his failures.

Only after Reggie takes a class with Mather does he become interested in Indian culture, but his interest, piqued by Mather, is misguided and becomes merely a facade. Together, the two attend traditional Indian cultural events like sweathouses, where Reggie discovers that being Indian offers him power over the other whites who attend and look to him for instruction and guidance. Consequently, he begins to act wise, all-knowing, and domineering. Alexie suggests that Reggie's experiences are not unique and that many Indians subscribe to mainstream codes for identity, which supplant their real identity, for doing so offers them rewards from non-Natives.

Still, it is Mather, rather than Reggie, whom Alexie ultimately vilifies as immoral and unethical. Their breaking point occurs when Mather finds audiotapes of Pacific Northwest Indian elders recorded in 1926. He plays them for Reggie, who insists that the tapes be erased because they are family stories, not meant for public consumption. While Mather wants to publish articles about the tapes, Reggie not only wants to keep the tapes from the prying hands of whites like Mather, but, like Mather, he also wants to keep the tapes for himself. To some extent Reggie's rationale is understandable, but it is extreme. Rather than considering giving them to a neutral third party, Reggie lets his anger and rage get the better of him. Mather is no better. In fact, his behavior is worse. After Reggie confronts him about the tapes, Mather denies their existence because of greed and selfishness. In

Mather's deluded world, he comes "to see those stories as his possessions, as his stories, as if it had been his voice on those tapes" (138). Mather's extreme immorality can be seen in that he continues to lie to the department chair about the existence of the tapes after Reggie lodges a complaint, leading Mather to selfishly keep the tapes for his own personal listening pleasures.

Furthermore, Alexie lampoons academic posturing and rationalization through Mather, who actually absolves the "Indian Killer" of responsibility and thereby denies him or her any agency. By blaming "capitalism," Mather's pseudo-Marxist rationale ignores race and ethnicity while theoretically encouraging the killing, as is demonstrated by his calling the Indian Killer a "revolutionary construct" (245). Losing the ability to take anything literally, Mather sees metaphors and representation when there really aren't any and makes sketchy analyses of the killings. Mather also represents poor literary analysis of the novel itself, evidenced by when he describes the kidnapping of Mark Jones as a metaphor for the Indian condition, an attempt to counteract centuries of oppression. Alexie, who in his poetry has previously lampooned literary critics for seeing metaphors and symbols in his work at places in which there aren't any or for overextending their meaning, uses the same technique here.

With Mather, Alexie also considers to what extent a non-Native can really be an expert of Native American studies. That Mather has, as he points out to Marie, lived on a reservation for several months and assisted the AIM movement during the late sixties and early seventies, improves his credibility. However, as a wealthy, white American, he lacks the firsthand knowledge of racism, discrimination, poverty and feelings of powerlessness. In essence, he is in too privileged a position to truly understand the "Indian condition" as he generalizes it.

While Mather is obtuse, arrogant, and immoral, he is not or does not appear to be physically violent, unlike most of the Rogers family, composed of the father, Buck, and two sons, Aaron, a vicious, violent ringleader, and David, a student in Mather's Native American literature class, who is thought to be killed by the Indian Killer but is actually killed by two random white men. The Rogerses own land near an Indian reservation and David recalls how Indians would "trespass" on his family's farm when David was a child to take camas root, "a traditional and sacred food of the local Indians for thousands of years" (62). David's father, Buck, having no use for camas root or the land where it grows, refuses to allow the Indians access to the land and the roots. Unconcerned about these Indians (and presumably all Indians), the Rogerses ironically regard them as trespassers, even shooting at them when they "invade" their land. Buck defends their actions to his children by claiming he is protecting his land from thieves. Buck, of course, doesn't realize the irony in his claim since the land was originally stolen from the ancestors of these Indians.

Representing far-right conservatism at best and a vicious, cold-blooded racist at worst, Truck Schultz, a white talk-show host reminiscent of Rush Limbaugh, helps stir up anti-Indian sentiment during the time of the killings. That Schultz, who espouses pro-white and anti-Indian rhetoric and is also the most popular talk-show host in the city, evinces a stern critique of Seattle, where the novel is set. Comparing Indians to spoiled children and savages, Truck claims that "we have coddled Indians too long and we've created a monster" (209). Truck, in many ways, is the most one-dimensional of all the characters in *Indian Killer*, which may be understandable given that as a radio talk-show host, his stage identity may have usurped his real identity.

What is shocking, then, is the extent of Truck's popularity. Even the seemingly innocuous Daniel Smith listens to Truck. Alexie implicates the city of Seattle for its lack of diversity and lack of equal opportunity for minorities. He describes Seattle as merely having a veneer of diversity when the city itself is largely ethnically segregated, with minorities residing in one part of the city and whites living in another. Further complicating matters is the friction between different minority groups. John Smith, for instance, recognizes common ground between himself and African Americans but finds it impossible to connect with the two

African American men (Paul and Paul Too) who work at Seattle's Best Donuts, where he is a frequent customer.

That Seattle is an ethnically polarized city becomes even more apparent as ethnic violence erupts after the police and media start calling the killer the "Indian Killer." Certain whites, angry at perceived attacks against them by the "Indian Killer," proceed to taunt and attack random Indians. Aaron Rogers, with two of his friends, leads random violent attacks against Indians as retribution for the murder of his brother David (although, as Alexie later reveals, he was not killed by Indians). Still, Alexie doesn't portray in a much better light extremist Indians, who, in their thirst for blood, glorify the Indian Killer as being a contemporary reincarnation of Crazy Horse, Chief Joseph, Geronimo, and Wovoka. One cheers on the killer, as in a sporting event in which the score is "ten million to three, in favor of the white guys" (220). Furthermore, Reggie assaults whites as mercilessly as Aaron Rogers does Indians.

Meanwhile, John grows steadily more unstable and, in his delusion and haze, becomes convinced that one death will rectify the wrongs committed against Indians. While this would seem to lend credence to the theory that John is the Indian Killer, the fact that he insists on a single death and the Indian Killer has already killed more than one person make the possibility that he is the Indian Killer less likely. Another suspect is Jack Wilson, an "Indian" mystery writer whom Mather assigns in his course and who also functions as a double of John Smith. Wilson's romanticized, misguided depictions of Indians can be seen through his protagonist, Aristotle Little Hawk, a Shilshomish Indian, shaman, and private detective in Seattle. Little Hawk possesses the stereotypical features of Indians, "a hawkish nose, walnut skin, and dark eyes," as well as a savage, emotional instability (162). It is significant that when Jack Wilson encounters John, he thinks John looks exactly like his fictional hero, Little Hawk, because Jack and John are virtually alter egos, their generic first names variations of the same name and both possessing generic last names. Furthermore, like Aristotle, John

Smith is all image and little or no substance, looking like a stereotypical Indian but internally possessing no real authenticity. Like John, Wilson is an orphan, isolated as an adult, and while Wilson is white and John Indian, they both overly romanticize Indian life and culture because they both believe that it offers a nurturing, supportive environment where all are welcomed (in contrast to how they view mainstream American society). Similar to John, Wilson conceives of himself as a romantic loner who is "in search of his family" (157).

Furthermore, just as John pretends to be from a certain tribe, Wilson concocts a half-baked story about having an Indian relative so that he can claim he is of mixed ethnicity. Alexie's sympathies lie more with John as John cannot fit into either the white or Indian world, whereas Wilson could easily live as a white man if he chose to do so. Alexie also uncovers the hypocrisy that allows whites to claim Indian status with a mere modicum of Indian ancestry (a reverse form of the one-drop rule), whereas Indians with a modicum of white ancestry, such as Marie, cannot really pass as white. When Wilson goes to an Indian bar (Big Heart's), Alexie points out Wilson's ignorance in that Wilson does not recognize that class distinctions do not matter as much as tribal distinctions to Indians. While Wilson believes himself to be accepted by other Indians at Big Heart's, he also does not realize that they are merely patronizing him and surreptitiously mocking him.

Still, in contrast to Alexie's depiction of racist police officers, Wilson appears almost heroic. Here, Alexie once again implicates Seattle; this time for discrimination and racism within the police department. When homeless Indians are killed, one officer tells a disconcerted Wilson that the crime isn't really worth being investigated and the perpetrator ought not to be actively sought because he views killing Indians as "pest control" (160). However, now that the victims are white and the perpetrator presumably Indian, the police take immediate action. Had the killer been a minority, Alexie suggests, there would not have been nearly as much concern, especially if the victims weren't white. Supporting this idea is the fact that there is an outpouring of grief for

David after he is found dead, whereas there is little or no concern for the Indian victims of Aaron's and other whites' rampages. In addition, whereas the police trust the testimony of a white man who was beat up by Reggie and his friends, when an Indian man reports an assault at the hands of whites, the officers believe he is probably delusional.

That most people insist that the Indian Killer is Indian is somewhat justifiable given the scalping and owl feathers, but it is by no means a certainty. While the police insist that an Indian is the killer, Wilson mentions that many non-Indians know about scalping. Furthermore, it is the common perception that an Indian is the killer, preying on white people, that sparks the extreme fear in Seattle, a fear Alexie would argue that Indians experienced during the settlement of the country and that, to some extent, they continue to experience up to the present day. While Wilson realizes there is a possibility that the "Indian Killer" is not Indian, he doesn't believe that possibility. However, it is conceivable that Wilson may be the killer himself, evidenced by how, in one dream, he thinks of John as the killer and then "Wilson saw himself with that knife. Wilson saw himself pushing the knife into one white body, then another, and another, until there were multitudes" (391). At the same time that Alexie suggests Wilson may be a possible suspect, he makes it less likely that John is the Indian Killer. At one point in the novel, two white men threaten John and Marie and then attack John. While John at first threateningly waves a golf club at the white men, he inexplicably gets frightened, screams, and runs away. In contrast, Alexie portrays Marie as more capable of violence. After learning of the random violence committed against Native Americans in Seattle, Marie is so infuriated that she "wanted to tear out their blue eyes and blind them" (375).

Aaron Rogers and his friends mainly commit these random acts of violence as supposed retribution for the death of Aaron's brother David, whom they mistakenly believe to have been killed by the Indian Killer. However, Aaron is not the only one responsible for inspiring the violence. Truck Schultz could also be held responsible due to his anti-

Indian rhetoric and for boldly announcing that the Indian Killer was responsible for Edward Letterman's death before possessing any legitimate evidence, leading to violence and rioting in Seattle.

Meanwhile, John decides that Wilson is the person who needs to be killed. Since Wilson is a virtual double of John, John's desire to kill Wilson may be a veiled desire to commit suicide, which he eventually does instead of killing Wilson. That Wilson keeps insisting to John that he is "Indian," not white, demonstrates how he has come to believe his own lies. Therefore, when John wonders "if Wilson knew the difference between dreaming and reality. How one could easily become the other" (403), it is clear that Wilson does not, especially as a writer. John comes to the conclusion that "Wilson was responsible for all that had gone wrong" (404). In essence, Wilson represents the desire on the part of certain whites to usurp Indian identity, and it is that same desire which may have led Daniel and Olivia to adopt John in the first place. It is not so much that Wilson is responsible for "all that had gone wrong," as John claims, but rather, like Mather, he is a metaphorical vulture plucking the last remnants of Indian identity and culture. John then slashes Wilson's face on the twisted, irrational logic that it will prevent him from claiming Indian ancestry because John believes the scar will forever mark him as an imposter and a symbol of white theft and perversion of Native culture.

After John's death, the police prematurely think of him as the chief suspect for being the Indian Killer, although they have no hard evidence linking him to the crimes. Wilson capitalizes on the incidents by writing a book about John, concluding, like the police, that John was the Indian Killer. Thus, even Wilson's disfigurement is not enough to counteract his distortions of Native American culture. That Wilson ends up being the ultimate authority on the killings is ironic, for it is in his literary nature to only obfuscate any illuminations of Indian life. Indeed, Wilson becomes even more arrogant after John's death as Wilson comes to believe not only that he is the only one who can understand who and what motivated the Indian Killer (whom he believes to be

John) but that his book would "finally reveal to the world what it truly meant to be Indian" (338). Similarly, Clarence Mather also capitalizes on the killings, writing a book about it and claiming that Reggie and possibly Marie were behind the killings. That Aaron Rogers and Barry Church only get six months in county jail for their violent assault and near-killing of several Indians in Seattle shows even more racial discrimination in the Seattle judicial system.

Some critics take fault with Alexie's uncompromising ending, which they interpret as justifying or glorifying violence against whites. At the end of the novel, an Indian, possibly the killer him- or herself, performs a Ghost Dance. The Ghost Dance, over five hundred years old, was performed in hopes that it would dispel the invading whites and resurrect dead relatives and loved ones, while returning the land to a precolonized state.[14] Earlier in the novel, Marie had castigated Mather for not understanding the full rationale behind the Ghost Dance. Whereas Mather views it as a benevolent, symbolic act, Marie interprets it literally as an expression of anger against the historical oppression of whites to the point of wanting them banished forever from the continent. Mather claims that the Ghost Dance was "about peace and beauty" (313), but Marie claims it is more about retribution and that in the late twentieth century, given the decrepit state of reservations and of Indian life both on and away from the reservation, there is more reason than ever to feel angry at the oppression of whites and to support the Ghost Dance. In the last chapter, during a final vision, when the killer begins to perform the Ghost Dance, other Indians (hundreds) come and dance it along with him. Alexie describes the killer as planning on "dancing forever" and that the surrounding trees grow "heavy with owls" (420). As established earlier, according to traditional Indian folklore, the owl is a sign of evil, sickness, or death. Alexie thus suggests that the killings will continue in the future. This is not to suggest that Alexie encourages an attempted violent revolution, for he surely recognizes that such an attempt would ultimately prove futile, but that the desire for revolt and revenge remains an important, albeit repressed desire for many Indians, a startling revelation for many who believe in the stereotype of Indians as docile, despondent, and nature-loving.

## Notes

1. Quoted in Joelle Fraser, "Sherman Alexie's *Iowa Review* Interview." http://www.english.uiuc.edu/maps/poets/a_f/alexie/fraser.htm. Originally published as "An Interview with Sherman Alexie," *Iowa Review* 30, no. 3 (Winter 2000): 59-70.

2. Quoted in Lynn Cline, "About Sherman Alexie," *Ploughshares* 26, no. 4 (Winter 2000/2001): 201.

3. Quoted in Duncan Campbell, "Voices of the New Tribe." *Guardian* (Manchester), January 4, 2003. http://books.guardian.co.uk/review/story/0,12084,868123,00.html.

4. Quoted in Campbell, "Voices of the New Tribe."

5. Quoted in Campbell, "Voices of the New Tribe."

6. John Skow, "Lost Heritage," *Time* 148, no. 19 (October 21, 1996): 88.

7. By naming the killer John Smith, Alexie probably refers to the original colonist and writer, John Smith, who was among the first settlers in Virginia and was abducted by Native Americans. Smith describes his encounters with Native Americans in *A General History* (1624). In a sense, the original John Smith was the first powerful, European colonizer in the New World.

8. Quoted in Tomson Highway, "Spokane Words: Tomson Highway Raps with Sherman Alexie." *Aboriginal Voices*, January-March 1997. http://www.fallsapart.com/art-av.html.

9. Bonnie Duran, Eduardo Duran, and Maria Yellow Horse Brave Heart. "Native Americans and the Trauma of History," *Studying Native America: Problems and Prospects*, ed. Russell Thornton (Madison: University of Wisconsin Press, 1998), 69.

10. Sherman Alexie, *Indian Killer* (New York: Warner Books, 1996), 114. Further references to this book are noted parenthetically in the text.

11. Ron McFarland, "Sherman Alexie's Polemic Stories," *Studies in American Indian Literature* 9, no. 4 (Winter 1997): 34.

12. Bobby Lake-Thom, *Spirits of the Earth: A Guide to Native American Nature Symbols, Stories, and Ceremonies* (New York: Plume, 1997), 117.

13. In an interview, Alexie further explains his criticism of some of these works: "The same man who wrote that book [*Lakota Woman*] also wrote *Lame Deer, Seeker of Visions*. Once again, these autobiographies are not really autobiographies, they're translations. Both writers of those books have freely admitted to poetic license. Poetic

license and manifest destiny are often the same thing" (quoted in "Spokane Words"). Alexie's claim about *The Education of Little Tree* has been substantiated; see Tom Gliatto's article "*The Education of Little Tree*" in *People Weekly* 37, no. 22 (December 15, 1997): 87-92; or Michael Marker's "*The Education of Little Tree*: What It Really Reveals about the Public Schools," in *Phi Delta Kappan* 74, no. 3 (November 1992). There is more dissent about *Black Elk Speaks*, with prominent Indian activist Vine Deloria Jr. calling it "a North American Bible for all tribes" (quoted in Carl Silvio, "*Black Elk Speaks* and Literary Disciplinarity: A Case Study in Canonization," *College Literature* 26, no. 2 [Spring 1999]: 138) while others, like Alexie, question the authenticity of the text. For a history of the academic disputes surrounding *Black Elk Speaks*, see Silvio's article. While it is true that a white man (Richard Erdoes) co-wrote or co-edited *Lakota Woman* and *Lame Deer: Seeker of Visions*, it is not clear how much power he had in shaping the novel or whether his influence perverted the actual content.

14. For more information about the Ghost Dance, see Andrew Macdonald, Gina Macdonald, and MaryAnn Sheridan, *Shape-Shifting: Images of Native Americans in Recent Popular Fiction* (Westport, Conn.: Greenwood Press, 2000).

# Sex and Salmon:
## Queer Identities in Sherman Alexie's
## *The Toughest Indian in the World*_____
Lisa Tatonetti

Contemporary queer Native American writing emerged circa 1976 with the publication of two pieces by Mohawk author Maurice Kenny: an essay, "Tinseled Bucks: A Historical Study of Indian Homosexuality," and a poem "Winkte."[1] This beginning was followed in 1981 by Laguna author Paula Gunn Allen's essay, "Beloved Women: Lesbians in American Indian Cultures." During that same year, Cherríe Moraga and Gloria Anzaldúa's landmark anthology *This Bridge Called My Back* brought two more gay Native voices to print: Hunkpapa writer Barbara Cameron, co-founder of Gay American Indians, and Menominee poet, Chrystos. Two years later, in 1983, Mohawk poet and short fiction writer Beth Brant (Bay of Quinte Mohawk) published *A Gathering of Spirit: Writing and Art by North American Indian Women*. The first Native-edited collection of American Indian and First Nation writing, Brant's collection included pieces by eleven Native lesbians. It would be five more years until Will Roscoe's *Living the Spirit* (1988), an anthology devoted entirely to the writing of gay Native people, appeared.[2] While there has been a steady rise in the publication of literary work by and about gay, lesbian, bisexual, transsexual/transgender, queer (GLBTQ), and Two-Spirit Native peoples since Roscoe's 1988 collection, critical investigations of this important body of literature are just now finding representation in scholarly forums on American Indian literature.[3]

Paralleling the reticence of the larger critical community regarding queer Native voices has been the troubling inclusion of both implicit and explicit homophobia in the work of influential Native writers such as Leslie Marmon Silko and James Welch. Both Silko's 1991 *Almanac of the Dead* and James Welch's 2000 *The Heartsong of Charging Elk* contain negative images of queer sexuality: in each text, gay male characters function as the site of seemingly unrelenting evil.[4] Against such a backdrop, the 2000 release of Spokane/Coeur d'Alene writer Sherman Alexie's collection of short stories, *The Toughest Indian in the World*, represents one of the most positive and explicit depictions of queer sexuality offered in the work of the more canonical contemporary American Indian fiction writers—Leslie Marmon Silko, Louise Erdrich, N. Scott Momaday, James Welch, and Alexie.[5] Alexie's work in *The Toughest Indian* is representative of his outspoken championship of queer issues. An ally to the GLBTQ/Two-Spirit community, Alexie frequently addresses the problems of homophobia in both his public speaking engagements (which often resemble stand-up comedy routines) and his numerous interviews. Alexie's 2002 independent film, *The Business of Fancydancing*, focuses on the fictional (but semi-autobiographic) experiences of a gay Native poet, Seymour Polatkin, as he negotiates the sometimes-difficult relationship between his reservation history and his present urban reality.[6] Given Alexie's prominent position in contemporary anthologies, in current syllabi, and in the eye of the reading public in the United States—Alexie has laughingly called himself the "Indian du jour"—his representations of queer Native identity have the potential for considerable impact.

My analysis here centers on the productive and markedly significant images of queer sexuality found in Alexie's *The Toughest Indian in the World* (2000). While Alexie's collection has at its heart the examination of human relationships in all their forms, two stories in particular bring queer identity to the fore: the title piece, "The Toughest Indian in the World," which tells the enigmatic story of a Spokane journalist's first sexual experience with a Lummi Indian man; and "Indian Country," which unravels the rambling tale of Low Man Smith's unplanned reunion with his white college friend, Tracy Johnson, who rescues Low Man by getting him out of jail and bringing him to the tumultuous dinner at which she meets her Spokane girlfriend's parents for the first time. In "The Toughest Indian in the World," Alexie forwards what Two-Spirit author/activist Qwo-Li Driskill (Cherokee/African/Irish/Lenape/Lumbee) has termed the "Sovereign Erotic" by using queerness as a potential foundation of Native cultural identification.

Both "The Toughest Indian in the World" and "Indian Country" ground themselves in the safety of the heterosexual relationship before they introduce queer characters and themes. The unnamed, first-person narrator of "The Toughest Indian" tells the story of his recent sexual relationship with his co-worker, Cindy, while "Indian Country" opens when Low Man Smith steps off the plane in Missoula, Montana, with the intention of asking Carlotta, a Navajo woman, to marry him. Although both Cindy and Carlotta appear only in flashback, their presences at the beginning of each narrative serve as a heteronormative safety net since each story's subsequent exploration of queer desire and identity are, at least to some degree, mediated by the narrator and main character's seemingly grounded heterosexual identity. This mediation is upheld with vigor in a number of the reviews of Alexie's book.

While some reviewers fail to mention Alexie's representations of queer relationships at all, others take the protagonist's heterosexuality as a given. Polly Paddock Gossett, for example, while calling Alexie's title story "masterful," sums up its plot by saying that "the [story's narrator], though straight, winds up sleeping with the hitchhiker. 'I wanted him to save me,' he explains."[7] Gossett's caveat—"though straight"—and her use of the verb "explains" to describe the narrator's depiction of his sexual encounter illustrate how the narrator's sexual identity can be represented as unequivocally heterosexual rather than bisexual or gay despite, or perhaps because of, the fact that the bulk of the story circles around what seems to be the narrator's first gay sexual experience. Ken Foster, the reviewer for the *San Francisco Chronicle*, reads the encounter in much the same way: "Over the course of the story, the narrator, who is straight, picks up a scarred Indian fighter, takes him to a hotel and ultimately has sex with him. What makes this so astonishing is that Alexie doesn't feel the need to tack on any kind of sexual epiphany: At the end of the story, the narrator is no more gay than he was at the start."[8] Alexie himself points out the ironies of such reader response in a discussion of the title story's reception:

> When I wrote it I honestly didn't think about the reaction people would have to it. It's funny—it really brings up the homophobia in people. When a straight guy like me writes about a homoerotic experience in the first person with a narrator who is very similar to me—I could see people dying to ask me if it was autobiographical. They always ask in regard to everything else, but no one's asked me about that story. In the Seattle paper here, the critic called it a "graphic act of homosexuality" and I thought "graphic?" There's nothing graphic about it at all. It was three sentences. He talked about me being a "literary rabble-rouser" again.[9]

In each of these cases, Alexie's story, or, more specifically, Alexie's inclusion of queer sex, provokes strong response among reviewers. On the most basic level, such responses reflect current dominant attitudes toward sexuality, in which heterosexuality is still compulsory and sexuality continues to be framed as a system of binaries. In such equations, the narrator is either straight (preferably) *or* gay (possibly), but not bi, nor queer, nor Two-Spirit. The choices are limited and both the categories and responses remain rigid.

Such limited choices evoke Qwo-Li Driskill's commentary on colonialism and sexuality. Driskill points out that "[a] colonized sexuality is one in which [indigenous people] have internalized the sexual values of dominant culture. The invaders continue to enforce the idea that sexuality and non-dichotomous genders are a sin, recreating sexuality as illicit, shocking, shameful, and removed from any positive spiritual context. Queer sexualities and genders are degraded, ignored, condemned, and destroyed."[10] Driskill focuses specifically on indigenous sexualities here, addressing the sometimes-virulent homophobia that has been part of the assimilation process in many indigenous communities. His argument, however, extends beyond the boundaries of indigenous communities: Driskill suggests that heterosexist and/or homophobic responses (like those in reaction to Alexie's investigation of the range of human sexualities) tie directly to ideologies of colonialism. Furthermore, Driskill points out that these attitudes are part of the colonial project of erasure, which silences non-dominant histories such as, in this case, the fact that many indigenous cultures traditionally included multiple gender categories and alternate constructions of sexuality. As Sue-Ellen Jacobs, Wesley Thomas, and Sabine Lang note, "Cross-cultural comparative studies have shown that genders and sexualities are not always fixed into only two marked categories. Institutionalized gender diversity is found throughout the world but not in all cultures. In Native North America, there were and still are cultures in which more than two gender categories are marked. There is more than a hundred years of writing on this subject (albeit sporadic until the mid-twentieth century)."[11] In Driskill's argument, this history of indigenous sexualities is not an aside or addition, but a point of departure. Both Driskill's theory and Alexie's story speak against the sometimes-virulent homophobia and the often invisible heterosexism that has been part and parcel of the colonial project.

In "The Toughest Indian in the World," the narrator's sexual identity is a great deal more ambiguous than Alexie's reviewers acknowledge. The narrator's description of his short-lived relationship with his co-worker Cindy, for example, one of the many stories the narrator shares in his rapid-fire monologue, appears to be a sort of locker-room story, a performance of masculinity designed to situate the teller firmly within an accepted version of heterosexuality:

> I dated [a co-worker] for a few months. Cindy. . . . In daily conversation, she talked like she was writing the lead of her latest story. Hell, she talked like that in bed. . . .
>
> During lovemaking, I would get so exhausted by the size of her erotic vocabulary that I would fall asleep before my orgasm, continue pumping away as if I were awake, and then regain consciousness with a sudden start when I finally did come, more out of reflex than passion.[12]

The details of the episode, however, undercut such simplistic identification. The narrator's reaction to his partner is inconsistent with expectations regarding the performance of heterosexual masculinity—the narrator is not titillated, but "exhausted" by his partner's eroticism, while his obligatory climax is, according to his own description, a result of "reflex" rather than "passion." The narrator's depiction of his last heterosexual experience serves, not as a marker of heterosexuality, as it has been read by some, but instead as a fitting prologue to his subsequent queer sexual experience with the Lummi hitchhiker who the narrator believes might be "the toughest Indian in the world."

From the outset, the narrator's description of the hitchhiker suggests a less-than-sublimated desire. The narrator says of his passenger: "Even before he climbed into my car I could tell he was tough. He had some serious muscles that threatened to rip through his blue jeans and denim jacket. When he was in the car, I could see his hands up close, and they told his whole story. His fingers were twisted into weird, permanent shapes, and his knuckles were covered with layers of scar tissue." The narrator's fascination with the hitchhiker's physicality, his attention to the small details of his passenger's appearance, portends the two men's impending intimacy. That intimacy hinges on more than simple sexual desire, however: the narrator's entire interaction with the hitchhiker is circumscribed by his need to perform, to claim, an "authentic" indigenous identity, as he explains in his self-conscious narration of their conversation:

> "Jeez'" I said. "You're a fighter, enit?"
>
> I threw in the "enit," a reservation colloquialism, because I wanted the fighter to know that I had grown up on the rez, in the woods, with every Indian in the world. . . .
>
> "What tribe are you?" I asked him, inverting the last two words in order to sound as aboriginal as possible.

In the midst of the exchange, the fighter offers the narrator deer jerky and, looking back on the moment, the narrator glows: "I felt as Indian as Indian gets, driving down the road in a fast car, chewing on jerky, talking to an indigenous fighter" (*TI*, 26-27).

While the narrator's monologue signals his awareness of his own cultural performance, he seems blissfully unaware of the constructed nature of the Native identity he idealizes. This tension between reality and representation is highlighted when the Lummi hitchhiker tells the story of his most recent fight, which he forfeited to an injured opponent who "was planning to die before he ever went down." The narrator's exclamation—"Jeez, . . . You would've been a warrior in the old days, enit? You would've been a killer. You would have stolen everybody's goddamn horses. That would've been you. You would've been it"— casts the fighter into the mold of a stereotypical Hollywood Indian. The fighter, however, seems to recognize the irony in the narrator's depiction, when he answers without making eye contact: "A killer, . . . sure." This noncommittal response points to the fighter's discomfort with the narrator's enthusiasm, which feeds off dominant narratives of Native identity by equating warrior traditions with the marauding Plains Indian of the popular imagination (*TI*, 29-30).

The narrator's need to be Indian does not stand alone in this story, however, since the narrator's desire for a certain representation of indigeneity is indelibly wed to his burgeoning feelings of sexual desire for the fighter. Thus the narrator's outburst about the fighter's "warrior" status is explained with a portentous, "I was excited. I wanted the fighter to know how much I thought of him." And, correspondingly, when the time comes for the two men to part, the narrator responds to the hitchhiker's potential departure with an almost desperate litany of need:

"Thanks for the ride, cousin," he said as he climbed out. . . .
"Wait," I said. . . ."
I wanted to know if he had a place to sleep that night. . . . I wanted to tell

him how much I cared about my job. . . . I wanted to tell the fighter that I pick up all Indian hitchhikers. . . . I wanted to tell him that the night sky was a graveyard. I wanted to know if he was the toughest Indian in the world.

The narrator's yearning to "know about" the fighter is merely one of many implicit signals of his ultimate decision to know the fighter sexually, and thus his internal monologue is followed by an invitation: "It's late, . . . You can crash with me, if you want" (*TI*, 30-31).

The fighter accepts the narrator's invitation and during the night the two men have sex in an encounter that, rather than being "surprising," is a predictable outcome to the sexual tension that has been building throughout the story. What I want to highlight here is not that Alexie depicts queer sexuality in the first place, which seems to be the center of many early reviews (whether in the presence or absence of acknowledgement), but that he intertwines his character's search for indigeneity with a simultaneous exploration of queer desire. In "The Toughest Indian in the World," then, Alexie figures gay male sex as an avenue for cultural renewal.[13]

A number of Native writers/critics have been theorizing the ties between indigeneity and sexuality in recent years, key among them Craig Womack (Muscogee Creek/Cherokee), Deborah Miranda (Esselen/ Chumash), and Qwo-Li Driskill. Each of these authors refers to the historical suture between American Indian and queer histories, examining the variety of ways in which examinations of sovereignty and sexuality come together. For example, when analyzing how mainstream HIV-prevention messages function (or fail to function) for tribal people, Womack suggests that American Indian people "need not accept limited definitions in [their] imaginings of [them]selves, in [their] actions, or in [their] prevention messages. Maybe tribal sovereignty, rather than a repeat of European nationalism based on triumphalism and supremacy, can be more flexible, rooted in dynamism rather than 'staticism'—looking to change as culture evolves. Maybe sovereign nations can make a part of their concern homophobia and the lack of AIDS services in their own homelands."[14] Deborah Miranda also recognizes the overlaps between indigeneity and sexuality in her examination of Native women's love poetry and erotics: "we cannot be allowed to see indigenous women in all their erotic glory without also seeing and acknowledging all that has been done to make those women—their bodies and cultures—extinct."[15] Driskill extends such contentions, forwarding the concept of erotic sovereignty: "A Sovereign Erotic is a return to and/or continuance of the complex realities of gender and sexuality that are ever-present in both the human and more-than-human world, but erased and hidden by colonial cultures." S/he explains that "healing our sexualities as First Nations people is braided with the legacy of historical trauma and the ongoing process of decolonization. Two-Spirits are integral to this struggle."[16] In these theories, the legacies of racism, colonialism, sexism, and homophobia function as a palimpsest. Rather than situating such legacies as separate and separated issues, and thus putting queer Native people in the position of having to choose allegiances, Womack, Miranda, and Driskill argue for a more nuanced resistance to colonialism and for fully articulated understandings of queer Native realities. I suggest that Alexie's work is part of this project.

Alexie's exploration of the liminal spaces in which queer desire and Indian identity meld is evidenced by his narrator's description of and reaction to his experience with the fighter in "The Toughest Indian in the World." Halfway through what is, for the narrator, a nearly sleepless night, the fighter joins him in the hotel bed and begins to caress him. Their foreplay sends the fighter in search of condoms while, as the narrator says in retrospect, "for reasons I could not explain then and cannot explain now, I kicked off my underwear and rolled over on my stomach." Once the condom is in place the fighter asks, "Are you ready?," to which the narrator replies, "I'm not gay." This exchange, which undoubtedly plays a large part in reviewers' heterosexist readings of Alexie's story, points to the ephemeral nature of sexual identity categories—at the very moment of penetration, the narrator is compelled to reject the possibility that his actions are sutured to any specific subject position. But while the narrator might deny a tie between his sexual identification and his actions, he acknowledges, on the other hand, a correlation between his desire for the fighter and his desire to reconnect with his ethnic heritage. He says, "I wanted him to save me. He didn't say anything. He just pumped into me for a few minutes, came with a loud sigh, and then pulled out. I quickly rolled off the bed and went into the bathroom. I locked the door behind me and stood in the dark. I smelled like salmon." Although the fighter departs shortly after their brief encounter, the narrator is left "feeling stronger" (*TI*, 32-33). And, despite his denial of a queer identity, the scent of salmon suggests that Alexie's protagonist is productively enabled by his sexual encounter with the fighter. Signifying birth and renewal, sustenance and interconnectedness, the salmon, for Northwest Indians like Alexie and his main character in "The Toughest Indian in the World," is both traditional food and, correspondingly, a regionally specific sacred symbol depicted in art and daily life.

In light of the text's references to salmon, I argue that the narrator's queer relationship to the fighter is situated as an avenue of transformation. Though the narrator initially constructs his understanding of indigeneity through references to dominant markers of Indian identity, he now augments that generic Plains-based vision with a more specific reference to his own Spokane background. In the final scene of Alexie's story the narrator experiences an undefined but undeniable epiphany that further links his sexual experience to a process of decolonialization:

I woke early the next morning, before sunrise, and went out into the world. I walked past my car. I stepped on to the pavement, still warm from the previous day's sun. In bare feet, I traveled upriver toward the place where I was born and will someday die. At that moment, if you had broken open my heart you could have looked inside and seen the thin white skeletons of one thousand salmon.

The concluding metaphor ties the narrator again to the salmon. According to the narrator's father, the "salmon—our hope—would never come back." But such "cruel" lessons are called into question by the text. The narrator's intention to return home, a place where, as he explains, "I hardly ever go," is triggered by queer sex with an indigenous stranger (*TI*, 33-34, 21, 27). And while the sex itself leaves him carrying the salmon's scent, the entire experience leaves him as the salmon embodied. Just as in Craig Womack's injunction, here we see an indigenous man who is suddenly able to see beyond "limited definitions in [his] imaginings of [him]self" because of his sexual experience.

While queer experience enables the narrator of "The Toughest Indian in the World" to begin a journey home, such is not the case for Sara Polatkin, the Spokane lesbian in Alexie's "Indian Country." In this story Alexie abandons the metaphor of cultural renewal, exploring instead the consequences of homophobia for familial relationships and, by extension, for Indian peoples and nations. The protagonist of the story, the heterosexual Coeur d'Alene Low Man Smith, acts as the reader's window into the fraught dinner encounter where Sara's parents, Sid and Estelle, meet Sara's white lover, Tracy Johnson. As the encounter unfolds, the intricacies of family, love, and sex are played out over salmon specials in the neutral territory of the Holiday Inn.

"Indian Country" does not attempt to offer a window into a specifically Native lesbian experience; instead, Alexie presents a highly mediated account in which Low Man takes center stage.[17] The story begins with the abrupt end to Low Man's romantic dream as he arrives in Missoula, Montana to discover that the woman he had hoped to marry has just married someone else. Low Man's subsequent search for validation leads him to the local book store where he is tracked and detained by police who have been alerted to his erratic behavior. And since, as Low Man explains to the one person he knows in Missoula, his college friend, Tracy, "The police . . . just don't want me to be alone tonight," Tracy is left with no choice but to bring him with her to meet Sara's parents (*TI*, 136). The tumultuous meeting, which Low Man exacerbates, sets up a classic confrontation in which Sara must choose between her partner and her sexuality on the one hand and her family and culture on the other.

Although Sara's choices are at the heart of my analysis of "Indian Country," the narrative also toys with the archetypal heterosexual male fantasy in which a man is at the center of a lesbian encounter. One example of this triad occurs when Low Man first meets Sara. After Tracy collects Low Man from the police station, the two then pick Sara up for dinner. In the truck, Low Man "watche[s] as the women lean over him to kiss each other. He could smell their perfume" (*TI*, 138). Low Man's voyeuristic intrusion into the two women's intimacy is followed by back-and-forth banter in which Low Man and Sara exchange barbs about the nature of their relationships to Tracy. The exchange highlights the fact that Low Man's romantic attachment to Tracy, despite never having been reciprocated, remains staunchly in place. Low Man's desire for Tracy underscores one of the limitations of the story: because the limited omniscient narrative perspective is largely tied to Low Man's point of view, the two women's relationship is circumscribed by an ever-present insistence on heterosexuality. As a reader, I initially read this limitation as a failure of vision on the part of the author. At first glance, "Indian Country" contains none of the sex or the more intimate sense of queer connection found in "The Toughest Indian in the World." On the most basic level, I thought: Alexie, a heterosexually identified male writer, has "got it wrong." But after returning to *The Toughest Indian in the World* repeatedly both in and out of the classroom, I have come to believe that rather than being inaccurate, this story's highly mediated perspective on queerness offers a useful window into the way contemporary U.S. society attempts to contain lesbian identities within dominant heterosexist narratives. Alexie's story suggests, rightly I would argue, that despite gains in theoretical understandings of sex, gender, and sexuality, we have not come far in the nearly twenty-five plus years since Adrienne Rich first offered her famous critique of compulsory heterosexuality.[18] In the end, Alexie's story is an object lesson about the consequences of homophobia—through the limited and limiting perspectives of Low Man and of Sara's parents, Alexie demonstrates the enormity of the obstacles often faced by contemporary queer folks in their everyday lives. And while such realities are not necessarily bounded by race or culture, Alexie shows how considerations of both can further complicate familial relationships.

When the discussion between Sara and Low Man concludes, Low Man is sitting between the two women across the table from Sara's parents. He serves as both a physical and a psychological barrier in the scene since his very presence incites Sid, Sara's father, to a display of sexism intended to silence the two women. Ignoring Sara and Tracy entirely, Sara's father focuses solely on Low Man, grilling him about his religious beliefs and telling him "Why don't you and I pretend we're alone here. Let's pretend this is a country of men." Sid peppers Low Man with a barrage of questions about Low Man's relationship to Christianity and to Jesus as a savior figure, finally "moving from question to command": "'Please, Low, tell me what you think about Jesus.'" Low Man's single, noncommittal answer—"I'm not a Christian. Let them have their Jesus"—does not deter Sara's father since Low Man, despite being the object of Sid's conversation, is clearly not the object of his intent. Sid's next question—"Tell me, then, what do you think their Jesus would say about lesbian marriage?"—clarifies the actual targets of his barbed religious rhetoric (*TI*, 140-42). And since, prior to the dinner, Sara had informed her parents of her intention to marry Tracy, Sid's question is by no means idle. His sexism, as evidenced in his insistent focus on Low Man to the exclusion of the three women at the table, is thereby wedded to the heterosexism and homophobia that underlies his conservative version of Christianity. The exchange serves to demonstrate how such oppressions routinely intersect.

Irony abounds in the ensuing scene, in which Alexie captures, in turn, the subtle interplay of race, gender, history, culture, and sexuality as all of the characters grapple with the way their own desires challenge the beliefs of those they love. Through it all, Low Man stands as the figure of heterosexual attachment; even as Tracy fights for the legitimacy of her relationship to Sara, Low Man continues to watch her, reading every word, every imagined sign, as the potential fulfillment of his poorly concealed desire for a romantic attachment to her. Low Man's failure to release his irrational hope demonstrates not the strength of his feelings, but instead, the strength of his belief in heterosexuality itself. The situation incites Low Man's flashback to a heated conversation with Tracy: "Low, she'd said to him in anger all those years ago, *I'm never going to love you that way. Never. Can you please understand that? I can't change who I am. I don't want to change who I am. And if you ever touch me again, I swear I will hate you forever.*" Low Man's memory is triggered by Tracy's flash of anger at Sara's mother's "'We came here with love, . . . We came here to forgive'" (*TI*, 142). Just as Tracy repudiated Low Man's sexual advances so many years before, so now does she repudiate the suggestion that her sexual object choice necessitates "forgiveness." Her anger in each case points to her recognition of the validity of her subject position as a lesbian. Low Man's relentless heterosexual desire and Estelle's less than implicit suggestion that lesbianism is inherently transgressive both act as attempted cultural constraints. Tracy casts each off, but like the process of coming out as queer, which one must replicate ad infinitum, so, it seems, must she continually reiterate the legitimacy of lesbian identity. In each case, Alexie demonstrates how dominant versions of heterosexuality can be wielded like weapons.

Low Man's position in "Indian Country," then, symbolized on one hand heterosexual privilege, and on another persistent heterosexist attempts at erasure. In each case, however, because readers are tied to Low Man's perspective, they see that he recognizes the impossibility of categorizing and thereby containing human relationships even as he reinforces dominant stereotypes. For example, as a Coeur d'Alene, Low Man is well aware of the historical irony of an Indian invoking

Christianity as a disciplinary mechanism. He openly mocks Sid's attempts to do so by queering Jesus and highlighting his status as outsider:

> "Just think about it, I mean, there Jesus was, sticking up for the poor, the disadvantaged, the disabled. Who else but a fag would be that liberal, huh? And, damn, Jesus hung out with twelve guys wearing great robes and great hair and never, ever talked about women. Tell me Sidney, what kind of guys never talk about women?"

In a moment of camaraderie over Low Man's religious irreverence, Tracy cries out in answer to his final question: "Fags!" Besides undercutting Sid's religious rhetoric and allying himself with Tracy, Low Man also draws attention to the sexism inherent in Sid's insistent denial of female agency. At the same time, however, he himself denies Tracy's subjectivity by refusing to accept her lesbianism. Thus, by the end of the story, Low Man's heterosexual desire for Tracy allies him not with her, as he so hopes, but instead with Sara's father and all he represents. Other moments in the story further reinforce this unlikely alliance: when Low Man looks at Tracy and Sara, he thinks that he, too, "want[s] to separate them"; later, Low Man explicitly tells Sid, "I want to take Tracy out of here. I want to take her back home with me. I want her to fall in love with me" (*TI*, 142-47). Like Sara's father, Low Man continually attempts to contain and control the inherently unruly nature of queer desire. His repeated failures to subsume Tracy's lesbianism beneath his more and more overt expressions of heterosexual desire become almost Foucauldian in their spiraling replication. Together, Sid's attempts to silence his daughter and her partner and Low Man's attempts to subsume queer desire within a heterosexual matrix represent a classic explosion, rather than repression, of discourse. Rather than silencing queerness, Low Man and Sid's speech acts make queerness doubly visible.

In the chaos at the dinner table, Low Man's insistence on heterosexual desire serves for Tracy's partner, Sara, as a reminder that hetero-sexism and problematic gender performances are by no means limited to dominant culture. For example, when Low Man exacerbates the al-ready fraught dinner conversation by asking sexually explicit ques-tions designed to shock her father, "Sara looked at Low and wondered yet again why Indian men insisted on being warriors. *Put down your bows and arrows*, she wanted to scream at Low, at her father, at every hypermasculine Injun in the world. *Put down your fucking guns and pick up your kids*." But as Sara recognizes, Low Man is far from com-ing to such an epiphany. Moreover, Sara sees that although Low Man's masculine posturing at the dinner table would seem to challenge Sid's homophobia, it ultimately replicates it, replacing homophobia with heterosexism. Sara quietly acknowledges this irony, "understanding that Indian men wanted to own the world just as much as white men did. They just wanted it for different reasons" (*TI*, 144-45). With this exchange, Alexie pulls the rug out from under readers who might ro-manticize Indian culture as an avenue of escape from dominant modes of gender performance.[19]

In the end, the intersections of culture and sexuality in "Indian Country" are defined in ways that diametrically oppose the same in-vestigations in "The Toughest Indian in the World": while queer sexu-ality engenders cultural affiliation in "The Toughest Indian," it is situ-ated as the barrier to such affiliations in "Indian Country." These lines are drawn early in the story when Tracy explains to Low Man, "I'm freaking out her parents. Completely. Not only am I a lesbian but I'm also white." The tie between whiteness and queer identity—which Low Man calls the "double whammy"—is a classic invocation of the stereotype in which "queerness" is cast a "white man's disease." Sid reinforces such connections when he categorically states: "My daugh-ter wasn't, wasn't a gay until she met this, this white woman" (*TI*, 137, 146). His denial, which implicitly situates Tracy as the "cause" of his daughter's queerness, invokes the historical erasure of accepted tradi-tions of gender variance in many indigenous communities.

Sid's suggestion that homosexuality is, like English or strong coffee, a product of assimilation into white society is untrue. As anthropologist Sabine Lang points out, reports of accepted gender variance practices among indigenous peoples in what is now the present-day U.S. have been recorded "[e]ver since Europeans came into contact with North American Indian cultures."[20] While Sid's Christianity *is* a product of assimilation, Two-Spirit identity is not.[21] But though such history might be undeniable, it holds little sway in the face of the homophobia that has come to characterize responses to non-dominant sex/gender categories in many Native communities. On a positive note, according to the 2000 U.S. census, "Native women on 43 different reservations told census interviewers that they lived in a female, same-sex partnered household . . . with the numbers totaling just over 4,000 lesbian couples in all."[22] But Cherokee-Choctaw journalist Diane Anderson-Minshall suggests that many indigenous urban queer folks doubt the accuracy of these numbers. Anderson-Minshall herself found that, in her own research for an article on Native lesbians, "tribal elders and reservation leaders weren't interested in talking about their queer citizens. . . . I contacted more than 100 tribal council members, museum curators and PR reps from reservations in Colorado, Connecticut, New Mexico, Oklahoma, Louisiana, Idaho and California, and none were willing to comment."[23] Such silences lead to the sort of typified responses Alexie presents in "Indian Country," the sort of responses that bring Qwo-Li Driskill to ask, "How do we as Two-Spirits remain whole and confident in our bodies and in our traditions when loss attempts to smother us?"[24]

As Driskill's comment emphasizes, Sid's suggestion that lesbianism is somehow alien to indigenous communities dichotomizes queer and Native American identities. Craig Womack invokes a Hank Williams analogy to describe the internal divisions such dichotomies create:

[T]here was something about those Hank Williams songs. . . . I don't know quite how to put my finger on it, but it has to do with alienation, loneliness, a shitload of pain, and not being able to speak to the one you love, remaining hidden and silent in the shadows for a lifetime. The songs have everything to do with being queer; the songs have everything to do with being Indian . . . the beauty and terror of both identities.[25]

In Alexie's short story, this division means that Sara is positioned between her family and the cultural ties they represent and her lover. After their dinner explodes into acrimony, Tracy gets up from the table, at which time Sara confronts a difficult decision; she looks at her parents, thinking, "Together, the three of them had buried dozens of loved ones. The three of them know all the same mourning songs. Two of them had loved each other enough to conceive the third. They had invented her! She was their Monster; she was surely going to murder them."

Angry and hurt, Sid leaves her no middle ground, saying, "If you leave now, . . . Don't you ever call us. Don't you ever talk to us again." For Sara, the "murderous" choice, at least as constructed in the heat of her father's anger, seems to be whether or not she will agree to remain "hidden and silent in the shadows" or whether she walks away. Thus, when Sara stands to follow Tracy, turning from the table and literally stepping "away from the salmon" on her plate, she figuratively steps away from the strictures and love of her family and all they represent in terms of her cultural ties (*TI*, 147). Her experience evokes a scene from Alexie's film *The Business of Fancydancing*, in which Seymour Polatkin's white lover tells him, "I'm your tribe now." Sid's ultimatum and the melee that follows reinforces the story's critique of homophobia, suggesting that such attitudes harm indigenous communities by forcing queer Native people to make radical and unnecessary choices.

Together, "Indian Country" and "The Toughest Indian in the World" bring conversations about queer Native literature and queer Native people to the fore in the larger field of American literature. Given Alexie's position as one of, if not most likely the most recognizable and most frequently taught American Indian author in current U.S. literature today, his work attains a kind of exposure that few Native au-

thors receive. And, whether an author embraces it or not, with exposure comes the power to influence public perception. In an era in which
stereotypical images of Indians are still used to sell butter and football,
and homophobia is being further codified by state laws, Alexie's representations of queer and Native and queer Native identities are important cultural artifacts and influences, forwarding complex understandings about the productive intersections of sexuality and culture. Craig
Womack talks about such intersections in personal terms: "I began to
see that every angle of vision from which I saw myself was refracted
through the larger lens of being Indian and fighting for survival. It was
no longer a matter of reconciling being gay with being Indian but of
being Indian, period, and understanding being gay in Indian terms."[26]
The melding of queerness with Indian identity is at its heart, as
Womack emphasizes, a political issue. "The Toughest Indian in the
World" addresses such concerns by depicting a character who does not
choose, as Sara must in "Indian Country," between queer desire and
American Indian community. Instead, Alexie's unnamed narrator in
"The Toughest Indian in the World" finds queerness an avenue for cul-
tural identification, thereby "braid[ing]" "the legacy of historical
trauma"—as evidenced by manifestations of homophobia—with what
Driskill calls the "ongoing process of decolonization."[27] By contrast,
"Indian Country," a story about both connection and misperception, is
not nearly so celebratory. It is, however, just as important to understanding the often difficult decisions faced by contemporary Two-
Spirit people. "Indian Country," like "The Toughest Indian in the
World," is ultimately an activist text that highlights the dangerous consequences homophobia can have for Indian people and communities.
Alexie's story points to the fact that it is not queerness, but negative
and uninformed reactions to queerness that can cause queer Native
people to be separated from their tribal communities. Alexie is not creating such a tradition of activism. Instead, he allies himself with those
Two-Spirit authors and activists—Beth Brant, Barbara Cameron,
Chrystos, Qwo-Li Driskill, Janice Gould, Joy Harjo, Daniel Heath

Justice, Maurice Kenny, Deborah Miranda, Janet McAdams, Vicki Sears, and Craig Womack, to name just a few—who have been and are writing and fighting for social justice and sovereignty.

From *Studies in American Fiction* 35, no. 2 (Autumn 2007): 201-219. Copyright © 2007 Northeastern University. Reprinted with permission of The Johns Hopkins University Press.

## Notes

I would like to offer thanks to Jane Hafen for encouraging me to write this essay.

1. I use "American Indian," "Native American" and "Native" interchangeably when referring to indigenous people of North America. As this essay focuses primarily on American Indians, I at times include First Nations, or indigenous Canadian writers, within these blanket terms as well. While sometimes necessary, such terminology is inherently inaccurate as it groups hundreds of differing Native nations with radically different languages, belief systems, and histories under a single name.

2. Will Roscoe, "Native North American Literature," *The Gay and Lesbian Literary Heritage* (Henry Holt: New York, 1995), 514-15.

3. The term "Two-Spirit" was coined at a 1990 Winnipeg meeting as, in part, a way to resist the history of colonization and homophobia that was tied to "berdache," a derogatory term historically used by non-Native anthropologists and missionaries to refer to indigenous people whose sexualities did not fit within the dominant heterosexual matrix. Referring to queer Native peoples in the U.S. and Canada, the term denotes the distinctly different histories that often separate queer American Indian people and histories from non-Native queer people and histories. For more background, see Sue-Ellen Jacobs, Wesley Thomas, and Sabine Lang's edited collection *Two-Spirit People: Native American Gender Identity, Sexuality and Spirituality* (Urbana: Univ. of Illinois Press), 1997.

4. The problem in these two texts, which I use as examples of a larger trend, is not the inclusion of negatively depicted queer characters, but the way that representations of non-normative sexualities are uncritically paired with psychological and social deviance as if one begets the other. Such pairings have long histories in literature and film where representations of not only queerness, but also of disability, race, and culture are represented as either dangerous or tragic if they do not align with dominant norms.

5. A notable exception to this claim can be found in the recent work of Louise Erdrich. Cyprian Lazarre, a queer Ojibwe circus performer, is central to Erdrich's *The Master Butcher's Singing Club* (New York: Harper Collins, 2003), while Erdrich's novel *The Last Report on the Miracles at Little No Horse* (New York: Harper Collins, 2001) includes references to the Ojibwe people's traditional acceptance of indigenous Two-Spirit traditions and a brief historical vignette in which a two-spirit character ap-

pears. Erdrich's earlier work also includes characters who are Native lesbians. For more on the queer characters in Erdrich, see Julie Barak, "Blurs, Blends, Berdaches: Gender Mixing in the Novels of Louise Erdrich," *Studies in American Indian Literatures* 8, no. 3 (1996), 49-62. While such inclusions are important. I would argue that Alexie's work is markedly different in light of the centrality of queer issues to both the two short stories examined here and to his film, *The Business of Fancydancing* (Wellspring, 2002).

6. Alexie is clear about his aims in *The Business of Fancydancing*. For example, in an interview with filmcritic.com, he says, "'I've spent more time in urban situations and in the art world. I've made more friends who are gay. So it's a huge part of my life. . . . Part of me writing about gay people in this movie was a larger social effort. I knew a lot of Indians will see this movie, and there's *a lot* of homophobes in the Indian world, so I wanted to slap them in the face a bit.'" Quoted in Aileo Weinmann, "Hold Me Closer, Fancydancer: A Conversation with Sherman Alexie," *Filmcritic.com*, 2002. http://www.filmcritic.com/misc/emporium.nsf/95a45e26914c25ff862562bb006a85f2/1adbe1e88680513188256c340015b7b9?Open Document.

7. Polly Paddock Gossett, "Tribal Past is a Strong Presence in Alexie's *Toughest Indian*," *The Charlotte Observer*, July 2, 2000, sec. Bookweek, 6F.

8. Ken Foster, "Bold, Sexy Stories from Alexie," *San Francisco Chronicle*, May 21, 2000. http://www.sfgate.com/cgi-bin/article.cgi?file=/chronicle/archive/2000/05/21/RV25336.DTL.

9. Joelle Fraser, "An Interview with Sherman Alexie," *Iowa Review* 30 (Winter 2000-2001), 59.

10. Qwo-Li Driskill. "Stolen From Our Bodies: First Nations Two-Spirits/Queers and the Journey to a Sovereign Erotic," *Studies in American Indian Literatures* 16, no. 2 (2004), 54.

11. *Two-Spirit People*, 2.

12. Sherman Alexie. *The Toughest Indian in the World* (New York: Atlantic, 2000), 26; hereafter cited parenthetically as *TI*.

13. This intertwining of ethnic and queer identities is also a place where Alexie's representations of queer identities depart from Erdrich's. While Alexie's narrator searches for identity through a queer encounter, Erdrich's characters tend to separate and/or minimize the relationships between queerness and indigeneity. For example, the Two-Spirit runner in *The Last Report on the Miracles of Little No Horse* is a minor, one-dimensional character who runs off into the sunset; Agnes DeWitt's explorations of gender/sexuality in the same text are bounded by her whiteness; and, in *Master Butcher's Singing Club*, Cyprian Lazarre initially hides both his queer desire and his Ojibwe heritage. Though Cyprian ultimately enters a same-sex relationship, he does so outside the boundaries of the text as he and his partner disappear from the storyline. While these representations merit further study, they present much less interplay between queerness and ethnicity than that depicted in *The Toughest Indian in the World*.

14. Craig Womack, "Politicizing HIV Prevention in Indian Country," in *Native American Religious Identity: Unforgotten Gods*, ed. Jace Weaver (Maryknoll, NY: Orbis Books, 1998), 215.

15. Deborah A. Miranda, "Dildos, Hummingbirds, and Driving Her Crazy: Search-

ing for American Indian Women's Love Poetry and Erotics," *Frontiers* 23, no. 2 (2002), 145.

16. Driskill, 56, 51.

17. Alexie himself said, "I pay attention to the stories of the least powerful group in the country: gay Native women. . . . We all feel lonely and isolated. Perhaps my work helps lesbian Native women feel less alone in the world." Qtd. in Diana Anderson-Minshall, "Without Reservations: Native American Lesbians Struggle to Find Their Way." *Curve* 13, no. 2 (2003): 37.

18. Adrienne Rich, "Compulsory Heterosexuality and Lesbian Existence," *Signs: Journal of Women in Culture and Society* 5 (1980). 631-60.

19. This disruption of romanticism is especially relevant in the context of Queer Native history in which GLBTQ/Two-Spirit traditions and identities are so often co-opted by dominant culture. See the introduction of *Two-Spirit People* and Womack's "Politicizing HIV in Indian Country" for two of the many existing discussions of this pattern.

20. Sabine Lang, "Various Kinds of Two-Spirit People: Gender Variance and Homosexuality in Native American Communities," in *Two-Spirit People*, 100.

21. I don't mean to invoke a romanticized, nineteenth-century version of identity in which Christianity is incompatible with Indian traditions. A large percentage of contemporary American Indian people are Christian. Instead, what I'm pointing to here is how certain aspects of Christianity are used in Alexie's story and elsewhere to deny the validity of Two-Spirit Native traditions that predate the introduction of Christian belief systems.

22. Anderson-Minshall, 36.

23. Anderson-Minshall, 34-35.

24. Driskill, 56.

25. Craig Womack, "Howling at the Moon: the Queer but True Story of My Life as a Hank Williams Song," in *As We Are Now: Mixblood Essays on Race and Identity*, ed. William S. Penn (Berkeley: Univ. of California Press, 1997), 38.

26. Womack, "Howling," 45.

27. Driskill, 51.

# The Trans/historicity of Trauma in Jeannette Armstrong's *Slash* and Sherman Alexie's *Indian Killer*_____

Nancy Van Styvendale

We're carrying a pain that is 400 years old.

—Alanis Obomsawin

The ongoing domestic colonization of North America has a specifically "traumatic" impact on the Native peoples of this land, but what is the "event" or referent to which such an effect can be traced? Is it possible to locate the traumatic event of a (post)colonial history that is, as Alanis Obomsawin makes clear in the epigraph, centuries old and, I would add, nations wide? Or, as this paper will argue, does the *trans/ historicity* of Native trauma challenge the very assumption of trauma as rooted in event, where "event" is defined, as it most commonly is, as a singular, recognizable, and chronologically-bounded incident? These questions draw attention to the commonplace understanding of traumatic events as singular, recognizable incidents, inviting our consideration of the problematics engendered by recent attempts to theorize the intergenerational colonial subjection of Native North American peoples through the lens of trauma theory—especially that which focuses on individual psychic trauma. Cumulative, collective, intergenerational, and intersubjective, the trauma of Native peoples, when understood as trans/historical, exceeds any attempt to fix its location or define its event, even as it demands our attention to historically specific atrocities. In order to explore the trans/historicity of trauma and, in particular, its unique articulation in Native North American literature, this paper situates two representative novels from the Native literary canon, Jeannette Armstrong's *Slash* (1985) and Sherman Alexie's *Indian Killer* (1996), within the nascent conversation between trauma theory and Native experience.

By using the word "trans/historical" to describe the trauma crafted in *Slash* and *Indian Killer*, I run the risk of reinstating, through my own diction, the idea of trauma as transcendent of historical conditions and material realities; indeed, the *Oxford English Dictionary* defines "transhistorical" as "(Having significance) that transcends the historical; universal or eternal." As a descriptor of the intergenerational trauma of Native communities, the word "trans/historical" thus fails to do justice to the complexity of this trauma. Still, I will maintain and nuance it here because of the way in which it gestures toward a trauma that takes place and is repeated in multiple epochs and, in this sense, exceeds its historicity, conventionally understood as its singular location in the past. Also, in its very failure to approach this excess as something other than transcendent or outside of the historical, the word "trans/historical" reminds us that the English language circumscribes the way in which we might think about and refer to a traumatic event-which-is-not-one.

As literary texts, *Slash* and *Indian Killer* both express and craft a distinct understanding of "traumatic temporality," a term coined by Cathy Caruth ("Interview" 78). Rooted in a psychoanalytic and poststructuralist methodology, this term refers to the way in which traumatic events, because they cannot be known or integrated by the survivor as they occur, are indirectly accessible only as symptom—that is, in their belated return to the survivor as repetitive dreams, flashbacks, and reenactments of the event. Caruth's notion of traumatic temporality famously challenges the assumption that the history of trauma involves a one-to-one correspondence of reference and event and ushers in a performative theory of trauma, which understands trauma as dis-located in its reiterative return rather than in its origin—an origin that therefore remains elusive at best. The trans/historicity of Native trauma, as constituted in the work of Armstrong and Alexie, nuances this theory, prompting an exploration of the temporal and spatial dis/location of a trauma that is centuries old and nations wide.

A note of clarification is necessary before I proceed: this paper analyzes the specifically literary cultivation of trauma as trans/historical and thus contributes to Jeffrey C. Alexander's approach to trauma as a performative reality rather than a natural occurrence.[1] However, along with looking to how literary constructions of trauma can advance the purview of trauma theory, I also argue that trauma theory, along with the recent sociological application of this theory to the post-contact experience of Native peoples, is crucial to the field of Native literatures. One of my functions as literary critic is to recognize the fact of trauma in Native literature (with all the attendant benefits and dangers of such a move) by using the lexicon of trauma to make sense of the constructions of history, woundedness, recovery, and temporality that I see expressed within this literature. There is, at present, little literary criticism that approaches Native literature as trauma narrative; in fact, while individual traumas suffered by individual characters might be referred to as such, there is no literary-critical work that theorizes collective Native trauma *per se* or that uses "trauma" as anything other than a transparent synonym for "oppression." Because of this dearth of critical work, it is necessary for me to delve first into the vicissitudes of contemporary trauma theory and its sociological application to Native peoples in order to show, on the one hand, that the study of Native literature would benefit from an encounter with trauma theory—an encounter I will then actualize through my reading of *Slash* and *Indian Killer*—and on the other hand, that trauma theory has much to learn from the trans/historicity of trauma articulated in these novels.

## The Meeting Place:
## Trauma Theory and Native North American Peoples

Researchers who have investigated the topic of trauma in relation to Native communities will know that this field of study is still relatively new, and while words like "oppression," "colonization," "subjugation," and "violation" are commonly used to explain the post-contact experiences of Native peoples in North America (and elsewhere), "trauma" is not. Sociologists Robert W. Robin, Barbara Chester, and

David Goldman acknowledge that there is "little representation of Native Americans among the . . . populations studied for PTSD [posttraumatic stress disorder]" (243) and that "traumatic . . . factors specific to many American Indian communities . . . have rarely been studied" (244), a conclusion echoed by Spero Manson et al., who assert that "despite the relative ease with which this construct [PTSD] has found a place in local [indigenous] lexicons, little systematic study of trauma, and PTSD in particular, has been conducted in these communities" (256). While the need for such study is great, Robin, Chester, and Goldman stress that the category of PTSD, which diagnoses the effects of individual psychic trauma, actually "fails to describe the nature and impact of severe, multiple, repeated, and cumulative aspects of trauma common to many [Native] communities" (246). They argue that a distinction needs to be made between long-term, cumulative trauma and "specific" trauma within the context of cumulative trauma.

A number of crucial insights arise from these findings. First, the increasingly popular language of trauma resonates with Native peoples and within Native communities. The deployment of this language provides Native communities with a means through which they can give expression to their collective and individual pain, doing so through linguistic and diagnostic categories that, because they are sanctioned within the dominant culture, hold out the hope of having this pain recognized, legitimated, and compensated for.[2] Secondly, the lack of sociological or psychological research on Native trauma, along with the scarcity of the term itself in other fields related to Native peoples (Native literature, for example), reveals an institutional complicity in larger, nationwide attempts to forget the trauma of Native peoples. This repression ameliorates "white guilt" for the theft of the North American land base and obfuscates the need for Euroamericans to take responsibility for privileges that continue to accrue from this theft—and its denial. Yet the paucity of research on Native trauma also reveals a necessary political resistance to the potential revictimization of Native peoples through the nomenclature of trauma—or, in other words, to the reification of Native victimhood and the pathologizing of Native communities through the imposition of yet another Euroamerican framework designed to "figure out" and "fix" Native peoples. The danger of institutionalizing the fact of trauma in Native communities, to which I referred in my introduction, is the danger of revictimization; and while I admit to having no easy safeguard to protect against this danger, my conviction is that it is necessary to proceed, aware of the possible pitfalls, to recognize post-contact Native experience as traumatic.

## The Trans/historicity of Native Trauma

In addition to the above dangers, the now pervasive language of individual trauma has established the traumatic event as an extraordinary occurrence, an assumption particularly troubling when invoked in relation to the trans/historical trauma of Native communities. As a discrete event outside of the norm, trauma, in the popularly-held view, shocks and frightens the individual who experiences it, causing the splitting off or dissociation of the memory of the event from the regular stream of consciousness, where events become integrated and narrativized through preexisting interpretive categories (van der Kolk and van der Hart 170-172). The intergenerational trauma of Native peoples raises serious questions about the assumption of trauma as rooted in event, where "event" is understood to refer to a distinct experience that happens in one specific location and time. Cumulative and collective, this trauma is more properly understood as both "insidious," in Maria P. P. Root's formulation of a trauma as the status quo of a particular group (240), and trans/historical.

Feminist theorist Laura S. Brown observes that the *DSM* III-R's narrow definition of trauma as "an event that is outside the range of human experience" (qtd. 100)[3] obscures the existence as such of long-term "repetitive" traumas (100), such as those sustained by incest survivors or battered women, to cite her examples, or by (post)colonial cultural, racial, and national groups. This obfuscation, Brown argues, permits the construction of a "mythical norm of human experience" (111) and reifies a form of trauma in which members of the dominant culture "participate [only] as a victim rather than as the perpetrator or etiologist of the trauma" (102). In other words, the assumption of trauma as an "event outside the norm" allows the "norm" itself to go unrecognized as the site of multiple traumas, an oversight that in relation to the systemic oppression of Native North Americans, justifies the status quo of domestic colonialism.

The related notion of trauma as (the effect of) a discrete event assumes an (un)knowable traumatic origin, which is then reflected in current posttraumatic behaviors. As with the presumption of trauma's uniqueness, the supposition of its temporal location in the past functions to obscure and perpetuate a status quo that abnegates responsibility for traumatic events of the past through their very location in the past. The commonplace notion that the wounds of colonization were inflicted in the past (a perception that does not automatically deny the idea that the effects of these wounds may reverberate in the present) precludes the recognition of a trans/historical trauma that exceeds—yet is grounded in—its articulation and repetition in a multiplicity of historical events and locations and, as such, demands a different kind of witness, response, and accountabililty in and for the present.

Using models of individual psychic trauma such as PTSD—or, drawing on Freud, what we might call the "accident model" of trauma[4]—to examine the effects of colonial oppression on Native communities is obviously fraught with difficulties; yet these models have been put to exactly this purpose. Briefly, I would like to review one such recent sociological attempt to show how its approach to collective trauma, albeit motivated by important political goals, locates colonial trauma in the forgotten event of post-contact epidemics and thus accomplishes the temporal removal critiqued for its obfuscation of the ongoing trauma of Native peoples. In their report for the Aboriginal Healing Foundation, *Historic Trauma and Aboriginal Healing*, Cynthia Wesley-Esquimaux and Magdalena Smolewski introduce the concept of Historic Trauma Transmission (HTT), arguing that the disease pandemics and depopulation of the Americas from 1493 to 1520 formed a "nucleus of traumatic memory" (10) that is "buried deep within [the] collective psyche" of Aboriginal peoples (24), who have continued to suffer from the return of this "dark nucleus" (23) in subsequent generations, including the present one. Taking the form of a PTSD flashback of massive proportions, this nucleus of unresolved grief returns to haunt contemporary Native peoples through its repetition in current posttraumatic behaviors, in themselves "new pathogens" (32) that infect the younger generation (see also Abadian).

By calling up PTSD to make sense of the collective trauma of Native peoples, Wesley-Esquimaux and Smolewski are clearly working within a recognizable lexicon to secure funding and attention for a variety of recovery projects in Native communities, a vital task indeed. But the difficulty lies in their location of colonial trauma at a safe remove from Euroamerican culpability for the extension of this trauma in the present, a move that could be seen as strategic in terms of garnering Euroamerican support for their project but which is problematic nevertheless. True, the model proposes the ongoing repetition of a traumatic origin and, in this sense, locates trauma in the present moment as well as the past, thereby problematizing its assumption that colonial trauma originates in the past. But the model's adherence to the accident model of trauma and its suggestion that the current trauma of Native peoples is located not in a situation of ongoing domestic colonization but in an indigenous rehearsal of the forgotten past make for a model that functions to displace and assuage Euroamerican guilt for the existent colonial situation in North America. Wesley-Esquimaux and Smolewski cite Cecil White Hat on the crucial difference between PTSD and HTR (Historic Trauma Response, the precursor to HTT), but their model appears to obscure—while paradoxically embracing— his observations: "PTSD happens around an event, an event with a beginning and end. For Native people, the trauma continues. There hasn't been an end" (White Hat qtd. in Wesley-Esquimaux and Smolewski 55). White Hat's trans/historical trauma, especially as it is expressed and cultivated in much Native fiction, not only demands recognition of but also ethical response to current conditions of neocolonial oppression.

## Redefining Trauma, History, and Event: Jeannette Armstrong and Sherman Alexie

My appellation of Native trauma and its reconstruction in Native literature as trans/historical might at first appear ironic, especially in light of the political necessity of history in much of this literature, including the work of Okanagan author Jeannette Armstrong and Coeur d'Alene/Spokane novelist, poet, and screenwriter Sherman Alexie. As a whole, Native literature is often characterized by its concern with counterhegemonic historical narratives. Critics commonly refer to Armstrong's first novel *Slash* (1985) as a historical novel with a didactic function, and rightly so, for its genesis was part of a curriculum project designed to produce pedagogical materials reflective of Native realities (Lutz 14). "My real quest," Armstrong says about writing the novel, "was to present a picture of that time" because, in the 1980s, "there were no books available about [the Indian movement in] . . . the 1960s and 1970s" (20). The story of Tommy Kelasket (a.k.a. Slash)—a young Okanagan Indian[5] who journeys across North America and experiences the rage, protest, and militant action of the movement but who ultimately returns home to practice the traditional ways of his people—*Slash* narrates the often foreclosed history of political resistance to the "two options" given Native peoples by the majority culture: "Assimilate or get lost." "A lot of us are lost," Mardi, Tommy's lover and political inspiration, explains. "We need to make a third choice. That's what Red Patrol is about" (70).

The journey to enact this "third choice," aligned in Mardi's words with militant responses to colonial trauma such as Red Patrol in Canada or, more famously, the American Indian Movement (A.I.M.) in the States, makes for much of the book's content, begging further investigation of the undertheorized relationship among trauma, militarism (or the desire for "action," as Tommy says [76, 107, 125, 143]), and rage. The Indian on the "warpath," while surely a stereotype, is also a discourse harnessed by Native peoples in response to colonial trauma, and although the idea of militant rage as a response to trauma might appear, to some, to muddy the victim status of the person who has been traumatized by complicating the division between "victim" and "aggressor," it is for this very reason that rage needs to be theorized as both an effect of and a method of resistance to trauma. (S)lashing out with rage, the text proposes, is one response to being slashed or wounded—in either a psychological or a physical sense. Tommy's barroom brawl, during which his attacker "thought to carve a few lines on [his] shoulder" and Tommy responds by "slashing around and yelling, 'I'll slash the nuts off anybody that tries that again!'" (59), metaphorizes the way in which trauma (here, a literal wound) engenders rage, itself another or further wounding. While Armstrong shows the third choice of anger and action to be necessary to Tommy's development, Tommy finally comes to feel "a need to stand for more than being just a mad Indian" (182) and realizes the truth of his cousin Chuck's premonitory words: "Anger, when it is uncontrolled and directed towards anything and everything, is dangerous even to itself" (141). Tommy's repeated emotional and physical exhaustion and self-inflicted abuse through alcohol and drugs bear witness to this danger.

Generally speaking, critics have analyzed the third choice in *Slash* as non-teleological, and, while this analysis makes sense given the novel's commitment to multiple perspectives and modes of resistance within the pan-Indian community, I would suggest that the text does hold out and affirm a clear goal: the return home and recovery of inherent indigenous ways and rights.[6] "Them ain't the only choices," Joe, one of Tommy's spiritual advisors in a dry-out center, says about the "two choices" of assimilation or termination: "There is another way. It's always been there" (198). At a conference on Indian religion, Tommy is reminded of the importance of "returning to the medicine ways of [his] people. . . . The young people were urged [by the Medicine men] to continue their struggle in finding their *true identity*" (190, emphasis added). Authentic Indianness is aligned here with the pursuit of tradition; indeed, it is the difference between action as protest (positioned against and thus always in relation to the colonizer) and practice as preservation (of indigenous ways existing before colonial influence) that Tommy learns through his journey, which repeatedly takes him both away from and back toward his home in British Columbia. Tommy ultimately finds his way(s), learning to follow a spiritual path that returns him to his rightful cultural inheritance (201) instead of continuing to pursue the roads, both material and metaphorical, that only took him further from home. As an alternative to (s)lashing out with rage, Tommy learns to turn his attention inward, to his people, and to cultivate and reenact the indigenous ways that have "always been there and had never gone anywhere" (202): "We just ha[ve] to do it," Tommy comes to realize. "[T]hat's what culture is" (211).

Alexie's *Indian Killer* holds out no such hope for a return to roots, but it does bear resemblance to *Slash*—and to the majority of Native literature—in its contextualization of the plight of its characters within a particular era of Native/non-Native relations in North America. The novel begins in the late 1960s, well before the Indian Child Welfare Act (ICWA) of 1978. The story of John Smith, a Native individual taken away from his mother at birth and forcibly relocated to the Seattle home of a white, upper-middle class couple, Daniel and Olivia Smith, provides fodder for Alexie's satiric indictment of cultural appropriation and paternalistic racism. Alexie thus situates his novel in the context of the American counterpart to the Canadian Sixties Scoop, an "[u]nwarranted" and "epidemic" removal of Native children from their birth families (Bensen 13) known, "in Bertram Hirsch's phrase, [as] the 'gray market' for Indian children, which developed under the pressure on local welfare agencies to provide Indian children for adoption" (12).

With the passing of the ICWA, the theft, removal, and relocation of Indian children would come to be recognized as a neocolonial assault on one of the "most valuable natural resource[s]" of Native communities—their children (Hollinger 456). The effect of this assault on John Smith, a synecdochic representation of these children, can be witnessed in his alienation from his tribal roots (which are unknown) and his feeling of being less than "real" (17, 19, 24, 35, 39, 40, etc.).[7] In an interview with Tomson Highway, Alexie notes that John "gently goes mad during the course of the book," and critics have elaborated upon this point, analyzing John's ostensible schizophrenia as a metaphor for the kind of fragmented and tortured subjectivity inculcated by deracination.[8] But John's madness also takes the form of an insatiable anger that is resonant with *Slash*'s rage. In the same interview, Alexie explains that the "identity crisis" of this "lost bird," a term used to refer to "Indians adopted out by non-Indian families," was the "germ of the novel." Alexie notes that even before he realized that the book was going to be a murder mystery, he knew that he "wanted to write a book about a character like that to get this [information] out into the public" ("Spokane Words"). John's invisibility—his inability to see and recognize himself as a "real" Indian—propels him to search for and reenact authenticity through a complex of colonial discourses of Indianness instilled in him by his adoptive parents and his mentor, the Spokane Jesuit Father Duncan. Through their performative reiteration, these discourses function to reinstall authentic Indianness as not only unrecoverable but also unachievable and, consequently, to fuel John's murderous rage at a society that has refused him not only his roots but even his own pain (411). Even John's rage, which finds partial expression in his failed attempt to inhabit a traditional warrior identity, is bound up with his reiteration of a colonial script of Native identity—the discourse of Native savagery to which he is introduced at the North American Chapel of Martyrs in the stained glass portrait of Indian "savages" killing "innocent" white men (13-16). John's rage is, therefore, a result both of his being appropriated and of his appropriation of an available discourse of Nativeness and, as such, begs a series of questions consonant with those articulated by Armstrong's text: how is rage related to trauma, how might this feeling be discursively constituted and reified, and what are the implications of articulating resistance through colonial discourse?

The profundity of John's rage prompts him to decide that he "need[s] to kill a white man" (25) in order to redress "everything that had gone wrong" (27); a "real Indian," in his estimation, would be able to kill a white man (24). "That's what I need to see," he meditates, "that's what will feed me. . . . Fear in blue eyes." Imagining the delectability of such fear, John daydreams that he is holding his boss, a construction foreman, over the edge of the last skyscraper in Seattle: "He would hold onto the foreman as long as possible and stare down into those terrified blue eyes. Then he'd let him fall" (25). At the novel's close, it is of course John himself who ends up "falling" from the skyscraper, a disturbing act of "taking back his pain" that points again to the im/possibility of claiming authenticity. John's jump echoes and fulfills his earlier desire to fall from the helicopter, "past the skyscrapers" (7) and back to his indigenous mother, as he is being transported to his adoptive parents in Seattle. In this sense, it is the ultimate return to roots, albeit a tragic and paradoxically unfulfilled return, which rehearses the discourse of the "vanishing Indian." Citing Patricia Penn Hilden, Arnold Krupat notes that John's final act can be read to align John with the novel's infamous Indian Killer (138)— quite simply because he kills himself, an Indian, despite the fact that he never kills a white man. As an aside, it is noteworthy that John's inability to fulfill the warrior/savage script by killing a white man is, in one sense, a further comment on authenticity as always—already unachievable, at the same time as it is yet another attempt at achieving the authentic. Indeed, John ends up being unable to kill Wilson, the white man he brings to the skyscraper for this purpose, a statement of character that reenacts Father Duncan's earlier lesson that ("real") Indians "didn't have the heart" (14) to kill all of the colonists who invaded their lands.

Clearly, John is not the Indian Killer, sought after in the story for murdering a series of white Seattle men and kidnaping an affluent white boy. Not only can John not kill a white man, but also such a character cannot be so singularly defined. The very name, which can be read as either "killer of Indians" (like Custer, the most notorious "Indian Killer") or "killer Indian," or both, invokes the interimplication of colonial genocide and Native vengeance, and suggests that this character encompasses a history larger than its individual parts. Krupat and James R. Giles have compared the traits and activities of the killer with those of the novel's main characters (John Smith, Marie Polatkin, her cousin Reggie, and even the wannabe Indian murder mystery writer Jack Wilson) in order to select or rule out these characters as potential Indian Killers, but this exercise has proven both futile and telling—futile in the sense that the characters do not quite match the descriptions we have of the Indian Killer, telling in the sense that they do. Alexie does indeed construct strategic parallels between the killer and each main character. For example, in a passage describing the killer's first murder, we are told that "[t]he killer saw the fear in the white man's blue eyes. The man's fear inspired the killer's confidence" (52), a description clearly resonant with John Smith's desire to see fear in blue eyes. But rather than pointing, as Giles suggests, to Alexie's perfection of the "false clues" characteristic of detective fiction (135), I would suggest that these parallels, when combined, underscore how the Indian Killer is all yet none of the novel's Indian characters. The killer, also referred to as "it" (323)—a genderless pronoun that allows this character to inhabit multiple bodies in the reader's imagination—gives an ineffable form to the pain and rage felt by Alexie's Indian characters as individuals, at the same time as it gives shape to a collective trauma that is larger than any one of them. While Euroamerican literary constructions of the "mad Indian/ unpredictable/ on the war path" (Dumont 12-14) have most often functioned to "turn [the native] into an animal" (Frantz Fanon, qtd. in Goldie 95) by situating his or her rage not as a "human response . . . to oppression," but rather as "an expression of [indigenous] nature" (95), Alexie critiques this maneuver through his construction of "warriors" like John Smith and the Indian Killer who illustrate the traumatic historical conditions constitutive of a collective, intergenerational anger. "The United States *is* a colony," Alexie emphasizes, "and I'm always going to write like one who is colonized, and that's with a lot of anger" ("Seeing Red" par 15).

In the field of Native literary studies, Armstrong and Alexie are not often mentioned in the same critical breath, owing mainly to the fact that the political projects of their literatures seem—and in some ways are—very different. Alexie is a postmodern satirist whose work challenges authenticity and highlights social issues. Because of this, he has been criticized by nationalist critics for participating in what Gloria Bird calls, in the title of her 1995 article, "The Exaggeration of Despair" and what Elizabeth Cook-Lynn refers to as the "deficit model of Indian reservation life" (68)—in other words, for portraying Native people as (stereotypical) victims rather than foregrounding a commitment to Native sovereignty (see also Owens 77). Armstrong, by contrast, is a realist writer interested in just such a commitment. Her work revolves around what I call the recovery project of Native literatures— that is, the project to recover, restore, heal, and return to a kind of Native identity that is land-based, traditional, nationalist, and tribally-specific. If there exists a continuum in Native literature between traditionalist/nationalist and postmodern/cosmopolitan perspectives (a false dichotomy but one that is nevertheless employed in much Native literary criticism), Armstrong would be poised at one end and Alexie at the other, although Alexie's explicit commitment to sovereignty complicates this simplification (see Alexie, qtd. in Moore 298). Despite the ostensible gulf separating Armstrong from Alexie, however, these authors share a deep concern with trans/historicizing the traumatic experiences of Native peoples—specifically, the trauma of dislocation and

rootlessness. Both *Slash* and *Indian Killer* are structured around a crucial tension in which the collective, cumulative trauma of dislocation,
a trauma that exceeds historical specificity, is in fact grounded in specific historical articulations. I would argue that the tension between
these two concepts is best seen as productive, as opposed to irreconcil-
able, and that the novels' trans/historicist approach to trauma should
not be thought of as an attempt to fix or recover the (post)colonial
trauma of Native peoples in any one time and place. Recently, a
historicist approach to trauma has been critiqued by postcolonial
trauma theorist Sam Durrant, who "argu[es] for the centrality of a
deconstructive, anti-historicist ethics of remembrance" (7). Durrant's
argument that postcolonial trauma exceeds representation is indispens-
able to my current analysis, as is his related assertion that the "immod-
erate grief" of individual postcolonial literary characters "needs to be
recognized as a precisely proportionate response to history, a way of
bearing witness to losses that exceed the proportions of the individual
subject" (11); it is the excess of this loss that disables its representation.
As allegorical and/or synecdochic characters, both Tommy Kelasket
and John Smith bear witness to a trauma—specifically, the trauma of
dislocation and rootlessness—that exceeds their individual experiences of this wound; in their respective narratives, these characters
testify to a collective, intergenerational trauma that exceeds—yet
informs—its unique articulations.

In *Slash*, a long history of traumatic removals and relocations
haunts and propels Tommy's separation from his Okanagan community. The something "missing" (84, 160, 180, 185) that Tommy tries to
locate through his travels is, in this reading, the symptom of a larger
trans/historical loss as well as its contemporary expression. Tommy's
movement from place to place—his "itchy feet" (168)—quite literally
follows in the footsteps of pan-Indian ancestors removed from their
land due to assimilationist policies and attempts to terminate their
communities. His inability to forget the trauma of this dislocation is
marked in actions that can be seen as somatic manifestations of "'un-

represented pasts' [that] haunt the present" (Bhabha, qtd. in Durrant 13). For example, during his participation in the Caravan of Broken Treaties, a nationwide march culminating in the occupation of the BIA (Bureau of Indian Affairs) offices in Washington, DC, Tommy and his fellow AIMers "cross historic sites where large massacres of Indian people occurred" (93), "retrac[ing] the route called the 'Trail of Tears.' This was the route taken in 1838 when Tribes in the southeastern U.S.A. were uprooted to give place to white settlers." Even though Tommy says that he "hadn't even heard of [the Trail of Tears]" before his participation in the Caravan and, significantly, that his own people "weren't pushed out of [their] land into another part of the country . . . like some of the people here were" (95), his actions demonstrate that he, like his girlfriend Elise, "cannot forget." "[W]hat they did burns in our hearts," she comments. "Some would like to forget and some try, but most of us don't forget ever" (96).

Tommy's Okanagan people do not carry the trauma of dislocation in the same way as other Native communities do, to be sure, but they experience a psychic dislocation, a relocation of their sense of Native identity and place that is resonant with the dislocation suffered by communities physically removed from their lands. Armstrong constructs the dislocation in Tommy's community as a morally-encoded "split" (110) between the traditionalists (embodied in Tommy's relations, who live "up" [16, 26] on the ranch and pursue traditional ways) and the assimilationists (embodied in Tommy's friend Jimmy, who lives "down" [16] in the village and whose anger and desire to acculturate are, as Cheryl Suzack argues, "constitutive effects of economic impoverishment and racism" [120]). Leaving Tommy divided and confused, the split in his community is an effect of the colonial effort to divest Native peoples of their sovereignty, not only through sustained conditions of economic and social oppression but also, Armstrong reveals, through the bitterly ironic promise that "equal rights" through "inclusion" or, more properly, assimilation will rectify these conditions. Armstrong situates various characters in relation to this assimilationist ideology of "equal rights" in order to trace its divisive effect and historical development in a Canadian context, from its expression in enfranchisement (18), the enforced education of Okanagan children in white schools (23), the legalization of alcohol on reserve land (43), and the termination of reserves and indigenous rights proposed in the White Paper of 1969 (60) to its complex articulation in the inclusion of Aboriginal rights in the 1982 Canadian Constitution. Although the fight to have Aboriginal rights enshrined in the Constitution was fueled by an anti-assimilationist agenda, for Tommy, the actualization of this goal participates in yet another—albeit more deceptive—attempt at absorbing Native peoples into a neocolonial society intent on robbing them of their inherent rights (238-51).[9] Through this ideological tracing, Armstrong shows the insidious process through which Native sovereignty is established as productive of inequality for Native people in Canada, a process instrumental to the continued land theft and cultural genocide of these peoples.

In this context, Tommy's constant movement is indicative of a psychological search for the traditional home or Native identity lost to him through a trans/historical dislocation that because it exists in advance of his experience of it, is constitutive of the very kind of home and identity he seeks. His search for a space "before" the violent dislocation that in fact precedes him bespeaks a repetition compulsion of sorts that is reflective of the trans/historical trauma of dislocation that unites Native peoples across tribes and nations. While the repetitive (or cyclical) structure and content of *Slash* is often thought to reflect traditional oral narrative conventions, I would argue that Tommy's recurring departure from and return home is also an "acting out" or return to the site of an intergenerational, intertribal trauma as well as an attempt to move beyond—or, more accurately, before—this trauma. This movement is both a behavioral symptom and a performative reiteration that, in an attempt to master the trauma, not only recites and reinforces it, but also repeats and thus relocates it in a particular time and community.

The trans/historical trauma of violent separation and dislocation can be witnessed in Tommy's repeated homecomings throughout the novel and not only in his frequent departures. A reading of Tommy's returns—especially his final return, which marks the recovery of his traditional Native identity—as indicative not only of recovery but also (paradoxically) of a continued traumatization complicates any reading of the novel that understands its conclusion as a straightforward expression of recovery's possibility. Tommy's attempt to return to the moment before the violent split and dislocation of his community (his attempt to return to what was always there) is, in this sense, an attempt to repress the very trans/historical trauma that renders such a return both impossible and desirable. But with each departure, the repressed returns; indeed, it is this psychic strategy of repression and return whose mechanisms the novel lays bare in its concluding pages: the death of Tommy's wife, Maeg, can be read as the necessary foreclosure on which the im/possibility—that is, the simultaneous possibility and impossibility—of Tommy's recovery and return is based. Although the novel positions Maeg as holding traditionalist values similar to Tommy's, her participation in the fight to enshrine Native rights in the Canadian constitution contributes, from Tommy's perspective, to the assimilationist designs of the state. Her death, which occurs on the road home from celebrating constitutional victory, reflects the terminal danger of fighting for inclusion (or assimilation) within the neo-colonial state and thereby consolidates Tommy's perspective, since the challenge her position poses to his is symbolically removed in this way. Her erasure is thus the mechanism through which Tommy's recovery is simultaneously secured and undone, for this erasure operates metonymically both to emphasize and excise the trans/historical trauma of dislocation, articulated in this context as a split between the assimilationists and the traditionalists. *Slash* provides a "precocious testimony" (21), to borrow Shoshana Felman's term, to the way in which recovery demands its own violent removals.

For Durrant, the forgetting or primary repression of the Other through which the European subject is consolidated renders impossible the historical representation of such Forgetting, where "representation" is understood as a "recovery" of the past: "To recover a history of the Holocaust [for example] as an event that took place during the Nazi era is to ignore the fact that this Forgetting does not take place in historical time. . . . Such a history would . . . not be capable of remembering the Forgetting of Jewish humanity that is foundational to the construction of European identity" (6). History, in this view, is the territory of the European subject. While I am sympathetic to Durrant's argument that the forgetting of the Other's humanity is the precondition of the European subject, I question both his location of this forgetting outside history and his assumption that a historicist approach to postcolonial trauma necessarily involves the "fantasy of recovering or retrieving the past" (8). Rather, I would argue that the challenge is to redefine the historicity of (post)colonial trauma as something other than its singular location in time and space. From my reading of *Slash* and *Indian Killer*, traumatic events locatable in specific historical eras, such as the adopting-out of Native children, can be seen as material incarnations of a repetitive trauma that takes place trans/historically or in multiple historical times instead of outside or as a sublime break with historical time. In this view, the removal of Native children is a traumatic calling up of other historic removals, a reenactment that nevertheless has its own historicity, understood here as a material specificity and temporal/spatial location. This approach complicates any easy assumption of the historical location of trauma, but it does not necessarily do away with this location; rather, it redefines it. Understanding (post)colonial trauma as trans/historical eschews a conventional historicist approach that assumes the possibility of fixing history or recuperating the lost other through representation and thus insists that postcolonial narratives "[bear] witness to the way in which the 'unrepresented pasts' haunt the present" (13). At the same time, a trans/historical ethics of remembrance (to borrow and modify Durrant's "antihistoricist ethics of remembrance") insists that we consider the material location of traumatic events even as it complicates the singularity of such a location. This is not to argue for the possibility of overcoming trauma by narrativizing or locating it within a historical chronology; instead, it is to suggest that trans/historical trauma, because of its very trans/historicity, renders im/possible such a recovery.

The first chapter of *Indian Killer*, "Mythology," provides an apt example of the historical dislocation of trans/historical trauma. "Mythology" is the first in a series of fantasies, ascribed to John but related indirectly by the third-person narrator (a further, strategic dislocation), in which John imagines his life had he not been taken away from his indigenous community. In this first fantasy, John recreates the scene of his birth and thus returns to the trauma of his kidnapping, reconstructing it as such rather than accepting its reconstruction as an adoption. Alexie's language condemns the criminal treatment of John and his mother by the multiple authorities that facilitate his removal: the remains of the placenta are referred to as "the evidence"; John's mother is "bleeding profusely" and "screaming in pain" (5); her "legs [are] tied in stirrups" and "[t]he white doctor has his hands inside her" (4). This is the scene of a crime—a rape and murder—accordant with the historic invasion of Native lands, the conquering of Native women as territory, and the imprisonment and genocide of Native peoples. After the delivery, John is taken away in a helicopter (a removal that parallels extra-tribal adoption and transnational baby-lifting,[10] as well as parodying the rescue/apprehension scenes of popular crime movies), and "[s]uddenly this is a war," complete with shells exploding from the aircraft: "Indians hit the ground, drive their cars off roads, dive under flimsy kitchen tables. A few Indians . . . continue their slow walk down the reservation road, unperturbed by the gunfire. They have been through much worse" (6). As Krupat observes, the war staged here not only calls up the Vietnam war, whose allusive presence underlines America's parallel treatment of indigenous people everywhere, but it also foregrounds the war waged daily on the Native peoples of North America (98)—a trauma that has become so thoroughly the status quo that some, as Alexie's narrator comments with bitter irony, remain "unperturbed" by it.

In its construction of a phantasmatic space in which the traumatic story of John's birth is overtly fictionalized, the scene alludes to the familiar tenet that trauma can only be known or represented indirectly through its narrativization. Fiction, the scene further implies, is a crucial space in which to articulate the trans/historicity of historical traumas, for it is the condensation of multiple historical events and resonances in the relatively small world of the fictional text that invites us to theorize the interimplication of such events in the world outside the text. In "Mythology," the story of John's origins is the "origin story"— or mythology—of the trauma of (his) removal while, at the same time, it questions the very assumption of "origins" as accessible and singular. The simultaneous universality and historical particularity of this removal is accentuated through Alexie's inconsistent usage of determiners. For example, although the first sentence, "The sheets are dirty" (3), employs a definite article, pointing to a specific set of sheets, other sentences in the scene use either indefinite determiners or none at all: "An Indian Health Service hospital in the late sixties. On this reservation or that reservation. Any reservation, a particular reservation. . . . Linoleum floors swabbed with gray water. Mop smelling like old sex. . . . Old Indian woman in a wheelchair . . ." (3). Alexie's diction reinforces the point: this could be any number of Indian Health Service hospitals in the late 1960s; John's situation is not unique. However, the scene also lends historical specificity to what it has revealed as the larger, trans/historical trauma of removal and relocation—it demonstrates that baby-lifting is the most recent act of removal in a long chain of historic removals and war crimes, and it reinforces this point through the occasional specificity of its articles: although "John's mother is Navajo or Lakota. She is Apache or Seminole. She is Yakama or Spokane," she is "*[t]he* Indian woman" (4, emphasis added), not "an" Indian woman, not any Indian woman. The text inscribes specificity at the same time as it marks its loss, a partial marking of specificity that functions not only to locate John's trauma within its larger historical narrative but also to underscore how this trauma, as the trauma of dislocation, severs the possibility of historical location: as Shandra Spears says of the experience of being adopted-out, "There is no future and no past, only a long, isolated now/ I am not connected to past relations/ I am not connected to future generations/ I am pulled from the flow of time" (1).

## Carrying the Weight of the People: Final Thoughts

In describing the traumatic event-which-is-not-one as such, I return to the insights that have grounded this paper: first, that the event of a trans/historical trauma is not an "event," where "event" is defined as a discrete occurrence in time and space; and, second, that this event is not singular but is repeated over or across time and space and is thus cumulative, proliferating, and unhinged from the assumed verifiability or specificity of history. To theorize the trans/historicity of such an event-which-is-not-one is to focus on the way in which the prefix "trans" attaches to the historicity of trauma a sense of moving across or through—rather than beyond—history.

Felman, Dori Laub, and Caruth have similarly problematized commonplace understandings of the event, origin, and history of trauma by arguing for a "traumatic temporality" (Caruth "Interview" 78) in which traumatic events, located as they are in a delayed psychic return in the present, explode any easy supposition of their temporal fixity. Based, at least in part, on the medical model of trauma, as well as in a poststructuralist approach to referentiality, these theorists hold in common the idea that an individual's inability to apprehend trauma as it occurs causes its reiterative—and performative—reenactment in the present. While critical of Caruth's work, Ruth Leys nevertheless provides an accurate summary of the medical model on which a Caruthian approach relies: "massive trauma precludes all representation because the ordinary mechanisms of consciousness and memory are temporarily destroyed. Instead, there occurs an undistorted, material, and—[Caruth's] key term–*literal* registration of the traumatic event that, dissociated from normal mental processes of cognition, cannot be known or represented but returns belatedly in the form of 'flashbacks,' traumatic nightmares, and other repetitive phenomena" (266). Caruth herself asserts, "What returns to haunt the victim . . . is not only the reality of the violent event but also the reality of the way that its violence has not yet been fully known" (*Unclaimed* 6). Laub adds, "Trauma survivors live not with memories of the past, but with an event that could not and did not proceed through to its completion, has no ending, attained no closure, and therefore, as far as its survivors are concerned, continues into the present and is current in every respect" (69). "[T]he impact of the traumatic event," Caruth elaborates, "lies precisely in its belatedness, in its refusal to be simply located, in its insistent appearance outside the boundaries of any single place or time" ("Introduction" 9).

In this view, trauma exists through its performative citation in the present rather than its fixity in the past and, as such, is a return to an unrepresentable past made present through its reiteration—in my argument, both within the Native text and as the Native text. In the same way that, for poststructuralist linguistics, there is no *a priori* referent to language (or for Caruth, following de Man, that reference must be rethought in nonrepresentational terms), there is, from the perspective of a poststructuralist trauma theory, no traumatic event prior to the subject's unwitting repetition of traumatic symptoms in the present. More accurately, Caruth maintains that traumatic symptoms interrupt representation; their return marks the unrepresentability of the traumatic past: they do not represent the past; they refer to it. Although poststructuralist theories of performativity and referentiality are crucial to my reading of traumatic temporality in Armstrong and Alexie, my argument, grounded as it is in the historical specificities of Native trauma, necessarily differs from them. In part because of its indebtedness to the accident model of traumatic effects, Caruth's version of traumatic temporality remains insufficient to describe the historical perpetuity or endurance of the trauma of Native peoples. The currency (or present-tense) of Caruthian trauma inheres in the incomprehensibility of this trauma in the past—its extraordinariness—whereas in Alexie and Armstrong, the currency of trans/historical trauma testifies not only to the possession of the present by "unrepresentable pasts" but also to continuing traumatic conditions. This is not to ignore that, for Caruth, trauma survivors experience their trauma as continuing in the present, but it is to suggest that, for Armstrong and Alexie, present-tense traumatic conditions exist outside of their repetition in symptom. Trans/historical trauma exceeds its temporal location not only because it psychically haunts its survivor in the present but also because it accumulates and repeats, across time, the residue of diverse historical circumstances.

Trans/historical trauma might be seen as closer in kind to Dori Laub's "second holocaust," especially given that the focus of Laub's model is on collective rather than individual trauma, but I would emphasize that the difference between this model and that articulated in Armstrong and Alexie is parallel to that which differentiates their model from Caruth's. Detailing the intergenerational repetition compulsion central to his concept, Laub explains that the trauma of the Holocaust is inherited by the children of Holocaust survivors, whose lives unwittingly bear witness to the trauma their parents are "attempting to repress and to forget." In one particular case study, "[b]oth the father and the daughter shied away from *knowing* and from grieving, a loss they could henceforth only *relive* as haunting memory in real life, at once through the actual return of the trauma and through its inadvertent repetition, or transmission, from one generation to another." Laub continues: "Through its uncanny reoccurrence, the trauma of the second holocaust bears witness not just to a history that has not ended, but, specifically, to the historical occurrence of an event that, in effect, *does not end*" (67). The Holocaust, as constructed in Laub's analysis and, indeed, in most of its representations, is similar in traumatic effect to Freud's train accident; understood as an "event outside the norm," the

Holocaust defies all comprehension and thus returns to haunt its survivor—and its survivor's heirs—in an ongoing historic present. This analysis owes much to a psychoanalytic model of individual trauma and its psychic belatedness, and although Laub works to problematize historical location, it is the very method of this problematization that serves to reinstill the Holocaust as a discrete and therefore bounded event. While the accident model constructs the Holocaust as ongoing in psychic life, it does not ask us to see the Holocaust as an ongoing material circumstance. (This is not to ignore the material dimension of psychic life; instead, it is to suggest that a distinction needs to be made between the materiality of cumulative psychological trauma and that of the trauma of sustained political and economic oppression.) Laub's language bears witness to a certain fixation of the trauma of the Holocaust in the past: trauma in the above case study might possess the present, but it is possessed or owned by the past; indeed, it is the parent's trauma that returns. Therefore, while Laub's model might appear amenable to a study of Native North American trauma, it is in fact quite different from that cultivated by Native authors, for as these authors suggest, the trauma of colonization is present not only in its psychic return but also in its continuation in everyday, material conditions.

The concept of trans/historical trauma has the potential to make a crucial intervention in trauma theory, invested as this concept is in an "event" that refuses historical location at the same time as it insists on being multiply lodged. In *Indian Killer* as well as in *Slash*, the trauma of dislocation and homelessness, along with the rage this trauma engenders, is an event of the present as well as of the past: it originates in distinct historical periods and events and is tied to diverse locales. While its present citation calls up its past rehearsals, it is not only-ever a repetition of the past but instead has its own materiality, its own conditions of production, its own traumatic effects.

From his decision to entitle individual "race wars" between white and Native characters with the names of historic-sounding battles, such as "The Battle of Queen Anne" (211) and "The Aurora Avenue Massacre" (255), to his novel's repeated alignment of the Indian Killer and the killer's acts of vengeance with the nineteenth-century Ghost Dance—an "act of warfare against white people" designed to "destroy the white men and bring back the buffalo" (185)—Sherman Alexie calls attention to the trans/historicity of Native North American trauma. "So maybe this Indian Killer is a product of the Ghost Dance," Marie Polatkin speculates. "Maybe ten Indians are Ghost Dancing. Maybe a hundred. It's just a theory. How many Indians would have to dance to create the Indian Killer?" (313). "Indians are dancing now," she later adds, "and I don't think they're going to stop" (418). The novel reinforces this point through its final depiction of the killer, who "sings and dances for hours, days. Other Indians arrive and quickly learn the song. . . . The killer knows this dance is over five hundred years old. . . . The killer plans on dancing forever" (420). Both a product and a part of the Ghost Dance, the Indian Killer is a present-tense expression of a trans/historic accumulation; he is "all those badass Indians rolled up into one," as a homeless Indian explains to John's father: "This Indian Killer, you see, he's got Crazy Horse's magic. He's got Chief Joseph's brains. He's got Geronimo's heart. He's got Wovoka's vision" (219). Daniel's response, "But who is he?" disregards the man's insight, thus betraying the refusal of (post)colonial society to acknowledge the trans/historicity of Native trauma. But the Indian man will not be deterred: "It's me" (220), he laughs. The trauma of homelessness, alienation, and dislocation—suffered in different ways not only by Crazy Horse, Chief Joseph, and Geronimo but also by John Smith, Marie and Reggie Polatkin, the homeless Indian man, and of course, Tommy Kelasket—is a trans/historical trauma located in the removals and relocations of the nineteenth-century reservation period as well as in the contemporary conditions and consequences of extra-tribal adoption, assimilationist policies, urban relocation, and the identity politics of authentic Nativeness. It is a "pain," Alanis Obomsawin reminds us, that is over "four hundred years old," a pain that is "carried" by the people. As Jeannette Armstrong, through Tommy, makes clear,

> I learned that, being an Indian, I could never be a person only to myself. I was part of all the rest of the people. . . . What I was affected everyone around me, both then and far into the future, through me and my descendants. They would carry whatever I left them. I was important as one person but more important as a part of everything else. That being so, I realized, I carried the weight of all of my people as we each did. (202-03)

## Notes

1. See Alexander et al., especially chapter 1. To propose that trauma is "not something naturally existing" (2) is not to suggest that it is not somehow grounded in material realities; rather, it is to maintain that "[t]rauma is a socially-mediated attribution," which may be made "as an event unfolds . . . before the event occurs . . . or after the event has concluded" (8).

2. For a similar analysis of the way in which the institutionalization of trauma functions to necessitate collective responsibility and compensation, see Hacking, who discusses the cultivation of PTSD in the wake of the Vietnam War.

3. The definition of a traumatic stressor underwent changes in the *DSM* IV (1994). While "criterion A for post-traumatic stress disorder will no longer require that an event be infrequent, unusual, or outside of a mythical human norm of experience, . . . [t]he DSM IV revision has failed to provide us with a diagnosis to describe the effects of exposure to repetitive interpersonal violence and victimization" (Brown 111). Even though the *DSM* definition has changed, I would advance that the earlier definition prevails in popular and academic discussions of trauma.

4. I use Freud's "accident model" as shorthand for the theory of trauma as a discrete event outside the norm. Elaborated upon in *Beyond the Pleasure Principle*, the accident model extrapolates from the symptoms of train-crash survivors to general principles of traumatic neurosis (see Section II).

5. "Indian" is Armstrong's term, as well as Alexie's. Along with "Native" or "Native North American," this designation will be used throughout my discussion. Note, however, that even though I do not differentiate between the terms, important distinctions are often made. Alexie himself has commented: "Thesis: I have never met a Native American. Thesis repeated: I have met thousands of Indians" ("Unauthorized" 13).

6. Alternative readings of the "third choice" can be found in Emberley 136-37, Godard 217-18, Green and Fee 174-75.

7. For more information on the ICWA and the conditions leading up to its passage, see Kiiwetinepinesiik Stark, Hollinger, and Mannes. See also Fanshel for a revealing look inside the BIA's Indian Adoption Project, which, in conjunction with the Child Welfare League of America, began in 1958 to promote the adoption of Indian children by non-Indian families.

8. Christie's "Renaissance Man: The Tribal 'Schizophrenic' in Sherman Alexie's *Indian Killer*" provides a critique of schizophrenia in the novel.

9. For Tommy, to fight to have Aboriginal rights included in the Constitution is to overlook the fact that inherent, pre-existing Aboriginal rights given by the Creator and upheld through practice cannot be "granted" by the Canadian nation. Granted rights are contingent rights, subject to possible redefinition outside the control of Aboriginal peoples. The split between those who desire to protect their rights through inclusion and those who understand these rights as non-negotiable replays, on a grand scale, the split between assimilationists and traditionalists in Tommy's community.

10. In her discussion of the ICWA, which includes a section on *Indian Killer*, Pauline Turner Strong coins the term "extra-tribal" adoption (rather than using "transracial" adoption) to "refer to the placement of an Indian child with adoptive parents who are not members of the tribe to which the child belongs." "[E]xtra-tribal adoption," she argues, "shares . . . the issues of sovereignty and citizenship with transnational adoption" (470).

## Works Cited

Abadian, Sousan. *From Wasteland to Homeland: Trauma and the Renewal of Indigenous Peoples and Their Communities*. Diss. Harvard University, 1999. Ann Arbor, MI: UMI, 1999. 9936187.

Alexander, Jeffrey C., et al. *Cultural Trauma and Collective Identity*. Berkeley: U of California P, 2004.

Alexie, Sherman. *Indian Killer*. New York: Warner, 1996.

_____. "Seeing Red." Interview with Gretchen Giles. *Sonoma Independent* 3-9 Oct. 1996. 23 May 2007. http://www.metroactive.com/papers/sonoma/10.03.96/books-9640.html.

_____. "Spokane Words." Interview with Tomson Highway. *17th Annual International Festival of Authors*, Toronto 28 Oct. 1996. 22 May 2007. http://www.2005.lang.osaka-u.ac.jp/~krkvls/salexie.html.

_____. "The Unauthorized Autobiography of Me." *One Stick Song*. New York: Hanging Loose, 2000. 13-25.

Armstrong, Jeannette. *Slash*. Penticton, BC: Theytus, 1985.

Bensen, Robert, ed. *Children of the Dragonfly: Native American Voices on Child Custody and Education*. Tucson: U of Arizona P, 2001.

Bird, Gloria. "The Exaggeration of Despair in Sherman Alexie's *Reservation Blues*." *Wicazo Sa Review* 11.2 (1995): 47-52.

Brown, Laura S. "Not Outside the Range: One Feminist Perspective on Psychic Trauma." *Trauma: Explorations in Memory.* Ed. Cathy Caruth. Baltimore: Johns Hopkins UP, 1995. 100-12.

Caruth, Cathy. Interview with Aimee L. Pozorski. *Connecticut Review* 28.1 (2006): 77-84.

_____. Introduction. *Trauma: Explorations in Memory.* Ed. Cathy Caruth. Baltimore: Johns Hopkins UP, 1995. 3-12.

_____. *Unclaimed Experience: Trauma, Narrative, History.* Baltimore: Johns Hopkins UP, 1996.

Christie, Stuart. "Renaissance Man: The Tribal 'Schizophrenic' in Sherman Alexie's *Indian Killer*." *American Indian Culture and Research Journal* 25.4 (2001): 1-19.

Cook-Lynn, Elizabeth. "American Indian Intellectualism and the New Indian Story." *American Indian Quarterly* 20.1 (1996): 57-76.

Dumont, Marilyn. "The Devil's Language." *An Anthology of Canadian Native Literature in English.* 2nd ed. Ed. Daniel David Moses and Terry Goldie. Oxford: Oxford UP, 1998. 391-92.

Emberley, Julia V. "History Lies in Fiction's Making and Unmaking: Jeannette Armstrong's *Slash*." *Thresholds of Difference: Feminist Critique, Native Women's Writings, Postcolonial Theory.* Toronto: U of Toronto P, 1993. 129-50.

Fanshel, David. *Far From the Reservation: The Transracial Adoption of American Indian Children.* Metuchen, NJ: Scarecrow P, 1972.

Fee, Margery. "Upsetting Fake Ideas: Jeannette Armstrong's 'Slash' and Beatrice Culleton's 'April Raintree.'" *Canadian Literature* 124-25 (1990): 168-80.

Felman, Shoshana. "Education and Crisis, or the Vicissitudes of Teaching." *Testimony: Crises of Witnessing in Literature, Psychoanalysis, and History.* Ed. Shoshana Felman and Dori Laub. New York: Routledge, 1992. 1-56.

Freud, Sigmund. "From *Beyond the Pleasure Principle*." 1920. *Beyond the Pleasure Principle and Other Writings.* Trans. John Reddick. London: Penguin, 2003. 45-102.

Giles, James R. *The Spaces of Violence.* Tuscaloosa: U of Alabama P, 2006.

Godard, Barbara. "The Politics of Representation: Some Native Canadian Women Writers." *Canadian Literature* 124-25 (1990): 183-225.

Green, Matthew. "A Hard Day's Knight: A Discursive Analysis of Jeannette Armstrong's *Slash*." *Canadian Journal of Native Studies* 19.1 (1999): 51-67.

Hacking, Ian. "Memory Sciences, Memory Politics." *Tense Past: Cultural Essays in Trauma and Memory.* Ed. Paul Antze and Michael Lambek. New York: Routledge, 1996. 67-87.

Hollinger, Joan Heifetz. "Beyond the Best Interests of the Tribe: The Indian Child Welfare Act and the Adoption of Indian Children." *University of Detroit Law Review* 66.3 (1988-89): 451-501.

Kiiwetinepinesiik Stark, Heidi, and Kekek Jason Todd Stark. "Flying the Coop: ICWA and the Welfare of Indian Children." *Outsiders Within: Writing on Transracial Adoption.* Ed. Jane Jeong Trenka, Julia Chinyere Oparah, and Sun Yung Shin. Cambridge: South End P, 2006. 125-38.

Krupat, Arnold. *Red Matters: Native American Studies*. Philadelphia: U of Pennsylvania P, 2002.

Laub, Dori. "Bearing Witness, or the Vicissitudes of Listening." *Testimony: Crisis of Witnessing in Literature*. Ed. Shoshana Felman and Dori Laub. New York: Routledge, 1992. 57-74.

Leys, Ruth. *Trauma: A Genealogy*. Chicago: U of Chicago P, 2000.

Lutz, Hartmut. "Jeannette Armstrong." *Contemporary Challenges: Conversations with Canadian Native Authors*. Saskatoon, SK: Fifth House, 1991. 13-32.

Mannes, Marc. "Factors and Events Leading to the Passage of the Indian Child Welfare Act." *Child Welfare* 74.1 (1995): 264-82.

Manson, Spero, et al. "Wounded Spirits, Ailing Hearts: PTSD and Related Disorders Among American Indians." *Ethnocultural Aspects of Posttraumatic Stress Disorder: Issues, Research, and Clinical Applications*. Ed. Anthony J. Marsella et al. Washington, DC: American Psychological Association, 1996. 255-83.

Moore, David L. "Sherman Alexie: Irony, Intimacy, and Agency." *Cambridge Companion to Native American Literature*. Ed. Joy Porter and Kenneth M. Roemer. Cambridge: Cambridge UP, 2005. 297-310.

Owens, Louis. *Mixedblood Messages: Literature, Film, Family, Place*. Norman: U of Oklahoma P, 1998.

Robin, Robert W., Barbara Chester, and David Goldman. "Cumulative Trauma and PTSD in American Indian Communities." *Ethnocultural Aspects of Posttraumatic Stress Disorder: Issues, Research, and Clinical Applications*. Ed. Anthony J. Marsella et al. Washington, DC: American Psychological Association, 1996. 239-53.

Root, Maria P. P. "Reconstructing the Impact of Trauma on Personality." *Personality and Psychopathology: Feminist Reappraisals*. Ed. L. S. Brown and M. Ballou. New York: Guilford, 1992. 229-65.

Spears, Shandra. "If I Pull Away." *Outsiders Within: Writing on Transracial Adoption*. Ed. Jane Jeong Trenka, Julia Chinyere Oparah, and Sun Yung Shin. Cambridge, MA: South End, 2006. 117-23.

Suzack, Cheryl. *Law, Literature, Location: Contemporary Aboriginal/Indigenous Women's Writing and the Politics of Identity*. Diss. U of Alberta, 2004.

Turner Strong, Pauline. "To Forget Their Tongue, Their Name, and Their Whole Relation: Captivity, Extra-Tribal Adoption, and the Indian Child Welfare Act." *Relative Values: Reconfiguring Kinship Studies*. Ed. Sarah Franklin and Susan McKinnon. Durham: Duke UP, 2001. 468-93.

van der Kolk, Bessel A., and Onno van der Hart. "The Flexibility of Memory and the Engraving of Trauma." *Trauma: Explorations in Memory*. Ed. Cathy Caruth. Baltimore: Johns Hopkins UP, 1995. 158-82.

Wesley-Esquimaux, Cynthia, and Magdalena Smolewski. *Historic Trauma and Aboriginal Healing*. Ottawa, ON: Aboriginal Healing Foundation, 2004.

# Building Cultural Knowledge in the Contemporary Native Novel_____

Sean Kicummah Teuton

I knew this was coming, so deal with it. Next thing is to call home. I call home and talk to my mother, tell her what happened. I had tried to warn her before hand that this was probably going to happen, but when she hears the bad news I could hear the change in her voice. It's hard to hide disappointment and hurt when over the phone. When *you* go to prison, the people that are near and dear to you also do the time with you. They feel the same things you feel whether bad or good. I had never thought of that before I was locked up, but now it is real. I also get to share two more years of prison with my mom and the rest of my family.

—Greg, Tuscarora prisoner, Auburn prison, April 1999

Except for the grey concrete floor, the holding tank was painted yellow. . . . Velma was a thin white whore with needle tracks up and down her arms. . . . Then there was Ethel, a black woman in a black velvet jumpsuit that zipped up the front. . . . Cecelia thought how strange it was that [Velma] was desired by men, often, and by many men, so very much desired, in fact, that she was able to earn her living the way she did. Yet—and she did not just realize this now; she had known it for some time and turned it over in her mind, decided it was not valid, and continued to do it anyway—it was through attracting handsome men that she, Cecelia Capture Welles, sought a measure of self-esteem.

—Janet Campbell Hale, *The Jailing of Cecelia Capture*

In town for our Green Corn ceremony, I pull into the Wal-Mart parking lot and notice all the vehicles, from brand-new sedans to beat-up trucks, with Cherokee Nation license plates. When the Nation began issuing tribal tags a few years ago, one's citizenship was suddenly on display while driving around Tahlequah. Emerging from cars with

Cherokee Nation tags were everyday Cherokee people, some dressed like cowboys, some with children, teenagers wearing hip hop attire, old people with disabilities, some dark, some light, all headed in to get a jug of milk or fishing tackle, as I was. In this moment I was struck by how "Cherokee-ness" is so variously represented. Looking around, I also saw Creek Nation and Sac and Fox Nation tags. The experience confirmed for me how truly multicultural Indian Country is, even though social and cultural diversity is often a value more lived than discussed in tribal communities. For centuries, Cherokees have married people outside the tribe and, often, brought their non-Cherokee spouses into their townships. Since around the 1980s, the Native novel has increasingly represented this expansive and interactive social world in an honest engagement with the diversity of class, gender, and sexuality, for example, found across Native America today. In addition, many of these novels elaborate the theoretical issues of Indigenous knowledge that I have been developing in previous chapters. Such growth in more recent Indian novels, however, would not have been possible without the imaginative literary strides of earlier Red Power literary texts. In this concluding chapter [of *Red Land, Red Power*], I would like to explore this legacy and its new social developments in the contemporary Indian novel. After extending some of my tribal realist claims to approach social diversity and interaction in today's Native communities and literature, I will briefly analyze several contemporary novels that I feel explore neglected social communities in Indian America.

As I note in my experience at Wal-Mart, just moving through the world often puts us in touch with people who lead lives different from our own. In the previous chapter, I explained that a historically grounded criticism can be pursued by interacting with those beyond our own worlds, and that we can draw on such experiences to inform our politics. From this idea of social interaction, we not only can develop a more comprehensive account of the American Indian world, but also be changed by and grow through that experience. When I began teaching in prisons, I was made to reconsider my views of criminality, race, power, and justice, and I was thus changed as a Native scholar. As Greg writes in the epigraph above, he of course experienced great change in prison and he also discovered that his family endures his prison sentence with him. In a similar manner, Cecelia Capture discovers that her world is not so different from those of other women, despite disparities in race and class. As a law student arrested for drunk driving, Cecelia considers a similar gendered relation of power in the United States that affects not only Indian women but all women in different ways. Such moments of social complexity and cultural interaction point to the emergence of a new and subtle narrative pattern in the American Indian novel from around the mid-1980s to the present.

In this concluding chapter, I thus investigate more recent Native literature that draws on the vision of the Red Power novel to extend the theoretical claims I have been making through the course of this work. For social transformation is achieved not only by recovering a past but also by preparing a future. In imagining a future for American Indian people, the authors I explore in this chapter help prepare a theory of culture adequate to the decolonization of Indian Country in the years ahead. The recent outpouring of creative work by Native writers counters the unrelenting image of the Vanishing American in popular culture, and it even suggests a future of social and creative flourishing. Here, I turn to this new wave of literature to outline how, in the past two decades since Red Power, the writers Sherman Alexie, Betty Louise Bell, Robert Conley, Janet Campbell Hale, Irvin Morris, Greg Sarris, Craig Womack, and Ray Young Bear seek a more comprehensive understanding of culture and social justice in Native America. These writers continue to represent what I find to be an empirical process—the task of recovering, revising, and building Indian cultural knowledge—as characters engage with personal and tribal history and memory and with suppressed social experiences.

## Social Knowledge in Indian Country

Throughout this work, I have proposed that a tribal realist view of knowledge may better serve critical studies of literature and culture and the real world social struggles of American Indian people. We recall that this approach to Indigenous art and life rests on a redefined model of objectivity, one I often see maintained in tribal oral traditions. Resituating philosophical and social inquiry in this intellectual framework enables Indian scholars not only to challenge dominant and inaccurate interpretations of Native literature and culture, but also to justify alternative and more accurate knowledge on tribal peoples and their creative work. In this vital respect, realism benefits from the constructivist critique that preoccupies contemporary theory, but it also promotes normative claims to the world. Realism thus confronts the conclusion stemming from skeptical approaches—that Native people, as colonized agents thoroughly mediated from their world, cannot know their world. When Native scholars adapt a tribal realist view of knowledge and interpret their social world with this alternative model of cultural normativity, they are able not only to locate the exploitations of colonialism, but also to affirm the viability of American Indian people and their communities. Because realism holds that our understandings of the world are certainly constructed but nonetheless constructed in different ways that entail quantifiable political consequences, the position allows us to say that such accounts of the world can, indeed must, be more or less objectively evaluated. Nonrealists frequently do not make such evaluations. As the world changes and American Indian people continue to gather social knowledge, we can revise our assessments. For this reason, this "fallibilistic" social theory can accommodate material change and cultural development without relying on a cultural essence. Rather, we can guide our growth by positing and revising normative claims regarding Indian life. I believe this achievement of cultural objectivity is *the* crucial intellectual goal for American Indians struggling to decolonize their nations.

In both current cultural studies and recent announcements in the popular media, Indians are said to be verging upon a new social moment in which they are interacting with people of other cultures perhaps more frequently than ever before. I imagine the years ahead to entail a tremendous infusion of other cultures among American Indians—an infusion that will not endanger but indeed may even benefit Native culture so long as we approach this opportunity of cultural interaction from the most enabling intellectual framework. Such dynamic social transformation will require a clear understanding of Native cultural change as a conscious process to assess and modify a collective identity. To develop culturally and to succeed politically, we will have to ask whether we can say anything objective about changing Indian culture. Native historians have already documented earlier events of cultural exchange, leading to this moment upon us, such as both nineteenth-century and twentieth-century displacements of Native groups to new lands or urban areas. But whether we recall "the Removal" of Native peoples to Indian Territory or "the Relocation" of American Indians to cities, we should emphasize the impressive agency of Native people, not only to adapt and survive, but also to devise creative solutions to their oppression through social and cultural cooperation among tribal and nontribal groups. While this sharing of knowledge is no doubt an old story in Indian America, between European Americans and Native peoples such cooperation is still strained by colonial relations.

Building on my understanding of cultural interaction and development from previous chapters, we can now reencounter the function of Native culture in an altogether new light: namely, as a "think tank" in which to generate and test new ideas. Satya Mohanty explains cultures as "fields of moral inquiry" in which social activity provides an opportunity for the production of knowledge: "Cultures are more like laboratories than anything else; they do not only embody values and beliefs, they also test and modify these values and beliefs in practical ways. Values, which involve more than our conscious beliefs, are the very substance of such experiments. New forms of living . . . help us interrogate old ideas and deepen new hunches. Hunches develop both into programs for action and into theories. Notions of the just society and of the moral status of individuals are developed out of institutions that arise in the practices of everyday social life. . . . Cultural practices embody and interrogate rich patterns of value, which in turn represent deep bodies of knowledge of humankind and of human flourishing" (1997, 240-41). Mohanty's theory of culture as a laboratory for the development of rich "patterns of value" supports my vision of social interaction in and beyond Indian Country not as a potential hazard but indeed as a social ideal. Indigenous peoples have long invented and tested new ways of life. Historians of science recognize the advanced pharmaceutical and medicinal knowledge of tribal peoples of the Americas upon invasion by Europeans who gathered this knowledge; other historians explore the influence of Native governments on the framers of the U.S. Constitution, for example.[1] It is quite possible that the rich production of Indigenous knowledge in North America owes a great deal to Native societies' ability to both enable and protect complex patterns of social expression. This is the Indian "freedom" or "liberty" romanticized by European intellectuals such as Montaigne and Rousseau, Franklin and Thoreau. The protection of social freedom allows for the production, experimentation, and development of new ways of life. For as we know, new practices, customs, and rituals to maintain social knowledge assure the preservation and flourishing of a tribal people. Early on, Native people likely understood the importance of maintaining free social and political conditions to ensure the production of more complete assessments of the tribal world. Mohanty encapsulates this claim about the relationship between culturally produced objective knowledge and social practice: "Objectivity is inextricably tied to social and historical conditions, and objective knowledge is the product not of disinterested theoretical inquiry so much as of particular kinds of practice" (213).

From this view of Native knowledge production as a social practice, we receive a twofold benefit: the promotion of social expression in Indian Country is not only a social good but also an empirical necessity. We thus may foster cultural diversity in Native America not out of any sentimental concern for "disadvantaged" groups but for clear epistemological reasons. In this realist view of cultural inquiry, we work to enable members of a particular group, such as Natives with disabilities who are often marginalized in inaccessible communities, to participate in the production and testing of new cultural values so we can better achieve normative knowledge. The development of social diversity is thus one part of a broader goal of social justice in what we call Indian Country. Even among our own people, the protection of cultural and social expression often inspires us to do political work. According to Caroline Hau, who employs a realist approach in post-colonial studies: "Attempts at objective explanation are necessarily continuous with oppositional struggles. Activism strives to create conditions for better knowledge" (2000, 161). In this view of knowledge production, the concepts of social identity, social practice, and social justice are interrelated, forming a dynamic synergy to support decolonization. We thus discover another benefit of adapting a realist theory of cultural identity: a sound theory of social identity in Native communities develops our bodies of Indigenous knowledge. From my earlier discussion of experience and its ties to identity, it now should be apparent how experience can contribute to this collective project of social inquiry. Drawn from our very lives and shared with others, our experiences and those of others can confirm or challenge our known worlds. In this regard, they shape not only personal but indeed collective identity. So when we introduce the various social identities that enrich the category of American Indian—say, Native lesbians, middle-class Navajo persons, impoverished Six Nations citizens, or Choctaw Baptists—we certainly complicate the way our cultural identities refer to the assumed world around us, but we also improve social inquiry in viewing Indian Country from this more laden vantage. In so doing, we reduce error and thus better complete the picture of modern Indian life. But how can we today promote the profound particularism, envisioned in this view of social diversity as an ideal of inquiry, and still speak of an Indian Country?

Leaders of social struggles in the Third World have often identified this goal of organizing disparate groups into a united force of resistance. Such a task, however, has drawn critique among scholars who question not only the exclusions required to streamline such a social movement but, more important, the unavoidable error in interpreting experience across different local communities. Organizing Indian Country thus presents an epistemological challenge. Hau describes this difficult role of the intellectual in social movements: "This position emphasizes the potential contribution that the intellectual can make as one whose epistemic access to and articulations of the experiences of others are crucial in generalizing—broadening, or, in the context of anticolonial struggle, 'nationalizing'—popular consciousness" (2000, 134). It is through intellectual process as well as political practice that activists and scholars come better to understand and clarify a collective destination for a subordinated group like Native America. As Hau suggests, movements succeed not on a reduction but an expansion of group interests. For this reason, the promotion of social diversity in Indian communities not only aids inquiry but also helps to produce a more collective vision, and it does so without reducing, but indeed building on, the political force of the particular. This is my view of social diversity in Indian Country as a goal to fortify a theory of justice and normative knowledge. Its achievement requires not only intellectual planning but also empirical practice. But as we encourage the contributions of particular social concerns on the one hand, we should not lose sight of universal moral claims on the other. Respect for the dignity of Native peoples from all walks of life as well as of the land and its creatures is one such principle on which a progressive vision of Indian social justice could be built.

This book's view of American Indian selfhood might help explain how, in recent Native literature, Indian people often inhabit more than one social identity. Previous chapters have explored how a Native person understands her or his world and perhaps reconsiders and improves that understanding and grows culturally. Through an ongoing process, Native people may awaken politically and recover cultural identity. Of course, such a broad category as "Indian" must also be contextualized in specific tribal groups with their clan and band affiliations, their histories and lands. All these cultural factors combine to constitute what we generally call Indigenous identity. This tribal complexity demands an account of the numerous social worlds encompassed in any approach to Indian America. The well-known social categories of sexuality, class, and gender, for example, often complicate our understanding of Native identity, and more recent scholarship in Leisure studies and Disability studies has introduced youth and age, body and mind, as crucial categories of social identity. So we might consider how elderly Native feminists, gay Indian men, and diabetic Ho-Chunk women with disabilities enrich our accounts of being Indian in the world today. Add the above social complexities to a theory of American Indian identity and some skeptical scholars might conclude that such a politics of identity cannot succeed without calculating strategic exclusions. There are just too many determinants; the shifting cultural, geographical, and historical—and now social forces, they say—mystify an identity we wish were stable. Contemporary theorists would now recommend that we should instead accept and represent this fragmentation to the hegemonic culture to disrupt colonialist constructions of "the Indian." I argue that we need neither enact essentialist exclusions nor embrace discursive fragmentation but instead we can expand, without erasing, the Indian experience. Such an understanding of identity can not only accommodate but also benefit from the complexity of multiple social identities.

Michael Hames-García's revised concepts of "multiplicity" and "restriction" provide a practical model for this expanded conception of American Indian group membership. He carefully explains the task often presented to those who belong to a cultural group that at times marginalizes those members who also belong to another social group.

---

Hames-García discusses the concern in Michael Nava's novel *The Hidden Law*, in which a gay Chicano protagonist bears strong allegiances to a Chicano community, even though that community is reluctant to include him. Of course, many people from a variety of groups experience a similar tension: "Black women, gay Chicanos, and Asian American lesbians are examples of people who have memberships in multiple politically subordinated groups in the United States" (2000, 104). Hames-García advances a crucial point for understanding the challenge of multiple group membership—that it will not do to explain social-cultural identity as a contributive formulation, as a mathematical equation: "One cannot understand a self as the sum of so many discrete parts, that is, femaleness + blackness + motherhood" (103). He argues that to do so would be to essentialize one aspect of one's identity to stabilize the construction of another. Imagine, for example, that an American Indian woman recovers from a marriage in which she was battered, after which she becomes a feminist. It would be wrong to suppose she developed a "new" feminist identity as an addition to a genderless American Indian cultural identity; conversely, she decides to become a feminist not from a preracialized cultural position but as a Native woman—a cultural location that likely has something to do with the radicalization of her femaleness. According to Hames-García, "the whole self is constituted by the mutual interaction and relation of its parts to one another. Politically salient aspects of the self, such as race, ethnicity, sexuality, gender, and class, link and imbricate themselves in fundamental ways. These various categories of social identity do not, therefore, comprise essentially separate 'axes' that occasionally 'intersect.' They do not simply intersect but blend, constantly and differently" (103). Hames-García's redefinition of multiplicity helps explain the political transformation of the woman above, avoiding simplistic or reified notions of how people participate in a variety of communities, changing and developing in fact as a consequence of complex allegiances. As Hames-García explains, social location is not immobile but rather moves and resituates, with the self often reconstituting in response to one's surroundings or moment in life.

Imbalances in social power, however, affect the potential benefit of this kind of fluidity of the self, through what Hames-García calls "restriction." This is a useful term for a situation in which many of us often find ourselves, a modern problem in a world that often seeks to reduce the complexity of social representation and recognition not only to simplify the challenge of knowing social others but also to serve political interests. Restriction occurs when one is viewed in terms of only one social identity at the expense of all others: "According to the fracturing logic of domination inhering in capitalist cultures, this multiplicity of the self becomes restricted so that any one person's 'identity' is reduced to and understood exclusively in terms of that aspect of her or his self with the most political salience" (2000, 104). A society often decides for us exactly which aspect of our complex self is to be recognized as the defining feature of our social existence. When one's own view of oneself is in agreement with that of the dominant cultural construction, one's interests are "transparent," explains Hames-García. But for those who do not assimilate or conform to the dominant white American construction of the citizen, this restriction is oppressive and reductive, thus limiting the possibility for fruitful social expression. According to Hames-García, those who experience this restriction of their social multiplicity have suppressed, "opaque" concerns.[2] Clearly, the challenge facing social theorists in Indian Country is to create conditions that allow a robust multiplicity of social identities to emerge. Hames-García explains that those with transparent interests occupy a privileged position in a cultural or social group, in which their desires for social expression are not questioned, and thus take for granted their ability to be fully expressive. But in an unequal world, this feeling of transparency is often an illusion produced by the very dominant social network that the transparent support, a false transparency in which desires for multiplicity can be unwittingly suppressed. In this regard, always recognizing and overcoming opacity is a vital process of a just society watchful of blockages to social expression and invention. Hames-García advocates a realist theory of social selfhood that allows for a whole yet multiple self without fragmenting the self so that one is always partly outside at least one social community. This view of multiplicity, he argues, best serves anticolonial and antiracist struggles because it understands the necessity of including particular interests in order to always reconsider and revise the goals for which we scholars and activists—and the writers I discuss below—collectively work.

## Indian Poverty

The worst poverty in North America exists among American Indians, and that poverty is a source of other socially destructive problems in Native communities.[3] Such maladies as health problems, depression, and criminality are not endemic, of course, but largely stem from U.S. colonial domination and economic privation. Any portrait of modern American Indigenous life that seeks cultural objectivity thus cannot avoid an account of Indian poverty. Having grown up in a low-income family with many social problems related to poverty—such as domestic violence, alcoholism, drug abuse, homelessness, incarceration, and mental illness—I feel I must address the issue of poverty in Indian Country. To do so, I turn to the representation of poverty and poor people in two recent works of Indian fiction, Sherman Alexie's *Reservation Blues* and Betty Louise Bell's *Faces in the Moon*. Specifically, I confront the image of poverty in these works, both as an often-internalized social value and as a reality to be overcome.

With the 1995 publication of his first novel, *Reservation Blues*, Spokane writer Sherman Alexie rapidly gained critical acclaim among Indian and non-Indian readers alike. As Stephen Evans writes, however, "Inevitably, perhaps, it is precisely the success of *Reservation Blues* among the mainstream literary establishment that has brought Alexie criticism from some Indian writers and scholars" (2001, 49). Indeed, American Indian scholars might be most concerned because Alexie presents an often-unpleasant portrait of Indians to this vast audience. Graphic shots of the worst reservation realities, delivered with the blunted emotions of a trauma survivor, offend some critics because they potentially reinforce Western assumptions that dysfunction in Native communities occurs "naturally" rather than as a result of colonial relations. Alexie, they claim, does not sufficiently contextualize this Indian poverty. In representing Indigenous people's poverty and its attendant social ills as a commonplace to dominant culture, *Reservation Blues* risks playing into the hands of mainstream readers who wish to believe Native people are socially degenerate. Native readers react to this display quite differently; I suppose we might at first feel our cultural privacy violated. What right does Alexie have to share with general readers our most painful realities of poverty and social dysfunction?[4] Critics are justifiably angry when in a cultural vacuum Alexie exposes only the most troubling aspects of the American Indian world today. Alexie's novel thus "is a partial portrait of a community wherein there is no evidence of Spokane culture or traditions, or anything uniquely Spokane," argues Spokane scholar Gloria Bird (1995, 51).

In the classroom, Indian students appear to benefit from the discussion of poverty in *Reservation Blues*. With mainstream students, however, I must work extremely hard to provide a colonial context to understand the deeper sources of poverty, which Alexie does not clearly introduce in the novel. Though we work to eliminate poverty, our experiences of it should nonetheless be accepted as a source of knowledge regarding what it means to be Native today in a community suppressed by the federal government. Crucial to this process, however, is the clarification that poverty itself is not an American Indian cultural value. Indeed, assuming as much risks leading young tribal people to internalize the dominant culture's frequent insistence that Indigenous people must remain poor in order to be spiritually pure and authentic. Eduardo Duran and Bonnie Duran discuss this internalization of poverty and its social problems: "After so many decades of abuse and internalizing of pathological patterns, these dysfunctional patterns at times [become] very nebulous. . . . The dysfunctional patterns at some point start to be seen as part of Native American tradition. . . . Therefore, many of the problems facing Native American people today—such as alcoholism, child abuse, suicide, and domestic violence—have become part of the Native American heritage due to the long decades of forced assimilation and genocidal practices implemented by the federal government" (1995, 35). In the program for decolonization, these scholars explain how poverty can and should be externalized as a colonial imposition—not internalized as evidence of Indian inferiority. But, regrettably, *Reservation Blues* does not communicate this message. Its characters do not identify their poverty and social dysfunction self-consciously and then attempt to overcome it. In the novel, members of the Spokane Indian Reservation often accept their poverty as an unexamined fact of Native life. Social poverty, the novel suggests, is to a large extent not a product of economic sanctions enforced by the federal government but rather one of envy and betrayal among members of the community.

In *Reservation Blues*, three Spokane men start a blues band they call Coyote Springs. Eventually they attempt to land a New York City record contract, but fail. Dominant readers might argue that they fail because they must remain poor to remain real Indians. From the opening pages, poverty is an unavoidable fact of Spokane reservation life. Thomas Builds-the-Fire, the tribe's unofficial and unappreciated storyteller, when asked about his community, remembers the layers of poverty they all suffer: "Thomas thought about all the dreams that were murdered here, and the bones buried quickly just inches below the surface, all waiting to break through the foundations of those government houses built by the Department of Housing and Urban Development" (7). Alexie is a master of such imagery. The excruciatingly visceral suggestion of bone poking through skin introduces readers to the colonial wounds Spokane people continue to feel "just inches below the surface," for their dispossession is more recent in U.S. colonial history. The federal government provides only gestures of care for these colonial wounds and suppresses the truth of the genocidal campaigns against Native peoples beneath BIA concrete. From the novel's beginning, Thomas is cognizant of the source of Indian poverty, but seems to wonder how his people can even begin to dig through such layers—to dress the wounds and to lay the bones to rest.

Far more than his friends and fellow band members Victor Joseph and Junior Polatkin, Thomas, though ignored, continues to explore the social meanings of economic strife—alcoholism, violence, suicide—as products of poverty imposed by dispossession of ancestral land, way of life, and economy. When Victor bullies him, Thomas accepts this cruelty and violence among community members: "Thomas was not surprised by Victor's sudden violence. These little wars were intimate affairs for those who dreamed in childhood of fishing for salmon but woke up as adults to shop at the Trading Post and stand in line for U.S.D.A. commodity food instead" (14). Throughout the novel, the external source of hatred and violence is rarely shown, but seems to originate from community members in the "little wars" that my students sometimes dismiss as "Indian-on-Indian" crime. In fact, the band is literally run off the reservation by its own hateful tribal members. This theme of internalized and self-inflicted violence in *Reservation Blues* peaks when the band loses its record contract and Junior, remembering a white woman who rejects him and their child because he is Native, kills himself: "Junior had turned and walked away from Lynn. He always wondered why they had been together at all. Everybody on campus stared at them. The Indian boy and the white girl walking hand in hand. Lynn's parents wouldn't even talk to him when they came to campus for visits. Junior walked away from Lynn and never looked back. No. That wasn't true. He did turn back once, and she was still standing there, an explosion of white skin and blonde hair. She waved, and Junior felt himself break into small pieces that blew away uselessly in the wind" (240). The "explosion of white skin and blonde hair" that causes Junior to come apart, to "break into small pieces," represents an underdeveloped moment of cultural collision. It seems he suddenly "wonders why they had been together at all" and feels foolish for ever hoping to be valued simply as a person. Junior begins to succumb to feelings of "uselessness."

The memory detailed above anticipates Junior's suicide only pages later, when he literally explodes: "A week after Coyote Springs staggered from Manhattan back onto the Spokane Indian Reservation, Junior Polatkin stole a rifle from the gun rack in Simon's pickup. . . . Junior strapped that rifle over his shoulder and climbed up the water tower that had been empty most of his life. . . . Junior unshouldered the rifle and felt the smooth, cool wood of the stock, set the butt of the rifle against the metal grating of the floor, and placed his forehead against the mouth of the barrel. . . . Junior remembered. . . . He flipped the safety off, held his thumb against the trigger, and felt the slight tension. Junior squeezed the trigger" (247). Portraits of Native sacrifice are not new to dominant representations of Indigenous people in film and literature. But here, Alexie serves the image of the Vanishing American to mainstream audiences in a way that "returns an image of a 'generic' Indian back on the original producers of that image," argues Bird (1995, 49). Though Alexie claims merely to portray Spokane community life as he well knows it, Native critics contend that he is nonetheless accountable for representing Native life to a broader culture, which often expects (or even wishes) American Indians to disappear. The novel represents other acts of self-destruction; many characters, such as Victor and Samuel Builds-the-Fire, Thomas's father, drink toward early deaths. But Alexie's explanation of Junior's suicide is most troubling. Because Alexie is not clear about the deeper, colonial cause of suicide in Indian nations, I fear that many readers are led to believe American Indians are simply doomed—that they are their own worst enemies. Certainly Victor, who reacts violently and is less aware than Thomas about postcolonial life and despair, needs to know why Junior commits suicide. However, when Victor encounters the ghost of his friend and asks Junior why he killed himself, Junior actively does not disclose the colonial cause of Native social dysfunction, and even sees no larger explanation for his Indian vanishing:

". . . Junior, why'd you do it?"

"Do what?"

"Kill yourself."

Junior looked away, watching the sunlight reflecting off Turtle Lake.

"Because life is hard," Junior said.

"That's the whole story, folks. I wanted to be dead. Gone. No more."

"Why?"

"Because when I closed my eyes like Thomas, I didn't see a damn thing. Nothing. Zilch. No stories, no songs. Nothing." (290)

The conclusion that "life is hard" avoids explaining such acts of self-destruction in their larger context. Indeed, all that Junior identifies as the source of his own despair is a lack of imagination. Since he could name the instances of racism and colonial oppression he relives shortly before pulling the trigger, it is puzzling that Junior finally sees "nothing." In the end, such nihilism evades contending with the federal sources of economic and cultural destruction on the Spokane Indian Reservation. In *Reservation Blues*, Sherman Alexie portrays poverty and social dysfunction in the Spokane community as the unexamined and unlucky consequence of being American Indian in the world today.

While we can certainly benefit from confronting and examining poverty, we often resist this painful topic. Perhaps this explains the reception of Cherokee writer Betty Louise Bell's 1994 novel *Faces in the Moon*, where we receive a harrowing American Indian life tangled with domestic violence and sexual abuse, the frequent products of poverty. But unlike the works of fiction written during Red Power, which represent poverty in tension with healthy cultural traditions—traditions that often aid characters in overcoming social illness, such as they do in *House Made of Dawn*—in *Faces in the Moon*, Indians must labor to discover few cultural roots. They do, however, have their immediately available and persistent stories. Bell's novel opens with a familiar portrait of Native women around a kitchen table, sharing stories:

"I was raised on the voices of Indian women. The kitchen table was first a place of remembering, a place where women came and drew their lives from each other. The table was covered with an oilcloth in a floral pattern, large pink and red roses, the edges of the petals rubbed away by elbows" (4). This pleasing image of gentle Indian ladies living well and passing on oral traditions to young women, however, soon deteriorates like the fading flowers, as the narrator, Lucie, begins to confront her memories of poverty and sexual abuse. She recalls the child she was and the mother she preferred to know: "As a child, I called the woman 'Momma,' slipping close to the photograph and tracing her outline with my fingers, whenever I passed through Lizzie's parlor. After my great aunt's death, it was harder and harder to put the pretty girl with the child together with the fat, beat-up woman who cursed and drank, pushed into her only threat, 'Maybe I'll just run away and leave y'all to yourself'" (8-9). *Faces in the Moon* is a courageous novel because it dares to contend with a troubling Native past that offers no readily available cultural history. Admirably, the novel engages memory and loss for the sheer sake of better knowing: to gain historical clarity, to understand the causes of poverty and abuse and to do so, if at all possible, through forgiveness: "But, long before [her mother's] letters began to arrive, long before she knew she had something to say, she had already lost me to her stories. And there, I loved and forgave her" (9).

In her creative acts of understanding and forgiveness, Lucie contends with her rage at Gracie, her abusive and abandoning mother. She deals with the loss of social and cultural rearing through story, a process that, ironically, "loses" Lucie to her mother but frees Lucie from her entanglements of an abusive childhood. She eventually escapes Oklahoma and the impoverished, cruel home of her childhood. She marries a wealthy man and feels that she has left her past behind her, though it is kept alive in pleasing stories of her upbringing. But strikingly, such stories prove inadequate to maintain this comfortable distance from a colonial past. In the safety of her own memory, Lucie has

mastered a separate kind of forgiveness, but when the real world con-
tradicts or challenges this more approving version of the past, she discovers the fear and rage that lay behind her memory. As Lucie approaches the truth of her past, forgiveness seems almost impossible.
She is thus challenged to deepen her notion of forgiveness into one that
can meet the painful reality of her lived experience. Lucie dares to
share her stories with her husband Melvin. She recalls a moment from
her childhood when she was thrilled to receive a gift from her aunt,
while preparing to enter a child beauty contest. She remembers gazing
in the window of a department store, and then her Aunt Lizzie stepping
in to buy her a leopard-patterned coat. Lucie cherishes this rare moment when she felt loved and protected, and even in adulthood she
views herself as a pretty, well-dressed child: "Lucie turned, took a few
steps down the isle, and turned on a point. 'I feel like Shirley Temple'"
(61). But when her husband views the old photograph of Lucie in the
coat, "on his first and final visit to Momma's house," he thoughtlessly
exclaims: "'You were a ragamuffin!'" (61). Interestingly, even in
adulthood Lucie cannot see her childhood poverty, and is thus shocked
and ashamed by Melvin's discovery: "With that one word, the leop-
ard coat left me. Flying into the past, a shameful thing, an unworthy
thing, it caught on its false promise and I never wore it with pride
again" (61-62).

So reflecting, Lucie is compelled to reconsider her relationship to
herself, her mother, and the past, as she works to achieve a more adequate understanding of herself as an adult woman. *Faces in the Moon*
thus describes a building process of personal growth through a creative
response to the trauma of poverty, abandonment, and sexual abuse, in
which the bounds of forgiveness are tested and redefined. In the above
moment, Lucie preserves her sense of self-worth, her "pride," by up-
holding the coat as an emblem of these feelings, only to have the
threadbare piece torn from her and unraveled to expose her feelings of
shame and lack of worth. Later, divorced from Melvin, visiting Oklahoma and alone at the home of her mother, Lucie admits the truth of the

coat's embarrassing spectacle: "Now, studying the picture, I can see that the coat had not fit well. Even *her* small four-year-old body was too large for the thing. The wonderful black cuffs ended well before the wrists, and the hem of the pink dress hung inches below the coat. But there they stood, in front of Momma's Packard, two girls proud of their purchase" (emphasis added, 61). Caught in the bind of either clinging to a safe yet inaccurate past or confronting its reality and her feelings of shame and self-hatred—a choice that offers no foreseeable benefit—Lucie is left with a complex mixture of despair, rage, and hopelessness. Yet she glimpses the possibility of forgiveness, cultural recovery, and even resolution in her struggle to focus the photographic image and to interpret the little girl Lucie through the eyes of the adult Lucie—to begin to call that child "Lucie."

At the age of four, Lucie suffers a desperate period of intense abuse when J.D., Gracie's new man, moves in.[5] Gracie, afraid to lose J.D., decides to abandon Lucie to relatives. Ironically, Lucie finds life in the woods with Aunt Lizzie and Uncle Jerry to be free of poverty and full of security, care, culture, history, and hope. In this safe space, Lucie discovers the richness of her Cherokee ancestry and the beautiful woman her mother once was:

> Her eye caught a glint in the room, and she went to the bureau. There was a small gold box with an Indian woman painted on it. The woman had long black hair and a face like Lizzie's. On either side were photographs of children and old people, in overalls and hats and a jacket. Lucie studied the photographs, wondering who all these people were. In one bent photograph a beautiful dark-haired woman held a baby up to her cheek; she was wearing a plain cotton dress and standing in a field before a wood.
>
> "That there's your momma." (82-83)

In this place of cultural and historical grounding, Lucie recovers the appropriate vitality of a child. She recovers the stories of her Cherokee ancestors' life in the Old Cherokee Nation in the Southeast, and their forced march to Indian Territory. Lucie gets a fever and experiences Indian medicine, and she gains a moral education from her great-aunt: "'The Cherokee always been a proud people. They took care of their children and families. That always come first. When my granddaddy come from Georgia he didn't leave no body behind'" (122). The abandoned Lucie has been reclaimed by her nation.

In this novel, readers will not find any supernatural processes that help a Native person recover from abuse. For Lucie, recovering from an impoverished and abusive upbringing and reclaiming a Cherokee history and identity are conscious, cognitive practices. In fact Lucie is quite honest about feeling an irrational sense of guilt when someone who is not Native asks her what it is like being Indian: "I wish I had Indian stories, crazy and wild romantic vignettes of a life lived apart from them. Anything to make myself equal to their romance. Instead I can offer only a picture of Momma's rented house, a tiny flat two-bedroom shack in a run-down part of town" (59). While Red Power writing of the 1960s and 1970s sometimes relies on an idealized conception of Native culture, in which history and belonging are readily available to those who seek it, contemporary American Indian literature often risks contending with cultural loss and poverty—even when no spiritual forces attract one to a community of belief. Such an honest engagement with domination and poverty perhaps represents a moment of growth in Native literature. Indeed, Lucie admits that her most influential cultural foundation rests on the Cherokee women of her family, around the table, smoking and telling stories:

I have tried to remember my life outside the remembering of that kitchen table. I have tried to circumvent the storyteller and know my life with an easy Indian memory, but I knew no Indian princesses, no buckskin, no feathers, no tomahawks. The Indians in westerns confused and frightened me. My mother and aunt chose high heels over moccasins; they would have chosen blue eyes over black eyes. I have tried to know Momma, Auney, and Lizzie as Indian women, but all that surfaces is tired, worn-out women, stooped from picking cotton and the hard work of tenant farming. I know women burnt by the hot Oklahoma sun and wasted by their men, women scared into secrets, women of solid and steady patience. But, mostly, I know them by their hunger to talk. (58-59)

In this profoundly expressive, confessional moment, Lucie grapples with the problem of an impoverished past that offers no romantic roots, no popularized Native body of cultural knowledge. Instead, the Indigenous women she knows would rather not be Native if it means suffering "black eyes." These women speak to resist and recover from their enforced silence by the men who control them. But in an uncanny sense this life is an Indian life; the poverty cannot be winnowed out of the history. Instead, as I argue, these categories blend and inform one another. In daring to contend with a painful past of neglect, Lucie comes to understand her mother's and her own life, and through a margin of forgiveness she finally reunites the child Lucie with the adult Lucie: "In a store window I caught a glimpse of the small Indian woman, and I eased forward to catch her, with the stealth of a cat, pushing my face into my own reflection" (187). *Faces in the Moon* invites readers to consider the sources and consequences of Indian poverty, and it offers, if not a solution, then at least a resolution, through a process of remembering and healing that all of us can understand.

## Notes

1. See Barreiro 1992; Johansen 1998; and the 1992 collection by Onondaga chief Oren Lyons and Seneca historian John Mohawk.

2. Michael Hames-García adapts his concepts of transparency and opacity from María C. Lugones's work on "transparent" versus "thick" group membership (1994, 474).

3. The Indian poverty rate is 25.3 percent compared to whites at 10.6 percent; see U.S. Census Bureau 2006b, 2. Indigenous health problems are often the highest nationally; see U.S. Centers for Disease Control and Prevention 2006, 2. Native suicide rates in the 15-24 age group are the highest nationally; see U.S. Centers for Disease Control and Prevention 2004, 2. Domestic violence is more common in Indian Country than in any other culture; see U.S. Bureau of Justice 2004, 1. Drug abuse is highest among American Indians, at 10.6 percent, compared to 7.7 percent for blacks, for example; see U.S. Census Bureau 2006a, 1.

4. I must admit I feel a twinge of shame, then take offense, when confronted with the image of American Indian alcoholism in this early passage from *Reservation Blues*: "WalksAlong had raised his nephew since he was a toddler. Michael's mother had died of cirrhosis when he was just two years old, and he'd never even known his father. Michael was conceived during some anonymous three-in-the-morning pow-wow encounter in South Dakota. His mother's drinking had done obvious damage to Michael in the womb. He had those vaguely Asian eyes and the flat face that alcohol babies always had on reservations" (39). On reading this passage, a student fled my classroom in tears. Alexie's often-comic portrayal of Indian social ills marks a divergence from Red Power representations of Native social dysfunction.

5. J.D. continually and sadistically taunts Lucie, and when Lucie calls him "scum," J.D. strikes her face with his fist, drags her across the floor by her hair, and then declares: "'I'm gonna teach ya a lesson you ain't gonna forget. Now'n you shut up or I'm a-gonna make it hard on ya'" (68). J.D. then sexually assaults the child. J.D. "teaches" Lucie the lesson of women's submission to men and the silencing of men's violence, declaring, "'T'ain't nothing but Injun trash. Your momma's trash, and you're trash too'" (68). Like the other women in the novel, Lucie, at four years old, discovers that impoverished Indian women often have little choice but to suffer the abuses of men, actually changing their names as each man comes to possess them.

## Works Cited

Alexie, Sherman. 1995. *Reservation Blues*. New York: Atlantic Monthly.

Barreiro, José, ed. 1992. *Indian Roots of American Democracy*. Ithaca, N.Y.: Akwe:kon.

Bell, Betty Louise. 1994. *Faces in the Moon*. Norman: University of Oklahoma Press.

Bird, Gloria. 1995. "The Exaggeration of Despair in Sherman Alexie's *Reservation Blues*." *Wicazo Sa Review* 10, no. 2: 47-52.

Duran, Eduardo, and Bonnie Duran. 1995. *Native American Postcolonial Psychology*. Albany: State University of New York Press.

Evans, Stephen F. 2001. "'Open Containers': Sherman Alexie's Drunken Indians." *American Indian Quarterly* 25: 46-72.

Hale, Janet Campbell. 1985. *The Jailing of Cecelia Capture*. Albuquerque: University of New Mexico Press.

Hames-García, Michael R. 2000. "'Who Are Our Own People?' Challenges for a Theory of Social Identity." In *Reclaiming Identity: Realist Theory and the Predicament of Postmodernism*, edited by Paula M. L. Moya and Michael R. Hames-García, 102-29. Berkeley: University of California Press.

Hau, Caroline S. 2000. "On Representing Others: Intellectuals, Pedagogy, and the Uses of Error." In *Reclaiming Identity: Realist Theory and the Predicament of Postmodernism*, edited by Paula M. L. Moya and Michael R. Hames-García, 133-70. Berkeley: University of California Press.

Johansen, Bruce E. 1998. *Debating Democracy: Native American Legacy of Freedom*. Santa Fe, N.M.: Clear Light.

Lugones, María C. 1994. "Purity, Impurity, and Separation." *Signs* 19, no. 21: 458-79.

Lyons, Oren, and John Mohawk, eds. 1992. *Exiled in the Land of the Free: Democracy, Indian Nations, and the U.S. Constitution*. Santa Fe, N.M.: Clear Light.

Mohanty, Satya P. 1997. *Literary Theory and the Claims of History: Postmodernism, Objectivity, Multicultural Politics*. Ithaca, N.Y.: Cornell University Press.

U.S. Bureau of Justice. 2004. *American Indians and Crime: A Bureau of Justice Statistics Profile, 1992-2002*. Washington, D.C.: Government Printing Office.

U.S. Census Bureau. 2006a. *Drug Policy Report 2003-2005*. Washington, D.C.: Government Printing Office, 1-5 September.

U.S. Census Bureau. 2006b. *Poverty Report 2003-2005*. Washington, D.C.: Government Printing Office, 2-4 August.

U.S. Centers for Disease Control and Prevention, National Center for Injury Prevention and Control. 2004. *Centers for Disease Control Report 2004*. Washington, D.C.: Government Printing Office.

U.S. Centers for Disease Control and Prevention, Office of Minority Health and Health Disparities. 2006. *Healthy People 2010*. Washington, D.C.: Government Printing Office.

# Sherman Alexie:
## Interview

Margo Rabb

The first time I saw Sherman Alexie speak I was 21 years old. He was 27, and his collection of short stories, *The Lone Ranger and Tonto Fistfight in Heaven*, had recently been published; it was one of his first readings in New York City, in a small bookstore crowded with several dozen people. I was going to lots of readings then, most of them so boring that staying home and sticking a pen in my eye would've been more fun. Then I went to his reading . . . and he didn't read. He *recited* one of his stories. I was smitten.

Now he's 42 years old and at the top of his game. His first young adult novel, *The Absolutely True Diary of a Part-Time Indian*, tells the story of Arnold Spirit Jr., a boy who leaves his school on the Spokane Indian Reservation to attend an all-white school. It won the 2007 National Book Award for young people's literature; his adult novel, *Flight*, was also published in 2007, and is a masterful time-traveling feat; his poetry collection, *Face*, published this month by Hanging Loose Press, is a staggering collection of both formal poetry and poems that defy formalism. This interview took place in College Station, Texas, before he spoke to a crowd of nearly a thousand. On stage, Alexie is a magnetic performer; when alone, he's warm, funny, unpretentious, and unassuming. We spoke about poetry, grief, fear, Stephen Colbert . . . and tacos.

\* \* \*

**Face *is your first full-length collection of poetry in nine years. You've said that you had a poetry dry spell for a year or two—what caused it?***

I had complete writer's block for almost two years, from 1999 through 2000 or so. It was from writing for Hollywood—I got so used to hearing producers' notes in my head that they started interfering with everything. I didn't write anything—I thought I was done.

*And in the last few months you said you've written over sixty poems—what do you think causes your more prolific periods?*

I think part of it this time was getting away from the YA world—the freedom of not having to think about what would or wouldn't be appropriate for a teenage audience. Or rather, what their parents and the adults around them would think was appropriate. The freedom of removing myself from that world resulted in this big explosion of writing.

**Face** *contains both formal poems and poems that play with form—sonnets interspersed with prose poetry, footnotes on a villanelle, a q&a in the middle of a poem, etc.—how did that evolve?*

Well, I've always sort of done that, just never so overtly before. But part of it is that I think the poems sort of replicate my personality. I'm not a writer of lyric poetry or difficult poetry, so I'm very interested in accessibility. So I think the forms I use are about accessibility.

*The collection was originally titled* **Thrash.** *Why did you change it to* **Face?**

Because when people would pronounce it and talk about the book in interviews they'd always call it *Trash.* And when my poetry editor emailed me once, even he typed *Trash* by mistake. So I thought, okay, I'm changing it. Although now whenever I get interviewed or talk about it people are calling it *Fate* instead of *Face.* And someone pointed out yesterday that if you look at the cover—I knew this was going to be a little bit of an issue, but I just let it go because the cover is so beautiful—someone pointed out that if you look at the title a certain way it looks like it says *Taco.*

*Which would be a great title for a collection of poems! You should write a taco poem.*

I'm going to now, actually! I have to.

*I love this phrase in the poem "Vilify": "Funny grief" being the best answer to the question "What is Native American poetry?" I'm Jewish, and "funny grief" is such a part of Jewish culture, too—do you think that's how mainstream WASPy American culture deals with death and grief also?*

I don't think so. I think that one of the problems with the United States is that people can't deal with contrasting emotions, with having two emotions at the same time. Mixing conflicting emotions like that is not a part of mainstream culture. And when it is mainstream, by and large it *is* Jewish culture. Because when you think about stand-up comedy and situation comedies and movies, you're talking Jewish people. In terms of the creation of comedy in the United States, the origin of comedy in the U.S. is Jewish. So even for those of us who are non-Jewish—funny grief is a Jewish concept still, even though it's also Native American.

*It's not innate to Indian culture as well?*

[Laughs] I don't know . . . was Crazy Horse a funny guy? I wouldn't bet on it. I don't ever recall anyone talking about whether Geronimo was great around the campfire.

*Something that I've been thinking about a lot lately is how teenagers experience grief differently than adults do—I lost my mom when I was young, and my father when I was older, and the grief was so different each time. You've written about your sister's death when you were a teenager, and your father's death when you were much older. Do you think teens handle grief differently than adults do?*

Yeah. I remember when I was a kid how adults were trying to control my grief, trying to tell me how I was supposed to feel or how I was supposed to behave . . . that there was a proper way to mourn . . . and I was interested in improperly mourning.

**How did you improperly mourn?**

Overt display of emotion I guess. In the Indian world there's a lot of humor, but . . . maybe the humor can get in the way, because sometimes there's not the out-and-out-absolute-weeping-from-the-center-of-the-world crying. That's what I was doing. I couldn't stop for weeks.

**And when you were older?**

Oh, man. When I got the news my father died I actually collapsed. That's the first time I fell or fainted when I heard news of some-body's death. I cried hard. I'm not over it. Not even remotely. So I guess . . . I healed as a kid. But now . . . I mean last night at a reading I gave, a kid asked me that question: "How are you dealing with your dad's death?" I said, "Obviously not very well!" My sister died so long ago . . . 29 years ago. It almost feels like an entirely different person who lost her. And I didn't know her that well—she was quite a bit older than me, she was out of the house, she was married . . . so she's a series of impressions at this point. I don't even know how ac-curate they are. She's almost become mythology.

**Reviewers are always describing you as a "fearless writer." What are you afraid of?**

[Laughs] They're always putting that in, aren't they? It's funny, because am I more fearless than any other given writer? I don't think so. I mean there are plenty of rowdy people. What am I afraid of? Heights, large bodies of water—I don't know how to swim—flying, and parties.

*You're afraid of parties?*

Yeah. Strangers. Groups of strangers.

*But you're such a good performer in front of a crowd.*

Because I'm in control. At a party, I don't know people's motivations. It's my introverted nature I guess. At a party I start acting.

*What are you afraid of as a writer?*

Nothing. [Laughs] Maybe I am fearless! There's nothing off-limits. I mean, the whole process itself can be terrifying—every time you sit down to write it's scary. But in terms of what I will or will not write about, nothing is terrifying.

*What about in terms of your career?*

I suppose in some sense I used to be afraid my career was temporary. But it's been sixteen years—I think I'm here to stay. I've had ups and downs and there are going to be other downs, but I'm not afraid of those. It doesn't affect my movement forward.

*Your next young adult novel,* **Radioactive Love Song,** *was originally scheduled to be published this spring, but it's been delayed. What's happening with it?*

We've tabled it because I'm working on the sequel to *True Diary* immediately. We decided to hold off on that because nobody wants something else—everybody wants the story of Arnold's sophomore year!

*Were you struggling with* **Radioactive Love Song?**

Yes, I think I was struggling with it because the narrator kept sounding like Arnold Spirit Jr.—it was Arnold Spirit Jr. on a road trip. It's the same sort of comedy . . . it just sounded like him. Partly I'm revising it to get away from the first person narration. I think that's it.

*Are you doing it in third person instead?*

No, it's going to be somebody else narrating.

*Who?*

The iPod.

*Wow.*

It'll be the first iPod-narrated novel.

*How are you going to do that?*

I don't know yet. I don't know yet. It's like HAL from 2001.

*How much do you have written in the iPod's voice?*

Not much. I might abandon the idea. It might not work. It's sort of a distant omniscient idea. Just think of it as god. iPod rhymes with god.

*Do you like going back to* **True Diary***?*

Oh yeah. I think I've spent enough time away from Arnold where I'm excited to see him again. A part of it is with *True Diary*, I love the response to it—when *True Diary* was published, it felt like the start of a career again. And it's nice to revisit him in new ways. Arnold kept talking to me. He wouldn't let me write the other book, he wouldn't let me finish it. He kept getting in the way of the other book.

*What happens during Arnold's sophomore year?*

It's a romance with Penelope . . . a will-they-or-won't-they romance.

*How down and dirty are they going to get?*

[Laughs] I don't know—that's the whole point of the book! Why am I going to tell you that?

---

*I want to know what pages to dog-ear.*

Well, you remember that whole high school back-and-forth-back-and-forth-back-and-forth . . .

*Is it going to be like* **Twilight,** *where they don't kiss till page 280?*

[Laughs] No, I think my version is sort of . . . not like that. Mine is a very realistic portrait of a teenage couple. It involves no vampires. It's two lefty kids in a little town . . . it's what happens when liberals get together.

*So is Arnold really in love with Penelope, or does he just want to have sex with her?*

He doesn't know. Both. The realism of it is that it's both things at the same time.

*How much do you have written? Do they have a pub date?*

About 100 pages. The pub date will probably be next spring.

*You wrote* **Flight** *during the same time that you were writing* **True Diary.** *Did you think about that as YA at all too?*

No—it's funny that people would even think so.

*But I would've loved that book when I was fifteen.*

But you were probably a crazy-ass fifteen-year-old. It wasn't the kids I was worried about, it wouldn't get past the teachers, the gate-keepers. There's genital mutilation in that book! No, I never thought of it as YA. It's way too violent. It's funny, people don't even re-member how violent it is. You know people will say that to me, "Why isn't that a YA?" I'll start listing everything that happens and they say, "Wait a second. That never would've made it past the school board."

---

***Well,* True Diary *didn't—***

*True Diary* didn't make it past the school board in a couple places! But it's so funny—the amazing thing is, it's certain communities, because tomorrow I'm reading from it in the George Bush Library here. I want to get a photograph of me reading at the George Bush Library and send it to that school and say, "At least a Republican president doesn't mind."

***Are you going to read the masturbation part?***

I might! No . . . I'll respect the library. But nobody even masturbates in the book! It's a metaphor! That's the thing . . . if someone had actually masturbated I could understand, but nobody masturbates. Nobody actually touches any sexual organ in my book.

***But you're going to rectify that in the sequel.***

I might, I might.

***Your next adult novel,* Fire with Fire, *recently sold to Little, Brown and is slated to be published in the Fall of 2010. What stage is it at now?***

It was sold with about half of it done. It's going to be about 600 pages. It's a mystery . . . I'm trying to write the great big American Native American novel. It's huge . . . it's apocalyptic, about everything. I'm trying to write the book about everything in the Indian world. It's big. I'm trying to make a huge statement. Indian writers, we write small. Small worlds, because we grew up tribal. As soon as you see an Indian writer writing big, you know they're not Indian. So here's my chance to prove that an Indian can write big. Extend the vision. I'm trying to be epic. It's about Thomas Builds-the-Fire and Victor from Smoke Signals on another road trip to solve a murder mystery. It starts on the rez and it ends up in Seattle. It's incredibly violent.

---

*You once said "Art is a young person's game," and you should give it up by the time you're forty. How do you feel about that now?*
I'm obviously doomed.

*So you changed your mind about that?*
One could argue I still keep writing the same shit.

*Really? Do you think that's true?*
In some regard, yeah.

*Don't you think you're doing it better?*
Equally as bad and equally as good.

*If sales of all your books were equal, what would you choose to keep writing? Poetry?*
If I could make a living just writing poems, if I could sell hundreds of thousands of copies of my poetry books, I would be a poet.

*You'd never write fiction at all?*
I doubt it. I doubt it.

*But maybe if poetry books sold hundreds of thousands of copies then you'd long to write fiction. You'd say, "If I could just sell some fiction I'd be so happy . . ."*
Oh god, no, no, no! If I could just write poems I would. It's how I think, how I look at the world. Everything else is a struggle, is a fight. No, god. That would be so great, making this living writing poems. In fact, I saw that the big lottery, the megamillions, is $212 million, and I thought if I won that, I'd just be a poet.

*But doesn't it make you happy, writing fiction?*
Oh yeah, but there's happy, and then there's just who I am. I mean, poetry is the thing I love to do most, and writing fiction is my

job. It's a great job, I love my job, but it's a job. Writing poetry's not a job, it doesn't feel that way at all.

**You were on the Colbert Report *in October—one of the only guests who's ever been able to make Stephen Colbert speechless. What was it like being on the show?***

It was great, but it's funny because Indians are so invisible and because my career has gotten so big that I think people . . . they don't forget that I'm Indian, but it becomes very secondary to the success. When I was on Colbert I had a double consciousness or triple consciousness about it . . . I was in the moment but then I was also thinking that this is really revolutionary for Indians . . . a rez boy holding his own verbally with one of the best in the business. It was big. I was proud that I also have that artistic ability. It was fun. He was a great guy. He came into the green room afterwards and congratulated me, which was very decent of him.

**So . . . are Arnold and Penelope going to do it in the sequel or not?**

[Laughs] That's the whole story! I'm not going to tell you that!

**I'm not going to buy the book if they don't do it.**

I'm still not telling you!

# RESOURCES

| 1966 | Sherman Joseph Alexie, Jr., is born on October 7 to Sherman Joseph Alexie and Lillian Agnes Cox Alexie at Sacred Heart Hospital in Spokane, Washington. |
|---|---|
| 1967 | Alexie undergoes an operation on his brain to treat his hydrocephalic condition; he suffers seizures for the next seven years and is treated with lithium and other sedatives. |
| 1972-1980 | Alexie attends school in Wellpinit on the Spokane Indian reservation. |
| 1981-1985 | Alexie enters Reardan High School, where he joins the debate team and Future Farmers of America and becomes captain of basketball team. |
| 1985-1987 | Alexie graduates from Reardan High School and attends Gonzaga University in Seattle; he begins excessive consumption of alcoholic beverages. |
| 1988-1991 | Alexie transfers to Washington State University and begins taking premedicine courses before changing his focus to creative writing. |
| 1988 | Alexie publishes eighteen poems in the *Journal of Ethnic Studies*. |
| 1990 | Alexie publishes the poem "Distances" in the journal *Hanging Loose*, the start of a continuing collaboration with the Brooklyn-based press. |
| 1991 | Alexie receives a Washington State Arts Commission fellowship ($5,000) for poetry and spends nine months with the People to People program as a student ambassador in Seattle. He completely stops drinking alcohol. |
| 1992 | Hanging Loose Press publishes *The Business of Fancydancing*, and Alexie receives a National Endowment for the Arts fellowship ($20,000). A New York Times Book Review essay on Native American literature calls Alexie "one of the major lyric voices of our time." |

| 1993 | *Old Shirts and New Skins*, a poetry collection, and *The Lone Ranger and Tonto Fistfight in Heaven*, a volume of linked short stories, are published. |
|---|---|
| 1994 | Alexie graduates from Washington State University with a B.A. in American studies. He marries Diane Tomhave (Hidatsa, Ho-Chunk, Powtawatomi). "This Is What It Means to Say Phoenix, Arizona" is selected to appear in Best American Short Stories 1994. Alexie receives the Lila Wallace-Reader's Digest Writers' Award ($105,000) for his work on an outreach project to organize writing workshops for Native peoples in Seattle. |
| 1995 | The novel *Reservation Blues* is published. |
| 1996 | *Reservation Blues* wins the Before Columbus Foundation Award. Alexie is named one of twenty best young American novelists by *Granta*. *Indian Killer*, a novel, and *The Summer of Black Widows*, a collection of poems and stories, are published. |
| 1997 | Alexie's son Joseph is born. |
| 1998 | The film *Smoke Signals*, screenplay by Alexie and directed by Chris Eyre, wins the Sundance Film Festival Audience Award. Alexie begins working as a "script doctor" for the mainstream film industry. He wins the first of four consecutive top prizes at the World Heavyweight Poetry Championship. |
| 1999 | Alexie is included in *The New Yorker*'s "Future of American Fiction" issue and is named one of "twenty best young fiction writers in America" by the magazine. He makes his debut as a stand-up comic at the Foolproof Northwest Comedy Festival. |
| 2000 | *The Toughest Indian in the World*, a collection of short stories, and *One Stick Song*, a hybrid poetry collection, are published. |
| 2001 | Alexie's son David is born. *The Toughest Indian in the World* shares (with Richard Ford) the PEN/Malamud Award for Short Fiction. |
| 2002 | The film *The Business of Fancydancing*, written and directed by Alexie, is shown at independent film festivals. |

| 2003 | Alexie appears on *The Oprah Winfrey Show*, where he is given reissued medals won by his grandfather in World War II. The short-story collection *Ten Little Indians* is published. Alexie receives the Regents' Distinguished Alumnus Award from Washington State University. |
| --- | --- |
| 2004 | Alexie is named artist-in-residence at Washington University; the appointment is renewed in 2006 and 2008. The short documentary film *49?*, featuring Alexie performing post-powwow songs, screens at the Sundance Film Festival. |
| 2005 | The short story "What You Pawn I Will Redeem" is included in *O. Henry Prize Stories 2005*. The poetry collection *Dangerous Astronomy* is published by Limberlost Press, and "Avian Nights" from the collection is included in *The Pushcart Prize XXIX*. |
| 2007 | *The Absolutely True Diary of a Part-Time Indian* is published and wins the National Book Award for young people's literature; *Flight*, a short novel, is published. Alexie receives the Western Literature Association Distinguished Achievement Award. |
| 2008 | *The Absolutely True Diary of a Part-Time Indian* receives the American Indian Youth Literature Award from the American Indian Library Association. |
| 2009 | *Face*, a hybrid poetry collection, is published; it becomes one of the year's top ten best-selling collections of poetry. *War Dances*, a collection of short fiction with some poetry, is published. |
| 2010 | *War Dances* wins the PEN/Faulkner Award for Fiction. Alexie works on a sequel to *The Absolutely True Diary of a Part-Time Indian* and publishes poems in many journals. He receives the Native Writers' Circle of the Americas 2010 Lifetime Achievement Award. |
| 2011 | *War Dances* is chosen by the One Book, One Philadelphia community reading program for its January 19-March 17 citywide festival. |

# Works by Sherman Alexie

**Long Fiction**
*Reservation Blues*, 1995
*Indian Killer*, 1996
*The Absolutely True Diary of a Part-Time Indian*, 2007
*Flight*, 2007

**Short Fiction**
*The Lone Ranger and Tonto Fistfight in Heaven*, 1993
*The Toughest Indian in the World*, 2000
*Ten Little Indians*, 2003
*War Dances*, 2009

**Poetry**
*I Would Steal Horses*, 1992
*Old Shirts and New Skins*, 1993
*Water Flowing Home*, 1996
*The Man Who Loves Salmon*, 1998
*One Stick Song*, 2000
*Dangerous Astronomy*, 2005
*Face*, 2009

**Poetry with Short Fiction**
*The Business of Fancydancing: Stories and Poems*, 1992
*First Indian on the Moon*, 1993
*The Summer of Black Widows*, 1996

**Screenplays**
*Smoke Signals*, 1998
*The Business of Fancydancing*, 2002

# Bibliography

Alexie, Sherman. Official Alexie Web site. http://www.fallsapart.com.

Belcher, Wendy. "Conjuring the Colonizer: Alternative Readings of Magic Realism in Sherman Alexie's *Reservation Blues*." *American Indian Culture and Research Journal* 31.2 (2007): 87-101.

Berglund, Jeff, and Jan Roush, eds. *Sherman Alexie: A Collection of Critical Essays*. Salt Lake City: University of Utah Press, 2010.

Cook-Lynn, Elizabeth. *New Indians, Old Wars*. Urbana: University of Illinois Press, 2007.
_____. *Notebooks of Elizabeth Cook-Lynn*. Tucson: University of Arizona Press, 2007.

Coulomb, Joseph L. "The Approximate Size of His Favorite Humor: Sherman Alexie's Comic Connections and Disconnections in *The Lone Ranger and Tonto Fistfight in Heaven*." *American Indian Quarterly* 26.1 (2002): 94-115.

Cox, James H. "Muting White Noise: The Popular Culture Invasion in Sherman Alexie's Fiction." *Muting White Noise: Native American and European American Novel Traditions*. Norman: University of Oklahoma Press, 2006. 145-99.

Dean, Janet. "The Violence of Collection: Indian Killer's Archives." *Studies in American Indian Literatures* 20.3 (2008): 29-51.

Evans, Stephen F. "'Open Containers': Sherman Alexie's Drunken Indians." *American Indian Quarterly* 25.1 (2001): 46-72.

Gilroy, Jhon Warren. "Another Fine Example of the Oral Tradition?": Identification and Subversion in Sherman Alexie's *Smoke Signals*." *Studies in American Indian Literatures* 13.1 (2001): 23-36.

Gordon, Stephanie. "The 7-11 of My Dreams: Pop Culture in Sherman Alexie's Short Fiction." *Studies in American Culture* 24.1 (2001): 29-36.

Grassian, Daniel. *Understanding Sherman Alexie*. Columbia: University of South Carolina Press, 2005.

Hausman, Blake M. "Alexie's Nutshell: Mousetraps and Interpenetrations in *The Business of Fancydancing* and *Hamlet*." *Studies in American Indian Literatures* 22.1 (2010): 76-112.

Hollrah, Patrice E. M. "'I'm Talking Like a Twentieth-Century Indian Woman': Contemporary Female Warriors in the Works of Sherman Alexie." *"The Old Lady Trill, the Victory Yell": The Power of Women in Native American Literature*. New York: Routledge, 2004. 121-54.

James, Meredith K. *Literary and Cinematic Reservation in Selected Works of Native American Author Sherman Alexie*. Lewiston, NY: Edwin Mellen Press, 2005.

Krupat, Arnold. "The 'Rage Stage'": Contextualizing Sherman Alexie's *Indian Killer*." *Red Matters: Native American Studies*. Philadelphia: University of Pennsylvania Press, 2002. 98-121.

Ladino, Jennifer K. "'A Limited Range of Motion?': Multiculturalism, 'Human Questions,' and Urban Identity in Sherman Alexie's *Ten Little Indians.*" *Studies in American Indian Literatures* 21.3 (2009): 36-57.

McFarland, Ron. "'Another Kind of Violence': Sherman Alexie's Poems." *American Indian Quarterly* 21.2 (1997): 251-64.

Moore, David L. "Sherman Alexie: Irony, Intimacy, Agency." *Cambridge Companion to Native American Literature.* Ed. Joy Porter and Kenneth M. Roemer. New York: Cambridge University Press, 2005. 297-310.

Newton, John. "Sherman Alexie's Autoethnography." *Contemporary Literature* 42.2 (2001): 413-28.

Peterson, Nancy J., ed. *Conversations with Sherman Alexie.* Jackson: University Press of Mississippi, 2009.

Purdy, John Lloyd. *Writing Native Conversations.* Lincoln: University of Nebraska Press, 2009.

Tatonetti, Lisa. "Visible Sexualities or Invisible Nations: Forced to Choose in *Big Eden, Johnny Greyeyes,* and *The Business of Fancydancing.*" *GLQ: A Journal of Lesbian and Gay Studies* 16.2 (2010): 157-81.

Teuton, Sean Kicummah. *Red Land, Red Power: Grounding Knowledge in the American Indian Novel.* Durham, NC: Duke University Press, 2008.

Treuer, David. *Native American Fiction: A User's Manual.* Saint Paul, MN: Graywolf Press, 2006.

Vizenor, Gerald. *Manifest Manners: Narratives on Postindian Survivance.* Lincoln: University of Nebraska Press, 1999.

_____. *Native Liberty: Natural Reason and Cultural Survivance.* Lincoln: University of Nebraska Press, 2009.

Wilmer, S. E. *Native American Performance and Presentation.* Tucson: University of Arizona Press, 2009.

Womack, Craig B., Daniel Heath Justice, and Christopher B. Teuton, eds. *Reasoning Together: The Native Critics Collective.* Norman: University of Oklahoma Press, 2008.

Youngberg, Quentin. "Interpenetrations: Re-encoding the Queer Indian in Sherman Alexie's *The Business of Fancydancing.*" *Studies in American Indian Literatures* 20.1 (2008): 55-75.

# CRITICAL
# INSIGHTS

# About the Editor

**Leon Lewis** is Professor in the English Department at Appalachian State University, where he directed the film program for twenty-five years. He studied humanities at Oberlin College and concentrated on contemporary American literature at the University of Pennsylvania and the State University of New York at Buffalo. After completing a Ph.D., he taught at Long Island University in Brooklyn, with visiting lectureships at New York University and the University College of Wales at Aberystwyth before joining the faculty at Appalachian. He is the author of *Henry Miller: The Major Writings* (1985) and *Eccentric Individuality in William Kotzwinkle's The Fan Man, E. T., Doctor Rat, and Other Works of Fantasy and Fiction* (2002), editor of *Robert M. Young: Essays on the Films* (2005), and translator of Gilbert Michlin's memoir *Of No Interest to the Nation: A Jewish Family in France, 1925-1945* (2004). He edited the spring 2008 issue of the *Cold Mountain Review*, and, among numerous analytical essays and reviews, published a study of Robert Frost's poem "The Star-Splitter" in the spring/summer 2008 issue of *Shenandoah* ("Famous Long Ago: Or, Frost Among the Infinities"), a consideration of Louis Zukofsky's *Eighty Flowers* in the February 2008 issue of *The Writer's Chronicle* ("Aural Invention as Floral Splendor: Louis Zukofsky's Vision of Natural Beauty in *Eighty Flowers*), a tribute to Jonathan Williams in the summer 2008 issue of *Appalachian Journal* ("In Memoriam: Wandering in the World of Jonathan Williams [1929-2008]"), and an examination of Michel Deguy's poetry in the spring 2011 issue of *Cerise Press* ("Michel Deguy and English Poesie: The [In]Compatability of Poetry and Philosophy").

# About *The Paris Review*

**The Paris Review** is America's preeminent literary quarterly, dedicated to discovering and publishing the best new voices in fiction, nonfiction, and poetry. The magazine was founded in Paris in 1953 by the young American writers Peter Matthiessen and Doc Humes, and edited there and in New York for its first fifty years by George Plimpton. Over the decades, the *Review* has introduced readers to the earliest writings of Jack Kerouac, Philip Roth, T. C. Boyle, V. S. Naipaul, Ha Jin, Ann Patchett, Jay McInerney, Mona Simpson, and Edward P. Jones, and published numerous now-classic works, including Roth's *Goodbye, Columbus*, Donald Barthelme's *Alice*, Jim Carroll's *Basketball Diaries*, and selections from Samuel Beckett's *Molloy* (his first publication in English). The first chapter of Jeffrey Eugenides's *The Virgin Suicides* appeared in the *Review*'s pages, as have stories by Rick Moody, David Foster Wallace, Denis Johnson, Jim Crace, Lorrie Moore, and Jeanette Winterson.

*The Paris Review*'s renowned Writers at Work series of interviews, whose early installments include legendary conversations with E. M. Forster, William Faulkner, and Ernest Hemingway, is one of the landmarks of world literature. The interviews received a George Polk Award and were nominated for a Pulitzer Prize. Among the more than three hundred interviewees are Robert Frost, Marianne Moore, W. H. Auden, Elizabeth Bishop, Susan Sontag, and Toni Morrison. Recent issues feature conversations with Jonathan Franzen, Norman Rush, Louise Erdrich, Joan Didion, Norman Mailer, R. Crumb, Michel Houellebecq, Marilynne Robinson, David Mitchell, Annie Proulx, and Gay Talese. In November 2009, Picador published the final volume of a four-volume series of anthologies of *Paris Review* interviews. The *New York Times* called the Writers at Work series "the most remarkable and extensive interviewing project we possess."

*The Paris Review* is edited by Lorin Stein, who was named to the post in 2010. The editorial team has published fiction by Lydia Davis, André Aciman, Sam Lipsyte, Damon Galgut, Mohsin Hamid, Uzodinma Iweala, James Lasdun, Padgett Powell, Richard Price, and Sam Shepard. Recent poetry selections include work by Frederick Seidel, Carol Muske-Dukes, John Ashbery, Kay Ryan, Mary Jo Bang, Sharon Olds, Charles Wright, and Mary Karr. Writing published in the magazine has been anthologized in *Best American Short Stories* (2006, 2007, and 2008), *Best American Poetry*, *Best Creative Non-Fiction*, the Pushcart Prize anthology, and *O. Henry Prize Stories*.

The magazine presents three annual awards. The Hadada Award for lifelong contribution to literature has recently been given to Joan Didion, Norman Mailer, Peter Matthiessen, John Ashbery, and, in 2010, Philip Roth. The Plimpton Prize for Fiction, awarded to a debut or emerging writer brought to national attention in the pages of *The Paris Review*, was presented in 2007 to Benjamin Percy, to Jesse Ball in 2008, and to Alistair Morgan in 2009. In 2011, the magazine inaugurated the Terry Southern Prize for Humor.

*The Paris Review* was a finalist for the 2008 and 2009 National Magazine Awards in fiction and won the 2007 National Magazine Award in photojournalism. The *Los Angeles Times* recently called *The Paris Review* "an American treasure with true international reach," and the *New York Times* designated it "a thing of sober beauty."

Since 1999 *The Paris Review* has been published by The Paris Review Foundation, Inc., a not-for-profit 501(c)(3) organization.

*The Paris Review* is available in digital form to libraries worldwide in selected academic databases exclusively from EBSCO Publishing. Libraries can contact EBSCO at 1-800-653-2726 for details. For more information on *The Paris Review* or to subscribe, please visit: www.theparisreview.org.

**Leon Lewis** is Professor of Film and Literature at Appalachian State University in North Carolina, where he directed the film program for twenty-five years. He is the author of *Henry Miller: The Major Writings* (1985), translator of Gilbert Michlin's memoir *Of No Interest to the Nation* (2004), and editor of *Robert M. Young: Essays on the Films* (2005).

**Georgie L. Donovan** is Associate Professor and Librarian at Appalachian State University. She has taught college-level English language and literature courses at universities in Texas, Tokyo, and Copiapó, Chile, since earning a master of fine arts degree in creative writing from the University of Texas, El-Paso. Her focus during her MFA studies was on poetry, and she completed a book of poetry for her thesis. She then earned a master's degree in information science and has worked in university libraries since 2003. She is coeditor of *Staff Development Strategies That Work* (2009) and has published several articles on scholarly communication and on leadership. She has also written encyclopedia articles on poetry and art for Salem Press's *The Eighties in America* (2008) and *Great Events from History* (2007) and reviews of poetry for *Counterpoise*. She has published poetry in *Figdust* and the *Rio Grande Review*.

**Barry Harbaugh** is an assistant editor at Harper, an imprint of HarperCollins Publishers.

**Tammy Wahpeconiah** (Sac & Fox) is Associate Professor and Assistant Chair of the Department of English at Appalachian State University, where she teaches American Indian, ethnic American, and early American literatures. Her research interests include early American Indian writers and contemporary American Indian literature.

**Michael Wilson** is Assistant Professor at Appalachian State University in Boone, North Carolina. His research and teaching interests include cultural studies, American literature, and humanities computing. He has published on a variety of topics, including American Indians in frontier literature, with entries on *Nick of the Woods* and *The Tennessee* for Salem Press's *Cyclopedia of Literary Places* (2003) and "Saturnalia of Blood: Masculine Self-Control in the Frontier Novel," first published in *Studies in American Fiction* (autumn 2005) and reprinted in Volume 197 of *Nineteenth Century Literary Criticism* (August 2008).

**Constance Bracewell** is a doctoral candidate in English literature at the University of Arizona, specializing in American Indian literature, diaspora studies, and twentieth-century American literature. She is the author of *Literary Removal and Repatriation: Diaspora and American Indian Literatures* (2012) and has published several articles on topics relating to American Indian literature. She is Cochair of the American Indian Literatures and Cultures Area of the PCA/ACA National Conference and also serves on the Distance Education Advisory Council of Rowan-Cabarrus Community College. She currently teaches courses in American and World Literature at Appalachian

State University and Rowan-Cabarrus Community College, both in North Carolina.

**Mark Vogel** is Professor of English at Appalachian State University in Boone, North Carolina. He has written consistently on emerging themes in young adult literature, on the theory and practice of writing, and on adolescent literacy. His writing has also focused on modern poetry in the classroom. His short stories have appeared in *Cities and Road, Knight Literary Journal, Whimperbang, SNReview,* and *Our Stories,* his poetry has appeared in *Poetry Midwest, English Journal, Slant, Dark Sky, Cold Mountain Review,* and numerous other journals. He has received the University of North Carolina Board of Governors Award for Excellence in Teaching.

**Cindy M. Spurlock** (Ph.D., University of North Carolina at Chapel Hill) has published work in *Environmental Communication, Enculturation,* and *Text and Performance Quarterly,* and she has a chapter in the forthcoming edited volume *Naturalizing Rhetoric: Environmental Politics and the Visual Poetics of National Parks and Monuments* (edited by Tom Patin). She currently serves as the lead editor of the Praxis Section of Environmental Communication and was the lead editorial assistant for Critical Studies in Media Communication from 2006 to 2009. Her research interests include the cultural politics of public memory, political and popular discourses of sustainability, and contemporary social movements. She received the J. Robert Cox Award for Outstanding Achievement in Scholarship at UNC Chapel Hill and is a recent recipient of a competitive Appalachian State University Foundation Fellows research grant on environmental public memory. She is a member of the graduate faculty at Appalachian State University, and she regularly teaches undergraduate and honors courses on environmental communication, rhetoric and persuasion, mass media and society, and ethics. She was the founding faculty adviser (spring 2010) for the Omega Theta chapter of Lambda Pi Eta, the national communication honor society.

**Richard Sax** is Professor of English at Lake Erie College in Painesville, Ohio. He received his bachelor of arts degree from Haverford College and his master's and doctoral degrees from the University of Michigan. His teaching and research areas include American literature, American studies, American Indian studies, interdisciplinary humanities, and medieval English outlaw poetry.

**Carrie Etter** is a Senior Lecturer in Creative Writing at Bath Spa University, England. Originally from Normal, Illinois, she has published essays on the work of Peter Reading and W. B. Yeats, as well as two collections of poetry, *The Letters* (2009) and *Divining for Starters* (2011). She has also edited an anthology, *Infinite Difference: Other Poetries by U.K. Women* (2010).

**Douglas Ford** is Associate Professor in the Language and Literature Department of the State College of Florida. He is a specialist in twentieth-century American literature, and his scholarly works have appeared in *MELUS, Modern Fiction Studies, Legacy,* and *Dissections.* He is active on the conference circuit and is a member of the International Association for the Fantastic in the Arts. His most recent exploration of Sherman Alexie's work involves an analysis of the zombie trope in the story "Ghost

Dance." His professional pursuits would not be possible without the support of his wonderful wife and children.

**Gloria Bird** is one of the founding members of the Northwest Native American Writers Association and has been a contributing editor for *Indian Artist* magazine. Her books of poetry include *Full Moon on the Reservation* (1993) and *The River of History* (1997). With Joy Harjo, she coedited the anthology *Reinventing the Enemy's Language* (1997) and was an editor of the journal *Wicazo Sa Review*. She is a member of the Spokane tribe of Washington State and has worked for the tribe in several capacities, including as a teacher at the Wellpinit Campus of Salish Kootenai College.

**Jennifer Gillan** is Associate Professor of English and Media Studies at Bentley University. She is coeditor of four award-winning multicultural anthologies: *Unsettling America* (1994), *Identity Lessons* (1999), *Growing Up Ethnic in America* (1999), and *Italian American Writers on New Jersey* (2004). Her analysis of literary responses to the "typical American" depicted on 1950s sitcoms led her to archival research on the era's programs. Among her six television studies anthology chapters is an essay in *The Great American Makeover* on the representation of southwestern tribes, the war in Iraq, and U.S. history in ABC-TV's *Extreme Makeover: Home Edition*. Her book *Television and New Media: Must-Click TV* (2010) examines the transformation of contemporary U.S. broadcast networks.

**Scott Andrews** has published book reviews, essays, poetry, and fiction. His recent work includes an essay on Sherman Alexie's short stories in *World Literature Today* (summer 2010) and a prose poem titled "I (Thunderheart) N.Y." in *Sentence: A Journal of Prose Poetics* (2009). He teaches American and American Indian literatures at California State University, Northridge, where he is also coordinator for the American Indian Studies Program and a faculty adviser for the American Indian Student Association. He is an enrolled member of the Cherokee Nation of Oklahoma.

**Meredith K. James** is Associate Professor of English at Eastern Connecticut State University. She is the author of *Literary and Cinematic Reservation in Selected Works of Native American Author Sherman Alexie* (2005). Her scholarship is mostly centered on Native American and American studies.

**Laura Arnold Leibman** is Associate Professor of English and Humanties at Reed College. She is the author of *Indian Converts* (2008) and the companion Web site "The Indian Converts Collection" (http:/cdm.reed.edu/cdm4/indianconverts). Her current research on Jewish mysticism, messianism, and material culture in the Atlantic World (1620-1820) is forthcoming in *Friendly Piranhas and Other Myths of First American Jews*. She is the Academic Director of the award-winning television series *American Passages* (Annenberg/CPB 2003) and the featured interdisciplinary expert on architecture and literature for *Artifacts and Fictions* (Annenberg/CPB). She currently resides with her family in Portland, Oregon.

**Åse Nygren** is affiliated with Blekinge Institute of Technology in Sweden, where she has taught English since 1995. After she studied for some time at the University of

California, Los Angeles, a research grant took her to the University of Oklahoma in 2001, where she met and worked with Professor Alan Velle. She finished her dissertation, *Tracing Trauma: The Narrative of Suffering in Sherman Alexie's Writing*, in 2007. As a part of Professor Jay Bolter's research group, she has more recently done research on digital migrations in Second Life. She is also an active pedagogical developer deeply engaged in quality work throughout all of the educational programs at Blekinge Institute.

**Daniel Grassian** is Department Chair of Humanities and Associate Professor of English at Nevada State College in Henderson. He is the author of *Understanding Sherman Alexie* (2005), *Hybrid Fictions: American Literature and Generation X* (2003), and *Writing the Future of Black America: Literature of the Hip-Hop Generation* (2009). His main research and teaching interests are in the fields of contemporary literature and ethnic studies, and he is currently working on a book about Iranian and Iranian diaspora literature and culture.

**Lisa Tatonetti** is Associate Professor of English and American Ethnic Studies at Kansas State University, where she studies, teaches, and publishes on Two-Spirit literatures and Native literatures. She is coeditor of *Sovereign Erotics*, a forthcoming collection of Two-Spirit creative work. She has essays forthcoming in *Out of the Cupboard: Critical Interventions in Queer Indigenous Studies*, *Gerald Vizenor's Poetry and Poetics*, *Sherman Alexie: A Collection of Critical Essays*, and *Strawberries in Brooklyn: Maurice Kenny, Mohawk Poet* and has published in a special issue of *GLQ:A Journal of Lesbian and Gay Studies* titled "Sexuality, Nationality, Indigeneity," as well as in numerous other journals. She is currently completing a book project titled *Queering American Indian Literature: The Rise of Contemporary Two-Spirit Texts and Criticism*.

**Nancy Van Styvendale** is Assistant Professor in the Department of English at the University of Sasketchewan. She specializes in Native North American literatures and has additional research interests in trauma theory, postcolonial theory, indigenous and diasporic citizenship theory and practice, community service learning, and Palestine literature. Her current work focuses on the discourse of recovery and the construction of identity and "home" in contemporary Native North American novels.

**Sean Kicummah Teuton** is Director of the American Indian Studies Program and Associate Professor of English at the University of Wisconsin-Madison. He is the author of *Red Land, Red Power: Grounding Knowledge in the American Indian Novel* (2008) and coauthor (with the Native Critics Collective) of *Reasoning Together: The Native Critics Collective* (2008). He is at work on a new book on human rights and diplomacy in the Native nineteenth century, titled *Cities of Refuge: American Indian Literary Internationalism*, a project funded by the Woodrow Wilson Foundation and the School of Advanced Research. He is a citizen of the Cherokee Nation.

**Margo Rabb** is the author of the novel *Cures for Heartbreak* (2007), which won the Teddy Book Award for young adult literature and was named one of the best books of the year by *Kirkus* and *Booklist*. Her short stories and essays have appeared in the *New York Times Book Review, Atlantic Monthly, Zoetrope, Our Story, Seventeen, Mademoiselle, Best New American Voices, New Stories from the South,* and elsewhere, and have been broadcast on National Public Radio. She has received the grand prize in the *Zoetrope* fiction contest, first prize in the *Atlantic Monthly* fiction contest, first prize in the *American Fiction* contest, and a PEN Syndicated Fiction Project Award. Her new novel, *Mad, Mad Love* will be published in 2012. A New York City native, she now lives in Austin, Texas, with her family.

# Acknowledgments _____

"The *Paris Review* Perspective" by Barry Harbaugh. Copyright © 2012 by Barry Harbaugh. Special appreciation goes to Christopher Cox, Nathaniel Rich, and David Wallace-Wells, editors at *The Paris Review*.

"Dialectic to Dialogic: Negotiating Bicultural Heritage in Sherman Alexie's Sonnets" by Carrie Etter. From *Telling the Stories: Essays on American Indian Literatures and Cultures*, edited by Elizabeth Hoffman Nelson and Malcolm A. Nelson (2001), pp. 143-149. Copyright © 2001 by Peter Lang Publishing, Inc. Reprinted with permission of Peter Lang Publishing, Inc.

"Sherman Alexie's Indigenous Blues" by Douglas Ford. From *MELUS: Journal of the Society for the Study of Multi-Ethnic Literature of the United States* 27, no. 3 (Fall 2002): 197-215. Copyright © 2002 by *MELUS*. Reprinted with permission of the journal.

"The Exaggeration of Despair in Sherman Alexie's *Reservation Blues*" by Gloria Bird. From *Wicazo Sa Review* 11, no. 2 (Fall 1995): 47-52. Copyright © 1995 by the University of Minnesota Press. Reprinted with permission of the University of Minnesota Press.

"Reservation Home Movies: Sherman Alexie's Poetry" by Jennifer Gillan. From *American Literature* 68, no. 1 (March 1996): 91-110. Copyright © 1996 by Duke University Press. All rights reserved. Reprinted with permission of Duke University Press.

"A New Road and a Dead End in Sherman Alexie's *Reservation Blues*" by Scott Andrews. From *Arizona Quarterly* 63, no. 2 (Summer 2007): 137-152. Copyright © 2007 by *Arizona Quarterly*. Reprinted with permission of *Arizona Quarterly* and Scott Andrews.

"'The res has missed you': The Fragmented Reservation of the Mind in *The Business of Fancydancing*" by Meredith K. James. From *Literary and Cinematic Reservation in Selected Works of Native American Author Sherman Alexie* (2005), pp. 79-86. Copyright © 2005 by The Edwin Mellen Press. Reprinted with permission of The Edwin Mellen Press.

"A Bridge of Difference: Sherman Alexie and the Politics of Mourning" by Laura Arnold Leibman. From *American Literature* 77, no. 3 (September 2005): 541-561. Copyright © 2005 by Duke University Press. All rights reserved. Reprinted with permission of Duke University Press.

"A World of Story-Smoke: A Conversation with Sherman Alexie" by Åse Nygren. From *MELUS: Journal of the Society for the Study of the Multi-Ethnic Literature of the United States* 30, no. 4 (Winter 2005): 149-169. Copyright © 2005 by *MELUS*. Reprinted with permission of the journal.

"*Indian Killer*" by Daniel Grassian. From *Understanding Sherman Alexie* (2005),

---